THINKING ABOUT THE ENLIGHTENMENT

Thinking about the Enlightenment looks beyond the current parameters of studying the Enlightenment, to the issues that can be understood by reflecting on the period in a broader context. Each of the thirteen original chapters, by an international and interdisciplinary team of contributors, illustrates the problematic legacy of the Enlightenment and the continued ramifications of its thinking since the eighteenth century to consider whether modernity can see its roots in the intellectual revolution of the seventeenth and eighteenth centuries.

The collection is divided into six sections, preceded by a comprehensive introduction to the field and the most recent scholarship on the period. Across the sections, the contributors consider modern-day encounters with Enlightenment thinking, including Kant's moral philosophy, the conflict between reason and faith, the significance of the Enlightenment of law and the gender inequality that persisted throughout the eighteenth century. By examining specific encounters with the problematic results of Enlightenment concerns, the contributors are able to illuminate and offer new perspectives on topics such as human nature, race, politics, gender and rationality.

Drawing from history, philosophy, literature and anthropology, this book enables students and academics alike to take a fresh look at the Enlightenment and its legacy in the modern world.

Martin L. Davies is Emeritus Reader in History at the University of Leicester. His publications include *Historics: Why History Dominates Contemporary Society* (Routledge, 2006) and *How History Works* (Routledge, 2016).

THINKING ABOUT THE ENLIGHTENMENT

Modernity and its ramifications

Edited by Martin L. Davies

LONDON AND NEW YORK

First published 2016
by Routledge
2 Park Square, Milton Park, Abingdon, Oxon OX14 4RN

and by Routledge
711 Third Avenue, New York, NY 10017

Routledge is an imprint of the Taylor & Francis Group, an informa business

© 2016 Selection and editorial matter, Martin L. Davies; individual chapters, the contributors

The right of the editor to be identified as the author of the editorial material, and of the authors for their individual chapters, has been asserted in accordance with sections 77 and 78 of the Copyright, Designs and Patents Act 1988.

All rights reserved. No part of this book may be reprinted or reproduced or utilised in any form or by any electronic, mechanical, or other means, now known or hereafter invented, including photocopying and recording, or in any information storage or retrieval system, without permission in writing from the publishers.

Trademark notice: Product or corporate names may be trademarks or registered trademarks, and are used only for identification and explanation without intent to infringe.

British Library Cataloguing-in-Publication Data
A catalogue record for this book is available from the British Library

Library of Congress Cataloging-in-Publication Data
Names: Davies, Martin L., editor.
Title: Thinking about the Enlightenment : modernity and its ramifications / edited by Martin L. Davies.
Description: London: Routledge, 2016. | Collection of 13 essays. | Includes bibliographical references and index.
Identifiers: LCCN 2015039730| ISBN 9781138801813 (hardback : alkaline paper) | ISBN 9781138801820 (paperback : alkaline paper) | ISBN 9781315627540 (e-book)
Subjects: LCSH: Enlightenment—Europe. | Enlightenment—Europe—Influence. | Europe—Intellectual life—18th century.
Classification: LCC B802 .T467 2016 | DDC 190.9/033—dc23LC record available at http://lccn.loc.gov/2015039730

ISBN: 978-1-138-80181-3 (hbk)
ISBN: 978-1-138-80182-0 (pbk)
ISBN: 978-1-315-62754-0 (ebk)

Typeset in Bembo
by diacriTech, Chennai

CONTENTS

Acknowledgements ix
Contributors xi

    Introduction 1
    The Enlightenment: Something to think about
    Martin L. Davies

PART I
Thinking about Kant and the Enlightenment   **29**

1   Kant's concept of Enlightenment: Individual and universal
    dimensions   31
    Olga Poznjakova

2   Rethinking Kant's 'immaturity' in Arendt's post-totalitarian
    reflection   48
    Tatiana Weiser

PART II
Thinking about Enlightenment and politics   **67**

3   The Enlightenment, encyclopedism and the natural
    rights of man: The case of the *Code* of *Humanity* (1778)   69
    Luigi Delia

4 Deliberative democrats as the heirs of Enlightenment:
   Between Habermas and Dewey   86
   John Min

PART III
Thinking about Enlightenment and religion   103

5 Christianity and Enlightenment: Two hermeneutical
   approaches to their relationship   105
   Salvatore Muscolino

6 The Enlightenment legacy and European identity:
   Reflections on the cartoon controversy   122
   Carsten Meiner

PART IV
Thinking about Enlightenment and gender   137

7 Between shadow and light: Women's education   139
   Christophe Regina

8 "Race", "sex", and "gender": Intersections,
   naturalistic fallacies, and the Age of Reason   153
   Carina Pape

PART V
Thinking about Enlightenment and its limits   171

9 Adoption as a limit-case for Enlightenment:
   Lessing's *Nathan der Weise* and Kleist's *Der Findling*   173
   David D. Kim

10 From unsocial sociability to antagonistic society
   (and back again): The historical role and social-scientific
   presence of an anthropological trope   188
   Tilman Reitz

PART VI
Postscripts: Thinking about Enlightenment thinking   **207**

11 Multiple Counter-Enlightenments: The genealogy of a polemics from the eighteenth century to the present   209
Theo Jung

12 'The proper study of mankind': Enlightenment and tautology   227
Martin L. Davies

Index   *270*

ACKNOWLEDGEMENTS

At Routledge I would like to thank Laura Pilsworth for inviting me to take on the project that produced this book and Catherine Aitken for her support and advice while it was proceeding. I very much appreciate their commitment to it.

I must also express my thanks to the contributors for their patience and understanding while this project was taking shape. Without their interest and cooperation this project would not have been possible.

MLD

CONTRIBUTORS

Martin L. Davies
Emeritus Reader, School of History, University of Leicester
Publications:
Identity or History? Marcus Herz and the End of the Enlightenment (Detroit: Wayne State U.P., 1995); *Historics: Why History Dominates Contemporary Society* (Abingdon: Routledge, 2006); *Imprisoned by History: Aspects of Historicized Life* (Abingdon: Routledge 2010); 'Moses Mendelssohn' in *The Bloomsbury Companion to Kant*, ed. G. Banham, et al. (London: Bloomsbury 2015); *How History Works: The Reconstitution of a Human Science* (Abingdon: Routledge 2015).

Luigi Delia
Research Fellow, Department of Modern French Language and Literature, University of Geneva
Publications:
*La vision nouvelle de la société dans l'*Encyclopédie méthodique, Vol. 1, *Jurisprudence*, Québec, Les Presses de l'Université Laval, 2012 (with Ethel Groffier); (co-editor) *L'Europe et le monde colonial au XVIIIe siècle*, Paris, H. Champion 2013; themed issue on capital punishment for the journal *Corpus*, 62, 2012; themed issue on concepts of punishment for the journal *Lumières*, 20, 2012; *Philosophie et droit à la lumière de l'*Encyclopédie (monograph in progress).

Theo Jung
Assistant Professor, Chair of Comparative Western-European History, History Department, Albert-Ludwigs-Universität Freiburg, Br.
Publications:
Zeichen des Verfalls. Semantische Studien zur Entstehung der Kulturkritik im 18. und frühen 19. Jahrhundert, Historische Semantik 18. Göttingen: Vandenhoeck & Ruprecht 2012;

'The Politics of Time: Zeitgeist in Early Nineteenth Century Political Discourse', in: *Contributions to the History of Concepts* 9, Nr. 1, (2014) pp. 24–49; 'Zeitgeist im langen 18. Jahrhundert: Dimensionen eines umstrittenen Begriffs', in: A. Landwehr (ed.), *Frühe Neue Zeiten. Zeitkonzepte zwischen Reformation und Revolution*. Bielefeld: transcript 2012, pp. 319–355.

David D. Kim
Assistant Professor, Department of Germanic Languages at UCLA
Publications:
Imagining Human Rights (with S. Kaul), De Gruyter (forthcoming); *The Postcolonial World* (with J. Singh), Routledge (forthcoming). Also in collaboration with the Center for Digital Humanities at UCLA, a digital project for modeling authorial, translational and literary networks.

Carsten Meiner
Professor of French Culture and Literature, University of Copenhagen
Publications:
Les Mutations de la clarté. Induction, exemple et schématismes dans l' œuvre de Marivaux, Honoré de Champion, 'Collection Les 18ème siècles', Paris 2007; *Roland Barthes. En antologi*, Ed. Carsten Meiner, Museum Tusculanum, København 2007; *Nouvelles topologies littéraires*, (ed with R. Ceserani), Revue Romane 42-2, København 2007; *Le Carrosse et l'invention du hasard. Essai de topologie littéraire*, Presses Universitaires de France, Paris, "Collection Lettres", 2008; *The Cultural Life of Catastrophes and Crises*, (co-ed. with K. Veel). De Gruyter 2012; *La Clarté à l'âge classique*. Actes du colloque international La Clarté à l'âge classique. (co-ed. with E. Bury). Garnier, 2013.

John B. Min
Full-time philosophy instructor at the College of Southern Nevada
Publications:
'Review of John Parkinson and Jane Mansbridge', eds., *Deliberative Systems: Deliberative Democracy at the Large Scale Journal of Public Deliberation:* 2014, 10(2); 'Epistocracy and Democratic Epistemology', *Politics in Central Europe*, 2015, 11(1).

Salvatore Muscolino
Lecturer in Political Philosophy at the University of Palermo
Publications:
Persona e mercato. I liberalismi di Rosmini e Hayek a confronto, Rubbettino, Soveria Mannelli 2010; *Linguaggio, storia e politica. Ludwig Wittgenstein e Quentin Skinner*, Carlo Saladino Editore, Palermo 2012; *Cristianesimo e società post-secolare*, Mimesis, Milano-Udine 2015.

Carina Pape
Post-doctoral researcher for the DFG-project on "Indignation / Empörung" at the Europa-Universität Flensburg

Publications:
'От воззрения Лютера на женщин к семейному праву Канта' (Luther, Kant und die Frauen. Von Luthers Frauenbild zu Kants Eherecht). In: *Almanach 'VERBUM'.Yearbook of the Centre for medieval culture*, Faculty of Philosophy, Saint Petersburg 15, 2013; 'Autonome Teilhaftigkeit und teilhaftige Autonomie. Der Andere in Michail M. Bachtins Frühwerk (Dissertation)'. In: *Übergänge*. Hrsg. von W. Eßbach und B. Waldenfels. München: Wilhelm Fink Verlag, 2015; 'Aufgeklärt?! Immanuel Kants pädagogische Überlegungen zur Sexualaufklärung', in *230 Jahre Beantwortung der Frage: Was ist Aufklärung?* (co-ed. with H. Sederström). In preparation.

Olga Poznjakova
Head of the Department of Philosophy and Political Sciences at the Belorussian State Medical University, Minsk
Publications:
'Kant's idea of a "cosmopolitan state" as a fundamental, universal world-view of contemporary civilization', in *Proceedings of international seminar: Immanuel Kant*, Baltic Federal University of Russia, 2013, pp. 132–135; 'I. Kant's cosmopolitanism vs contemporary regionalism: two aspects of a world development project', in *International conference "Lomonosov-2015"*, Russian State University, Moscow, 2015, pp. 1–3; *Kant's philosophy of history: anthropological and socio-political aspects*. Minsk, 2015, 104 pp.

Christophe Regina
Lecturer at Jean Jaurès University, Toulouse, and member of the UMR 5136 FRAMESPA (France Méridionale Espagne)
Publications:
(co-ed.) *La culture judiciaire. Discours, représentations et usages de la justice du Moyen-âge à nos jours*, Dijon, Presses Universitaires de Dijon 2014; (co-ed.) *Récit et Justice. France, Italie, Espagne XIVe–XIXe*, Aix-en-Provence, Presses Universitaires d'Aix-Marseille 2014; *Genre, mœurs et justice. Les Marseillaises et la violence au XVIIIe siècle*, Aix-en-Provence, Presses Universitaires d'Aix-Marseille 2015; *Dire la violence. Les femmes et la justice à Marseille au XVIIIe siècle*, Paris, Classiques Garnier, « Esprit des Lois, Esprit des Lettres », 2015; *La manipulation: droit, justice, société de l'Ancien Régime à nos jours*, Paris, Classiques Garnier, 2015.

Tilman Reitz
Professor for the sociology of knowledge and theory of society, Institute of Sociology, University of Jena
Publications:
Bürgerlichkeit als Haltung. Zur Politik des privaten Weltverhältnisses, Wilhelm Fink Verlag Munich 2003; (with C. Lupton) 'New Grub Street's Self-Consciousness', in: M. Ryle and J.B. Taylor (eds.): *George Gissing. Voices of the Unclassed*, Ashgate:

Aldershot 2005, pp. 133–144; *Das zerstreute Gemeinwesen. Politische Semantik im Zeitalter der Gesellschaft*, Wiesbaden: VS Verlag für Sozialwissenschaften 2015.

Tatiana Weiser
Reader in Social and Political Philosophy, Russian Presidential Academy of National Economy and Public Administration; Chair of the Masters Programme in Political Philosophy, The Moscow Higher School of Social and Economic Sciences, Moscow. Publications:
'Human Science and Social Health', in *Experience and Theory: Reflection, Communication, Pedagogy*. Moscow: Delo 2012, pp. 103–114; "Unity and Singularity in Community Studies", in *Collections of Essay 12 of Russian Anthropological School*. Moscow: Russian State University of Humanities 2013, pp. 33–48; 'Traumatography of Logos: Languages of Trauma and Language Deformation in the Post-Soviet Poetry', in *New Literary Observer*, 2014, 125(1), pp. 245–265; 'Logic of Intersubjective Limits within Habermas' Community (or Why We Should Not Be a Unified Whole)', in *New Sociological Review (Borders: Merging, Emerging, Emergent)*, 2014, 13(4), pp. 80–93.

INTRODUCTION

The Enlightenment: Something to think about

What does thinking about the Enlightenment mean?

Thinking about the Enlightenment has several meanings: (a.) It evokes the intellectual revolution that occurred in Europe from the late seventeenth to the late eighteenth century. (b.) It attempts to ascertain how it looks from within the prevailing horizon of consciousness, from within the current world-situation. It implies, therefore, (c.) a re-evaluation of its actual significance, as a cultural "legacy", as the foundation of modernity; and (d.) a reassessment of its original cognitive and cultural intentions.

Further, before this, "thinking about" raises the question of thinking's own cognitive intention, of its purpose and its envisaged outcome. It accounts for the persistence of interest in the Enlightenment. It also perpetuates the Enlightenment's self-interest.

That is to say: the Enlightenment vindicates academic work. The Enlightenment must vindicate it, if it is now 'impossible to imagine any aspect of contemporary life in the West without it' (Pagden 2013: 345). But what justifies Pagden specifically leaving history – after all now, and even then, the dominant mode of world-comprehension – off the list of those human sciences, those 'academic disciplines', with their 'beginning' in the Enlightenment and still 'dictating much of how we view, and attempt to control, our lives today' (Pagden 2013: viii)? Academic work is itself justified ultimately by Enlightenment values, such as freedom, truth, democracy, tolerance, open discussion, evidence, criticism, honesty, observance of ethical codes both personal and professional – in short: the attributes of humanity, and with them the transcendental humanism inferred from them. Hence, for Todorov the spirit of the Enlightenment is 'humanism or, if you prefer, [. . .] anthropocentrism'.

This matches Nussbaum's 'spirit of the humanities' promoting a studious ethos: 'searching critical thought, daring imagination, empathetic understanding of human experiences of many different kinds, and understanding of the complexity of the world we live in' (Todorov 2007: 17; Nussbaum 2010: 7).

That is also to say: interest in the Enlightenment (interest *ipso facto* in the Enlightenment's self-interest) promotes professional studiousness – academic self-interest – as a socially affirmative, species-essential value. Hence, vindicating 'the middle station of life' Hume asserts that 'there are more natural parts, and a stronger genius requisite to make a good lawyer or physician, than to make a great monarch'. He maintains that only this social position permits studiousness, that only it 'is more favourable to the acquiring of wisdom and ability, as well as of virtue'. Consequently (he concludes) only 'a man so situate has a better chance for attaining knowledge, both of men and things, than those of a more elevated station' (Hume 1971b: 581). In principle, therefore, Hume advocates 'a league between the learned and conversible worlds'. He recognises that 'learning has been [. . .] a great a loser by being shut up in colleges and cells, and secluded from the world and good company'. Philosophy, in particular, to avoid 'this moping recluse method of study' needs to 'consult experience [. . .] where alone it is to be found, in common life and conversation' (Hume 1971a: 569).

Thus for academic work the Enlightenment offers a regulative idea, a wider cultural ethos, as when Pagden defines it as 'creating a field of values, political, social, and moral, based upon a *detached and scrupulous understanding* – as far as the mind is capable – of what it means to be human'. And this culture of studiousness means that 'today *most educated people*, at least in the West, broadly accept the conclusions to which it led'. Moreover, this studiousness is – naturally – self-vindicating, which is – naturally – why 'most believe that it is possible *to improve, through knowledge and science*, the world in which we live'. This studiousness too affirms ethical ideals (Pagden continues): 'Because they [i.e., *most educated people*] believe this, they also believe that there exists a "human nature" [. . .] which is *much the same everywhere*' (Pagden 2013: 343–344 (my emphasis)). Inevitably academic comprehension culminates in the most comprehensive category ("human", "humanity"). Thus, with its authoritative, correctional academic evaluations, with its historiographicalm bickering, Enlightenment scholarship puts its fundamental cognitive intention beyond criticism: its comprehensive clarity derives directly from, and so *a priori* affirms, the Enlightenment paradigm its own procedures enact, the very paradigm it proposes to evaluate. It leaves nothing else.

Even so, the studiously vindicated humanism that justifies Enlightenment scholarship and affirms Enlightenment values forecloses on thinking about it. It has already done the thinking: it is pre-emptive. So too, in its own way, has its symmetrical opposite, the Counter-Enlightenment which affirms faith, tradition, orthodoxy – unquestionable knowledge, knowledge already known. In so far as the Enlightenment congeals into a "tradition", a "process", let alone an abstract universal ("humanity"), it becomes its own orthodoxy, its own antagonist – 'a paradoxical disenlightening at the heart of the Enlightenment project' (Allott 2002: 144).

Further (to follow also Gray's argument in *Enlightenment's Wake*), thinking about the Enlightenment must face the nihilism it implies – the 'groundlessness' of thought in itself evinced in 'the post-modern condition of plural and provisional perspectives, lacking any rational or transcendental ground or unifying world view' (Gray 1997: 153, 166). It is a question of not just relinquishing humanism as a universal value or virtue as an end in itself because they rest on a "hollowed out" rationality, but also the indeterminate nature of any value. The current cognitive situation reveals that, even if promoting humanism and virtue – or even a plurality of values – were imperative, nothing identifies which cognitive attitude (cf. variants (a.) – (c.) above) would suit that purpose (and, even if they all did in different ways, which one would be preferable). Moreover, to regard this situation as 'an historical fate, which we are wise to make the best of', anaesthetizes thinking (Gray 1997: 146, 153). It denies any differentiation between an individual's ontological essence [*Wesen*] and the contingent reality of his or her existence [*Dasein*]. It inhibits the 'constant capacity of reason to construct new forms of thought, perception, preference, and value': it thus discounts the cognitive procedures that lead to new forms of ideation, 'that – be it deliberately or unconsciously – operate as what could be termed a technology for *suspending reality as the character* of things, of the world' [*eine Technik, die man als* [. . .] Aufhebung des Wirklichkeitscharakters *der Dinge, der Welt bezeichnen kann*' (Scheler 1978: 52). Crucially it would deprive the individual of the power strenuously to refuse his or her immediate reality (ibid.).

Reflecting on how and what to think about the Enlightenment recognises that human beings are already endowed with the capacity to think, even if – as Kant remarks – they still need to know how to use it autonomously. Specifically they need to know how to orientate themselves in their own mind so as to be immunised against the emotional plagues – the social constraints, the superstitions, the zealotry, the idolatry, the licentiousness, the dogmatism – that poison the public realm (cf. Kant 1982b: 53; 1977: 280–282). For this reason thinking is inherently dissident: if it were not, it would be merely mental dressage, the mechanical indoctrination of conventional responses. Rather thinking is reservation, analysis, inference, differentiation, evaluation – not as a "tradition going back to Socrates", nor as the sole invention of the Frankfurt School, but as a species-essential capacity. Dissident and reserved *a priori*, thinking actually in itself creates the freedom its cognitive procedures demand.

Thinking about the Enlightenment: the ideational entity produced is mercurial, protean. It was "an age of reason" that also included "Sensibility" and "*Sturm und Drang*" as literary movements. It required various forms of rational idealism (as with Descartes or Leibniz) but it could not foresake radical empiricism (as with Locke). Now its natural theology and the evidence of divine providence ensured metaphysical complacency (as with Bonnet); now its radical materialism provoked political outrage (as with La Mettrie or Helvétius). It represents a rupture, a new beginning, "a turning point" in history, a new civilisation; but it also stands in a "long tradition", including the Renaissance, the Reformation, and even a secularised, scholastic nostalgia for the worldview of Augustine and Aquinas. It appears as a pan-European movement or programme; conversely, as the expression of state and nation-specific modernising initiatives, it hardly exists as a unity in itself. In short, any of the recognised classical accounts can refine the Enlightenment's kaleidoscopic mutations – particularly the controversialist approach taken by Israel in *Radical Enlightenment* and its sequels that chart the points of friction both between competing values within the Enlightenment and between these competing values and those affirmed by the advocates of political hierarchy and religious orthodoxy (Israel 2001; 2006; 2013). Hence, precisely because the tools for scholarly thought derive from the spirit of the Enlightenment, its historiography wrapped up in itself apparently offers an accumulating mass of heterogeneous approximations.

The Enlightenment exactly?

It seems self-evident, therefore, primarily to explore how (cf. (a.) above) the intellectual revolution that occurred in Europe from the late seventeenth to the late eighteenth century is defined, what constitutes an adequate definition. That seems logical: thinking about it presupposes knowing what it was. The history, the account of the past, of what it was, that – historically – preceded the cognitive subject, surely takes precedence. So, Ferrone intends to uphold both 'the autonomy and prerogatives of historical knowledge in this field' and 'the epistemological status of historical knowledge' (Ferrone 2015: 58, 63). Blocking any philosophical reflection on the Enlightenment, he wishes to 'distinguish with true intellectual honesty and philological rigor between the specific historical identity of the eighteenth-century phenomenon and its legacy in the following centuries, down to our own times' (Ferrone 2015: 57). So, like Ferrone (but advocating a 'controversialist', intellectual historical approach he rejects), Israel aims to discover 'what exactly the Enlightenment was and what it socially and intellectually involved', since 'the Enlightenment has been and remains by far the most positive factor shaping contemporary reality' (Israel 2006: v). This means that '*any scholar* discussing Enlightenment in broad terms has *a clear responsibility* to render as accurate, carefully delineated, and *complete a picture* of the phenomenon as possible' (Israel 2013: 2 (my emphasis)). It means too – as for Pagden also – that scholarship as socially affirmative behaviour naturally, like a self-fulfilling prophecy, promotes the Enlightenment, since '*anyone wishing to live in accord with reason* would want to support and contribute to' the 'strands of modernity' the Enlightenment 'shaped' (Israel 2006: v (my emphasis)).

However, thinking like this fulfils neither the aspiration of accuracy and comprehension it promises nor its own self-imposed disciplinary commands. To begin with: in Ferrone's case it discounts the *a priori* existence – the ontological precedence – of an existing cognitive subject prerequisite for recognising historical precedence at all. In this it reveals a questionable mental habit so deep-seated that it mimicks self-evident logical 'rigour'. Israel's aspiration leaves the reader wondering how "complete" a 'complete picture' could be, particularly since formulating that injunction already, surely, presupposes knowing what complete knowledge looks like – which, therefore, cancels aspiring to achieve it. Since only narrative can make sense of the various intellectual controversies through which the Enlightenment articulated itself, almost inevitably 'one of the most important shifts in the history of man' comes down to a grandiose, but still monotonous soap-opera of human relationships, – for each thinker an endlessly reiterated pattern of biographical summary, relations with associates or critics, and brief paraphrases of his thinking and its consequences – a psychologistic amalgam of personalities, beliefs, and motives (Israel 2001: vi).

Further, these historical accounts are lodged on two internal contradictions. Common to both: the very method to bring the Enlightenment into focus, to amplify it, to affirm its current humanistic value, to establish its identity, at the same time, in the recourse to historical "context", effectively neutralises it, isolates it. The first: insisting on 'a detached [...] understanding' of an 'eighteenth-century phenomenon' as the approved disciplinary method of determining 'what exactly the Enlightenment was' is a conventional "truth-strategy" of historical scholarship, specifically of historicism. In order the better to comprehend its object, the cognitive principle of the present historical account must place it at a temporal-historical distance from itself, in (what Ernst Bloch calls) 'the remoteness of the preterite' [*Abgeschiedenheit des Präteritums*] (Bloch 1979: 330). This affirms knowledge traditionally (since Aristotle) as the contemplative preoccupation [*theoria*], of a spectator, with things having been the way they were – all the more capable of being 'scrupulously' 'delineated' for being extricated from any ideologically particular, currently prevailing application (the catch-all, *passe-partout* humanism excepted), for being in the safe custody of the 'clearly responsible' historian thanks to the (mysterious but absolutely unquestionable) 'prerogatives of historical knowledge'.

The second: the Enlightenment concepts worthy of historical interest, particularly for ramifying into 'our own times', for "shaping" modernity, undergo a semiotic re-functioning when identified by their place, by their role, in the "process", the historicist category that *a priori* produces the Enlightenment as a knowledge-object in and for history. Certainly (as Deleuze and Guattari argue) the task of philosophy is to create concepts: so concepts *are* created at certain moments in world-time (in history). However, they can never be pinned down historically: (i) Concepts are events, hence orientated towards, and with cognitive consequences and opportunities for, an unknown future. They should 'not be confused with the state of things in which they were incarnated'. (ii) Concepts organise a vast quantity of otherwise heterogeneous data. (iii) Concepts thus elude the "before / after", the "from / to" linear structure of history. They co-exist a-temporally through their own structural and cognitive affinities (Deleuze and Guattari 1991: 24–26, 28, 36, 58–59). Thinking (i.e., the production of concepts) is, therefore, experimentation, and 'experimentation is always busy with itself – with the new, the remarkable, the interesting which replace the appearance of truth and are more demanding than it is' [*le nouveau, le remarquable, l'intéressant qui remplacent l'apparence de vérité et qui sont plus exigeants qu'elle*]. Hence, 'history [...] is only the totality of the almost negative conditions which facilitate experimentation with something that eludes history' [*L'histoire [...] est seulement l'ensemble des conditions presque négatives qui rendent possible l'expérimentation de quelque chose qui échappe à l'histoire*]. The point is: 'without history, experimentation would not be determined or conditioned; but the experimentation itself is not historical, it is philosophical' [*mais l'expérimentation n'est pas historique, elle est philosophique*] (Deleuze and Guattari 1991: 106). The point is, further: unless the history of philosophy proposes 'arousing a dormant concept, getting it to play on a new stage, even at the cost of turning it against itself', it becomes 'totally uninteresting'. In fact, 'the most universal concepts, presented as eternal forms and values [e.g., humanism, humanity], are the most skeletal, the least interesting'. Content just to 'to stir up old, ready-made concepts', history is doing 'nothing positive': the historian 'might just as well be polishing and scraping away at old bones' (Deleuze and Guattari 1991: 80–81).

Thus the history of ideas proves intellectually perverse – not just immobilizing thought, but appropriating original, experimental, or intellectually liberating concepts only to embalm them in a historicist preservative: their 'documentary value'. As Mannheim explains, documentary value is something other than the 'objective' or (subjectively) 'expressive character' of an art-object or an idea. Rather it represents an 'intentional object only for the [. . .] spectator' (Mannheim 2007: 55). Ascertaining an object's documentary value is an administrative task since it is a category (or class) of meaning both incidental to the object or idea and unintentional subjectively for its creator or author. To the spectator's administrative gaze it discloses 'an identical, homologous pattern underlying a vast variety of totally different realizations of meaning', something in these realisations that is 'culturally characteristic' (Mannheim 2007: 57–58). In the particular case of the Enlightenment, this would be the means of organising it into 'a single highly concentrated intellectual and cultural movement' (Israel 2001: v, 715). Consequently documentary interpretation 'gathers the scattered items of documentary meaning together in overarching concepts' such as '*Weltanschauung*' or 'spirit'. Hence terms such as "Shakespearian" or "Goethean" – or here in historical accounts, "Enlightenment" – refer not to a specific author or texts but 'to an ideal essence' epitomised in them (Mannheim 2007: 58–59). A 'systematic analysis of documentary meaning' is an administrative-academic task, an organisational procedure, the application of instrumental reason. Its aim is to 'distill the spirit of an epoch from the various "objectifications" of that epoch'. It means 'detaching certain elements [. . .] of meaning from their concrete setting and fusing them into validly ascertainable objects of higher generality by using appropriate categories and conceptualizations'. The concepts used must be 'applicable [. . .] to every sphere of cultural activity alike'. Further, 'since culture is in the process of historical evolution', they must also 'serve the purpose of a "longitudinal" analysis of successive temporal stages'. But supporting all this is flimsy tautology that Mannheim disregards, maintaining that 'in the cultural sciences the part and the whole are given simultaneously': the '"spirit of the epoch" derives from its individual documentary manifestations' while 'we interpret the individual documentary manifestations on the basis of what we know about the spirit of the epoch' (Mannheim 2007: 73–74). Thus the historicist marrow in history, let alone intellectual history, is inimical to thinking – and not just in the way Deleuze and Guattari suggest. The notion of documentary value — achieved through the interdependence of part and whole — is in itself a fallacy, an example of the 'vicious bifurcation of nature': 'assertions about things which don't exist [i.e., the abstract, "spiritual" whole] in order to convey truths about things which do exist [i.e., the tangible objective or subjective part]' whence the "spiritual" whole was abstracted in the first place; dividing knowledge into immediate perceptions and sensations (on the one hand) and abstract 'mental excitements' or 'psychic additions' meant to "explain" them (on the other). In fact (Whitehead insists), 'so far as reality is concerned all our sense-perceptions are in the same boat, and must be treated on the same principle' (Whitehead 1920: 42, 44–45, 148). On this line of argument, the historicist logic driving historical processes, the historical concepts categorising their documentary justification (as with the Enlightenment), are sophistical attempts to resolve the crucial 'problem [namely] to discuss the relations *inter se* of things known, abstracted from the bare fact that they are known' (Whitehead 1920: 30).

The Enlightenment's historiographical make-up

Hence, pinning down the identity of the Enlightenment also resorts — as a form of insurance — to an apparently different truth-strategy: it sees how it looks from within the prevailing horizon of consciousness, from within the current world-situation (cf. (b.) above).

This too has logical plausibility. The Enlightenment implies a sense of finality. As Kant said, the age of Enlightenment was not an enlightened age: that had still to be realised, and history in its progress would testify to it (Kant 1982b: 59–60; Kant 1982a: 47ff.). This Foucault construes as occurring through testing and transgressing the prevailing historical limits of one's cognitive and social situation (Foucault 2001: 1387, 1390ff.). Consequently, Enlightenment historiography regards the world as it now is as the eighteenth century's future (obviously: the Enlightenment went before, now its historians have come afterwards), so that the Enlightenment offers itself as a "legacy" to modernity or as modernity's "heritage". But here too historical scholarship operates in the Enlightenment's own self-interest. As Diderot confirms, to succeed the Enlightenment must make a pre-emptive claim on the future, on those who come afterwards. As he explains in his article 'Encyclopédie', collating the existing knowledge of Man, elaborating its comprehensive system only makes sense if the outcome is passed on to posterity — a posterity grateful to its predecessors for their effort — for it to complete (cf. Diderot 1994a: 363, 374). But though this intellectual legacy is the very vital, experimental concept of Enlightenment, what modern historians receive is a ready-made thought-structure, a documentary value finally to assess.

Here too the clarifying procedures and intentions of Enlightenment historiography *a priori* rely on the very cognitive stance, the Enlightenment, it intends to validate. So the technique it employs is the very opposite of resorting to 'the remoteness of the preterite', of seeing the Enlightenment principally as an eighteenth-century phenomenon. Instead, it counter-balances the present's *historical link* to its 'remote' past by the past's close *ethical attachment* to its proximate present. As a past documentary value the Enlightenment is re-functioned so as to gauge the present's ethical propriety.

Hence, a marked characteristic of Enlightenment historiography: documentary evidence and values become a spring-board into ethical propriety underwritten by academic comprehension. Conventionally coordinating the most heterogeneous material, it has no qualms about projecting documentary values as indices of ethical achievements.

In Pagden's case it even exerts a form of blackmail: desiring the opportunities that come with modernity must mean affirming Enlightenment values. 'Without the Enlightenment modernity would not have taken place' or at least 'not [. . .] in the way and where it did' – though this is a self-evident verdict implying equally it might have turned out better or possibly worse (Pagden 2013: viii). This procedure culminates in self-contradiction. The global political and economic organisation of the world since 1945 might well be a legacy of the Enlightenment; but since the world is still 'populated by [. . .] very far from enlightened regimes, *this may not be very much*' (Pagden 2013: xiii (my emphasis)). Consequently (as Pagden's argument demonstrates) a set of documentary values implying world-improvement through knowledge is enlisted to affirm 'admittedly somewhat ramshackle, often ineffective [. . .] cosmopolitan institutions', even if they are 'not utterly unlike the kind that Kant hoped for' (Pagden 2013: 350). Thus moral idealism as an Enlightenment documentary value is reduced to affirming the world in its prevailing desolate condition – at the moment of writing the corpse of a young Syrian refugee found washed up on a Turkish beach and ancient Palmyra being destroyed – based on the documentary coordination of 'central Enlightenment beliefs in a common humanity' evinced in it, 'shakily primitive and incomplete' though they evidently are (Pagden 2013: 349). Thus the ethical ideals implied by the Enlightenment as a documentary value come down ethically to this 'miserable moralism in the name of which we are being constrained to accept the way of the world and its absolute injustice' [*le moralisme misérable au nom duquel on veut nous contraindre à accepter le train du monde et son injustice absolue*] (Badiou 2003: 13).

The structure of this kind of argument is fallacious, in three respects. First: (as Mannheim said) documentary interpretations and values define a historical epoch and are epoch-specific. Hence, the documentary character and values of eighteenth-century culture do differ from those of the twentieth or twenty-first century. Superimposing past values on the present's own documentary values destroys their original, distinctive historicist worth and with that the apparent validity of superimposing them to start with.

Second: documentary values are (as Mannheim also said) a class in themselves, evident to the contemplating spectator, coordinated by the historian's comprehensive, administrative gaze – a theoretical situation transcendant to the heterogeneous data being documented, categorised. Given that they can endorse value-free knowledge (particularly in Weber's sense: indisposed to any ideological agenda), documentary values have nothing to do with ethical values unless it be to extract a comprehensive documentary value from their formulation (Weber 1988: 608–609, 612–613). Conversely, ethics is objective action, subjective commitment, both excluded by the historian's 'detached' administrative gaze – unless writing a history is a politically subversive action due to personal (not just professional disciplinary) commitment (e.g., against a prevailing ideological party-line or institutionalised orthodoxy). Since human beings are integrated into the same global system, the same rationalised order, beyond their control, ethical capacity cannot arise from personal self-refinement, personal self-development – the conception of humanistic sameness – systematised integration itself displaces and negates. Rather it manifests itself in an intuitive appreciation of the plight of someone other, their vulnerability, their ethical demand expressing their difference (cf. Lévinas 1987: 51–53, 96–97).

Third: the re-functioning of Enlightenment documentary values as twenty-first century ethical norms is based on a historicist fallacy (which is why it ultimately erases their historical or epochal value). It justifies the superimposition of the documentary past on the documentary present not just by insisting on a causal relationship between the Enlightenment and modernity, but also on (allegedly) incontrovertible historical continuity, an absolutely indestructible temporal bond between them. For these documentary values there is, apparently, a 'true line of causal descent from the Enlightenment to the modern western world' (Reed 2015: 219). Curiously the fact that epoch-making documentary values do not convert into modern ethical values involves questioning the respective types of value rather than the alleged temporal bond between them – particularly since here the presumption of historical continuity obfuscates the crucial problem (defined by Whitehead): 'the relations *inter se* of things known, abstracted from the bare fact that they are known'. In the *World We Want*, Louden, 'with the benefit of two centuries' hindsight', is dismayed to discover 'the large gap that exists between Enlightenment ideals and contemporary realities'. He intends, therefore, to examine 'how our present world [is] both similar to and different from the world they wanted,' and 'how and why [. . .] the ideals of the Enlightenment still elude us' (Louden 2010: vii, 6–7). The result is truly an account: the historian-accountant reckoning credits and debits to both sides, to Enlightenment and to modernity. But 'drawing attention to the enormous gap that often exists between Enlightenment ideals and current realities,' both diminishes the Enlightenment's documentary value and misrepresents the present's moral destitution (Loudon 2010: 126). There is, in one sense, little point in dwelling on the 'enormous gap' between ideals and realities: that is why – in Loudon's context – an ideal *is* "ideal" and a reality "real". In any case, however impressive the documented philosophical achievement of the Enlightenment was in its own epoch, the desolate present need not rely solely on it for its moral and intellectual self-orientation. It has its own epochal resources (exemplified amongst others by Hannah Arendt, Emmanuel Lévinas, or Alain Badiou). Rather the narrow, rigidly historicist vindication of the comparison is dubious: if there is a 'true line of causal descent' from the Enlightenment to the present, there is too for everything else, not least as its shadow anything uninterested in, or opposed to, Enlightenment.

Thinking about the Enlightenment in this way – especially since in taking documentary values for ethical values it functions affirmatively – implies not just that the present is otherwise diminished and disorientated but also that this questionable realisation of documented Enlightenment values should automatically motivate perpetuating them into the future. But this ethical predicament derives from a historicist syndrome most accurately defined (by Ernst Bloch) as 'commodity thinking' [*Denkform Ware*]. As these ways of thinking about the Enlightenment confirm, 'the rigid distinctions between future and past collapse by themselves, unrealized future shows itself in the past, avenged and inherited, mediated and fulfilled past in the future.' Hence, 'grasped in isolation and held onto, the past is merely a category of commodity, a reified fact unconscious of how it comes to be and its ongoing process' [*Isoliert gefaßte und so festgehaltene Vergangenheit ist eine bloße Warenkategorie, das ist ein verdinglichtes Factum ohne Bewußtsein seines Fieri und seines fortlaufenden Prozesses*] (Bloch 1979: 7). It is as though the "stream of history" is halted so that the immobilized, documented epoch offers itself as mental artefact or object – that history has "shaped" – to be made over with all kinds of historicist applications any interest can customise.

'To change the common way of thinking' [*changer la façon commune de penser*] was for Diderot the principle of a good encyclopedia as an agency of Enlightenment (Diderot 1994a: 403). From this the ethical inference would suggest no point in thinking about the Enlightenment in common academic ways well within the historical limits of the present (cf. (a.) and (b.) above). This way the Enlightenment becomes its own constraining scholastic orthodoxy, its own self-contradiction, stifling the human species-interests it otherwise advocates. But it thus poses a crucial, apprehensive question: whether or not currently available forms of thinking can come to terms with it. It suggests – though this is not at all surprising – that the mind can produce eidetic constructions other minds subsequently cannot comprehend as adequately as its creators believe they themselves do. The Enlightenment allegedly anticipates modernity, but it is not self-evident that that allegation gives modernity any cognitive advantage in defining the Enlightenment: the identity principle [A = A; i.e., Enlightenment = modernity] is here deceptive. More generally why should hindsight, two centuries of it, be construed as a scholastic benefit when the 'gap' between Enlightenment past and post-Enlightenment present is a euphemism for species's self-indictment, if not the sign of incompatible documentary values? Because Enlightenment attitudes inform scholastic procedures and presumptions, they pre-empt documentary evaluations of the movement itself. Particularly now, just after the seventieth anniversary of the destruction of Hiroshima and Nagasaki by atomic bombs, why assume (like many *philosophes*) that history is progress? As arguably this event signified the beginning of a new epoch, the atomic epoch, with its own documentary value, the 'close of the epoch in which epochs succeeded each other' [*die Epoche der Epochenwechsel* [*ist*] *vorüber*], inhabited henceforth by 'the first generation of last human beings' [*der ersten Generation letzter Menschen*], why not bet rather – in the name of the Enlightenment but not *like* the Enlightenment – on history being a permanent exhibition of species self-incrimination (Anders 1986a: 20; 1986b: 174)? Why not at least admit that "reason", for the *philosophes* the decisive human faculty, but in some of its subsequent instrumental-technological manifestations absolutely lethal, will never determine where the "historical process" is heading – if it exists now at all.

Enlightenment finality

The Enlightenment cannot dispense with a sense of its finality: otherwise it would be unthinkable. Condorcet's *Esquisse d'un tableau des progrès de l'esprit humain* (1793) would demonstrate that the inauguration of a world finally permitting the realisation of human beings' infinite potential is imminent. In line with his own empiricist conviction he insists: 'the epoch of one of the great revolutions of the human species is within *touch*' [*nous* touchons à *l'époque d'une des grandes révolutions de l'espèce humaine*] (Condorcet 1971: 86 (my emphasis)). With its speculations ended, with no hypotheses to form any more, 'philosophy has nothing left but to gather and order facts and to demonstrate the useful truths arising from their combinations and their comprehensive totality' [*il ne lui reste qu'à rassembler, à ordonner les faits, et à montrer les vérités utiles qui naissent de leur enchaînement et de leur ensemble*] (Condorcet 1971: 83). For Condorcet's optimism it is axiomatic that history is an exact science disclosing progress as one of the general laws of nature, evinced 'at the *same* time [*en même temps*] in both the development of the individual's faculties and in a great number of individuals existing together in societies' (Condorcet 1971: 76). Condorcet's *Tableau* insists that the progress made so far since the beginnings of civilisation by the human species will continue into the future. His conviction presumes that these 'general laws, be they known or unknown, [. . .] are necessary and constant' [*les lois générales, connues ou ignorées* [. . .] *sont nécessaires et constantes*] (Condorcet 1971: 253).

Like Condorcet Kant too envisages an end, a purpose – for individuals, societies, and states – to being enlightened, to behaving in an autonomous, enlightened manner: the establishment of a world offering all human individuals equally global citizenship. Certainly he is here attempting to universalize a Stoic disposition: 'that the mind should not be a bondsman to any one place', and that the individual is born 'not for one corner of the universe' since 'its country is the whole world' [*patria mea totus hic mundus est*] (Seneca 2006: 200–201; XXVIII, §§4–5). He aims to establish some philosophical principles conceived to elicit from the ever accumulating mass of historical erudition documentary interpretations and values that will affirm this moral end (Kant 1982a: 49–50). In contrast to Condorcet, for whom an enlightened world was already discernable, Kant's own ethical finish to the Enlightenment as a cultural concept is projected onto a (from his perspective) still distant future.

The Enlightenment as a historical process

The historical self-projection of the Enlightenment underpins both the claim (as by Pagden) that it 'still matters' and 'why it is important to understand just what it was' (Pagden 2013: xiv). These two principles inform any re-evaluation of the Enlightenment as the foundation of modernity, hence as a cultural "legacy" for our own times (cf. (c.) above). They are inevitably reciprocal: on the one hand, 'the key terms of almost every modern conflict over how we are to [...] understand humanity [...] ultimately refer back to some understanding of the Enlightenment;' on the other, 'we are all, *inescapably*, the heirs of the architects of the Enlightenment "science of man"' (Pagden 2013: 5, 351 (my emphasis)). But this 'inescapable' reciprocity is constituted not by humanity as an ethical value as such: that value could be derived from moralists historically prior to the Enlightenment (e.g., amongst others Plato, Aristotle, Cicero, Seneca, Montaigne). Rather it is produced by a documentary evaluation that recognises the Enlightenment as a 'top down process', an 'intellectual process', 'as an open-ended, continuing progression, subject to constant scrutiny and re-evaluation' (Pagden 2013: xiii, 8, 10). This evaluation is confirmed by the Enlightenment, as described by the *philosophes*, regarding itself as progressive development, as gradual, even arduous self-realisation that needs history as its transmission-system. For Condorcet as for Kant (as for others too) it works as a "universal coupling" eidetically connecting present reality as unrealised ideals with realised ideals as future reality. Tellingly for Condorcet: almost – figuratively – within touch is not the imminent 'great revolution' but its 'epoch'. Thus too (as already mentioned) the Enlightenment becomes not just the paradigmatic historical topic, but also a topic that vindicates an essential historical paradigm. Thinking like this about the Enlightenment and its finality displays historicism in its crudest form.

Historical comprehension relies on basic eidetic paradigms – that could be called "categorical coordinators" – (such as "causes", "linkages", "traditions", "legacies", "heirs", "frameworks", "contexts", "roots", "forces", "impulses", "impacts"; "shaping", "making") to structure its historical account, to articulate its argument. For making meaningful connections between facts in the heterogeneous material it already knows, for coordinating them, these 'psychic additions' are indispensable. Without them history would not work, mechanically useful but semantically redundant though they are.[1] Arguably the most basic, the most essential is "process" or "historical process", as in these examples (amongst many, e.g., Pagden above):

- 'Examining controversies in detail provides a means of testing possible answers to the most pertinent questions *objective to the historical process* itself [...]. As a methodology it employs the *general historical process* itself to locate the key ideas and sift out those superimposed [...] by later [...] historians' (Israel 2006: 25 (my emphasis)).
- 'For Peter's successes opened the way to *a wider process* of renewal and rationalization, embracing the whole Orthodox world' (Israel 2006: 295 (my emphasis)).
- 'The French nobility's tenacious promotion of its power and privileges, however crucial to the *mechanics* of the *historical process* that made the Revolution possible, was entirely secondary [...] in *shaping* the revolutionary outcome (Israel 2013: 16 (my emphasis)).
- 'A *process* was set in train in the *late eighteenth century*, a democratic enlightenment based on liberty, equality, and the "general good", which was then [...]

driven back, but which *resumed* after a fashion in the *post-Second World War era*' (Israel 2013: 951(my emphasis)).

Conversely, seeing itself as still to be realised, as still in development (as illustrated by Condorcet and Kant), the Enlightenment itself invests "process" with affirmative semantic significance, thus reinforcing its otherwise purely connective function – as acknowledged in these examples:

- 'among all enlighteners, Henry Home, Lord Kames (1696–1782), was one of the first to analyse and explore the stages of history, to view human development as *a complex process* and attempt through studying history and society to widen our understanding of what humanity is' (Israel 2013: 248 (my emphasis)).
- '[Lessing] sought to redefine revelation, converting it from a miraculous event into a development understood only non-miraculously and historically as *a long-term process*, the progressive emergence of the rationality and moral consciousness of man in society' (Israel 2013: 325 (my emphasis)).

Hence, academic evaluation of the Enlightenment is self-referential. It operates with academic strategies (i.e., forms of "process") the Enlightenment created for itself: it is a mirror absorbing academicism in its self-reflection. As a result the Enlightenment is comprehended in terms not just of the "natural precedence" of the past for the present (modernity) but also of their necessary reciprocity. The relationship (as suggested earlier) may be close: 'the Enlightenment stands at the threshold of the modern age, and these answers [i.e., to "What is Enlightenment?"] inevitably tell us a good deal about how we make sense of our own situation;' or remote, given 'the *historical distance* that separates us from the Enlightenment', despite 'the ties of tradition and usage that still bind us to it' (Schmidt 1996: xi (my emphasis)). Thus the historiography of the Enlightenment works with an apparently fail-safe, rigid historicism. Certainly the documentary interpretation historicism offers is provisional, needing constant revision, since 'any single interpretation is profoundly influenced by the location within the historical stream from which the interpreter attempts to reconstruct the spirit of a past epoch' (Mannheim 2007: 61). However, even if highly conflicted in its modern interpretation, 'the subject of irate and furious debates', the Enlightenment's significance, far from thereby being rendered provisional, is only reinforced (cf. Pagden 2013: 5). The reason is: the historiographical paradigm for making sense of the Enlightenment – its "process", its "project" – not only derives from it, but is also integral to modern (conventionally historicized) thinking (as the examples cited above demonstrate). It makes up the optic modernity sees it with. The Enlightenment can, therefore, be read into any aspect of the modern world, find itself implicated in the most egregious, the most disastrous consequences resulting from the self-same historicist structures that enable it to make sense of itself. In its modernity the Enlightenment has achieved a – somewhat dubious – form of finality. It 'still matters' even if its political realisation really is 'admittedly ramshackle, often ineffective' and its envisaged 'future cosmopolitan world [. . .] still [. . .] some way off' (Pagden 2013: 350). Thus functioning 'after a fashion', its underlying historicist determinism looks more like a variable 'trend' than a necessary historical or evolutionary "law" (Israel 2013: 951; Popper 1974: 115-6). In these desolate circumstances its pristine, abstract humanism, though predicated on its 'science of man' as the most self-evident form of human comprehension, never was a realistic objective. Rather, in view of the *moralisme misérable* it tolerates, with which it has always co-existed, it holds out apologetically an illusory, always deferred compensation.

If this outcome is disappointing, the fault lies less with the Enlightenment as such than with the historicism it depends on. In its egregious political manifestations in the twentieth century, specifically in promoting totalitarianism, historicism has been ruinous: there is, therefore, no point in arguing for a "good", humanistic historicism (e.g., in Condorcet's *Tableau*, or Herder's *Ideen*). There isn't one. Even conceived with the best intentions, its basic, flawed assumption is that its laws are indeed constant (as, e.g., Condorcet asserts), that, therefore, 'society will necessarily change but along a predetermined path that cannot change' (Popper 1974: 51). 'The historicist,' says Popper, seems 'deficient in imagination, for he cannot imagine a change in the conditions of change': after all, there is 'no valid reason to expect of any repetition of a historical development that it will *continue* to run parallel to its prototype' (Popper 1974: 111, 130). However (by contrast), the Enlightenment specifically betrays *both* a certain apprehension, the awe-inspiring realisation of the ramifications of its intention to move beyond or, more critically, to project the demise of the existing world-order; *and* the immediate need, therefore, for intellectual and moral reassurance, the need for the *philosophes* 'to compensate themselves for the loss of an unchanging world by clinging to the faith that change can be foreseen because it is ruled by an unchanging law' (Popper 1974: 161). But this holistic stance – manifested typically in eighteenth-century notions of providence or of natural theology – is 'inescapably' ideological. In political and social terms, it diminishes the public sphere as Kant formulated it. As Popper remarks, 'the appeal for a *common purpose*' is 'an appeal to abandon rational thought' since it is 'an appeal to abandon all rival moral opinions and the cross-criticisms and arguments to which they give rise'. It thus undermines the freedom of thought, specifically what here depends on it: the effectiveness of crucial strategies for testing sociological and scientific propositions by attempting to falsify them (Popper 1974: 159). In cognitive terms (from Deleuze's and Guattari's perspective), historicism pre-empts the immanence, the experimentation, the inventions of other concepts, the formulations of different truths, and with them a still open future essential for philosophical conceptualisation, not least for reconceptions of the Enlightenment. Instead, as both Israel and Pagden demonstrate, the Enlightenment operates as a form of historical pre-emption. It comes down to reiterating what about it has been unchanging, what about it is always same: for Israel it is a process that 'resumes' as well as a 'programme [that] could perhaps be completed yet' (Israel 2013: 951); for Pagden it is predicated on the belief 'that there exists a "human nature" [...] which is much the same everywhere' (a principle that plausibly seems to explain so much but in effect 'explains nothing') (Pagden 2013: 344; cf. Popper 1974: 154). In thus asserting the Enlightenment's 'commanding centrality', proposing it as a model for 'anyone wishing to live in accord with reason', deriving from it what (allegedly) 'most educated people' accept and believe – statements tanked up with disciplinary authority and academic correction – the historiographical consensus surreptitiously exerts social and intellectual control: that 'most educated people' should recognise 'what the present owes to the past', and, absorbed in the reiterated interpretation of the same, adjust their thinking to conform with it (Israel 2013: 1; 2006: v; Pagden 2013: xiv, 343–344; cf. Popper 1957: 53–54).

Enlightenment perpetually postponed

If historical phenomena behaved like natural phenomena they would evince not static, 'constant' "laws" but dynamic situations unfolding in chaotic, unpredictable ways as their momentum falters and disperses. This helps explain the Enlightenment's modern dilemmas as evinced in its dialectical transmutations: its implication in the intimidating disenchantment of the world explored by Horkheimer and Adorno in *Dialektik der Aufklärung* (1947), or, 'materializing in [. . .] the virtual assemblage of the interconnections preprogrammed and predetermined by the universe of intelligent machines,' a digital counterfeit of Absolute Knowledge, originally a Hegelian derivation from the Enlightenment's comprehensive rationality (Berardi 2009: 73). Saving the Enlightenment would, therefore, mean cancelling its historicist self-conception. To redeem its essential finality, might it not be better – paradoxically – for it to be perpetually incomplete, always postponed, never quite realised?

This rationale produces the proposition that 'Enlightenment [. . .] immensely larger and richer without the capital letter' is 'never outdated because never completed'. It never will be because 'there will always be new problems to face, the old unenlightened forces of interest and power to oppose, and a new generation that has to tackle them' (Reed 2015: 219–220). Thus the Enlightenment dissolves into the historicist "stream" of history, into things being the way they are, the way they will be, the same 'old' things. It thus offers not just Pagden's 'most educated people' but also the common-sense 'ordinary person' 'a way of living in history' by pushing a somewhat vain hope as a prophylactic against the 'despair and inertia' this endless situation otherwise produces (Reed 2015: 215, 218). Viewed thus the open-ended commitment by humanity to realise Enlightenment optimism resembles the unending labours of Sisyphus, 'after all the Enlightenment's patron saint' (Reed 2015: 215). But this identification speaks volumes: it completely inverts the Enlightenment's philosophical significance, negating its moral claims. Choosing Sisyphus is, in one sense, particularly apt: his name is understood to mean 'very wise'. But like his son, Odysseus (as Horkheimer and Adorno stress), his knowledge made him clever and cunning, even tricking and deceiving the gods. Hence, his sentence in the underworld: to roll a weighty stone uphill that then 'bounces back to the very bottom once more; where he wearily retrieves it and must begin all over again' (Graves 1966: 216–220, §67).

The analogy transforms the Enlightenment: (i) What is proposed as motivating the hope it vouchsafes, is in fact eternal forced-labour, a brutal, physical form of punishment, Sisyphus incurred through thinking instrumentally for himself, in his own self-interest. (ii) So cancelling historicist structures such as "progress", "process", or "project", leaving the Enlightenment always incomplete, at the "degree zero" of historicism, still cannot remove their or the Enlightenment's characteristic sameness. It still discounts any 'change in the conditions of change': Sisyphus's pointless labours continue always the same. (iii) Thus Sisyphus symbolises the sheer desolation of human life not just in a natural world completely, constantly indifferent to it but also in the exhausting, incarcerating routines of the socio-economic world: its *absurdity*, in other words (Camus 1972: 26–29, 44, 80). Nothing could be further from the anthropocentrism of Enlightenment, from Man as the necessary, central pivot, the *copula*, of its entire *Weltanschauung*, or from the humanism it implies. Conversely, if Sisyphus nevertheless represents reiterated, but vain attempts to realise its 'programme', if it really is the case that it is 'never outdated because never completed', it is still self-negating. With its sense of finality the Enlightenment's humanistic agenda may well offer human beings an indispensable rational goal, all the while as an end in itself leading them into a historicist trap, kettling them in a historical cul-de-sac. The Enlightenment's finality in this case would demonstrate an unexceptional truth: that for the best reasons human beings can nurture ideals so sublime, so demanding, that their dismal realisation triggers nothing but self-punishing frustration and dejection.

Evaluation in itself implies finality, something terminal, as modernity demonstrates as with hindsight it attempts to assess the Enlightenment's continuing relevance, why it 'still matters', appraising its historicist documentary value, thus blocking any future, different conceptualisation. The Enlightenment's current 'ramshackle ineffectiveness' thus displayed can only, therefore, turn finality back on itself. It proposes instead the inference that modernity's fixation on the Enlightenment's current value is itself symptomatic of a terminal condition – if not Spenglerian in scope, 'the prelude to an irreversible [. . .] Western decline', then apparent at least in current misgivings about the survival of the Western world (Gray 1997: 183; Debray and Girard 2014; cf. Davies 2002: 32-4).

The demise of a 'great truth'

For d'Alembert, if it could be surveyed from a single, comprehensive point of view 'the universe would be nothing but a unique fact and a great truth' [*ne seroit* [. . .] *qu'un fait unique . . . une grande vérité*] (D'Alembert 2011: 88). The *Encyclopédie* he and Diderot edited relied on a comprehensive scheme based on a similar single viewpoint to reveal the totality of human knowledge as interconnected (D'Alembert 2011: 99). Now, though, this form of comprehension – manifested still in the historian's '*clear responsibility* to render as [. . .] *complete a picture* [. . .] *as possible*' – is unobtainable: 'it is not possible for us to observe or to describe a whole piece of the world [. . .]; in fact, not even the smallest whole piece may be so described, since all description is necessary selective' (Popper 1974: 77). Its claim to encompass everything on a systematic foundation is meaningless: 'Knowledge is based on no foundation; what drives ideas and truths is sustained by their continual movement and interaction' [*Das Wissen ruht eben auf keinem Fundamente; das Getriebe der Ideen und Wahrheiten erhält sich nur durch fortwährende Bewegung und Wechselwirkung*] (Fleck 1980: 70).

So thinking about the Enlightenment that would reassess its original cognitive and cultural intentions (cf. (d.) above) must depend on its own future-orientated, conceptually experimental interests. For example, in 'The New Enlightenment' – an essay hardly recognised by orthodox Enlightenment historiography – Allott affirms Kant's concept of world-citizenship, encoded as 'the international society of the whole human race, the society of all societies' (Allott 2002: 144, 148). At the same time, he avoids historicist determinism by stressing law and legislation as means of realising the choices human beings have to make in order to create the world they wish to live in: 'Law,' he says, 'defeats the passage of time by retaining choices made in society's past, in a form – the law – which can take effect in society's future.' 'Retained from society's past' and 'taking effect in a society's present' as it is 'interpreted and applied in the light of actual circumstances', law 'helps make society's future'. Thus law 'resolves that infinitely fruitful dialectic between stability and change which is the nature of human society' (Allott 2002: 134, 150ff.).

Thus Allott's argument avoids historiographical cliché ("what the present owes the past"; "Enlightenment as a legacy", "modernity as heir to the Enlightenment"). Certainly, Allott confirms the 'millennial potential of human beings' – as illustrated in the light of current knowledge by it now being 'hard to believe that, in the year 1000, we in Europe did not know of the idea of zero' (Allott 2002: 135). But this human potential is hardly historically deterministic, even if history manifests it: human choice directs it. Further, he also avoids the *moralisme misérable* evinced in the 'ramshackle, often ineffective' or 'shakily primitive and incomplete' realisation of Enlightenment principles prinked up by their indispensable humanistic cosmetic. He is well aware that his thinking must confront powerful, entrenched ideologies: '*Great-power hegemony. Inter-state rivalry. Global capitalism. Science-led social progress*' (Allott 2002: 136). He confronts the 'de-humanizing humanity' they cause. He acknowledges a 'planet-wide phenomenon, a pandemic of social evil implicit in current social systems, which is, therefore, 'more than merely an aggregation of the dysfunctioning of subordinate societies': 'the globalizing of social systems is also a globalizing of social morbidity', and in effect 'the collective self-wounding of the half-formed society of all-humanity' (Allott 2002: 138–139). He recognises capitalism as a form of 'totalitarian integrating of human effort, including the totalitarian integrating of human consciousness', not least because the individual is now solely an 'economic actor', so that aided by liberal democracy it 'becomes the most advanced form of social oppression ever invented' (Allott 2002: 139–140). Hence, his rejection of historicism: 'if the present condition of democratic-capitalist societies' – societies in their morbid, diseased state – 'is the end of the history of human self-evolving, it is a tragic, if not farcical, end to the long experiment of human biological evolution' (Allott 2002: 149).

But Allott is also aware of the paucity of philosophical and cognitive resources available to inform the choices future human development in the sense of the Enlightenment depends on.

First, he recognises 'the *intellectual* de-humanizing of humanity'. This results from the unrealistic expectation that the human sciences would provide human truths. Instead, two centuries of the Enlightenment project have produced dangerous illusions – essentially normative attributes – that for that very reason need negating: 'There is no such thing as *human nature*. There is no such thing as a *natural human condition*. There is no such thing as *natural human progress*' (Allott 2002: 141). Hence, the crucial inference that negates the basic assumption of Enlightenment historiography: 'The dissolving of the comfortable illusion of *Human naturalism* is the greatest intellectual challenge which the twenty-first century has inherited from the Enlightenment project' (ibid.). Here, too, with its illusory, ideal norms the Enlightenment triggers 'fatalism, defeatism, [. . .] and general despair': in suggesting that human biological, psychological, and social nature cannot be overcome, 'they powerfully re-enforce the idea that social evil is natural and inevitable' (ibid.). Viewing the Enlightenment with this naturalism as generating "processes" and "forces" removes moral responsibility from individuals, by denying them the use of their own minds. Vitally threatened here, the source of the apprehension modernity triggers, is the self-creating potential of human beings through the 'amazing power of subjective consciousness', repressed in two key respects (ibid.). On the one hand, capitalism and science – products of the Enlightenment, 'compatible with terrible horrors and miseries' – drive 'natural human progress' that displaces 'human choice', 'the 'intelligent and courageous use of our capacity for self-transcending and self-surpassing'. On the other, the human sciences themselves 'have tended to alienate humanity from itself, because they tend to deny the essential and overwhelming subjectivity of human beings' (ibid.).

Second, and as an example of a human science denying subjectivity, he acknowledges the modern 'poverty of philosophy': that it, 'as one of humanity's greatest glories, came to be treated as a sort of human science, a professionalized activity within universities', so that thought appeared 'incapable of transcending the conditions of its production'. Symptomatic of this de-humanizing impoverishment are Marx, Freud, and Wittgenstein. Nevertheless their significance (Allott asserts) is ambiguous: they stress respectively the undeniable social, unconscious and symbolic vectors of human consciousness (Allott 2002: 144–145).

With this situation in mind Allott proposes a 'New Enlightenment project of *reconceiving the human mind*' which 'includes the task of reconceiving the way in which we form our ideas, our values, and our purposes', and which requires 'a new intellectual discipline – *international philosophy* – in which minds from all traditions and cultures across the world can contribute to a reunderstanding of what it is to be a thinking being' (Allott 2002: 154). For Allott, philosophy is the sole means of surpassing the de-humanizing tendencies in modernity and of producing a re-humanized good place (*eutopia*) sustained by good social order (*eunomia*) (Allott 2002: 152ff.). To this end, it alone stimulates, sustains, and coordinates 'the self-transforming power of *law*', 'the re-imagining our ideas and ideals of human self-socialising (*society*), and 'human self-contemplating' (*mind*) (Allott 2002: 144). Underpinning this philosophical initiative is the premise that 'the public mind of society and the private mind of the human individual are extensions of each other'. Here, manipulated by the social, unconscious, and symbolic vectors of thought, social evil arises as individual mind and will encounter public mind and will. Precisely here, though, the 'pursuit of social good and of a better form of human society must originate'. On this, Allott is insistent: 'transnational justice is not possible except as an ideal of a self-conscious society of all humanity' (Allott 2002: 148). Significantly Allott rejects the spurious conflict between individual and society: rather 'the self-constituting of the private mind – our personality' and the 'self-constituting of the public mind – the constitution of a society' are interdependent: in the self-reconception of human consciousness that philosophy offers the individual both are radically implicated (Allott 2002: 155). Certainly, too, he advocates idealism: not as an unrealistic or unrealisable aspiration, but as an immediately effective capacity of consciousness itself, specifically as 'the wonderful instrument of human self-evolving and self-prefecting'. The ideal, he affirms, functions as 'a dialectical *negation* of the actual which nevertheless affirms a *potentiality* of the actual. [. . .] the perfectiblity of the actual' (Allott 2002: 156). The ideal is thus no endlessly deferred, historicist objective. Rather it works immediately as a controlling principle of personal and social action, 'giving us the self-transcending power to overcome both social totalitarianism and social evil at every level of social organization' (ibid.). Here Allott's view seems to coincide with Scheler's: the mind, human self-consciousness for its own sake, has the capacity to reject or deny the contingent reality confronting it. Like Diderot in *Le rêve de d'Alembert* (1769 / 1830) (whom he cites), Allott rejects 'the sophism of the ephemeral' [*le sophisme de l'éphémère*], 'the belief held by a transient being that things are immutable' [*c'est celui d'un être passager qui croit à l'immutabilité des choses*], 'the belief [i.e., from within short-term, limited horizons] that what happens to exist now is inevitable and permanent' (Allott 2002: 154; cf. Diderot 1994c: 633).

The Enlightenment's vital energy

In respect of the current situation of the Enlightenment's ethical and global political possibilities, to orientate itself, thinking – particularly the thinking about the Enlightenment demonstrated by the essays in the present volume – relinquishes the administrative evaluation of documentary interpretations in order to re-connect with the immediate energies of its constitutive texts and the dilemmas they pose.

Thinking has no other option. It remains incontrovertible: however much modernity knows *about* the Enlightenment, however "complete" its picture of it, the immediate moment, *now*, in which subjectively each person must decide and act, is a "blind spot", shrouded in darkness [*das Dunkel des gerade gelebten Augenblicks*] (Bloch 1985: 82). More than this (as Allott also recognises): the dominant, academic expert-culture with its elucidation of documentary values, its disciplinary management of cultural systems, ensures that the entire realm of purely subjective truth beyond its jurisdiction is devalued (cf. Husserl 2012: 58). As if the present were not dark enough, it supplies a blindfold.

Hence reading, cultivating immediate contact with Enlightenment texts themselves, is, on the one hand, a means of defying the ideological claim by science [*Wissenschaft*] to be the sole ground of intelligibility, a way of overcoming its 'psychic additions' and 'vicious bifurcations' of comprehension. It challenges 'the false universality of cultural historical method' since it need not automatically be 'about presenting literary works in the context of their time', but instead about 'bringing out in the time in which they were created the time – our own time – that responds to them'. This prevents literature from becoming nothing but 'history's source material' (Benjamin 1988: 452, 456). Reading can in itself block automatic calculations of documentary values. It is, in other words, a means of self-orientation, the Platonic turn towards the light.

On the other, reading establishes the legitimacy of subjective experience; it reinforces the confidence to think for oneself; it encourages the mind to surpass its present state of consciousness. However, the question of how one reads is wide open: how to respond to texts then dissident, scandalous, and forbidden, but now essential constituents of the literary-philosophical canon? Reading is basic, indispensable: the immediate apprehension. However the text is categorised, be it "shocking" or "classic", the reading must be properly – simply, honestly – 'carried out' [*une lecture bien faite*] (to use Péguy's phrase) (Péguy 1961: 105). Readers (as Péguy stresses) bear an immense responsibility. Only they ensure the continuing cultural transmission of the text. In the *act of reading* they become custodians of the author's intentions, crucial to their being accomplished, and of the text's destiny, thereby recharging it with vital significance. Hence reading is nothing passive or receptive, but an active, productive attitude towards the text – to identify its discursive rules, its strategies of codification, its thought-style, to deconstruct them to elicit from it further, implied reserves of signification.

Reading, therefore, means 'organically assimilating the text, being nourished by it, [. . .] never *to work with it* for the sake of a social profile in the century'; but [. . .] to *enter into it* [. . .] not just with sympathy but with love; [. . .] and literally to collaborate with the author' [*pour s'en alimenter, pour s'en nourrir,* [. . .] *nullement pour travailler avec, pour s'en faire valoir, socialement, dans le siècle;* [. . .] *c'est entrer dans;* [. . .] *non seulement avec sympathie, mais avec amour;* [. . .] *et littéralement collaborer avec l'auteur*] (Péguy 1961: 105). Reading explores what the text means: unread or improperly read, it remains inert. For this reason the text dispenses with its context. As Péguy urges (in connection with reading Homer, 'the greatest, the oldest, the *patron*' – the most Classic classic), 'there should be no history between you and the text' [*Qu'il n'y ait aucune histoire entre vous et le texte*]: rather it should be read unceremoniously 'as though it had just been published' [*comme si ce fût la dernière* nouveauté], as though Homer's rhapsodies appeared every fortnight, just like his own *Cahiers* (Péguy 1961: 254). Historical information about the text occludes the critical responsibility every reader bears and the act of reading tests. Reading is not about skimming from the text historical-documentary features as its ready-made sense, nor about showcasing the scholar's reputation as its exemplary interpreter, the authoritative assayor of its documentary value. It repudiates the 'dessicated' philological identification of manuscript sources, the construction of frameworks for dating and framing the author (Péguy 1961: 196). This scholastic indifference towards the text, the failure to respond to it, a 'zero reading' [*un zéro de lecture*], 'opens the door to forgetfulness' [*ouvre la porte à l'oubli*] (Péguy 1961: 110). Péguy insists: thus confining texts to oblivion does the work of history for it. Unlike proper readings that can never be final, never finish with the text, worthless, improper readings are what centuries consume, what time consumes: 'they accomplish a final, supreme disaggregation' [*elles accomplissent la désagrégation suprême, la désagrégation finale*]; 'they enact a first, temporal Last Judgement, they act like a (first) temporal image of a Last Judgement' [*elles réalisent comme un premier jugement dernier, temporel, elles font comme une (première) image temporel, d'un jugement dernier*] (Péguy 1961: 113).

In other words, *une lecture bien faite* excludes historians from being the literary or philosophical text's implied readers. Their research into its documentary values operates with historicist simulacra of it objectively and subjectively inaccessible to its author. In so doing they become not readers 'organically assimilating the text, being nourished by it', but (as Mannheim and Pagden confirm) 'detached spectators' – especially now with their research pre-requisite for professional qualifications or promotion, sponsored by corporate funding, and ready with its preconceived objectives and measurable eventual "impact". Moreover, this exclusion is confirmed precisely by an Enlightenment text, the *Lettres persanes* (1721) by Montesquieu, who (Valéry observes) 'did not envisage the kind of readers we are. He did not write for us as he did not foresee us being so primitive' [*n'a pas entretenu les lecteurs que nous sommes. Il n'écrit pas pour nous, qu'il ne prévoyait pas si primitifs*] (Valéry 1957: 516). Affording his readers 'the pleasure of elegant intelligence' [*les plaisirs de l'intelligence élégante*], Montesquieu envisaged them as 'being more nimble-witted' [*plus déliés*] in contrast to 'people now who take offence if asked to make the slightest mental effort' [*des personnes à qui de demander le plus petit effort de leur esprit on inflige une sorte d'offense*] (ibid). Dispensing with historicist structures, Valéry sees him producing with his novel a liberating historical interregnum in which manners once naturally taken for granted can be playfully exposed, questioned, and ridiculed – an apprehension nevertheless of approaching disorder (Valéry 1957: 515). On the one hand, it challenges the old order maintained by purely fictional, magical means (that 'the sacred, the just, the legal, the decent, the praiseworthy' actually are) as well as the state institutions traditionally supporting them (Valéry 1957: 509). On the other, it senses that something more barbaric is imminent, the 'era of the scientific fact' – a society that 'eliminates anything vague and irrational to rely on what is measurable and verifiable', hence 'the entire modern era displaying a continuous increase in precision' rendering 'anything intangible, anything incapable of precision insignificant' (Valéry 1957: 511). Thus Valéry enters into Montesqieu's text, collaborates with it: it is, after all, a 'preface'. What better demonstrates modernity as the Enlightenment's Nemesis?

Reading the Enlightenment

Since reading – *une lecture bien faite* – does affirm subjective experience, reinforcing the confidence to think for oneself, to dissent from the 'false universality of cultural historical method', it does offer an alternative cognitive value: eclecticism. Eclecticism is a form of knowledge formulated by the Enlightenent but contrasting with the disciplinary technologies of academic comprehension derived from the Enlightenment and essential to modernity. According to Diderot, eclecticism has a certain immediacy: it is 'a particular, domestic philosophy' [*une philosophie particulière et domestique*] created from all the philosophies the eclectic philosopher has analysed. On this personal basis he would be more a disciple to the human species than its teacher, rather reform himself than reform others, rather know truth than educate others with it. So, 'relying on nothing but his own, subjective experience and reason, he tramples on anything that subdues the minds of the masses' [*foulant aux pieds* [. . .] *tout ce qui subjugue la foule des esprits, ose* [. . .] *n'admettre rien que sur le témoignage de son expérience et de sa raison*], such as prejudice, tradition, antiquity, universal consent, authority. Enacting what would be Kant's concept of autonomy, he thus 'dares to think for himself by going back to the clearest general principles to examine and discuss them' [*ose penser de lui-même, remonter aux principes généraux les plus clairs, les examiner, les discuter*]. In short: 'the eclectic philosopher [. . .] acknowledges no-one as his master' [*l'éclectique* [. . .] *est un homme qui ne reconnâit point de maître*] (Diderot 1994b: 300).

Consequently, eclecticism's apparent "undisciplined" disadvantage proves cognitively advantageous. As Cioran observes, it liberates the theoretician 'because it expands [his or her] horizon and enables [him or her] to take advantage of every tradition [*nous permet de profiter de toutes les traditions*]' (Cioran 2006: 150). In practice, according to its Classical Greek etymology, eclecticism involves seeing, selecting, reading, speaking, arranging – being intellectually, aesthetically discriminating.[2] This Xenophon's *Memorabilia* confirms with Socrates's remark that '[. . .] the treasures that the wise men of old have left us in their writings I open and explore with my friends. If we come on any good thing, we extract [*eklegometha*] it, and we set much store on being useful to one another' (Xenophon 1979: 75 (I.vi.14)). Eclecticism opposes the cynicism of specialized, but promiscuous expertise, its occlusive rationalisations, its pre-emptive conceptualizations, its historicist-documentary values. It dismantles comprehension and the administrative gaze producing it. Eclecticism is, therefore, vindicated since it is clear that 'the pursuit of objectivity in the human sciences no longer depends on our ability to find a uniquely correct standpoint from which to arrive at proper judgements' because 'no such unique viewpoint is to be found'. It is, therefore, synonymous with the 'multiplicity of procedures', employed by 'productive rational activities', dependent on 'the multiple tasks we set ourselves in the course of all our different enterprises. It thus meets the need of 'learning to counter our own biases' and to 'make explicit [. . .] the interests and values that we ourselves bring to our research' (Toulmin: 2001: 84–86).

Immediate occasions for knowledge

Eclecticism, therefore, informs the selection of topics presented in the essays that constitute this book. Produced by authors of different nationalities, from different cultural backgrounds, with different academic practices, they sample Enlightenment thinking and they are samples of thinking about the Enlightenment. That is to say: the book does not attempt a panoptic or synoptic, holistic or comprehensive conception of the Enlightenment. That is because (after Popper) it is unobtainable, but also because (after Whitehead) 'things directly observed are, almost always, only samples'. Certainly (Whitehead continues) 'we want to conclude that the abstract conditions, which hold for samples, also hold for other entities which, for some reason or another, appear to us to be of the same sort' – in this case the products of other perceptions of the Enlightenment. But this induction – 'reasoning from the sample to the whole species' – is not self-evident. Though 'all our activities are based on it', it is 'the despair of philosophy' (Whitehead 1967: 23). Hence, the essays themselves are instead 'immediate occasions for knowledge'. They rest inevitably upon a metaphysically problematic 'antecedent rationalism': as Whitehead points out, 'you cannot have a rational justification for your appeal to history [e.g., Enlightenment] till your metaphysics has assured you there *is* a history [e.g., Enlightenment] to appeal to'. Hence induction permits not 'the derivation of general laws', holistic or comprehensive "frameworks", but the assemblage of a 'community of occasions'. Rather it is the 'divination' in these occasions of a 'general nature' or common features: to them something recognisable as "Enlightenment", something philosophy, 'the critic of abstractions', has already identified, can be attached (Whitehead 1967: 44, 87).

Further, precisely because this eclectic range of essays is by authors from different nationalities and academic backgrounds, it cannot help demonstrating – as the selection of topics shows – that if the Enlightenment is a "legacy" to modernity, if modernity is its "heir", it can be problematic, awkward. Its 'line of descent', far from true, is tangled – so that to define the Enlightenment by 'the prerogatives of historical knowledge in this field' is just a convenient way of eliminating its problematic characteristics that alone make it currently interesting (Ferrone 2015: 58). So the arrangement of the essays in this book, the different voices they express, identify by subheadings a selection of topics illustrating this problematic reception.

'Thinking about Kant and the Enlightenment' contains two contrasting essays on Kant's moral philosophy. Olga Poznjakova's essay explores its conceptual coherence. It elucidates Kant's argument that personal freedom and autonomy can morally improve society as a whole and produce as a political ideal – that carries conviction now more than ever – a globalised society for all humanity. To this end the Enlightenment offers a human moral potential that informs the future course of history from the start. Tatiana Weiser's essay reflects on a 'theoretical lacuna' in Kant's moral philosophy exposed subsequently by totalitarianism: if a person passively accepts professional constraints on reason as well as the state's law, how should he or she behave morally when state law itself is criminal? Hence it argues that Kant's categorical imperative needs to be supplemented by Arendt's concept of civil disobedience.

In 'Thinking about Enlightenment and politics' Luigi Delia's essay on De Felice and the encyclopedic *Code of Humanity* focusses attention on the central importance for the Enlightenment of law – a crucial term that links nature, human thought and behaviour, social order and the governance of states. As his essay shows, in human affairs law is precisely where reason and practice can coincide, where the present thinking has future, modern ramifications. Some of these ramifications, identifiable in political terms as 'deliberative democracy', are explored in John Min's essay. The work of Habermas and Dewey, he argues, reconceives ideas formulated by Locke, Rousseau, and Kant and proposes how these reconceptions may feasibly be realised in modern democracy so that they sustain the hope that the project of modernity might yet be completed.

The essays in 'Thinking about Enlightenment and religion' reveal that the conflict between reason and faith, toleration and orthodoxy remains undiminished in the modern world. In his essay Salvatore Muscolino shows how its attitude to the Enlightenment has produced an unresolvable dichotomy within contemporary Catholicism: a conservatism that would reject it while still affirming faith's transcendent relevance for modernity (on the one hand); and a political theology assimilating the Enlightenment legacy to express Christian values in social practice (on the other). In his essay Carsten Meiner shows how current religious controversy does not just produce conflict between crucial Enlightenment principles, principally between freedom of expression and toleration, but also exposes that since the eighteenth century Enlightenment thought has been sustained by tensions and conflicts between its core values.

The essays in 'Thinking about Enlightenment and gender' reflect on a notorious blind-spot of Enlightenment thought: its affirmation of gender inequality. As Christophe Regina argues, there was controversy about how women could be better educated, but at the same time in deferring to nature – as much a liberating concept as an inevitably ordered structure – many *philosophes* only reinforced their own prejudice of inequality. In her essay, informed by social anthropology, Carina Pape shows how for the Enlightenment thinking on gender, race, and theology intersected, producing in the name of science a 'naturalistic fallacy', a scientifically induced illusion, that sanctioned both gender and cultural discrimination.

In 'Thinking about Enlightenment and its limits' David Kim in his essay reveals the vulnerability of Enlightenment values of reason, morality and identity when confronted by individual sin, religious conflict, institutional corruption. The confrontation suggests an unfathomable genetic dimension to human behaviour, inaccessible to Enlightenment rationality and morality, that disrupts sociability. In his essay Tilman Reitz explores the ways in which Kant's concept of unsocial sociability has been interpreted by subsequent social philosophy and social psychology – the ways in which responses to unsocial, psychopathological forms of behaviour reaffirm and re-define sociability.

In 'Thinking about Enlightenment thinking' the two essays consider semantic and rhetorical aspects of the Enlightenment. In his essay Theo Jung examines the development of the Counter-Enlightenment as a response to its construction of the *philosophes* as a clearly defined antagonistic group and traces its subsequent development into a polemical expression of a multi-facetted critique of the modernity projected by Enlightenment thought. My own essay – not an attempt, after all, to cast Pope as a metaphysician – takes his *Essay on Man*, an anthology of the Enlightenment's philosophical commonplaces, as the cue for exploring a figure of speech, hence also a mental trope – tautology, identity, "sameness" – controlling and directing Enlightenment thinking despite (or perhaps because of?) its radical character.

Notes

1 In the examples cited, "process" is redundant because it occurs with words that in themselves already signify it, e.g., 'renewal', 'rationalization'. In any case, what is a "historical process" if not history itself?
2 Eclecticism comes for the Greek *eklego*, 'to pick out', 'to choose for oneself'; *eklektos* meaning 'chosen out', 'selected'. One of the meanings of *lego* is 'to lay in order', 'to arrange', 'to gather'. German makes the connection between 'reading' and 'extracting' quite clear: *lesen* means 'to read' but also 'to gather', 'to collect'; e.g., *auslesen*, 'to pick out'.

References

(All translations are my own unless otherwise stated.)
Allott, P. 2002. 'The New Enlightenment', in *The Health of Nations: Society and Law beyond the State*. Cambridge: Cambridge University Press, pp. 132–157.
Anders, G. 1986a. *Die Antiquiertheit des Menschen. Zweiter Band: Über die Zerstörung des Lebens im Zeitalter der dritten industriellen Revolution*, 4th edn. Munch: C.H. Beck.
—. 1986b. *Die atomare Drohung. Radikale Überlegungen*, 5th enlarged edn. of *Endzeit und Zeitenende*, Munich: C.H. Beck.
Badiou, A. 2003. *L'éthique. Essai sur la conscience du mal*. Caen: Nous.
Benjamin, W. 1988. 'Literaturgeschichte und Literaturwissenschaft' [1931], in *Angelus Novus. Ausgewählte Schriften 2*. Frankfurt am Main: suhrkamp taschenbuch, pp. 450–456.
Berardi, F. 2009. *The Soul at Work: From Alienation to Autonomy*, preface by J. Smith; trans. F. Cadel and G. Mecchia. Los Angeles: Semiotext(e).
Bloch, E. 1979. *Das Prinzip Hoffnung* [1959]. 6th edn. Frankfurt am Main: suhrkamp taschenbuch wissenschaft.
—. 1985. *Philosophische Aufsätze zur objektiven Phantasie*. Frakfurt am Main: suhrkamp taschenbuch wissenschaft.
Camus, A. 1972. *Le mythe de Sisyphe. Essai sur l'absurde* [1942]. Paris: idées / gallimard.
Cioran, E. M. 2006. *La tentation d'exister* [1956], Coll. Tel. Paris: Gallimard.
Condorcet, J. A. N. Caritat, marquis de. 1971. *Esquisse d'un tableau historique des progrès de l'esprit humain* [1793], edited by M. and F. Hincker. Paris: Éditions Sociales.
D'Alembert, J. 2011. *Discours préliminaire de l'Encyclopédie et articles de l'Encyclopédie*, edited M. Groult. Champion Classiques. Paris: Honoré Champion.
Davies, M. L. 2002. 'Wissenschaft und Ambivalenz: Zur Rezeption der Aufklärung in Großbritannien', *Das achtzehnte Jahrhundert*, 26.1, pp. 18–34.
Debray, R. and Girard, R. 2014. *Que reste-t-il de l'Occident?* Paris: Éditions Grasset et Fasquelle.
Deleuze, G. and Guattari, F. 1991. *Qu'est-ce que la philosophie?* Paris: Les Éditions de Minuit.
Diderot, D. 1994a. 'Encyclopédie' [1755], in *Œuvres. Tome I Philosophie*, edited L. Versini. Paris: Éditions Robert Laffont, pp. 363–436.

—. 1994b. 'Éclectisme' [1755], in ed. cit., pp. 300–362.
—. 1994c. *Le Rêve de d'Alembert* [1769/ 1830], in ed. cit., pp. 611–676.
Ferrone, V. 2015. *The Enlightenment. History of an Idea*, with a new afterword by the author, translated by Elisabetta Tarantino. Princeton and Oxford: Princeton University Press.
Fleck, L. 1980. *Entstehung und Entwicklung einer wissenschaftlichen Tatsache. Einführung in die Lehre vom Denkstil und Denkkollektiv* [1935], edited by L. Schäfer and T. Schelle. Frankfurt am Main: suhrkamp taschenbuch wissenschaft.
Foucault, M. 2001. 'Qu'est-ce que les Lumières?', in *Dits et écrits II, 1976–1988*, edited D. Defert et. al. Paris: Gallimard Quarto, pp. 1381–1397.
Graves, R. 1966. *The Greek Myths: Volume One*, rev. edn. Harmondsworth: Penguin Books.
Gray, J. 1997. *Enlightenment's Wake: Politics and Culture at the Close of the Modern Age*, pb. edn. (London and New York: Routledge).
Hume, D. 1971a. 'Of Essay Writing', in *Essays Moral, Political, and Literary* [1741/1742]. The World's Classics. Oxford: Oxford University Press, pp. 568–572.
Hume, D. 1971b. 'Of the Middle Station of Life', in *Essays Moral, Political, and Literary* [1741/1742]. The World's Classics. Oxford: Oxford University Press, pp. 579–584.
Husserl, E. 2012. *Die Krisis der europäischen Wissenschaften und die transzendentale Phänomenologie: Eine Einleitung in die phänomenologische Philosophie* [1936/1956], edited by E. Ströker. Philosophische Bibliothek. Hamburg: Felix Meiner Verlag.
Israel, J. I. 2001. *Radical Enlightenment. Philosophy and the Making of Modernity* 1650–1750. Oxford: Oxford University Press.
—. 2006. *Enlightenment Contested: Philosophy, Modernity, and the Emancipation of Man* 1670–1752. Oxford: Oxford University Press.
—. 2013. *Democratic Enlightenment: Philosophy, Revolution, and Human Rights* 1750–1790. pb. edn. Oxford: Oxford University Press.
Kant, I. 1977. 'Was heißt: sich im Denken orientieren?' [1786], in *Werkausgabe*, edited W. Weischedel. 12 vols. Frankfurt am Main: suhrkamp taschenbuch wissenschaft, V, pp. 265–283.
—. 1982a. 'Idee zu einer allgemeinen Geschichte in weltbürgerlicher Absicht' [1784], in *Werkausgabe*, XI pp. 31–50.
—. 1982b. 'Beantwortung der Frage: Was ist Aufklärung?' [1784], in *Werkausgabe*, XI, pp. 51–61.
Lévinas, E. 1987. *Humanisme de l'autre homme* [1972]. Livre de Poche: biblio essais. Paris: Fata Morgana.
Louden, R. B. 2010. *The World We Want. How and Why the Ideals of the Enlightenment Still Elude Us*. pb. edn. Oxford: Oxford University Press.
Mannheim, K. 2007. 'On the Interpretation of *Weltanschauung*' [1923], in *Essays on the Sociology of Knowledge* [1936], edited by P. Kecskemeti. Abingdon: Routledge, pp. 33–83.
Nussbaum, M. C. 2010. *Not for Profit: Why Democracy Needs the Humanities*. Princeton and Oxford: Princeton University Press.
Pagden, A. 2013. *The Enlightenment and Why It Still Matters*. Oxford: Oxford University Press.
Péguy, C. 1961. 'Clio. Dialogue de l'histoire et de l'âme païenne' [1909], in *Œuvres en Prose, 1909–1914*, edited by M. Péguy. Bibliothèque de la Pléiade. Paris: Gallimard, pp. 93–308.
Popper, K. R. 1974. *The Poverty of Historicism* [1957]. London: Routledge and Kegan Paul.
Reed, T. J. 2015. *Light in Germany. Scenes from an Unknown Enlightenment*. Chicago and London: University of Chicago Press.
Scheler, M. 1978. *Die Stellung des Menschen im Kosmos* [1928]. 9th edn. Bern: Verlag A.G. Franke AG.
Schmidt, J. (ed.). 1996. *What Is Enlightenment? Eighteenth-Century Answers and Twentieth-Century Questions*. Berkeley and Los Angeles: University of California Press.

Seneca. 2006. *Epistles* 1–65. Translated R.M. Gummere. Loeb Classical Library. Cambridge, MA and London: Harvard University Press.
Todorov, T. 2007. *L'Esprit des Lumières*. Le Livre de Poche / Biblio Essais. Paris: Robert Laffont.
Toulmin, S. 2001. *Return to Reason*. Cambridge, Mass. and London: Harvard University Press.
Valéry, P. 1957. 'Préface aux *Lettres persanes*' [1926] in *Œuvres. I*, edited J. Hytier, Bibliothèque de la Pléiade, Paris: Gallimard, pp. 508–517.
Weber, M. 1988. 'Wissenschaft als Beruf' [1919], in *Gesammelte Aufsätze zur Wissenschaftslehre* [1922], ed. J. Winckelmann. 7th edn. Tübingen: J.C.B Mohr (Paul Siebeck), pp. 582–613.
Whitehead, A. N. 1920. *The Concept of Nature*. Cambridge: Cambridge University Press.
—. 1967. *Science and the Modern World* [1925]. New York: Free Press.
Xenophon. 1979. *Memorabilia*, in *Memorabilia, Oeconomicus, Symposium, and Apology*, translated E.C. Marchant and O.J. Todd. Loeb Classical Library. Cambridge, Mass.: Harvard University Press and London: Heinemann, pp. 1–359.

PART I
Thinking about Kant and the Enlightenment

1
KANT'S CONCEPT OF ENLIGHTENMENT: INDIVIDUAL AND UNIVERSAL DIMENSIONS

Olga Poznjakova

In this essay I plan to outline two dimensions within Kant's concept of the Enlightenment: the individual and the universal.

First I will demonstrate a traditional interpretation of Kant's idea of the Enlightenment based on the context of his essay 'An Answer to the Question: What Is Enlightenment?' Then I will show the importance of the Enlightenment on a specifically individual level. I will emphasise the difference between the internal and the external motivational impulse of a human being to be enlightened. I will demonstrate that the fact of an external motivation to the Enlightenment contradicts Kant's teaching about the universal character of human nature.

After that I will underline the significance of Kant's concept of the Enlightenment on a unsiversal level. Giving a brief summary of Kant's philosophy of history, I will show the role of the Enlightenment in the life of people on their way to the 'perpetual peace', a 'world-civil society', and a cosmopolitan world order within Kant's philosophical system. Finally I will argue that Kant's concept of the Enlightenment should become one of the main principles of the doctrine of international cooperation in the twenty-first century.

Introduction

Immanuel Kant is probably the most important philosopher of the past 2,000 years. He lived near the end of the Enlightenment, a European cultural movement that spanned the eighteenth century. Enlightenment figures such as Voltaire and David Hume sought to replace the traditions and superstitions of religion and monarchy with a world-view that relied primarily on the powers of reason. Kant's work belongs to this tradition. His three *Critiques* investigate the scope and powers of reason and emphasise that the proper study of metaphysics is our own rational faculties, not the sort of theological questions that occupied earlier generations.

The Enlightenment drew from, and furthered, the development of the new science that had begun during the Renaissance and inspired the republican revolutions in France and America. Kant was at his most productive around the time of these two great revolutions, but as he spent his entire life in eastern Prussia, he was largely untouched by the world events unfolding around him. Nevertheless, he wrote a number of important essays on political questions, particularly one discussing the possibility of perpetual peace.

Kant's influence has been immense. No philosopher since Kant has remained entirely untouched by his ideas. Even when the reaction to Kant is negative, he is the source of great inspiration. German idealism, which arose in the generation after Kant, draws heavily on Kant's work even as it rejects some of his central ideas. Similarly, the tradition of analytical philosophy, which has dominated the English-speaking world for the past century, takes its start from Gottlob Frege's criticisms of Kant.

In this essay we will try to investigate Kant's attitude towards the Enlightenment process beginning from its traditional interpretation based on the context of Kant's essay 'An Answer to the Question: What Is Enlightenment?' (Kant 1983: 29–37). It will be shown that there are at least two dimensions within Kant's concept of the Enlightenment: individual and universal. Both of the interpretations will be based on the understanding of the main principles and aims of Kantian philosophy as a whole system.

The traditional interpretation of the idea of the Enlightenment within Kant's philosophical teaching

While analysing Kant's idea of the Enlightenment within its individual and universal dimensions it is important to reveal the essence of its traditional interpretation based on Kant's fundamental essay 'An Answer to the Question: What Is Enlightenment?' (Kant 1983: 29–37). It should be considered in the context of the intellectual atmosphere that prevailed in Europe in the eighteenth century.

By that time in Germany, as well as in France, England, and Scotland, the process of the Enlightenment was already widespread. However, there was still no consensus on a fundamental theoretical level about the answer to the question 'What is Enlightenment?' This problem was raised for the first time in France by Diderot in 1755 in the fifth volume of his *Encyclopedia*. In Germany, it becomes a matter for discussion only in the 1780s, on the eve of the French Revolution.

The thing is that Kant gives his answer to the question 'What is Enlightenment?' from a point of view completely different from the vision of his contemporaries. His intellectual position was presented as original and rather sophisticated. His way of thinking reached Berlin from distant Königsberg, but that had little to do with the debate conducted by his colleagues in the capital of Prussia. Kant makes an appeal for freedom of thought because 'When one does not deliberately attempt to keep men in barbarism, they will gradually work out of that condition by themselves' (Kant 1983: 33). This idea has saved the life of the Kantian interpretation of the Enlightenment, while all the rest discussed in the 1780s had to disappear in the crucible of history.

Kant characterises the world historical process as a plan of Nature intended for the human race, for the full development of all the best human abilities. He defines the Enlightenment as a turning point, one of the most exciting stages of the development of human mind. In revealing its essence as another mechanism for overcoming the natural status between individuals and for achieving a society of world-citizens, he elucidates the fundamental *principles* that should guide people towards achieving the Enlightenment.

First, there is the principle of judgement based on one's own reason. Kant shows that before the Enlightenment humanity was not used to applying its rational capacity independently. In his opinion, people have previously been unable to use their intellect without guidance from someone else. He defines such a condition as 'tutelage' (Kant 1983: 35) and explains its characteristic feature as 'willing to remain for a lifetime adolescent' because of 'laziness and cowardice' (Kant 1983: 34). Moreover, Kant says that tutelage is exhibited most shamefully in respect to the sciences and the arts.

The Age of Enlightenment, in the opinion of Immanuel Kant, has made possible a new type of culture based on the ability to form reasonable judgements, the ability to use your own intellect without guidance from other people. Hence, Kant says that 'Enlightenment is man's emergence from his self-imposed tutelage' (Kant 1983: 29) which produces a 'true transformation of the way of thinking' (Kant 1983: 31). The ability to form judgements for oneself is a fundamental characteristic of a human 'adult', guided by the rule 'Sapere Aude!' – 'Have the courage to use your own understanding!' (Kant 1983: 29), marked by Kant as the motto of the Enlightenment.

Second, there is the principle of free rational judgement. Kant argues that freedom is a necessary condition for the implementation of the Enlightenment process intended to transform the way people think. He also notes: 'It is more nearly possible, however, for the public to enlighten itself; indeed, if it is only given freedom, enlightenment is almost inevitable' (Kant 1983: 36). The task to provide people with this freedom belongs to a new type of society that Kant calls 'a society of world-citizens'. Moreover, the philosopher regards the restriction of freedom of judgement as a restriction of freedom in general, and declares it a major crime against humanity.

Third, there is the principle of freedom and obedience. Kant's arguments about the need for restricting freedom must be of particular interest. In his opinion, not all kinds of freedom can be useful for the Enlightenment process and not every restriction of freedom prevents people from being enlightened. Speaking about the problem of the co-existence of civil and spiritual freedom, Kant concludes that the more civil liberty people get, the less spiritual freedom is left for them, and vice versa. Further, Kant makes a distinction between the 'public' and the 'private use of reason' (Kant

1983: 31), and attributes to them varying degrees of freedom. By the public use of one's reason he means that use 'which a man, as *scholar*, makes of it before the reading public' (ibid.). For Kant the public use of reason is an expression of spiritual freedom, exemplified by the relationship between a scientist or academic and his readership. As far as its private use is concerned, Kant calls it a 'use which a man makes of his reason in a civic post that has been entrusted to him' (ibid.). Under the private use of reason Kant understands reasoning concerning matters of an 'official' character, and believes that its degree of freedom should be limited for reasons of compliance with the official order. So, Kant comes to the conclusion that for an enlightened state the private use of freedom is not acceptable, and puts forward the following formula which describes the proper condition of affairs: 'Argue as much as you like, and about what you like, but obey!' (ibid.).

It should be added that Kant considered his age to be not yet 'enlightened' because 'it is still far from true that men are already capable of using their own reason in religious matters confidently and correctly without external guidance. Still, we have some obvious indications that the field of working toward the goal [of religious truth] is now opened. What is more, the hindrances against general Enlightenment or the emergence from self-imposed tutelage are gradually diminishing. In this respect this is the age of the Enlightenment and the century of Frederick [the Great]' (Kant 1983: 33).

Defining Enlightenment as a mechanism for overcoming the natural state of the people, the German thinker aims to answer the question of how pure reason can determine the human will. Since it does not contain anything empirical, and human actions are always based on empirical assumptions and are intended to achieve the objectives of the empirical world, pure reason must act on its own fundamentally different level, prescribing the necessary laws for action. The necessity of empirical behaviour is always hypothetical; that is, it always aims to achieve a particular, meaningful purpose. Therefore, from Kant's point of view the law of pure reason cannot contain anything empirical and generally cannot contain any specific content. Consequently, the subject for which pure reason legislates must be only its form. This explains Kant's formulation of his famous, fundamental law of pure practical reason, according to which a person should act so that the maxim of his or her will at all times could also be set as a principle of universal law. Therefore, the moral law is certainly important for every rational being, or, in other words, the law is certainly important for each person to the extent that he or she is guided by reason. Kant is well aware of that fact that human actions are determined most of the time by their empirical motives, and above all – by human egotism and selfishness in their very different ways. Moreover, Kant has no illusions about the fact that this circumstance can be fundamentally changed because it is only holy people who ultimately are capable of acting always in accordance with the moral law and solely on the basis of pure reason. However, every person has the ability to control his or her actions, which requires only the freedom to make decisions, supported by the process of Enlightenment in society.

It should be emphasised that, according to Kant, Nature wants people to be enlightened about how to use freely the ideas of pure reason in empirical conditions, that is, to act in accordance with the categorical imperative. As a result, Kant anticipates the full development of the best qualities of an individual as a representative of a human race. And even if the 'society of world-citizens', determined by reason, can never be achieved, it should still be an ideal purpose for us, meant for creating the most favourable conditions for the existence of civilisation in the future. Therefore, the process of the Enlightenment cannot be reduced to simple historical and political action. The process is important within itself: a person should enlighten him- or herself, rather than the educated elite enlighten uneducated people. Moreover, a human intention towards Enlightenment comes from the trouble [*die Not*] people cause for each other without proper guidance by the laws of Reason. Ultimately, this situation will force people to create a legal civil order in which they will be able to enlighten themselves. After all, the implementation of a permanent Enlightenment process promotes the highest value of a human being – his or her dignity, which in Kant's philosophy of history is directly related to the implementation of morality, of the categorical imperative, and the establishment of a 'society of world-citizens'.

Kant's idea of the Enlightenment on the individual scale

In order to get the full understanding of Kant's idea of the Enlightenment it would not be enough to investigate its traditional interpretation based only on Kant's essay 'An Answer to the Question: What Is Enlightenment?'. To depict fully its meaning within Kant's philosophical teaching, the idea of the Enlightenment needs to be considered on not just a universal but also an individual level. In this section we will reveal the essence of the controversial character of the Enlightenment process on the individual, transcendental, and empirical scale. For this purpose we will need to explicate Kant's concept of the universal character of human nature.

Kant's teaching about the universal character of human nature

It is well known that the question 'What is a human?' plays a fundamental role in the Kantian philosophical system. The answer to this question can be summarised in Kant's teaching about the universal character of human nature. The essence of this teaching will be analysed further.

Speaking about human nature in general, one must admit that almost all the philosophers somehow touched upon this problem during different historical periods. Thus, in pre-Kantian philosophy European thinkers were mostly concerned with the issue of whether a man is by nature a good or, on the contrary, an evil being. Some philosophers (for example, Hobbes) argued that human beings are evil by nature, so that civilisation and civil society are given to them to restrain their evil inclinations. Other philosophers (like Rousseau, for instance) were convinced that human beings are originally good and all the evil comes from the perversion of human nature. The third group of philosophers believed that human beings are neither good nor evil by nature, but they would become one or the other depending on the social environment. This, in particular, was the point of view of the French materialists of the eighteenth century.

Where the Kantian doctrine about the universal character of human nature is concerned, it doesn't belong to any of those trends shown above. Kant rather argues that a human being has an opportunity to be moral *a priori*, but he or she has to develop this skill during all their life. In essence, one can distinguish two levels in Kant's teaching about the universal character of human nature: the epistemological and the ethical.

The epistemological level

On the epistemological level Kant shows that it is the knowledge *a priori* that makes a human different from all the other creatures in the world. Thanks to the discovery of *a priori* forms of sensibility and reason, Kant develops his doctrine which will be later called the 'Copernican revolution'. According to this idea objects must conform to our knowledge but not vice versa. This thesis means that a number of fundamental characteristics of objects depends on the nature of our (human) cognitive abilities. It also means that any object of our knowledge must obey the universal forms of sensibility and reason, as a condition of the possibility of human experience. Kant's concept of space and time, the theory of the deduction of categories and the theory of imagination and schematism play here the fundamental role.

Moreover, the notion of the transcendental unity of self-consciousness and the transcendental unity of apperception, this central element of a human nature on its transcendental level, creates a background for our understanding of human nature. Ascribing the ability of reason to the synthesis of categories, Kant is able to explain the unity of consciousness of a thinking subject. He declares that the 'transcendental unity of self-consciousness' is given us *a priori*, which means that it doesn't need to be proven. He also calls this 'subjective unity of consciousness' which has an *a priori* character – 'the supreme principle of any cognition' (Kant 1998b: 183).

Apart from that, Kant develops his theory of *a priori* ideas of pure reason (cf. *The Critique of Pure Reason*, Transcendental Dialectic, Book I, Section II) (Kant 1998b: 399–405). These ideas act as a regulator of moral activity and people's behaviour. The fact that they are equally common to all the members of the human race regardless of their traditions, religious beliefs, and customs, proves the possibility of the universal character of human nature. Following this statement Kant creates his ethical concept which is based on the notion of the categorical imperative.

The ethical level

In fact the Kantian ethical position on the universal character of human nature radically differs from the beliefs of Hobbes and his predecessors. All of the pre-Kantian thinkers speak about human nature postulating its essential features as inborn, immutable, and completely independent from reason and will. According to their teaching, human beings have no control over their nature.

Kant analyses these ideas and shows that if we consider human nature as objectively good or evil we cannot consider a person to be responsible for his or her actions. This means that only freedom must determine human activity and each person must determine whether his or her nature is good or evil. Otherwise a person can be neither good nor evil-minded.

At the same time Kant considers a human being to belong to two different worlds: the phenomenal and the noumenal. As an empirical being a person is entirely determined by the laws of nature. It means that a person doesn't control his or her actions: deprived of free will, he or she is, therefore, essentially insane. A human being is just a phenomenon of nature, subject to its inexorable laws.

On the other hand, human beings are 'things in themselves' [*Dinge-an-sich-selbst*] that cannot be subject to the laws of nature. They are endowed with reason and do not depend on sensuality and environmental conditions. Real human beings can be responsible for their actions because they have free will and, therefore, can make themselves either good or evil-minded.

Furthermore, because all human actions are determined in the natural world and therefore are not free, Kant introduces the concept of a 'transcendental subject', the function of which is, regardless of the empirical circumstances, to determine human behaviour. Some human actions are consistent with the moral laws, while others represent a deviation from them (i.e., evil actions). The notion of a transcendental subject reveals a complicated indirect relationship between people's inclinations that cannot be simply determined by their motives. Thus, according to Kant, human behaviour should not be a direct response to the empirical situation. Between the empirical situation and human action there must always be the activity of practical reason with its ideas of the highest good and moral duty. These ideas must be the basis for public morality and people's social behaviour.

In other words, the ethical essence of Kant's teaching about the universal character of human nature is based on the idea that human beings are subject to the natural as well as the moral world. Kant justifies the fact that a person has the ability to be moral only if he or she makes a free moral choice.

To sum up, on the one hand Kant reveals an epistemological mechanism that makes it possible to create the world of nature by means of human intelligence. On the other hand, Kant shows how individuals can create themselves. Choosing the transcendental ideas of pure reason as a regulator of their behaviour, individuals thus show their ability to make a free choice in favour of moral behaviour, each one demonstrating in this way his or her difference from the animal world.

However, there's still a contradiction in Kant's teaching about the universal character of human nature. It becomes transparent when we speak about the internal and external motivation impulse of an individual towards the process of Enlightenment. Let's take a look at it more precisely.

The contradiction between the internal and external motivation impulse of an individual towards the process of Enlightenment

When analysing Kant's teaching about the universal character of human nature it is essential to pay attention to one unresolved contradiction within this concept. As it was shown above, Kant proves the possibility of moral self-improvement on an individual level. Pure reason is intended to create the absolute synthesis of all empirical knowledge. The result of such a synthesis is a set of transcendental ideas which serve as a moral regulator of a human being's activity. If a man acts in accordance with these transcendental ideas he becomes capable of breaking the chain of cause-and-effect, thus showing his independence from the world of physical nature.

However, the German philosopher deliberately ignores the problem of a mechanism that would possibly influence a person to choose moral behaviour. This idea might be urgent in view of the problem of moral politicians and political moralists. If all the people have free will to act according to the categorical imperative, why do some of them still prefer to stick to their natural inclinations rather than to rational (moral) norms? At first sight it looks obvious that the only thing we need to do is to work out a mechanism that would help people to follow the moral rules. However, thinking in this way we forget that it is only free will and free independent choice that can make an individual different from the entire animal world. The implementation of such mechanisms would only manipulate people's decisions, thereby suppressing their mental activity and leaving no chance for freedom of choice.

The same controversy can be observed within the process of Enlightenment when we speak about the necessity of educating people in the different spheres of their life. According to Immanuel Kant, Enlightenment is man's release from 'tutelage' (Kant, 1983: 29). Enlightenment is the process by which the public could rid themselves of intellectual bondage after centuries of slumbering. After providing a careful analysis of the causes why tutelage occurred, he proposes the requirements for Enlightenment. He wants the public to think freely, act judiciously, and be 'treated in accordance with their dignity'. 'Enlightenment is man's emergence from his self-imposed immaturity. Immaturity is the inability to use one's understanding without guidance from another. This immaturity is self-imposed when its cause lies not in a lack of understanding, but in the lack of resolve and courage to use it without guidance from another. "*Sapere Aude!* [dare to know] Have courage to use your own understanding!" – that is the motto of enlightenment' (Kant 1983: 29).

On the one hand, these issues demand from an individual a certain amount of free will so that he or she has the courage to use his or her own understanding. On the other, the process of the Enlightenment is impossible without external motivation induced by other people, thus suppressing an individual's free will. Moreover, the antinomial character of Kant's teaching about the Enlightenment can be clearly seen in his thesis 'Argue as much as you want and about anything but obey!' (Kant 1983: 31). Consequently, an individual can produce free will and think for him- or herself as a human being different from the animal world only on the theoretical level. As far as empirical reality is concerned, there will always be someone who will restrain our free will for some reason or another.

Such theoretical inclinations in all Kant's works can be explained only in one way. It is well known that eighteenth-century Germany was marked by socio-economic and political conflicts. The German Enlightenment could not openly disapprove of the real things that were happening in the country during that time. That is why most of the philosophers had to express their criticism with the help of theoretical philosophical constructions. From the height of metaphysical contemplation they supported the idea of the unity of the nations while their condemnation of the German governmental system could only be veiled, and appeals for its destruction were absolutely impossible.

So we must strictly differentiate between Kant the empiricist and Kant the metaphysician. This is a criterion for analysing Kant's attitude not only towards the universal character of human nature, the problem of war and peace, the French revolution, but also towards the understanding of the process of the Enlightenment within its individual and universal dimensions.

As has been noted, Kant does not introduce to his reader the idea of a mechanism for influencing individual choice towards either moral actions or the process of Enlightenment. The paradox is that as soon as we start manipulating an individual's will, that individual loses his or her freedom of choice and, therefore, his or her dignity. Only free moral choice can make an individual different from all living beings. After all, Kant has shown how majestic and powerful people can act according to the categorical imperative and that free will both constructs the essence of the universal character of human nature and determines society in its development.

Kant's concept of the Enlightenment on the universal level

In the previous sections we have revealed the essentially antinomial character of Kant's teaching about the Enlightenment on an individual level. In order to demonstrate the universal meaning of Kant's teaching about the Enlightenment it is vital to study his philosophy of history. It is within Kant's vision of the direction of the development of humankind that the role of the Enlightenment for all the people in the world becomes evident. Moreover, it becomes possible to justify Kant's idea of the Enlightenment as one of the universal values as well as one of the main principles of the doctrine of international cooperation in the twenty-first century.

Kant's philosophy of history

According to Kant's teaching humanity arises together with people's capacity for rational (moral) behaviour. Taking this criterion as the background of our theoretical reconstruction, we can distinguish three periods in the history of human society:

i. the dominance of the condition of nature when people are only at the start of developing their tendency to moral behaviour;
ii. the confrontation between savage and reasonable (moral) human nature;
iii. the prevalence of reasonable actions over people's savage inclinations and the establishment of a legal 'society of world-citizens' and 'perpetual peace' in the world.

A point often overlooked is that Kant considered moral and political processes to be the main moving force of human history. The interdependence of these two factors has a direct impact on how history proceeds. On the one hand, it is practical reason that determines the universal character of human nature and makes it possible for all humans to act in accordance with the categorical imperative. On the other, a political process in society aims to create legal conditions that permit people freely to follow the categorical imperative in their daily practice. Moreover, Kant shows the possibility of a 'world-civil society', where in a distant future the need for a legal regulation might be dismissed, in which people will be guided solely by moral norms.

Accordingly, Kant's philosophy of history evinces anthropological and socio-political aspects. Anthropological aspects include:

i. morality as a transcendental feature of all human beings;
ii. Enlightenment as a fundamental regulator of an individual's moral behaviour;
iii. human dignity as an indicator of human moral behaviour.

Socio-political aspects include, respectively:

i. the idea of 'perpetual peace';
ii. the idea of a 'society of world-citizens';
iii. the idea of a cosmopolitan world order.

Another key point is that Kant was the first one to reveal the *a priori* character of knowledge about the future. This means that any philosophical-historical model is always transcendental and that its implementation depends on people's good will and good intentions. With this in mind, the fact that we didn't observe moral progress in the past doesn't prove that it is impossible in the future. Therefore, the idea that the future of humanity depends on the free will of individuals makes Kant's philosophical-historical model highly anthropocentric.

Theoretical remarks on Kant's philosophy of history

It is important to note that when we speak about Kant's philosophy of history we mean its contemporary reconstruction, so that its ideas don't contradict the total Kantian philosophical system. Why does it have to be only a reconstruction? Because Immanuel Kant has not left for us a separate volume of writings entitled 'philosophy of history', as Hegel did, for instance. Nevertheless, Kant writes about the history of humankind, its goals and moving forces. These ideas can be found practically in all his essays and treatises. If we try to gather them all into one concept we will get a reconstruction of Kant's philosophy of history. It must be basically different from a so-called reminiscence, a free retelling of the author's thoughts without referring to his conceptual methodological background. The reconstruction of Kant's philosophy of history and its main principles should correlate with Kant's whole philosophical system and must look as if Kant himself would have written it if he had had that intention.

The main stages of human history are described by Kant in his essay 'Speculative Beginning of Human History' (Kant 1983: 38–55). Here the German thinker shows that human rationality was the first step in the development of humankind. It is also vital to emphasise that for Kant the notion of rationality is equal to morality. Human society begins its movement only when people get the ability to think and behave rationally (according to the categorical imperative) and to act morally. As far as the last stage of human history is concerned (the establishment of a 'society of world-citizens), it is described in Kant's essay 'Idea for a Universal History with a Cosmopolitan Intent' (Kant 1983: 12–28). Certainly one can find in the contemporary literature such a division of history into stages like those in Kant's philosophy of history: 'a natural order; a legal, constitutional state order; a legal, civil world order'. Such a vision of historical development doesn't contradict a certain model of the philosophy of history. But it does contradict the whole Kantian philosophical system, because Kant's philosophy is strictly all about reason and how it constructs the empirical and moral world. That is why it would be more correct to classify the stages of history from the point of view of the development of reason (which is the main criterion of the classification) but not from the perspective of the development of political structures. This latter case looks as though Kant might have been interested in political philosophy. But he could not because in the eighteenth century the subject of political philosophy had not yet been formulated. Moreover, as already shown in the previous sections, Kant could not discuss political questions openly because of the political regime in eastern Prussia at that time.

Besides, the classification of history into stages according to the development of reason (morality) reveals more clearly that all knowledge about the future is always given us *a priori*. It means that there must be a final goal in human history which is never to be achieved in the empirical sense but always directs human activity. This knowledge makes the logical step to the last stage of human history possible, namely the stage where there will be no need for legal regulation, the stage where people will be governed by the categorical imperative.

Apart from that, Kant's philosophy of history has a set of principles that make it possible to explicate certain laws of historical development, namely:

i. A transparent concept of development. Generally speaking, Kant's concept of development is the first theoretical, evolutionary concept in the history of human ideas. Its most important theses are continuity of the development; gradual changes that come from the course of the interaction of opposing elements; the triadic structure of the evolutionary process: the domination of one of the opposite elements, their existence in relatively the same manner, and the dominance of the second opposing element that initially played a secondary role.
ii. The principle of moral and social identity. The specifically Kantian understanding of this principle is represented by his anti-natural understanding of the moral and, consequently, the social world. Anti-natural ethical dualism results from the worlds of freedom and of nature, and it belongs to the theoretical core of Kant's philosophical system.
iii. The principle of a substantial difference between the capabilities of an individual and those of the entire human race. Kant writes: 'In man (as the only rational creature on earth) those natural capacities which are directed to the use of his reason are to be fully developed only in the race, not in the individual' (Kant 1983: 14).
iv. In his general philosophical system Kant's philosophy of history directly relies on a teleological method. This method complements the metaphysical concept of development since the latter is unable to explain a qualitative change in the link between physical world and social life. It also explains the possibility of self-movement within an organic, as well as within a social system.

All in all, in this section we have studied briefly the context of Kant's philosophy of history as well as its theoretical propositions. This material will help us to justify the importance of the Enlightenment on the universal level within Kant's teaching. It will also give us an opportunity to show that Kant's idea of the Enlightenment may become one of the main principles of the doctrine of international cooperation in the twenty-first century.

The Enlightenment in Kant's system of universal values

The reconstruction of Kant's philosophy of history makes it possible to explain the system of universal values on the transcendental level. The list given below shows that the Enlightenment is just as important as the other components extracted from Kant's philosophical-historical teaching. The content of Kant's system of universal values is summarised here.

The universal character of human nature suggests the existence of a *universal morality* based on the formal principle of the categorical imperative:

a. 'Act only according to that maxim whereby you can, at the same time, will that it should become a universal law' (Kant 1998a: 196). This formula may become one of the fundamental principles of the doctrine of international cooperation in the twenty-first century. It is aimed at preventing the imperial policies of some contemporary states that demonstrate a bad pattern of behaviour to their descendants.
b. Immanuel Kant anticipated the environmental problems awaiting mankind in the twenty-first century. Since the natural world of the individual cannot be perfect, the conflict between humankind and nature can at times lead to crises. Therefore Kant formulated the so-called environmental categorical imperative, the rule of our attitude to nature: 'Every rational being must so act as if he were through his maxim always a legislating member in the universal kingdom of ends' (Kant 1998a: 195).
c. 'Act in such a way that you treat humanity, whether in your own person or in the person of any other, never merely as a means to an end, but always at the same time as an end' (Kant 1998a: 205). This variant of the categorical imperative appeals for the rejection of the utilitarian attitude towards a human being in the context of contemporary international politics.

The *Enlightenment* plays a fundamental role in achieving peaceful conditions on a planetary level. It is another universal value within Kant's philosophical model. According to Kant, Enlightenment is a permanent process that develops the individual's ability to be guided by the ideas of practical reason in his or her daily practice. Thus, possessing intelligence is not enough to make moral actions. In this sense every person needs guidance (Enlightenment), which is to teach a person to be brave enough to use his or her own mind and to be guided in behaviour by a categorical imperative.

- The idea of *human dignity* justified by Kant may also become a fundamental value of the modern doctrine of international cooperation. According to Kant, a human being as a moral subject is above all price. Such factors as ethical arguments for happiness, sinfulness, etc. are not essential for the recognition of the unconditional value of human dignity. Human dignity is priceless; it cannot be taken away and it does not depend on any social group a person belongs to, whether he is a sinner or a saint, a believer or an unbeliever.

It is vital to note that the concept of human dignity appears today not only as an ethical principle but also as a legal category. A number of mechanisms of international law, as well as the constitutions of European countries, have introduced the concept of human dignity as a basic principle of all constitutional order. Thus, the protection of human dignity becomes the main criterion for the legitimacy of national political, social and economic interests.

- The idea of a legal 'society of world citizens' is considered by Kant as a universal value in the context of his philosophy of history, and, therefore, may become one of the principal targets of the doctrine of international cooperation in the twenty-first century. To avoid violation and wars and to end the natural condition of sovereign states, Kant offers a transition to the legal 'society of world citizens' in which people should overcome their distrust, their desire for domination and profit, and accept the status of being cosmopolitan. Thus, a legal 'society of world citizens' is the idea of the final form of a human community. It can be at the level of both micro-society that is directly embedded in the structure of civil society within a particular nation-state and public association on the interstate scale. As for the nation-state, its task is to mediate between these two extremes and to function to its legal extent in such a system of political relations.

- The project of 'perpetual peace' developed by Kant in the eighteenth century is a universal value for all the people in the world and it should become an integral component of contemporary international relationships. Kant justified the theoretical and practical interdependence needed to achieve 'perpetual peace' and the idea of a moral and legal 'society of world citizens'. He showed that in order to prevent war it is necessary to implement the idea of a legal society on a global scale. Thus Kant opened a new system of legal coordination in which states relate to each other as friends. Rejecting the original idea of a state, he moved to the idea of a free league of nation-states that would prevent war through the peaceful arbitration of conflicts.
- Kant's idea of a *cosmopolitan world order* may also become a universal value for all the people in the world, as well as a fundamental principle of the doctrine of international cooperation in the twenty-first century. In the context of Kant's philosophical-historical model, cosmopolitanism is an integral step towards the realisation of the project of 'perpetual peace' and legal 'society of world citizens'. Its adequate implementation means that that society will acquire an international responsibility for the violation of the law in every corner of the planet.

So far as is known, this approach is often criticised by opponents of eurocentrism, who stand against imposing the values of the European Enlightenment outside contemporary Europe. Nonetheless, the main argument to support this idea is the formality of the categorical imperative and its total detachment from any particular empirical reality. Kant shows the universal character of both theoretical and practical reason without any references to specific behavioural stereotypes in multi-cultural society (which is usually criticised in Kant's ethical system). This may be the reason for assigning to the categorical imperative the status of a universal principle in the context of the modern doctrine of international relationships.

Kant's idea of the Enlightenment as one of the main principles of the doctrine of international cooperation in the twenty-first century

It is widely known that in recent years the interactions between different social groups within a nation-state as well as on the intergovernmental level have become highly interdependent. Because of that fact an urgent need to review the basic principles of the doctrine of international cooperation has become the priority agenda issue for contemporary humanitarians and scientists.

Experts suggest that any doctrine aimed to coordinate the actions of people in society should not simply declare itself scholastically. Evidently it should rather be based on a common understanding of a direction in historical development. The role of estimating the purpose, direction and the moving forces of humankind belongs to the philosophy of history. This seems to be the dominant argument why we need to extract the fundamental principles of the doctrine of international cooperation from a certain philosophical-historical model. Moreover, a certain philosophical-historical model (in our case-study it is Kant's philosophy of history) must always undergo expert interrogation in ethical, ontological, epistemological, etc. terms. It means that all the positions about the order of humankind's development are to be proved and justified theoretically (morally) but not postulated scholastically.

While representing Kant's philosophy of history as a background for a contemporary doctrine of international cooperation, I mean it to be in opposition to the theories of state cooperation *with an ideological background*.

It is also important to underline that Kant presents a positive perspective for the development of humankind, giving people the hope to survive in the future. Moreover, he gives an explanation why it is possible to survive – because of the universal character of human nature that gives people the possibility to be moral. He also shows how to do it in the shortest way – to follow categorical imperatives in your daily life.

According to the list of the universal values that were extracted from Kant's philosophy of history, it is possible to formulate the main principles of the doctrine of international cooperation in the twenty-first century, namely:

- The principle of the universality of morality based on the formal principle of the categorical imperative.
- The principle of the universality of the idea of the Enlightenment as a permanent process for transforming the categorical imperative into the fundamental regulation of human behaviour.
- The principle of focussing on the idea of human dignity in the national and international legal space.
- The principle of the implementation of the idea of a legal 'society of world citizens' in the global political world order.
- The principle of the focussing on the idea of 'perpetual peace' in the context of a global strategy of the survival of humanity.
- The principle of the implementation of the idea of a cosmopolitan world order within the project of the legal 'world-civil society' and the concept of 'perpetual peace'.

The role of the Enlightenment within this list of principles of the doctrine of international cooperation is hard to underestimate. As shown above, the

Enlightenment is a permanent process of the development of individual rational qualities, the mechanism for overcoming the natural inclinations of people on the way to the establishment of the 'society of world citizens'. Enlightenment includes the principle of judgement based on one's own reason, the principle of free rational judgment, and the principle of freedom and obedience. In general, Enlightenment is aimed at increasing the capacity of the individual to be guided not only by rational thinking, but also by the ideas of pure reason. Thus, Enlightenment is aimed at developing the ability of an individual to use his or her reason, resulting in people's awareness of the need to follow the moral categorical imperative, to form skills of free thinking, moral choices and behavior. According to Kant, the process of the Enlightenment gives people the possibility to realise that the future of humankind depends only on each and every person in society. All the contradictions on the international level could be easily resolved as soon as people start avoiding their natural inclinations and begin to use the ideas of practical reason as a regulator of their own behaviour.

Conclusion

To summarise: we have elucidated the main contents of the Kantian idea of Enlightenment and discovered that its traditional interpretation is based on Kant's fundamental essay, 'An Answer to the Question: What Is Enlightenment?' According to this essay, Enlightenment is a permanent process intended to develop an individual's ability to be guided by the ideas of practical reason in their daily practice. This process includes the principle of judgement based on one's own reason, the principle of free rational judgement, and the principle of freedom and obedience.

Further, in the context of the individual the process of the Enlightenment reveals a contradiction. Since the universal character of human nature involves only the independent choice of the individual towards moral actions (including Enlightenment), an external impulse to the Enlightenment can be interpreted as a manipulation of the individual's will, which in turn deprives him or her of the status of being endowed with reason. According to Kant, what makes a human being different from the animal world is the free rational choice of moral action. It means that human beings are only human when they are able to abandon all their bad inclinations in order to act as moral subjects.

On the universal level Kant's concept of the Enlightenment is constructed as a philosophical-historical model and plays the role of one of the universal human values. Guided by the value of the Enlightenment, mankind will be able to overcome its tutelage and reach the 'society of world-citizens' in which everyone can freely follow the categorical imperative in their daily practice without violating the freedom of others. This will allow humanity to eliminate the threat of war, terrorism and armed conflict.

Moreover, Kant's model of the philosophy of history, along with the system of universal values embedded in it, allows us to formulate the basic principles of the doctrine of international cooperation in the context of current events at the beginning of the twenty- first century. Enlightenment plays an integral role in the system of these principles, for it is intended to guide humanity on the way to the 'society of world citizens', 'perpetual peace' and cosmopolitan world order.

Thus, Immanuel Kant has built a metaphysical bridge between the eighteenth century and the modernity, showing the way to help people to find the hope to survive.

References

Kant, I. 1983. *Perpetual Peace and Other Essays on Politics, History and Morals*, edited by Ted Humphrey. Indianapolis, IN: Hackett.
—. 1998a. *Groundwork of the Metaphysics of Morals*, translated and edited by Mary J. Gregor. Cambridge: Cambridge University Press.
—. 1998b. *The Critique of Pure Reason*, translated and edited by Paul Guyer. Cambridge: Cambridge University Press.

2
RETHINKING KANT'S 'IMMATURITY' IN ARENDT'S POST-TOTALITARIAN REFLECTION

Tatiana Weiser

Kantian 'immaturity' and Arendt's faculty of judgement

Among various facets of the Enlightenment's heritage, the Kantian appeal '*Sapere aude!*' is as relevant in modern philosophical reflection as it is controversial. It becomes particularly important in the context of totalitarian regimes and mass ideologies of the twentieth century. But just because of these contexts, the way Kant articulates this appeal reveals its ambiguity and poses more questions than it answers.

I will briefly describe Kant's concept of 'maturity' (in various translations also: competence or being of age). 'Enlightenment' – Kant begins his famous essay 'An Answer to the Question: What Is Enlightenment?' (1784) – 'is mankind's exit from his self-incurred immaturity. Immaturity is the inability to make use of one's own understanding without the guidance of another. Self-incurred is this inability if its cause lies not in the lack of understanding but rather in the lack of the resolution and the courage to use it without the guidance of another. *Sapere aude!* Have the courage to use your *own* understanding! is thus the motto of enlightenment' (1996a: 58).

What makes Kant different from philosophers of previous epochs is his idea that we are free to use or not to use our reason. We can be mere functionaries of the existing social order or independent thinkers courageous enough to criticise it. The freedom to make public use of one's reason is what evinces dignity in an individual. The free use of public reason alone can bring about Enlightenment among people. In this text, Kant first conceptually differentiates between authoritatively prescribed or the automatic reproduction of knowledge, on the one hand, and independent enlightened thinking, on the other: 'It is so easy to be immature. If I have a book that has understanding for me, a pastor who has a conscience for me, a doctor who judges my diet for me, and so forth, surely I do not need to trouble myself. I have no need to think, if only I can pay; others will take over the tedious business for me' (1996a: 58).

I will try to show that, when put in another context, namely, in a totalitarian context, this principle, framed by a restrictive Kantian logic that I will explain below, loses its force and requires to be both specified and replenished with new reflexive energy. Thus, the purpose of this article is to make explicit the limits of Kant's Enlightenment concept *sapere aude* and to demonstrate how it is reconceptualised in Arendt's post-totalitarian reflection. After briefly outlining Arendt's inheriting of Kant's principle of maturity in this introductory section (1), I will then demonstrate divergences between Kant's and Arendt's understanding of obedience to law (2); and will finally clarify how modern democracy can (and does) re-use Kant's principle of maturity by reconceptualising Kant's trust in state law through Arendt's post-totalitarian reflection (3).

Why compare Kant to Arendt? If we take Arendt's anti-totalitarian critique, we will see that she resorts to the same argument as Kant. She describes the Germans serving Nazi ideology as functionaries incapable of using their own reason. When Nazi propaganda embraced the whole country, they appeared to be 'helpless' in front of the new system and were forced to act as 'cogs in the mass-murder machine'. For those accused of cooperation or complicity with Nazis and who were afterwards judged for their crimes, the latter was a commonly used argument of self-defence. When Arendt analyses the situation that made it possible to involve the whole country in a large-scale systematic practice of mass murders, she arrives at the conclusion that 'in contrast to the earlier units of the SS men and Gestapo, Himmler's overall organisation relies not on fanatics, nor on congenital murderers, nor on sadists; it relies entirely upon the normality of jobholders and family men' (Arendt 1994: 129). Jobholders and good family men were primarily concerned with their security, pension, and the welfare of their families. Being 'guided' by Nazi ideologists, they did not feel anything to be 'wrong' with the new values of the organised mass killers, they just automatically changed one system of values for another. As Arendt infers, this new type of functionary killed not out of a passion to kill, but just because it was their professional duty which gave them an alibi for being exempted from any responsibility. Their lack of thinking entailed the incapacity to make any moral judgements necessary in that particular situation. In Kant's terms, being incapable of making use of their reason, they did not cast doubts on what the Nazis did and what they personally did, since the constant and reliable 'tutelage' of the Nazi bureaucratic organisation protected them from any excessive questions and throes of guilty conscience.

'Rules and formulas,' wrote Kant in 'What Is Enlightenment?', 'these mechanical instruments of a rational use (or rather misuse) of his natural gifts, are the fetters of an everlasting immaturity' (1996a: 59). 'Unfortunately it seems to be much easier to condition human behavior and to make people conduct themselves in the most unexpected and outrageous manner,' wrote Arendt two centuries later, 'than it is to persuade anybody to learn from experience […]; that is, to start thinking and judging instead of applying categories and formulas which are deeply engrained in our mind, but whose basis of experience has long been forgotten and whose plausibility resides in their intellectual consistency rather than in their adequacy to actual events' (Arendt 2003: 37).

Both Kant and Arendt thus criticize the unthinking masses and both protest against monopolies of dogmatic knowledge and the state treating people as machines. Both suggest freeing our minds from the blind and mechanical following of others' ideas. In this sense, two centuries after the Enlightenment, Arendt inherits Kant's critical tradition, and does so by reconstructing and renovating the value of mature independent thinking.

Kant's obedience to the law and Arendt's imperative to follow conscience

As we can recall, in 'What Is Enlightenment?' Kant suggests differentiating between the private and public use of reason. The private use of reason is appropriate when a person exercises their civil duty. The public use of reason gives people the freedom publicly to argue and to criticise a state of affairs that they might not agree with while exercising their duty. By attributing to our reason two different modes, Kant freed our faculty of judgement from the state of immaturity when we depend on others in our thinking. As H. L. Dreyfus and P. Rabinow put it: 'Kant's *maturity* consists in showing us how to save the critical and transcendental power of reason and thus the triumph of reason over superstition, custom, and despotism – the great achievement of the Enlightenment' (Dreyfus and Rabinow 1986: 110).

As we will see, problems with Kant's concept of reason free of dogmatism begin at the moment when he starts to associate the private use of reason with a civil post or a civil duty entrusted to a person. 'The private use,' writes Kant, 'I designate as that use which one makes of his reason in a certain *civil post* or office which is entrusted to him. Now a certain mechanism is necessary in many affairs which are run in the interest of the commonwealth by means of which some members of the commonwealth must conduct themselves passively in order that the government may direct them, through the destruction of these ends. Here one is certainly not allowed to argue; rather, one must obey. But insofar as this part of the machine considers himself at the same time as a member of the entire commonwealth, indeed even of a cosmopolitan society, who in the role of a scholar addresses a public in the proper sense through his writings, he can certainly argue, without thereby harming the affairs in which he is engaged in part as a passive member.' Kant offers some examples of this situation. One – of particular interest in the current context – concerns military orders: 'it would,' Kant says, 'be very destructive, if an officer on duty should argue about the suitability or the utility of a command given to him by his superior; he must obey. But he cannot fairly be forbidden as a scholar to make remarks on failings in the military service and to lay them before the public for judgement'. Another concerns civil obedience: 'the citizen,' Kant says, 'cannot refuse to pay the taxes imposed on him; even an impudent complaint against such levies [...] is punished as an outrage (which could lead to general insubordination). This same individual nevertheless does not act against the duty of a citizen if he, as a scholar, expresses his thoughts publicly on the inappropriateness or even the injustice of such taxes' (1996a: 60).[1]

The idea that 'the citizen cannot refuse to pay the taxes imposed on him' was, however, contested in 1849 by H. Thoreau in his famous essay *Resistance to Civil Government* (or *Civil Disobedience*). Thoreau makes a revolutionary claim that not only am I morally allowed to resist my government when it acts illegitimately (e.g., unleashes an immoral war or upholds slavery using my taxes), but I morally should resist (cf. Thoreau 2008). Kant apparently takes a step forward in freeing our potential for independent thinking, but immediately restricts himself to a law-abiding citizen. Usage of reason is free until we are limited by our civil duties. That the idea of a duty (no less than the moral law) is essential for the Kantian world-view is obvious from all his moral writings. Here, however, we come to the point where obedience to the law collides with the ability to think with one's own reason. Namely, they confront each other at the point where one's civil position or post implies a civil duty. The Kantian public use of reason as the major achievement of his Enlightenment project is not in the focus of our reflection; our primary concern will be with the imperative *sapere aude* when a person is limited by their civil duty.[2] Why this limitation is important for understanding Kant's imperative becomes clear when we regard him being conditioned by his particular historical context. Appealing to the latter, Kant critically exclaims: '[...] I hear from all sides the cry: *don't argue*! The officer says: "Don't argue, but rather march!" The tax collector says: "Don't argue, but rather pay!" The clergyman says: "Don't argue, but rather believe" (Only one ruler in the world says: "*Argue*, as much as you want and about whatever you wanr, *but obey*!")' (1996a: 59). The prince mentioned above was Friedrich II, who allowed for some considerable degree of public freedom during his reign from 1740 to 1786. Why Kant invested so much trust in the civil legality and the legal state can be explained by the fact that the state legal system was epitomised for Kant in Friedrich himself. And Friedrich's position – to allow for free thinking while inducing obedience to law – coincided with the position of Kant, whose whole philosophical paradigm testifies to subjugating rational thinking to moral law.

When we move into Arendt's totalitarian context, we encounter, however, quite a different situation with regard to the relationship between one's faculty of judgement and one's imperative to follow the state law. The characteristic defining the context that produces Arendt's reflection was that the Nazis (who initially were just terror organizations) intentionally blurred the boundaries between criminals and non-criminals. This meant that the constitution of the regime could incriminate everybody in Germany for being complicit with it, including those who might have wanted to escape from the Nazis' totalitarian policy. As Arendt describes it in her text 'Organized Guilt and Universal Responsibility', Nazi crimes were induced as everybody's guilt and by that the total bureaucratic organisation managed to embrace the whole country. The striking fact, though – and that is what makes Arendt's dramatically distinctive from Kant's context – is that the whole state regime of Nazi Germany enforced what are normally considered criminal activities. Crimes were committed within the context of legality and any act of the state was in fact criminal. People in Germany 'acted under conditions in which every moral act was illegal and every legal act was a crime', where 'the boundaries dividing criminals from normal persons, the guilty from the innocent, have been so completely effaced that nobody will be able to tell in Germany whether in any case he is dealing with a secret hero or with a former mass murderer' (Arendt 2003: 40; 1994: 125).

All of this explains why the faculty of judgement means for Arendt not only making use of one's reason publicly with the purpose of criticising an imperfect law, but using one's reason *in spite of* and *against* the law itself. To obey the law in Arendt's totalitarian context meant *not* to use one's own reason and to delegate this responsibility to the tutelage of the Other. But exactly that was the most commonly used argument of all those accused in cooperation with Nazis: 'I only obeyed the law', 'it was not my responsibility', 'I was only a cog in the machine' etc. 'The argument from the Nuremberg trials to the Eichmann trial and the more recent trials in Germany,' writes Arendt, 'has always been the same: every organization demands obedience to superiors as well as obedience to the laws of the land. Obedience is a political virtue of the first order, and without it no body politic could survive. Unrestricted freedom of conscience exists nowhere, for it would spell the doom of every organized community. All this sounds so plausible that it takes some effort to detect the fallacy' (Arendt 2003: 46). The fallacy, according to Arendt, lies in the equation of *consent* with *obedience*. Germans confused obedience with support and by pretending to obey the Führer or other Nazi bureaucrats they in fact supported the whole system of mass murders and concentration camps. As – for Arendt – where one does not refuse or protest against an apparently criminal law, one supports it. 'If I obey the laws of the land, I actually support its constitution, as becomes glaringly obvious in the case of revolutionists and rebels who disobey because they have withdrawn this tacit consent' (Arendt 2003: 47). The Germans did not have enough courage to refuse or protest as they simply did not think with their own reason. Arendt did not reproach them, though, that they did not have enough courage, but that they were so rooted in automatic thinking that when the Nazi regime started to gain strength, they just changed one set of morals, customs and manners for another and ended in automatic killing. '[…] The total moral collapse of respectable society during the Hitler regime may teach us that under such circumstances those who cherish values and hold fast to moral norms and standards are not reliable: we now know that moral norms and standards can be changed overnight, and all that then will be left is the mere habit of holding fast to something. Much more reliable will be the doubters and skeptics, not because skepticism is good or doubting wholesome, but because they are used to examine things and to make up their own minds' (Arendt 2003: 45).

Thus, she criticizes the very non-reflexive passivity with which the new ideological system was accepted and supported by the German bourgeois. Paradoxically, Kant describes his law-abiding citizen in terms of such passivity required by law for the purpose of the coordination of the social order, as in the abovementioned defintion: 'A certain mechanism is necessary in many affairs which are run in the interest of the commonwealth by means of which some members of the commonwealth must conduct themselves *passively* in order that the government may direct them, through, an artificial unanimity, to public ends [...]' (1996a: 60).³ In their role of citizens, individuals appear in Kant as *passive* members responsible for supporting social order. This passivity is legitimised, in Kant's logic, by the absolute imperative to obey one's duty: 'For what [a scholar] teaches as a consequence of his office as an agent of his church, he presents as something about which he does not have free reign to teach according to his own discretion, but rather is engaged to expound *according to another's precept and in another's name*' (1996a: 60).⁴ That is, when one has a superior authority, induced by the civil law, one could not but obey its commands. Moreover, for Kant, this obligation has always moral implications, which justifies one's actions whatever one does in the name of a duty. You are allowed to use your reason only when and where you are discharged of duty. For Arendt, in her context, one should have used one's reason while (and in this sense *against*) carrying out one's duties. Hence, the second paradox is that, contrary to Kant, whose free and open use of reason required publicity, Arendt's use of reason, in that particular context, required complete withdrawal from the public space: '[...] Nonparticipators in public life under a dictatorship are those who have refused their support by shunning those places of "responsibility" where such support, under the name of obedience, is required' (Arendt 2003: 47). And in another place: 'the simple truth of the matter is that only those who withdrew from public life altogether, who refused political responsibility of any sort, could avoid becoming implicated in crimes, that is, could avoid legal and moral responsibility' (Arendt 2003: 34).

Although both Kant and Arendt elevate our faculty of judgement to an absolute value, Kant subjugates this faculty to obedience to the law, while Arendt, in her context, criticises the type of legal system that justifies such subjugation. To blind and automatic obedience to the law she opposes conscience by which she understands the ability to think independently. Where Kant appeals to unconditional abidance by the law, Arendt appeals to following one's conscience as a regulative mechanism of the choice between doing morally right and doing morally wrong. She elucidates a particular type of situation when obedience to the law cannot and should not conform to, or be reconciled with, using freely one's own reason.

Eichmann's Kant: Did Eichmann really distort the categorical imperative?

There was an extended discussion on whether Kantian moral philosophy implicitly leads to Nazism or not. The incentive for this discussion was Eichmann's reference during the Nuremberg trial to Kant's imperative to obey one's duty. In Eichmann's view, he acted according to, and consistent with, Kant's moral theory. By implementing the 'Final Solution' he did what he conceived to be the duty of a law-abiding citizen. When being asked on trial why he *personally* had to send people to death, he answered within Kant's paradigm of responsibility: '[...] I became responsible in this matter [...] I was ordered to do it. I had to carry out orders.

Whether people died or not, orders had to be carried out in accordance with the administrative procedure. An officer makes a declaration of loyalty. If he breaks it, he is a scoundrel. I still adhere to that opinion. And I believed so at that time: an oath is an oath'.[5] The discussion whether Eichmann indeed followed Kant's moral credo (or whether Kant allows such interpretations and practical implementations of his theory) was initiated by Arendt herself, who believed that Eichmann, in fact, distorted Kant's categorical imperative. In her *Eichmann in Jerusalem* she mentions that during the police examination Eichmann clearly made references to Kant's moral ideas and afterwards developed them during the trial. He understood Kant so that 'the principle of [his] will must always be such that it can become the principle of general laws' (Arendt 1983: 136). But, as she writes, he has misunderstood the Kantian formula, since 'Kant's moral philosophy is so closely bound up with man's faculty of judgment, which rules out blind obedience' (Arendt 1983: 136) (though I will try to show further that it is not completely so). He had also 'distorted it to read: Act as if the principle of your actions were the same as that of the legislator or of the law of the land', – and, taking into account that the law of the Third Reich land was based on the Führer's will, that imperative turned out to be as Hans Frank formulated it: 'Act in such a way that the Führer, if he knew your action, would approve it' (cited in Arendt 1983: 136). At the same time, she admits that 'whatever Kant's role in the formation of "the little man's" mentality in Germany may have been, there is not the slightest doubt that in one respect Eichmann did indeed follow Kant's precepts: a law was a law, there could be no exceptions' (Arendt 1983: 137). She does not go further in this admission, however, and does not show how exactly the Kantian value of faculty of judgement comes to terms with the absolute imperative character of law (that I will also try to make explicit later).

In the reflection that follows on from Arendt there are two major positions – one trying to justify Kant and to purge his moral theory from the shadow of its implicit pro-Nazi assumptions; and the other admitting that Kant's theory is logically compatible with them. I will briefly compare these two positions as they are expressed in two articles: 'Eichmann's Kant' by C. B. Laustsen and R. Ugilt and 'Kant's Radical Evil' by R. J. Bernstein.

In 'Eichmann's Kant' Laustsen and Ugilt address Arendt's interpretation of the nature of Eichmann's evil that paradoxically might be connected with or follow from Kantian ethics. They advance two arguments against using Kant in Eichmann's sense. The first one is that the moral subject (including Kant's) is driven by a feeling of never having acted morally enough (and that is, according to them, the very nature of moral sense), while Eichmann, following the Führer's will, was secure in his conviction to have acted morally. The second one is that, though Eichmann in a sense practically fulfils the Kantian moral project (he integrates the universal moral law into the practical sphere), it does not mean that he follows Kant in his comprehension of the moral law. As they put it, 'the moral law does not tell me *what* my duty is, it only tells me *that* I must do my duty' (Laustsen and Ugilt 2007: 177). Then, referring to Žižek, they claim that, according to Kant, it is the full responsibility of the subject to translate ethical precepts into concrete actions: '"The ethical subject bears full responsibility for the concrete universal norms he follows'" (Žižek 1997: 221, cited by Laustsen and Ugilt 2007: 177).

They conclude that 'the target of criticism should hence not be Kant's formalism' (Laustsen and Ugilt 2007: 176). The problem, in their view, emerges from practical reason, and this problem resides in the fact that the practical sphere can never give any guarantees for morality or establish any secure moral foundations (nor should it be required to by the critique of practical reason). Therefore, if we want Kantian ethics to come to terms with itself, we should leave out the presumption that reason can once and for all establish which practical acts are moral and which are not. And that means that the categorical imperative itself can be a moral frame, but cannot be *the ultimate justification* for any practical action whatever.

In the article 'Kant's Radical Evil' R. J. Bernstein takes an alternative position. The author certainly admits that it would be anachronistic to expect that Kant anticipated the horrors of the twentieth century which radically changed our comprehension of what evil might be. But he also writes, 'some of Kant's reflections on duty – especially the "absolute" duty of a citizen to obey the sovereign power and the duty of a soldier to obey the orders of a superior – are more than disappointing; they are extremely disturbing'. He specifically refers to the case of Adolf Eichmann, 'who cited Kant (with reasonable accuracy) at his trial in Jerusalem in order to justify his conduct in sending victims to death camps'. While not blaming Kant, 'the great champion of human dignity, for this perverse appropriation of the categorical imperative', he nevertheless concurs with John R. Silber, whom he quotes: '"It may seem outrageous to find Kant's ethical doctrine, grounded as it is in the dignity of the moral person as end-in-himself, used to exculpate a confessed accomplice to mass murder. But it should come as no surprise to Kant scholars, for Kant's views on the citizen's obligation to the sovereign strongly support Eichmann's position."' And Bernstein continues: 'Kant's "official" doctrine is that the ban on resisting any supreme lawmaking is *absolute,* and also that a soldier must always obey the orders of a superior. (Let us not forget that for all the violence of the Nazis, "Hitler was made Chancellor in a constitutionally proper manner.")' To illustrate this point Bernstein quotes (from Silber) three of the many passages that Eichmann might have cited from Kant to justify his acceptance of the *Führerprinzip* (Bernstein 2001: 76–77):

1. '[A]ny resistance to the supreme lawmaking power, any incitement of dissatisfied subjects to action, any uprising that bursts into rebellion—that all this is the worst, most punishable crime in a community. For it shatters the community's foundations. And this ban is *absolute,* so unconditional that even though that supreme power or its agent, the head of state, may have broken the original contract, even though in the subject's eyes he may have forfeited the right to legislate by empowering the government to rule tyrannically by sheer violence, even then the subject is allowed no resistance, no violent counteraction' (quoted from Silber 1991: 186).
2. '[T]here is no right of sedition much less a right of revolution, and least of all a right to lay hands on or take the life of the chief of state when he is an

individual person on the excuse that he has misused his authority [...]. It is the people's duty to endure even the most intolerable abuse of supreme authority' (quoted from Silber 1991: 189).
3. 'Thus it would be ruinous if an officer, receiving an order from his superiors, wanted while on duty to engage openly in subtle reasoning about its appropriateness or utility; he must obey' (cf. 1996b: 18–19).

So, we have two opposite views on Kant's imperative of obedience: one saying that the Kantian subject is fully responsible for what they did while obeying law or duty; the other saying that Kant himself did not give any opportunity to disobey law or duty. In my last sections, I will show that the question is not whether we should accuse Kant of allowing misuses and misinterpretations of his moral principles, but what aspects of his moral theory, having passed through the tragic experiences of the twentieth century, we should rethink.

To be morally irreproachable while sacrificing others

In my own criticism of Kant I share Bernstein's position when he writes that Kant cannot be blamed for misappropriation and distortion of his ideas and that it makes no sense to extract them from their historical context. Bernstein says that he 'certainly [does] not want to judge Kant by the way his statements have been misappropriated and distorted –especially when they are taken out of context'. He thinks that it is not 'fair to criticize Kant for his failure to anticipate the type of systematic terror and violence practiced by the Nazis', especially as 'it is difficult to think of any philosopher whose ethical doctrines have not lent themselves to gross distortions'. In other words, he has 'no doubt that Kant would find ample grounds to condemn the conduct of the Nazi regime.' 'Nevertheless', he insists, 'the consistency and even harshness with which Kant opposes any active resistance against "the supreme law-making power," no matter how tyrannical and violent it may be, should at least make us question his rigorism – and his insistence that this ban is *absolute* and *unconditional*' (Bernstein 2001: 77).

Like Bernstein, I do not aim to accuse Kant of implicit pro-Nazi presuppositions. At the end of the eighteenth century Kant did not (and could not) yet attribute to the state the ability to be an organised criminal institution. But it seems to me crucial to reveal those presuppositions of his theory that might be (or really were) used in this sense. Let us examine how the absoluteness Bernstein speaks of penetrates all Kant's reasoning on duty. My own arguments against Kant's position or, rather, in favour of rethinking it, are the following.

Kant does not give us a clear understanding of what we should choose if obedience to law or duty contradicts the second part of his categorical imperative: 'Act in such a way that you treat humanity, whether in your own person or in the person of another, always at the same time as an end and never simply as a means' (Kant 1993: 429). If we follow the second part of Kant's imperative – to treat people as an end – we will not kill them as a means for purifying the allegedly superior race. But Kant believes it to be imperative to obey the moral law (embodied in an external duty in this case) as well as to treat people as an end. While appealing to Kant, Eichmann will not find enough theoretical odds in favour of treating people as an end but enough for killing them as an exercise of his duty, since both options have the same weight for Kant himself.

What if obedience to the universal moral law or one's duty comes into conflict with treating a human being as an end?[6] Then we have two answers from Kant: a theoretical and a practical one. A theoretical answer from Kant denies the very opportunity that there may be a collision of duties. As he says, 'A collision of duties or obligations would be the result of such a relation between them that the one would annul the other, in whole or in part. Duty and Obligation, however, are conceptions which express the objective practical *Necessity* of certain actions, and two opposite Rules cannot be objective and necessary at the same time; for if it is a Duty to act according to one of them, it is not only no Duty to act according to an opposite Rule, but to do so would even be contrary to Duty. Hence a *Collision* of Duties and Obligations is entirely inconceivable'. Kant does, however, concede that here may be 'two grounds of Obligation, connected with an individual under a Rule prescribed for himself,' and that 'neither the one nor the other may be sufficient to constitute an actual Obligation,' which means that 'one of them is not a Duty'. In this case, he concludes that 'if two such grounds of Obligation are actually in collision with each other, Practical Philosophy does not say that the stronger *Obligation* is to keep the upper hand, but that the stronger *ground* of Obligation is to maintain its place' (Kant 1887: 32–33).[7]

Notwithstanding, Kant believes treating human beings as an end to be as much a moral obligation as obeying one's professional duty. But he gives neither an example, nor a criterion according to which we could judge one foundation for action as more valid than another in case of a choice. In another text, 'On a Supposed Right to Lie Because of Philanthropic Concerns' [*Über ein vermeintes Recht, aus Menschenliebe zu lügen*] (1797) we find Kant's practical answer to our question: he analyses a hypothetical, though quite empirically possible, situation where we have a choice between following the moral law and saving human life (or at least not exposing it to risk). And the answer is not in favour of the latter. The text was written as a reaction to a surprised reproach made by Benjamin Constant in the journal *France* to Kant's readiness unquestionably to obey the moral law: 'This philosopher', wrote Constant on Kant, 'goes so far as to assert that it would be a crime to lie to a murderer who has asked whether our friend who is pursued by him had taken refuge in our house' (cited by Kant 1993: 425). Kant answers with the following: 'Truthfulness in statements that cannot be avoided is the formal duty of man to everyone, however great the disadvantage that may arise therefrom for him or for any other. And even though by telling an untruth I do no wrong to him who unjustly compels me to make a statement, yet by this falsification, which as such can be called a lie (though not in a juridical sense), I do wrong to duty in general in a most essential point. That is, as far as in me lies I bring it about that statements (declarations) in general find no credence, and hence also that all rights based on contracts become void and lose their force, and this is a wrong done to mankind in general' (Kant 1993: 426).

What Kant is saying here is that when having choice between following the moral law and saving human life (or at least not exposing it to risk), we should choose the moral law. And that means that on the level of practical considerations we have enough grounds to justify letting people die for the sake of moral immaculacy. While not being put under such pressing conditions, we would surely choose treating the same person as an end and so saving their life. However, when, for example, we would choose between killing a human being in order to steal their property or saving their life, we would be in perfect accordance with both parts of his categorical imperative. The same situation (to save or to sacrifice a human life) being reframed by a higher moral value derived from following the moral law will entail an opposite result without betraying Kant's logic.

My other counter-argument is that Kant does not give us a clear account of how exactly different aspects of a maxim should be universalised through the test of the categorical imperative. If we take a simple and rather abstract maxim and ask whether I could wish killing should become a universal law, the answer would be evident, given we share the presumption of the value of humankind or the necessity of survival. But there can be more than one option for universalising a maxim. Following Kant's test of logic, Eichmann can ask: 'could I wish obeying Führer's will should become a universal law?', or 'could I wish killing people should become a universal norm?' Had Eichmann asked himself such questions, he would presumably have answered positively to the first one and negatively to the second.[8] Kant does not tell us clearly which aspect of a maxim we should check through the test of the categorical imperative, given our maxim implicitly contains different facets. If we answer the first question positively and trust it to be our duty (as Eichmann did), then why ask the second question? Then we only have to resort to the argument by Laustsen, Ugilt and Žižek that the moral subject is fully responsible for what they choose to be their duty. But then it is presupposed that the subject would have an intuition of humanistic conscience or of Christian love for the Other and will have enough propensity to follow them *despite* doing his duty or obeying the moral law.

Two aspects of great importance for Kant in his attitude towards the moral imperative to obey are worth paying attention to. The first one is conceiving one's civil duty as the realisation of the Other's will. As a priest, says Kant in 'What Is Enlightenment?', one 'is not and cannot be free, because he conforms to the orders of another' (1996a: 61). And several lines before this: 'For what [a scholar] teaches as a consequence of his office as an agent of his church, he presents as something about which he does not have free reign to teach according to his own discretion, but rather is engaged to expound *according to another's precept and in another's name*' (1996a: 60). It seems to be a kind of rhetorical paradox as Kant completely contests the same figure of the Other's authority while speaking about using one's own reason as a public person. Though the demarcation between the two spheres is clear, the same rhetoric of the unconditioned obedience to authority used within the same text ('What Is Enlightenment?') with two opposite meanings is still rather challenging. Why act as if we did not have the capacity to use our reason *at the very point of* exercising a civil duty? Why not protest against certain concrete social norms being satisfied by criticising them *somewhere else*?[9]

Trying to defend Kant, Žižek writes: 'What we encounter here is the properly perverse attitude of adopting the position of the pure instrument of the big Other's Will: it's not my responsibility, it's not me who is effectively doing it, I am merely an instrument of the higher Historical Necessity [...]. The obscene jouissance of this situation is generated by the fact that I conceive of myself as exculpated from what I am doing: isn't it nice to be able to inflict pain on others in the full awareness that I'm not responsible for it, that I am merely fulfilling the Other's Will? [...] This is what Kantian ethics prohibits' (Žižek 1997: 222, cited by Laustsen and Ugilt 2007: 176). But he forgets what Kant explicitly says on this matter. In 'What Is Enlightenment?' Kant grants us the right to leave our post if it contradicts our values, but denies our right to disobey the Other's will if we have this post. And, as we will see now, he resorts to the argument that in obeying our duties or following moral laws we not only can, but also should, be free from personal moral responsibility.

From this comes the second aspect worth paying attention to – Kant's unconditional desire to be morally irreproachable. A person is inevitably guided by this desire regardless of any concrete empirical situation in which he or she might be confronted with a moral dilemma. In fact, no moral dilemma exists at all within Kantian logic, if we have enough courage and motivation to be guided by the principles of the moral law. 'However,' he insists further in 'On a Supposed Right', 'this well-intentioned lie can become punishable in accordance with civil law because of an accident; and that which avoids liability to punishment only by accident can also be condemned as wrong even by external laws. For example, if by telling a lie you have in fact hindered someone who was even now planning a murder, then you are legally responsible for all the consequences that might result therefrom. But if you have adhered strictly to the truth, then public justice cannot lay a hand on you, whatever the unforeseen consequence might be' (Kant 1993: 426–427). In other words, it would be preferable to stay morally irreproachable in the eyes of the law rather than taking responsibility for saving a life'. To hold rigorously and *regularly* (and in Arendt's terms, *mechanically*) to the moral law has a higher moral status and will have higher moral consequences for him than to have a *casual* opportunity to save human life.

In her article 'On the Justification of Lying from Altruistic Motives' Olga Artemjeva writes that for Kant, telling the truth is an obligation irrespective of circumstances and persons, as if they all were indifferent or similar. She remarks that we should understand Kant's words as being 'regardless of circumstances and persons' literally, not in an elevated Lutheran sense of strength of mind, but in the sense that in a situation of choice only moral principles are essential and no significance might be given to the concrete moral subject making the choice, nor to the concrete people involved in the situation, nor to the relationship between them, in other words, to anything that constitutes the situation as a particular or even singular event. It is as if moral principles mark out a moral space within which the moral subject has the right to do whatever it thinks fit, provided it stays within the moral frame. Within this disposition there is no need, of course, to ponder over the differentiated circumstances of an action or the persons towards whom the action is being done (Artemjeva 2008: 45).[10]

To sum up this section, I argue that these two points – to follow one's duty and to be morally irreproachable with regard to the moral law – are as valid for Kant as the second part of his categorical imperative: to treat human beings as an end and not as a means. There are no grounds for considering the former being of less value or importance for Kant than the latter. I do not claim that obeying one's duty or striving for moral immaculacy is bad. I just stress that these two points may come into conflict with the principle of treating people as an end under some specific circumstances and that Kant does not provide a sufficient conceptual framework that would allow us to avoid this conflict in such circumstances. In my last sections I will show that the probability of Kant's moral theory being misused in a certain type of situation is strongly intertwined with the limits of his concept *sapere aude* imposed by his unconditional belief in state law and legal authority. I will show that in her anti-totalitarian critique Arendt frees us from this pressure of an alleged absoluteness of a moral law. And that she does it by freeing our capacity for maturity and for its sake.

Rethinking obedience to law after twentieth-century catastrophes

Since Carl Schmitt we have been operating with the well-known distinction between legality and legitimacy and have been learning to put any legal system under question (Schmitt 2004).[11] Nazi Germany seems to be a perfect example of the crisis of a state legal-system that has tried to legitimise its criminal regime in every cell of national, political, social and juridical life. It not only criminalized law to the greatest extent possible, but also elevated obedience to the law as such to the status of the *absolute*. Obedience to the law and unconditional readiness to do one's duty became a form of legitimisation of the individual itself: you may not have right to life unless you obey. As Arendt diagnosed it: 'The moral point of this matter is never reached by calling what happened by the name of "genocide" or by counting the many millions of victims: extermination of whole peoples had happened before in antiquity, as well as in modern colonisation. It is reached only when we realise that this happened within the frame of a legal order and that the cornerstone of this "new law" consisted of the command "Thou shalt kill" [...]' (Arendt 2003: 42). And earlier in the text she wrote about the paradox that the categories of 'lawful' and 'unlawful' did not work anymore in the context where every unlawful act appeared to be lawful: '[...] men who did wrong were very well acquainted with the letter and the spirit of the law of the country they lived in, and today, when they are held responsible, what we actually require of them is a "feeling of lawfulness" deep within themselves to *contradict* the law of the land and their knowledge of it' (Arendt 2003: 42).

Therefore, what would be morally valuable for Kant in his unconditioned obedience both to the moral law 'within us' and to an external civil duty, would have lost its moral value in Arendt's context. The problem seems to reside in two different understandings of what the moral law is. While for Kant it is a universalisable maxim, for Arendt it is conscience that, amongst other things, is capable of resisting any imposed or internalised normativity. And this is the principal moment of divergence in their approaches. What in Kant's view would be definitely moral, can easily be turned into an eviscerated formula in Arendt's view: 'Nonparticipants [in Nazi Germany] were those whose consciences did not function in this, as it were, automatic way – as though we dispose of a set of learned or innate rules which we then apply to the particular case as it arises, so that every new experience or situation is already prejudged and we need only act out whatever we learned or possessed beforehand' (Arendt 2003: 44).

Though Arendt does not criticise Kant's moral steadfastness and even defends him against Eichmann's misuse, in inheriting his Enlightenment project she goes two steps further than Kant. Firstly, she introduces the notion of conscience as an instrument to stop automatism in thinking. Kant's 'you do not need to think' (while obeying law or exercising your duty) is reformulated by her as you do need to think, particularly when you obey the law or exercise your civil duty. You need to think always, in any situation, under whatever circumstances. *Sapere aude* only makes sense when its implementation is unrestricted by external limitations or the Other's will. And this explains why, according to Arendt, we have reasons to hold 'cogs in the machine' *responsible* for what they did: nobody, no authority may forbid you from using your own reason, no law may require you to have it, you are the only person responsible for using it or not and when to use it or not. In this sense, her 'conscience' may be conceived of as a means of producing a reflective rupture in (and resistance to) any imposed disposition of knowledge.

The second important step she takes is that for the first time since Thoreau and Gandhi she conceptualises *civil disobedience* as a positive social and political value. In her chapter 'Civil Disobedience' in *Crises of the Republic* she defines civil disobedience as a nonviolent protest openly performed in public in order to restore justice, often exercised by minorities ready to accept punishment for their defiance. Civil disobedience presumes acceptance of the frame of established authority as well as of the constitution and the legitimacy of the law-system in general. At the same time, it aims to draw public attention to an injustice and appeals for the restoration of violated human rights.

In recent times, Arendt states, civil disobedience becomes a more and more widespread phenomenon as a reaction to the loss of confidence in the existing authorities. It points to the fact that any human community regulated by law is based on a mutually binding social contract. If an established authority does not keep to the original conditions of consent (horizontal social contract), the right to dissent is not only possible, but also politically desirable. It is and *should* become the basic organising principle of any political community. And history shows that examples of governments breaking the original contract, in other words, of governments' illegal and unconstitutional acts, are becoming more and more numerous (illegal and immoral wars, increasing claim to power, chronic political deception or systematic lying etc.). When we face the erosion of governmental authority, when we doubt its legitimacy, 'when the established institution of a country fails to function properly and its authority loses its power', then, according to her, the time for civil disobedience has come (Arendt 1972: 101–102). In this case not only *may* we not disobey the law, but we are *morally obliged* to contest it, precisely because, as mentioned above, there are situations or regimes where any legal act turns out to be criminal, or, as she formulates it, we encounter 'criminalization of the whole governmental apparatus' (Arendt 1972: 80). Then, 'the establishment of civil disobedience among our political institutions might be the best possible remedy for this ultimate failure of judicial review' (Arendt 1972: 101).

Thus, for her, our political aim today is to find a home for civil disobedience in our political language and our political system. 'It would be an event of great significance,' she concludes, 'to find a constitutional niche for civil disobedience' (Arendt 1972: 83). But once civil disobedience turns out to be a necessity for fighting the illegitimacy of the legal system, the key question of her reasoning is: with what concept of law could it be compatible? And that is the sort of question that was not at all possible within Kant's moral paradigm. And that means that the *sapere aude* principle is not only *allowed parallel to* an intact law, but strives to *find its own place within* the law and claims to be the measure of its very legitimacy and morality. Law, in Arendt's conception, stops being immunized from uncomfortable and disturbing reflection: it becomes the very site of reflexivity, the site *within which* the eye of reason opens.[12]

Arendt makes a crucial contribution to both the post-Kantian and anti-Kantian Enlightenment project. Inheriting and reformulating his *sapere aude* in her conception of faculty of judgement, she was not satisfied (a.) with (only) criticising law when possible and allowed and (b.) with being morally irreproachable while being morally automatic. She believed not only that our duty is to resist dogmas (like Kant), but also that to resist an allegedly moral law is our moral duty. Not only did she make thought an instrument of the fight against dogmas, but she also made resistance to an illegitimate law a moral, social and political value. She conceived of it as one of the moral foundations of modern democracy. By that, Arendt paved the way for the contemporary philosophy of civil disobedience and of civil protest inherited in the last third of the twentieth century by such thinkers as J. Rawls, J. Habermas and others and which is now considered one of the most effective tools against the illegitimacy of the state legal system.[13]

To return to my own thesis, I argued that Kant himself does not give us enough theoretical resources that could orientate us towards a humanistic solution while having a choice between following the moral law and saving human life. In his own practical considerations he gives us a counter-example. And this position may very well be explained by the fact that one of the key principles of Kantian philosophy – *sapere aude* – is submitted to the absolute value of obedience to the law. As a consequence, the clear understanding that the *final solution* is so far from being a humanistic solution should once again direct our attention to this theoretical lacuna. This imperative Enlightenment principle, *sapere aude*, and the way we advance this imperative should be revised and questioned in each new historical context, in each new epistemological disposition. Only by reframing it in various ways can we see the blind spots that otherwise make us morally perfect machines feeling quite comfortable with their perfectly automatic functioning.

'If it is asked "Do we now live in an *enlightened* age?" the answer is, "No, but we do live in an age of *enlightenment*"', asserted Kant (1996a: 62). The twentieth century's extreme horrors and catastrophes demonstrated that not only do we not live in an enlightened age, but certainly the Enlightenment we have achieved through the last centuries permanently alternates with the most barbaric evil the humankind ever witnessed. As Hannah Arendt stated in *The Origins of Totalitarianism*, 'totalitarian solutions may well survive the fall of totalitarian regimes in the form of strong temptations which will come up whenever it seems impossible to alleviate political, social, or economic misery in a manner worthy of man' (Arendt 1973: 459). Therefore, the role of the Enlightenment project in the contemporary world should consist in the everlasting motivation to re-think ourselves, to question all the possible assumptions of our thought. When we reflect on the Enlightenment epoch today, we should address this very principle: we can only dare to claim that we use our own reason without self-incurred tutelage when we indefatigably re-think ourselves and question the limits of our thinking again and again. This would mean to acknowledge that enlightened thinking consists in the willingness to subject to criticism what seems to be the most reliable foundations of our life and moral credo.[14]

Notes

1 It is interesting that Kant uses 'mechanism' and 'machine', the very words that occur in the discussion of complicity with Nazism.
2 This topic would require separate fundamental research and a deeper insight into the whole tradition of the public sphere inspired by Kant and represented by H. Arendt, M. Foucault, J. Habermas etc.
3 My emphasis.
4 My emphasis.
5 Cited according to documentary shots from Margaret von Trotta's film *Hannah Arendt* (2012).
6 Or we should first ask if there is any difference between obedience to the moral law and to a duty for Kant. Though he differentiates between external laws which are obligatory and based on legislation, on the one hand, and internal moral laws 'within us', on the

other, there seems to be no difference for him with regard to the extent to which he has propensity *unconditionally* to obey to both.
7   The quotation omits the numerous Latin equivalents inserted by Kant in this passage.
8   Margaret von Trotta stressed this point in her film on Arendt devoted mostly to Arendt's visit to Eichmann's trial in Jerusalem. The camera fixes on her bitterly, ironically grinning face and a suddenly stunned gaze when Eichmann, being asked 'Did anybody prove to you that Jews should be exterminated [i.e., did you have any reasons to exterminate Jews besides the Führer's will]?', answered with the confidence of common sense, 'Ich habe sie nicht vernichtet' ['I did not exterminate them']. See M. von Trotta, *Hannah Arendt* (2012).
9   Though in general Kant would protest against any communitarian dictatorship and, had he lived in the twentieth century, against the *Reich*: 'But would not a society of clergymen, such as a church synod or a venerable classis [...], be justified in binding one another by oath to a certain unalterable symbol, in order to hold an unremitting superior guardianship over each of their members, and by this means over their people, and even to make this eternal? I say that is completely impossible' (1996a: 61).
10 Artemjeva makes reference to, among others, Lawrence Blum, who stated that the key moral attitude by Kant is not towards a concrete other, but towards morality itself, to the morally right act and principle only (Blum 1988).
11 Carl Schmitt (1888–1985) is a German jurist and political philosopher, with Heidegger and others engaged in establishing the philosophical legitimacy of Nazi policies. In his famous work *Legality and Legitimacy* (1932) he states that if a legal state concentrates all power in its law but dissociates the law from reason, justice, and the majority principle, any law can become legal; that a political party can use legal procedures to cancel all those guarantees of rights and freedoms due to which it had previously got power without being in contradiction with the state's constitution. And that was exactly what Arendt pointed out when she described the paradox of the Nazi legal state: that as soon as NSDAP come to power the demarcation between the Führer's will and the state law was intentionally blurred: 'the Führer's words, his oral pronouncements, were the basic law of the land' (Arendt 1983: 148). So for Eichmann, 'there existed no difference between Führer's will and moral law or, in more general terms, between legality and morality' (Laustsen and Ugilt 2007: 177).
12 See, e.g., Felman 2002, which analyzes 'ways in which the law remains professionally blind' while 'seeing [is] crucial to the very practice and the very execution of the law' (Felman 2002: 57, 80). What Arendt is trying to do is directing our reflexive and critical attention to the blind spots of law *within* law itself, while Kant draws a line around it, trying to keep it immunized and untouched.
13 See, e.g., Rawls 1971, Habermas 1985 and others.
14 As we know, the notion *conscience*, which Arendt takes to be an alternative to automatic thinking, is not immunized from misuse and can easily be turned into a powerful instrument of manipulation as it was, e.g., within the ideology of the Soviet totalitarian regime that used to appeal to conscience as its most basic moral foundation.

References

Arendt, H. 2003. 'Personal Responsibility Under Dictatorship', in *Responsibility and Judgment*, edited by J. Kohn. New York: Schocken Books, pp.17–48.
—. 1993. 'Organized Guilt and Universal Responsibility', in *Essays in Understanding*, 1930–1954, edited by J. Kohn. New York: Harcourt, Brace and Co.,

—. 1983. *Eichmann in Jerusalem: A Report on the Banality of Evil*. Revised and enlarged edition [1963]. New York: Penguin Books.

—. 1982. *Lectures on Kant's Political Philosophy*, edited by R. Beiner. Chicago: University of Chicago Press.

—. 1973. *The Origins of Totalitarianism*. New York: Harcourt Brace and Company.

—. 1972. 'Civil Disobedience', in *Crises of the Republic*. London, New York: A Harvest Book, pp. 49–103.

Artemjeva, O. 2008. 'Ob opravdannosti lzhi is chelovekoljubija' [On the Justification of Lying out of Philantrophy], *Logos* 5(68): 40–59.

Bernstein, R. J. 2001. 'Radical Evil: Kant at War with Himself', in *Rethinking Evil: Contemporary Perspectives*, edited by María Pía Lara. Berkeley: University of California Press, pp. 55–86.

Blum, L. A. 1988. 'Gilligan and Kohlberg: Implications for Moral Theory', *Ethics* 98(3): 472–491.

Breton, A. and Wintrobe, R. 1986. 'The Bureaucracy of Murder Revisited', *Journal of Political Economy* 94(5): 905–926.

Dreyfus, H. L. and Rabinow, P. 1986. 'What Is Maturity? Habermas and Foucault on "What Is Enlightenment?"' in *Foucault: A Critical Reader*, edited by D. Couzens Hoy. Oxford; New York: B. Blackwell, pp. 108–121.

Felman, S. 2002. 'Forms of Judicial Blindness, or the Evidence of What Cannot be Seen: Traumatic Narratives and Legal Repetitions in the O.J. Simpson Case and in Tolstoy's The Kreutzer Sonata', in Felman, S., *The Juridical Unconscious: Trials and Traumas in the Twentieth Century*. Cambridge: Harvard University Press, pp. 54–106.

Foucault, M. 1984. 'What Is Enlightenment?', in *The Foucault Reader*, edited by P. Rabinow. New York: Pantheon, pp. 32–51.

Gasparyan, D. 2011. *Vvedenije v neklassicheskuju filosofiju* [*Introduction to Non-classical Philosophy* – Rus.]. Moscow: Rossijskaja politicheskaja entsyklopedia.

Habermas, J. 1991. 'Publicity as the Bridging Principle Between Politics and Morality (Kant)', in Habermas, J., *The Structural Transformation of the Public Sphere: An Inquiry into a Category of Bourgeois Society*. Cambridge, MA: MIT Press.

—. 1985. 'Civil Disobedience: Litmus Test for the Democratic Constitutional State', *Berkeley Journal of Sociology* 30: 95–116.

Kant, I. 1996. 'An Answer to the Question: What Is Enlightenment?' (1784), *What Is Enlightenment?: Eighteenth-Century Answers and Twentieth-Century Questions*, ed. J. Schmidt. Berkeley: University of California Press, pp. 58–65.

—. 1996b. *Practical Philosophy*. The Cambridge Edition of the Works of Immanuel Kant, edited and translated by M. J. Gregor. Cambridge: Cambridge University Press, 1996.

—. 1993. *Grounding for the Metaphysics of Morals* [1785]. With 'On a Supposed Right to Lie Because of Philanthropic Concerns'. Indianapolis, IN: Hackett Pub. Co.

—. 1887. *The Philosophy of Law*, translated by W. Hastie. Edinburgh: T. & T. Clark.

Laustsen, C. B. and Ugilt, R. 2007. 'Eichmann's Kant', *The Journal of Speculative Philosophy*, New Series 21(3): 166–180.

Neiman, S. 2002. *Evil in Modern Thought: An Alternative History of Philosophy*. Princeton: Princeton University Press.

Norris, C. 1994. '"What Is Enlightenment?": Kant According to Foucault', in *Cambridge Companion to Foucault*, edited by G. Gutting. New York: Cambridge University Press, pp. 159–196.

Rawls, J. 1971. *A Theory of Justice*. Cambridge: Belknap Press of Harvard University Press.

Schmitt, C. 2004. *Legality and Legitimacy*, translated and edited by J. Seitzer. Durham: Duke University Press.

Schrift, A. D. (ed.). 2005. *Modernity and the Problem of Evil*. Bloomington: Indiana University Press.
Silber, J. R. 1991. 'Kant at Auschwitz', in *Proceedings of the Sixth International Kant Congress*, edited by G. Funke and T. M. Seebohm. Washington, DC: Centre for Advanced Phenomenology and University Press of America.
—. 1960. 'The Ethical Significance of Kant's *Religion*', in E. Kant, *Religion within the Limits of Reason Alone*, translated by T. M. Greene and H. H. Hudson. New York: Harper Torchbooks, pp. vii–ix.
Thoreau, H. D. 2008. *Civil Disobedience: Resistance to Civil Government*. Waiheke Island: Floating Press.
Žižek, S. 1997. *The Plague of Fantasies*. London: Verso.

PART II
Thinking about Enlightenment and politics

3

THE ENLIGHTENMENT, ENCYCLOPEDISM AND THE NATURAL RIGHTS OF MAN: THE CASE OF THE *CODE OF HUMANITY* (1778)

Luigi Delia

Published during the Enlightenment in 1778, during the period between Diderot and D'Alembert's *Encyclopedia* and Panckoucke's *Methodical Encyclopedia*, the *Code of Humanity* (referred to as *CH* in the citations) is a densely packed anti-materialistic anthology specialising in the rights and justice of mankind. In the history of juridical encyclopedism the *Code of Humanity* is unique in that it is the first alphabetical collection to make natural justice its focal point (Delia 2015).

Compiled by an international body of lawyers, moralists, publicists, and Protestant theologians – under the direction of Fortuné-Barthélémy De Felice – the *Code of Humanity* is an ambitious, large-scale project comprised of thirteen volumes, each one around 750 quarto pages each with two columns. The grandchild of the *Encyclopedia* of the Enlightenment, this massive collection totaling nearly 10,000 pages has almost completely fallen into oblivion over the years. Although it is still found in the collections of some European libraries, the *Code of Humanity* is seldom referenced by legal and political historians, or in scholarly works relating to eighteenth-century dictionaries (Burnand and Cernuschi 2006: 253–267).

Naturally, a work of this magnitude would overlap with other sources in some instances. The entries regarding the technical aspects of the law are derived from Yverdon's "Protestant" *Encyclopedia*, with the *Code of Humanity* functioning more as a type of specialised dictionary. The articles related to the notions of natural rights and political rights within the *Code of Humanity* can be considered a central part of the shift towards modern natural rights in encyclopedic history. This observation is primarily based on the spatio-temporal relationship: for instance, the publication location fits this scenario as Switzerland played a key role in spreading a culture of jusnaturalism. It was through the teaching of natural rights, usually in the context of legal studies, and through commentaries on, and then translations of, the treatises of Grotius and Pufendorf, that Switzerland functioned as a type of intellectual mediator between German culture (Pufendorf, Thomasius, Wolff) and French culture

(Montesquieu, Voltaire, the *Encyclopedia*). Crucial in this regard were the courses offered by Jean Barbeyrac at the Academy of Lausanne (1711–1717) along with the French translations of Grotius and Pufendorf and the teachings of Jean-Jacques Burlamaqui at the Academy of Geneva as well as his works of synthesis. Let us not, of course, forget the influence of Emer de Vattel (1714–1767) from Neuchâtel, author of the treatise that defined public international rights during the time: *Le droit des gens ou principes de la loi naturelle appliqués à la conduite et aux affaires des Nations et des souverains* [*The Law of Nations or the Principles of Natural Law Applied to the Conduct and to the Affairs of Nations and of Sovereigns*] (2 vols., 1758). Largely influenced by the philosopher Christian Wolff, Vattel defined the law of the nations as an autonomous system of juridical rules with the sole purpose of regulating the relations between states. This treatise was very influential on both sides of the Atlantic as evidenced by the United States' *Declaration of Independence* (1776) which employed Vattel's definition of the State, taken literally from the article STATE (*political right*) of the *Code of Humanity* (cf. *CH*. vol. VI, 116a) : 'Toute nation qui se gouverne elle-même, sous quelque forme que ce soit, sans dépendance d'aucun étranger, est un état souverain' ['Any nation that governs itself, whatever form of governance that may be, without any foreign dependence, is a sovereign state'] (*Droit des gens*, I, I, ch.I, n. 4. Cf. Good 2011; Chetail and Haggenmacher 2011).

Furthermore, the *Code of Humanity* was published during a pivotal time in history – the period between the Declarations of American rights (1776) and of French rights (1789).

These observations relating to the publication of the *Code of Humanity* invoke two important questions: First, how did this dictionary contribute to the intellectual history of natural rights? Second, can De Felice's *Code of Humanity* be considered the first European dictionary of the natural rights of mankind?

In order to provide answers to these questions, in this article the following aspects of the *Code of Humanity* will be thoroughly examined: the programmatic texts (including the editor's preface and dedication); the jusnaturalist inclination of De Felice, the notions of modern natural law by which De Felice attempts to orient the dictionary; and, finally, the initial reception of the *Code of Humanity* in Europe and the United States.

The programmatic texts

Both of the titles that De Felice chose for the dictionary are rooted in the tradition of natural rights. The first edition appeared in 1777 under the title *Dictionnaire universel raisonné de Justice naturelle et civile* [*Universal rational dictionary of natural and civil justice*]. Written by a group of moralists, legal experts and publicists, the draft was edited by De Felice before publication (De Felice 1777–1778, vol. 13). The similarity between De Felice's *Dictionary* and the jurist Guyot's *Répertoire universel et raisonné de jurisprudence* [*Universal and rational directory of jurisprudence*] is quite evident, although Guyot's publication focuses more on French positive law. A second edition of the *Dictionary*, identical to the first except for its title, went to print the following year with the new title, *Code de l'humanité* [*Code of Humanity*], and the subtitle, *ou la Législation universelle, naturelle, civile et politique* [*or universal, natural, civil and political legislation*]. Was the updated title part of a new business strategy or, perhaps, a means of being more precise about the conceptual framework of the dictionary? De Felice's dual role as editor and "philosopher" leads one to assume that the two are not mutually exclusive. It is also important to note the continued use of the terms 'Justice naturelle' ['Natural Justice'] and 'Législation naturelle' ['Natural Law']. These expressions are emphasised in order to assert the primacy of 'natural rights' and 'universal morality' within the numerous legal divisions that the anthology covers: international law, political law, public law, Roman law, feudal law, and canon law. This last section was entrusted to the Aix canonist Pierre Toussaint Durand de Maillane. Following in the footsteps of the masters of the modern school of natural rights, De Felice sought to use the category of moral law as the basis for natural law. However, this was also contingent upon the existing legal system and rules and requirements. This moral order that imposes duties towards other individuals, and the legal order, which implies mutual obligations among all human beings were, for him, inseparable.

But, what is a "code of humanity"? This expression, reminiscent of the title of Etienne-Gabriel Morelly's utopian treatise the *Code de la Nature* [*Code of Nature*] (1755), remains remarkably ambivalent. De Felice plays upon the multiple meanings of the concept of humanity, now implying virtue, now the collective concept of humankind: a 'terme générique' ['generic term'] the article *Humanité* (*Morale*) proclaims, 'qui embrasse toutes les qualités, tous les caractères et toutes les façons d'agir qui conviennent à l'homme, en tant qu'il est homme, et qu'il vit avec d'autres hommes' [that embraces all of the qualities, characteristics and behaviours that are suitable for man, as he is a man, and lives with other men]' (*CH*, VII, 511a). More precisely, from a legal perspective, the expression "code of humanity" refers to both a rulebook dictated by nature for all members of humanity, and a set of natural rules regarding relations between groups: a code of natural rights and a collection of 'natural rights of man' (*CH*, I, v).

The dictionary's preface further testifies to the importance of justice and rights. The *Code of Humanity* is presented as a monument to the glory of morality, 'cette science raisonnée qui nous apprend ce qui est permis et ce qui est défendu, ce qu'il est à propos que l'homme fasse ou qu'il évite dans quelques circonstances qu'il soit placé' ['this rational science that teaches us what is allowed and what is forbidden, what a man does and what he avoids in given circumstances'] (*CH*, I, i). The extensive article *Morale* (*Morale, Ethica*) ranks morality as the most noble branch of philosophy. It is morality

> qui expose les vrais principes des devoirs, qui en propose les règles, qui montre les moyens de les remplir [. . .]. Il est donc de la plus grande évidence que la *morale* [. . .] est la première des sciences, la plus importante, la plus universellement utile, celle qu'il faut enseigner avant toute autre à la jeunesse et au peuple, celle sur laquelle auraient dû insister de préférence les théologiens,

les ministres de la religion, les docteurs de l'église dans leurs écrits [...] [that exposes the true principles of duty, that provides rules, that shows how to fulfill them [...]. It is therefore of the utmost clarity that morality [...] is the first of the sciences, the most important, the most universally useful, the branch that should be taught before any other to youths and to the people, the one prefered by theologians, ministers of religion, and doctors of the church in their writings [...]

(*CH*, IX, 426b et 431b).

Several branches of the law are reviewed within the preface. The objective of the dictionary is also clearly articulated: to provide a comprehensive set of articles on ethical and legal issues in one single collection: 'Combien sera utile et commode un ouvrage dans lequel on pourra facilement chercher et promptement trouver tout ce qu'on désire d'apprendre ou de se rappeler relativement à chaque objet de la morale, ou des divers droits connus' ['How convenient and useful a work will be when one can easily search and quickly find everything one is looking to learn or remember with respect to each article of morality, or the various known rights'] (*CH*, I, 7).

The notion of natural rights resurfaces in the *Dedication* to Gustave III. The monarch, a cultivated supporter of the Enlightenment, was the king of Sweden from 1771 to 1792. He had been king for six years when De Felice paid tribute to him in the *Code* and was regarded as an enlightened ruler. During his rule, Gustave III redefined principles of justice and finances, outlawed torture by the State, promoted primary education, and improved conditions for the peasantry. He also partially liberalised the grain market. On the other hand, in 1774, he promulgated a royal decree that limited the freedom of the press. A life-long Francophile, the king was responsible for the reorganisation of the Académie des Belles-Lettres following the model of the Académie Française. In 1789, he asked the Riksdag to reduce the privileges of the nobility. He declared a new constitution (Union and Security Act) that granted equal rights to all Swedish citizens, including the ability to serve in public offices (Nordmann 1986; Gunnar von Proschwitz, 1986). Just as Voltaire did with Frédéric II of Prussia and Diderot with Catherine II of Russia, De Felice addresses a foreign monarch in the *Dedication*. The *Code of Humanity* is offered to the Swedish monarch as a type of alphabetized meta-constitutional philosophy that serves as a source of civil law, both public and private, in view of 'un renouvellement admirable de la constitution de ce government' ['an admirable renewal of the constitution of this government']. The *Code of Humanity*, intended to facilitate the 'bien physique et moral' ['physical and moral well-being'] of States, thus has as its primary goal to guide state powers towards the usage of a Constitution of the State. In order to avoid simply being a philosophical dream, a project such as this requires the "support" of the established authority:

C'est en vain que les philosophes dans leurs écrits, saisissent les vrais principes de la justice naturelle et de la morale universelle [...]; toutes leurs peines

[. . .] restent sans fruit et sans effet, si elles ne sont pas propagées et soutenues par l'autorité et l'exemple des Princes [. . .]. Je rassemble dans [. . .] le *Code de l'Humanité*, les diverses décisions de la justice naturelle et civile, et les droits réels ou prétendus que les hommes des différents ordres se sont attribués [It is in vain that the philosophers in their writings capture the true principles of natural justice and universal morality [. . .] all of their efforts [. . .] remain fruitless and without effect, if they are not propagated and supported by the authorities and the example of the Rulers [. . .]. I bring together in [. . .] the *Code of Humanity*, the various decisions by natural and civil justice, and the actual or alleged rights that men of different orders have awarded themselves]

(*CH*, *Dedication* to Gustave III, 24 March 1777).

Both De Felice and Gustave III were Protestant. This adherence to reformed Christianity is a key element in understanding the interests that the encyclopaedists of Yverdon showed in modern natural rights. First, the Reformation is, without a doubt, one of the 'matrices des droits de l'homme' ['matrices of the rights of man'] (Kérvégan 1995: 647–649). By revolutionising the relationship of the Christian to scriptural, clerical, and political authorities, the Reformation regarded the individual as an autonomous subject, free to choose to study the Scriptures and solely responsible for his own salvation in front of God. Additionally, the end of religious homogeneity contributed to the weakening of the communitarian concept of society, while also feeding the demand for freedom of thought, the first of the natural human rights: 'Aucun souverain n'a le droit de contraindre par la violence un sujet à participer au culte de la religion de l'État, si ce sujet croit en sa *conscience*, que ce culte est mauvais, ou qu'il ne peut être agréable à la divinité' ['No sovereign has the right forcefully to compel a subject to participate in the religious worship of the State, if the subject believes in his conscience that this worship is bad, or cannot agree with the divinity'] (*CH*, *Conscience, Liberté de* [*Droit naturel, Politique*], III, 474b). One should also recall that the discussions regarding freedom of thought occurred during an era of confessional peace that began in Switzerland in 1712 and resulted in "tolerance" being a key concept of this period.

Secondly, the *Code of Humanity* devotes "literary references" – often quite detailed – to many of the great authors of reformed jusnaturalism. Here are just a dozen examples: Abbadie, Barbeyrac, Buddaeus, Burlamaqui, Cumberland, Grotius, Leibnitz, Locke, Pufendorf, Thomasius, Wolff, Wollaston.

The jurisnaturalist orientation of De Felice

It is also important to keep in mind De Felice's compliance with the Calvinist confession, his 'Protestant choice', which helps to explain his selection of the fifteen contributors (Donato 2005: 89–120; Ferrari 2010: 87–105). Among these scholars, there was the chevalier de Jaucourt, the Vaudois pastor Elie Bertrand, from the French Church in Berne, a 'member of the major academies in Europe', the permanent secretary of the Academy of Berlin Jean-Henri-Samuel Formey and the

Calvinist theologian Gabriel Mingard, author of several hundred articles in Yverdon's *Encyclopedia* – making him one of De Felice's main contributors. A separate point of recognition should be reserved for the magistrate and canonist from Aix, Durand de Maillane (Basdevant-Gaudemet 2007: 294–295). Author of the two-volume *Dictionnaire de droit canonique et de pratique bénéficiale* [*Dictionary of Canonic Law and Beneficial Practices*] (Paris, 1761), the Gallican convert to Ultramontanism was deputy to the Estates-General of 1789 and had an active role in the work of the Constituent Assembly. He would have been one of the first to work on the draft of a declaration of rights as the preface to the constitution.

Nevertheless, the most prolific writer of articles for the *Code of Humanity* was De Felice himself. Educated by the Jesuits at the Roman College, a former Philosophy Professor at Rome and Experimental Physics Professor at the University of Naples, De Felice left Italy for Berne in 1757 (attracted by the Prestige of Haller), before settling in Yverdon in 1762. Once in Yverdon, he opened a printing company that soon became, and remained until his death, one of the most influential printing companies in Switzerland (Pejrone 1993: 57–62). Most famous for his role as editor of Yverdon's *Encyclopedia*, De Felice was not just an encyclopedist, publicist, cultural mediator, as well as an important publisher in Europe during the Enlightenment (having notably presided over the *Estratto della letteratura europea* from 1758 to 1766). He was also the author of half a dozen philosophical and pedagogical works: *Discours sur la manière de former l'esprit et le cœur des enfants* [*Discourse on how to educate the heart and mind of children*] (Yverdon, 1768), the *Leçons de logique* [*Lessons in logic*] in two volumes (Yverdon 1770) and the *Tableau philosophique de la religion Chrétienne, considérée dans son ensemble, dans sa morale, et dans ses consolations* [*Philosophical chart of the Christian religion, considered as a whole, in its morality, and its consolations*] (1779). Up until now these works have still not been the subject of any detailed studies. De Felice's interest in natural justice preceded the drafting of the *Code of Humanity*. Between 1766 and 1768, he published a prefaced edition of unprecedented stature, the *Principles du droit de la nature et des gens* [*Principles of natural law and of men*] by Burlamaqui, in eight volumes (Burlamaqui 1766–1768). The edition completed the well-known *Principes du droit naturel/ Principles of natural law* (1747), 'l'ouvrage le plus récent, le plus précis, & le plus méthodique que nous ayons sur le *droit naturel*' ['the most current, precise, and methodical work that we have on *natural law*'], according to Boucher d'Argis (*ENC, Droit naturel ou Droit de la nature*, V (1754), 133). After noting that Burlamaqui's treatise is divided into two parts, the first one focused on the general principles of law and the second on natural laws, Boucher d'Argis remarked that

> l'avertissement qui est en tête de l'ouvrage annonce que ce traité n'est que le commencement d'un ouvrage plus étendu, ou d'un système complet sur le *droit de la nature & des gens*, que l'auteur se proposait de donner au public ; mais qu'ayant été traversé dans ce dessein par d'autres occupations & par la faiblesse de sa santé, il s'est déterminé à publier ce premier morceau. Quoique ce soit un précis excellent du *droit naturel*, on ne peut s'empêcher de désirer que l'auteur achève le grand ouvrage qu'il avait commencé, où l'on verrait

la matière traitée dans toute son étendue [the notice at the front of the work announces that this treatise is just the beginning of a larger work, of a comprehensive system on the *laws of nature and of men*, that the author intends to share with the public; but having come upon this plan through other pursuits and through the weakness of his health, he determined to publish the first part. Even though it is an excellent handbook of *natural law*, one cannot help wishing that the author had completed the great work that he had started, so we could have seen the subject matter to its full extent]

(*ENC*, V, 133).

With this enlarged edition, De Felice fulfilled the wishes of Boucher d'Argis. The article *Burlamaqui* in the *Code of Humanity* also evokes this aspect: '[with Burlamaqui] n'ayant pu donner la dernière main à la seconde partie du *droit naturel*, M. de Felice, ayant obtenu son cannevas, a donné du tout une édition très complète, et a augmenté de près de trois quarts l'ouvrage du savant professeur de Genève [having not been able to finalize the second part of the *natural law*, M. de Felice, who obtained his framework, gave everyone a completed edition, and increased the work of the learned professor of Geneva by almost three quarters]' (*CH*, II, 344a).

But how did De Felice go about putting together this edition? Details of how he compiled it can be found in a letter to Formey from 19 November 1765:

> Ayant déterré un M[anu]s[crit] du célèbre Burlamaqui qui contient le reste de son Droit Naturel, j'ai pensé de donner une édition complète de ses œuvres. Mais comme ce M[anu]s[crit] est tout décharné, et presqu'une analyse de ses leçons, j'ai pris le parti d'y travailler, en ajoutant ce que je crois nécessaire non seulement au M[anu]s[crit] mais aussi à tout ce qu'il y avait d'imprimé c'est à dire les Principes du Droit Naturel et le Droit des Gens; de manière que je pense pouvoir donner [...] un cours complet et systématique du Droit Naturel et des Gens de la façon de Burlamaqui, qui est surement celui qui a mieux que tous les autres lié les idées de cette science [Having unearthed a manuscript of the famous Burlamaqui that contains the rest of his Natural Law, I thought to give a complete edition of his works. But since this manuscript is quite emaciated, and more like an analysis of his lessons, I took to work on it, by adding what I thought necessary not only to the Manuscript but also to everything that he had printed on the Principles of Natural Law and the Rights of Men; in this manner I think that I can give [...] a comprehensive and systematic course on Natural Law and the Law of Nations in the manner of Burlamaqui, who is surely the one who knows better than others the ideas associated with this science]
>
> (De Felice to Jean-Henri-Samuel Formey on 19 November 1765, Berlin, Staatsbibliothek, Preussischer Kulturbesitz, Nachlass Formey).

Moreover, De Felice relied on this editorial work to compose the two volumes of the *Leçons de Droit de la Nature & des Gens* [*Lessons of Natural Law and Law of*

Nations]. Published in Yverdon in 1769, these jusnaturalist lessons – that would be quite interesting to study in detail – open with terminology that gives a sense of his rationalism as less Platonic than Cartesian, according to which the principles of justice and injustice, of good and bad, of honesty and dishonesty, are naturally in the minds of all men. Human beings can discover and recognise all of these principles of natural rights through their own enlightenment, which is not something static, but rather a force of thought:

> On a défini l'Homme un être raisonnable. Nous adoptons avec plaisir une définition qui flatte si fort notre amour propre, & nous nous regardons comme des êtres raisonnables, c'est-à-dire comme des êtres qui dans toutes leurs démarches suivent les lumières de la raison. Trompeuse illusion ! L'homme n'est pas un être raisonnable, il s'en faut bien. Ce n'est qu'un être capable de raison [...]. Voilà ce qui m'a engagé à publier ces *Leçons de Droit de la Nature & des Gens* [We define Man as a rational being. We happily adopt a definition that strongly flatters our our own self-esteem and ego, and we regard each other as reasonable beings, that is to say, beings who in their own endeavours follow the light of reason. What a false illusion! Man is not a reasonable being, it takes much more. He is not a being capable of reason [. . .]. This is what inspired me to publish these *Lessons of Natural Law and Law of Nations*]
>
> (De Felice 1769: vol. I, i.).

An alphabetized collection of the natural rights of mankind

One must also take into account the programmatic texts as well as the intellectual contexts and cultural networks of the time. Nevertheless, it still may prove quite difficult for the researcher to 'entrer dans la forteresse' ['enter the fortress'] of the dictionary, to use a favorite expression of the great scholar Jacques Proust. However, this task fully confirms the jusnaturalist inspiration of the collection. From *Autorité, Citoyen, Code* to *Peine, Société, Sujet,* via *Egalite, Liberté, Lois fondamentales,* there are numerous articles that testify to this grand effort. Within this study, we shall focus on four main ideas in modern natural law that are found throughout the *Code of Humanity*: the absorption of the fundamental principles of Christianity into a moral philosophy; the rationalist understanding of the law; the affirmation of rights inherent in human nature, which every individual is entitled to, enforced by the ruling body; and, lastly, a conception of the origin of society as based on the notion of the natural sociability of man (Ippolito 2013: 3–20). These four theories, both interrelated and interdependent, allow De Felice to put together the overarching format, despite the fragmentation of his work.

An anti-dogmatic Protestant and humanist philosopher, De Felice sought to combine revelation and reason. He strove to transform Christianity from a dogmatic to a moral attitude. Specifically, he attempted to root it in reformed theology, free from dogmatism and from any sort of fanatical attitude, but rooted it instead in a moral philosophy dependent upon the modern conception of jusnaturalism. In the preface of the *Code of Humanity*, this "moral philosophy" is specifically highlighted as well as the divine origin of natural rights, with emphasis placed on individual conscience and, therefore, on "common sense," such as in the context of Descartes, i.e., the natural ability to discern right from wrong. Like both Barbeyrac and Burlamaqui, De Felice establishes the authority of natural law over reason and religion, the two things that God bestowed upon man in order for him to conduct himself. Rather than remaining mutually exclusive, common sense and Christian morality serve to complement one another. This complementary relationship proceeds from the laws of conscience and the divine laws being identical. Thus, the search for universally binding rules of conduct does not take place under the guidance of theology. De Felice and his colleagues agreed on reformed Christianity as the basis of natural morality: 'Toutes les vérités essentielles du *christianisme* tendent à la vertu, sont les principes ou les motifs de la morale, servent de sanction aux lois morales, en sorte que l'on peut dire que le *christianisme* est une religion toute morale' ['All of the essential truths of *Christianity* leaning toward virtue, are the principles and the grounds of morality, which serve to sanction moral laws, so that we can say that Christianity is a completely moral religion'] (*CH*, *Christianisme* [*Morale*], III, 32b. The article is not signed). Such an approach is not without repercussions for the promotion of religious tolerance (see *CH*, *Tolérance* [*Morale, Droit naturel*], XIII, 335–360), along with the subordination of society to the individual and the affirmation of the individual rights of mankind. Moreover, this interweaving of philosophical and Protestant cultures throughout the articles in the *Code of Humanity* which we have consulted moves in the direction of a fading religious spirit in favour of a type of broad humanism – a spiritualism with a strong moral connotation, quite at ease with its contribution to reason, modernity, economic liberalism, and Masonic ideals. This tendency can be clearly seen in the articles *Calvin, Calvinisme* and *Calviniste* by the pastor Bertrand. A "modern" mind, anxious to display his freedom of opinion, without being reckless, Bertrand carefully crafted these articles for Yverdon's *Encyclopedia*. Though not included in the *Code of Humanity*, Bertrand's articles take into account the biography of Calvin and his doctrine, starting with the *Institution de la religion chrétienne* [*Institution of the Christian religion*] (art. *Calvin* et *Calvinisme*). In the *Calviniste* article, Bertrand does not hesitate to distance himself from this great man of the sixteenth century, 'respectable sans doute [. . .] mais point du tout un docteur infaillible ni un maître qu'ils [les calvinistes] suivent sans examen' ['respectable without a doubt [. . .] but not an infallible doctor at all nor a master that they [the Calvinists] follow unquestionably']. De Felice and his colleagues adhere to the Reformed confession without sacrificing their right to exercise freedom of thought and judgement. On the other hand, in the article *Rigorisme* (*Morale*), it suits Gabriel Mingard to denounce any religious doctrine that is outside the precepts of natural morality and that 'choque tous les penchants' ['shocks all natural dispositions']: monastic rules, the Jansenists and, among the Protestants, the 'dévots, et ceux qu'on connaît en Hollande sous le nom de *fins*, et en Angleterre sous celui de *méthodistes*' ['the devotees, and those known in Holland as *fins,* and in England as *méthodistes*'] (*CH*, XII, 324b, italics in original text). Overall, De Felice, Mingard, Bertrand, and Jaucourt participated in a form of liberal Protestantism equally distant from the politicized Catholicism their adversaries described as clericalism, as well as from movements that were sceptical, indifferent, or hostile to religion. However, this connection between reformed and philosophical training was not always conducive to a secular conception of law, particularly to criminal law: it does not appear that De Felice and his colleagues clearly distinguished between a legal offence and a crime (cf. *CH*, VIII, 657b).

With modern jusnaturalism, the appeal to the law of reason acquires a new sort of centrality. Reason has the capacity to discover the principles of natural normality without necessarily using Revelation. The fact is that, according to De Felice, 'Le fondement général du système des lois naturelles, c'est la nature de l'homme prise avec toutes les circonstances qui l'accompagnent' ['The general basis of a system of natural laws is the nature of man and all of the circumstances that accompany it'] (*CH*, Loi naturelle, VIII, 527b).

Grotius's intellectual claim to have treated the law just as mathematicians consider numbers, by abstracting them from bodies, becomes a scientific programme. It would be useful to view the reflections on justice as a game of concurrent opinions and to elevate the knowledge of the rules of human actions to the same level as the certainty of geometric equations. The difficulty of mathematical equations is, thus, for the first time applied to the study of natural rights: 'notre Grotius est le premier qui ait traité cette matière méthodiquement' ['our Grotius is the first to have treated this matter methodically'], De Felice wrote (*CH*, Grotius [*Hist. litt.*] VII, 276a). Another article borrows from Wolff's systematic approach:

> Ce qui caractérise principalement les écrits philosophiques de ce savant homme, c'est la méthode [. . .]. Il a donc entrepris de faire de toutes les connaissances philosophiques un vrai système, qui procédât de principes en conséquences, et où toutes les propositions fussent déduites les unes des autres avec une évidence démonstrative'
>
> [What primarily characterises the philosophical writings of this learned man, is the method [. . .]. He therefore undertook to make all philosophical knowledge a real system, that developed from principles and their consequences, and in which all proposals were derived from one another through demonstrative evidence]
>
> (*CH, Wolff, Christien* [*Histoire littéraire*], XIII, 733a).

An offshoot of the Cartesian method, to which De Felice pays homage in his article *Cartésianisme, Philosophie morale de Descartes*, this rationalist approach clashes with the state of uncertainty and confusion found during the former common system of law, characterised by the heterogeneity of its normative sources and by the excessive variety of its judgements and sentences (commentaries, decisions, interpretations. . .) (*CH*, II, 419–430). This school of rationalism served to inspire the technical works of the jurist Jean Domat, whose treatise *Les lois civiles selon leur ordre naturel* (1997) [*Civil laws according to their natural order*] presented the French legal field as a systematic plan. According to De Felice, none of the books that had 'embrassé l'universalité' ['embraced the universality'] of jurisprudence had dealt with it adequately, specifically as regards the choice of legal principles, their usage, disposition, and the sub-categories as well (*CH*, *Domat* Jean [*Histoire littéraire*], V, 26b). Rationalism also inspired the ideology of codification. Unknown prior to the nineteenth century, codification nevertheless stresses the projet of the Enlightenment to establish justice on law. Further, this conceptual framework explains De Felice's choice of the notion of a "code" in the work's title. Code calls for ordered legislation, composed of clearly stated rules, both general rules and those taken from the *dictamina rectae rationis*. The article *Code criminel* (*Jurisprudence*), a subfield of the main article *Code*, displays the rationalist ambitions of De Felice, editor, correspondent, and propagator of the punitive ideas of Beccaria. Succinct and programmatic, this article proposes guidelines for developing a system for categorising crimes and punishments:

> Pour que le *code criminel* soit complet, il doit avoir pour but les six objets suivant : 1°. la nature des délits et des peines; 2°. les personnes capables de délit; 3°. le degré du délit dans le principal délinquant ou dans l'accessoire; 4°. les diverses espèces de délits avec les peines à y attacher; 5°. les moyens de prévenir les délits, et 6°. la manière d'infliger les peines [So that the *criminal code* is complete, it should aim for the following six items: 1. The nature of the offences and the penalties; 2. The people capable of these offences; 3. The degree of the offence by the main offender or the accessory; 4. The different kinds of offences with the offences attached; 5. The ways of preventing the crime; 6. The means to impose penalties]
>
> (*CH*, III, 122–123).

Five references to concepts of criminal law can be found in the articles: *Droit criminel, Délit, Crime, Délinquant, Peine*. This section provides a body of specific articles that determines the conceptual references for reorganising criminal legislation according to the recommendations of Beccaria.

A third concept concerns the assertion of 'individual rights' (Villey 2009). Unlike the former vision of natural law as part of an objective order, modern jusnaturalism is aimed at individuals on whom it imposes obligations and confers rights. Backed by writers from the late seventeenth century like Locke, this doctrine helped facilitate the natural law of the right to life (security), to freedom (political, civil, opinion, conscience) and to property. This doctrine makes the protection of these individual rights the foundation of the legitimacy of political power. The notion of the inalienability and the sacredness of natural rights spreads into the eighteenth century. It permeated the discourses of both American and French revolutionaries. With the *Bill of Rights* of the former British colonies and the *Déclaration des droits de l'homme et du citoyen* [*Declaration of the rights of man and the citizen*] of 1789, the demand for an individual sphere of fundamental liberties shifted from the discourses of philosophers to a political reality: with this movement, modern positive law began to take shape. The *Code of Humanity* is part of this intellectual history. The article *Personnes* (*Jurisprudence*), after observing that the 'Romains ne mettaient pas leurs esclaves au rang des personnes, mais des choses, parce qu'ils entraient dans le commerce' ['Romans did not regard their slaves as people, but as things, because they were traded'], states that 'les personnes sont le premier objet du droit' ['people are the first subject of law'] (*CH*, X, 588a). The article advances a universal notion of man: if human rights are inherent in human nature, all men therefore have the same rights, whatever their origins (*CH*, *Egalité naturelle*, V, 454–457). Blacks cannot be an exception to this rule: seeking to reduce them to slaves and into a type of commodity is a violation of the rights of humanity. In the article *Nègres, esclavage ou commerce des* (*Droit naturel*), the so-called Right to Slavery and the treatment of slaves are vehemently condemned. Signed by Gabriel Mingard, this revolutionary text reproduces excerpts from the *Histoire des deux Indes* (*CH*, IX, 625–629). The "people" are equally recognised by De Felice and granted certain fundamental legal rights, such as the right never to be tortured by the judiciary (see *CH*, *Question* [*Jurisprudence*], XI, 669–673), as well as the right not to be arbitrarily imprisoned: 'C'est une erreur non moins répandue que contraire à la fin de l'établissement de la société, qui est *la sureté personnelle*, de laisser le magistrat, exécuteur des lois, maître d'emprisonner un citoyen, d'ôter la liberté à celui qu'il hait, sous de frivoles prétextes' ['It's a mistake no less widespread than it is contrary to the end of the establishment of society, which is *personal security*, to leave the magistrat, the executers of the law, the master of the imprisoned citizen, to take away the freedom of whom he hates, under frivolous pretexts' (*CH*, *Emprisonnement*, en *Jurisprudence*, V, 569a; my italics).

The death penalty is also banned because it is contrary to natural law: 'Le droit de donner la mort [. . .] n'est donné à personne sur la terre. Il est si souverain, qu'il est réservé à Dieu seul. Les despotes l'ont usurpé: il ne leur appartenait pas. Il est contre les lois de la nature, que la mort dépende de la volonté et du caprice d'aucun mortel' ['the right to inflict death [. . .] is not given to any man on the earth. It is so sovereign that it is reserved for God alone. The despots have usurped it: it does not belong to them. It is against the laws of nature that death should depend on the will and whim of any mortal'] (*CH*, *Droit de vie et de mort*, V, 179b).

Lastly, natural law requires human beings to be property owners. At the end of the dense article *Propriété* (*Droit naturel et Politique*), consisting of dozens of pages analysing the origin and the foundation of property rights, De Felice concludes that, 'Rien' ['nothing'] is 'plus conforme à la droite raison, et par conséquent au droit naturel, que l'établissement de la propriété des biens, puisque sans cela il aurait été impossible que les hommes vécussent dans une société paisible, commode et agréable' ['more in accordance with the right of reason, and thus natural law, than establishing the ownership of property, since otherwise it would be impossible for men to live in a peaceful, suitable, and agreeable society]' (*CH*, XI, 530b).

A fourth idea concerns the development of human societies. Neither a type of natural political organisation nor the result of a divine investiture, the State stems from a social pact. The sovereignty of the state must be legitimised by the consensus of its members. This vision of social origins rests on individualistic principles and is based on three fundamental concepts in particular: the state of nature, where men live without political links yet hold the same natural rights; civil society, where men are dependent upon a common authority with the power to enact laws and reinforce them; and the social contract, which ensures the passage of the state of nature to civil society. From Hobbes to Kant, the natural law theorists disagreed in various ways with this natural schema that suggested the political origin of the State (Rodeschini 2012). The *Code of Humanity* places a great deal of importance on the doctrines of Locke and Burlamaqui, at the expense of Hobbes's political principles that were consistently rejected by the *Encyclopedia* of Yverdon: for example, the adaptation of the state of nature to a state of war, the denial of the natural sociability of men, the legitimisation of the unlimited authority of the sovereign, and so on. In the article *Hobbes, Thomas* (*Histoire littéraire*), Bertrand points to 'ses principes pernicieux [qui] travestissent l'homme en bête, le rendent ennemi de toute société, et ne donnent des magistrats que pour la vie animale, et nullement pour la morale' ['its pernicious principles that turn man into an animal, making him an enemy of all of society, and only providing judges for animal life, and in no way for morality]' (*CH*, VII, 404–408). Going against Hobbes, Locke dispels the traditional terms associated with political obligation: obedience takes the place of deontology, stipulating the duty of the subject to obey the commands of the sovereign. In this case, it is the duty of the sovereign state to respect and protect the rights of the subject. However, in the article *Liberté politique* De Felice optimistically points out that the rulers of well-constituted states 'sauront proscrire un jour les systèmes des instigateurs du despotisme, pour se renfermer dans les justes bornes de la puissance représentative et des droits du peuple et de la gloire des souverains' ['will one day outlaw the systems of the instigators of despotism in order to confine themselves to the proper limits of representative power and the rights of the people and the glory of the sovereign'] (*CH*, VIII, 419a). But, what should one do under the yoke of a tyrannical ruler? In various articles, De Felice and Jaucourt claim that any abuse of power that infringes upon natural rights justifies a resistance to this oppression as well as the deposition of public authorities. Meanwhile, De Felice speaks out in favour of the principle of resistance to oppression in the articles *Despotisme* (*Droit politique*) (IV, 467–468) and *Droit du plus fort* (V, 179ab), in which Chapter I, 3 of Rousseau's *Social Contract* is reproduced in full without naming the author.

When faced with an oppressor, the citizen has the duty and the right to revolt. In the *Code of Humanity*'s richly crafted article *Sujet* (*Morale, Droit civil et politique*), Jaucourt asserts that, in the tradition of jusnaturalism which sees the source of all positive laws within a universal and immutable right based on reason, 'les lois sont faites pour les hommes, et non les hommes pour les lois' ['laws are made for men, and not men for laws'] (*CH*, XIII, 186b). Portalis expresses his support for this idea as well: 'les lois ne sont pas de purs actes de puissance; ce sont des actes de sagesse, de justice et de raison. Le législateur exerce moins une autorité qu'un sacerdoce. Il ne doit point perdre de vue que les lois sont faites pour les hommes, et non les hommes pour les lois' ['laws are not pure acts of power; they are acts of wisdom, of justice and of reason. The legislature is rather a priesthood than an authority. One must not forget that laws are made for men, and not men for laws'] (Portalis 1827: 466).

The fundamental principle of the right to resist oppression is clearly stated in the *Code of Humanity*: 'La justice serait vraiment bannie de la terre, si les ordres des princes étaient des lois auxquelles il ne fût jamais permis de résister [Justice would truly be banished from the earth, if the ruler's orders were the laws to which he was never allowed to resist]' (*CH*, *Sujet*, XIII, 185b; cf. Burrati 2006: 85–170). This passage announces the last article of the French Declaration of the Rights of Man: 'Quand le gouvernement viole les droits du peuple, l'insurrection est pour le peuple, et pour chaque portion du peuple, le plus sacré des droits, et le plus indispensable des devoirs' ['When the government violates the law of Nations, the insurrection is for the people, and for each section of the people, the most sacred of rights, and the most indispensable of duties']. One famous historical example of the legitimisation of the right to revolt is the contractualistic justification of the American Revolution, articulated by Thomas Jefferson in the *Declaration of Independence*: if the State is not fulfilling its obligation to protect the fundamental rights of its subjects, the people are permitted to reclaim their sovereignty in order to form a new government with legitimate authority based on the consensus of the governed. For his part, Gabriel Mingard, in the article *Autorité* from the first volume, writes:

> C'est des lois que dépend la légitimité du *pouvoir*; c'est du mérite qu'elles supposent, que naît l'autorité qui rend respectable, et qui obtient l'obéissance volontaire ; c'est de la réunion du mérite connu, et des lois, que naît cet empire suprême, auquel tout cède sans résistance et avec plaisir, et qui fait des princes légitimes et estimables, les images visibles de Dieu [It is on laws that the legitimacy of *power* depends; it is from the merit that they presuppose, that the authority that makes voluntary obedience respectable and obtains it, is born; it is from the bringing of this known merit together with laws, that this supreme empire is born, to which all yield without resistance and with pleasure, and renders all rulers legitimate and esteemed, visable images of God]
>
> (*CH*, I, 729a).

De Felice echoes Mingard's sentiments in the article *Monarchie*, where the absolute and inherited power of the monarchy, often a source of political violence and, therefore, the 'ennemi de la Justice et de la Raison' ['enemy of Justice and Reason'] as well as of 'la liberté licencieuse de la démocratie' ['the licentious freedom of democracy'], is abandoned in favour of a monarchical form of government whose powers are restricted by intermediary bodies (*CH*, IX, 374–375).

Recent research on unpublished letters by De Felici allows us to appreciate better the efforts by this encyclopaedist in promoting the *Code* among European intellectuals (Burnand 2013: 77–90; cf. De Felice 2013). Certainly, the *Code of Humanity* was a relative commercial failure and its publication did not make much of a dent at all. Yet, it would be wrong to believe that the work has gone completely unnoticed. In France, it suffered, without a doubt, from the hostility between De Felice's influential printing house and the bookseller Panckoucke. The extremely combative relations between these two publishers is revealed in the letters (in particular, see the Letter from F.-B. De Felice to Charles-Joseph Panckoucke from 14 April 1769). By the late 1760s, De Felice's proposed Encyclopedia project found itself in direct competition with the editorial ambitions of Panckoucke, which was focused on the publication of Robinet's *Suppléments à l'Encyclopédie* [*Encyclopedia Supplements*] (Darnton 1973: 1331–1352). Ten years later, the commercial war moved into the field of legal dictionaries: De Felice published the *Code of Humanity* and Panckoucke published two major collections: Guyot's *Répertoire* [*Directory*] and the *Dictionnaire de Jurisprudence* of the *Encyclopédie méthodique* [*Dictionary of Jurisprudence* of the *Methodical Encyclopedia*].

With stiff competition from France, De Felice's dictionary barely made an impact on the market of the Italian states, still under the influence of Catholic culture. Less popular in the Mediterranean than in the reformed Northern European countries, Yverdon's *Code* was well received by the papers of the time. This can be seen in the reviews in *L'Esprit des journaux, français et étrangers*, from December of 1779 (XII, 414–418) and in the *Journal des Savants*, Paris, from October of 1778, page 2286:

> L'ouvrage que nous annonçons, en exposant les décisions de la justice civile, fait sentir jusqu'où elle se conforme à la justice naturelle, et où elle s'en écarte. La Morale fait la base de ce grand Ouvrage. Jamais ses vérités n'ont été présentées avec plus de candeur, de solidité, de profondeur et de franchise, qu'elles le sont dans ce Dictionnaire, qui jusqu'ici nous manquait, et qui est bien digne d'occuper une place dans toutes les bibliothèques publiques et particulières; c'est le Code de l'Humanité; il devrait être le manuel de ces respectables Magistrats, qui ne prononcent que d'après les arrêts infaillibles de la justice naturelle et de l'équité [The work that we are announcing, exposing the decisions of civil justice, shows where it complies with natural justice and where it deviates from it. Morality is the basis of this great Work. Its truths have never been presented with more candour, strength, depth, and sincerity than they are in this Dictionary which, until now, we were lacking, and is well worthy of occupying a place in all public and private libraries; it is the *Code of Humanity*; it should be the manual of those respectable magistrates who deliver their judgements only in accordance with the infallible decisions of natural justice and of fairness].

Forty years later, in 1820, the *Code* was once again grouped among 'les livres les plus précieux et les ouvrages les plus utiles' ['the most valuable and useful works'] by the *Manuel du libraire et de l'amateur de livres* established by Jacques-Charles Brunet (Brunet 1820: 37). An extensive bibliographical directory, the *Manual* categorizes De Felice's collection among the 'traités généraux du droit de la nature et des gens' ['general treatises of the law of nature and law of nations']. In reality, the *Code of Humanity* was not a treatise. It was more an encyclopedic dictionary. At most, due to some particularly well-developed articles spanning dozens of pages, it can be likened to a type of alphabetical collection of very condensed treatises. Still, since its publication, the *Code of Humanity* has been looked upon as a work of natural law.

Lastly, the influence of the *Code of Humanity* spread beyond Europe's borders and captured the attention of the founding fathers of the United States. Thomas Jefferson himself obtained a copy to add to his impressive private library collection.

Moreover, he praised the work and shared it among his colleagues. A copy was sent to Edmund Randolph, the future U.S. Secretary of State, accompanied by a letter from Jefferson, sent from Paris on 20 September 1785:

> I therefore send you by way of Havre a dictionary of law Natural & municipal in 13. vols 4to. Called le *Code de l'humanité*. It is published by Felice, but also written by him & several other authors of established reputation. It is an excellent work. I do not mean to say that it answers fully to its title. That would have required fifty times the volume. It wants many articles which the title would induce us to seek in it. But the articles of which it does treat are well written. It is better than the voluminous *Dictionnaire diplomatique*, & better also than the same branch of the *Encyclopédie méthodique* (Jefferson 1952–1959: 73).

This letter confirms that the *Code of Humanity* was looked upon as an 'excellent work' of 'natural and civil law'. A major part of the legal culture of the Enlightenment as well as a strong influence on the founders of the United States who sought to create a new society with a limited body of political power, the *Code of Humanity* became the first European dictionary of natural human rights. It addressed a variety of topics concerning the individual's right to life, liberty and property. Therefore, it represented a pivotal moment in the encyclopedic history of modern jusnaturalism, during which the traditional problematic of natural rights transformed into a politics of human rights.

References

Basdevant-Gaudemet, B. 2007. 'Durand de Maillane', in *Dictionnaire historique des juristes français*, édited P. Arabeyre, J.-L. Halpérin and J. Krynen. Paris: Presses universitaires de France, pp. 294–295.

Brunet, J.-C. 1820. *Manuel du libraire et de l'amateur de livres* Paris, vol. IV, n°1537.

Burlamaqui, J.-J. 1766–1768. *Les Principes du droit de la nature et des gens avec la suite du 'Droit de la nature' qui n'avait point encore paru; le tout considérablement augmenté par M. De Felice*. Yverdon: 8 volumes.

Burnand, L. and Cernuschi, A. 2006. 'Circulation de matériaux entre l' *Encyclopédie* d'Yverdon et quelques dictionnaires spécialisés', *Dix-huitième siècle* 38: 253–267.

Burrati, A. 2006. *Dal diritto di resistenza al metodo democratico: per una genealogia del principio di opposizione nello stato costituzionale*. Milan: Giuffrè.

Chetail, V. and Haggenmacher, P. 2011. *Vattel's International Law in a XXIst Century Perspective*. Leiden-Boston: Brill.

Darnton, R. 1973. 'The Encyclopédie Wars in Prerevolutionary France', *American Historical Review* 78: 1331–1335.

De Felice, F. B. 1769. *Leçons de Droit de la Nature & des Gens*. Yverdon, s.n., 2 vols.

De Felice, F. B. 1777–1778. *Dictionnaire universel raisonné de justice naturelle et civile. Ouvrage composé par une société de moralistes, de jurisconsultes et de publicistes; le tout revu et mis en ordre par M. De Felice*. Yverdon: dans l'imprimerie de M. De Felice, 13 vols.

De Felice, F. B. 2013. *Correspondance*, online edition by L. Burnand. Lausanne: Université de Lausanne (www.unil.ch/defelice) (accessed 10 August 2014).

Delia, L. 2014. '*Justice* et *Conscience* selon le *Code de l'Humanité* (1778)', in B. Garnot and B. Lemesle (eds.) *La justice entre droit et conscience: du Moyen Âge au XVIIIᵉ siècle*. Dijon: Éditions universitaires de Dijon, pp. 61–70.
—. 2015. *Droit et philosophie à la lumière de l'* Encyclopédie. Oxford: Voltaire Foundation.
Domat, J. 1997. *Les lois civiles selon leur ordre naturel*. Paris: Imbert Debats.
Donato, C. 2005. 'Religion et Lumières en Italie, 1745–1775: le choix protestant de Fortunato Bartolomeo De Felice', in *L' Encyclopédie d'Yverdon et sa résonance européenne. Contextes, contenus, continuités*. Genève: Slatkine, pp. 89–120.
L'Esprit des journaux, français et étrangers, 1772–1817. Paris-Liège: Valade, Tutot.
Ferrari, S. 2010. 'La conversione "filosofica" di Fortunato Bartolomeo De Felice', in G. Cantarutti and S. Ferrari (eds.) *Illuminismo e protestantesimo*. Milan: FrancoAngeli, pp. 87–105.
Good, C. 2011. *Emer de Vattel (1714–1767). Naturrechtliche Ansätze einer Menschenrechtsidee und des humanitären Völkerrechts im Zeitalter des Aufklärung*. Zürich: Nomos Verlagsges.
Guyot, J.-N. 1775–1783. *Répertoire de jurisprudence civile, criminelle, canonique et bénéficiale, ouvrage de plusieurs jurisconsultes*, 64 vols. Paris: Panckoucke.
Ippolito, D. 2013. 'Giusnaturalismo: elementi filosofici e lineamenti storici', in G. Pino, et al. *Filosofia del diritto. Introduzione critica al pensiero giuridico e al diritto positivo*. Turin: Giappichelli, pp. 3–20.
Jefferson, T. 1952–1959. *Catalogue of the Library of Thomas Jefferson; Compiled with Annotations by E. M. Sowerby*. 5 vols. Washington, DC, The Library of Congress: vol. II (Philosophy – Moral, chapter XVI 'Law of Nature and Nation').
Journal des Savants. 1778. Paris, Lacombe.
Kervégan, J.-F. 1995. 'Les droits de l'homme', in *Notions de philosophie*. edited by D. Kambouchner. Paris: Gallimard, vol. II, pp. 647–649.
Morelly, E.-G.. 1755. *Code de la nature ou Le Véritable Esprit de ses lois*. Amsterdam: Partout/ Chez le vrai sage.
Nordmann, C. 1986. *Gustave III. Un démocrate couronné*. Lille: Presses universitaires de Lille.
Pejrone, G. 1993. 'Fortunato Bartolomeo De Felice: éducateur, publiciste, éditeur', *Annales Benjamin Constant* 14: 57–62.
Portalis, J. E. M., 1844. *Discours, rapports et travaux inédits sur le* Code civil. Paris: au Dépôt.
Proschwitz, G. von, 1986. *Gustave III par ses lettres*. Stockholm: Vorstedts, Paris: J. Touzot.
Rodeschini, S. 2012. *Stati di natura. Saggi sul contrattualismo moderno e contemporaneo*. Rome: Carocci.
Vattel, E. de. 1758. *Le Droit des gens ou Principes de la loi naturelle appliqués à la conduite et aux affaires des nations et des souverains*. Leide: De´pense de la Compagnie, 2 vols.
Villey, P. 2009. *Le droit et les droits de l'homme*. Paris: Presses universitaires de France.

4
DELIBERATIVE DEMOCRATS AS THE HEIRS OF ENLIGHTENMENT: BETWEEN HABERMAS AND DEWEY[1]

John Min

Introduction

This essay argues that deliberative democrats are the heirs of the Enlightenment. Deliberative democracy, though there are competing visions, at its core asserts that democracy is an exercise of public reason among free and equal citizens. One of deliberative democracy's commitments is that democracy is capable of producing not only acceptable decisions to all citizens, but they are also just and wise. In other words, democratic decisions are not only legitimate, but they also have the presumption of rationality or reasonableness. Although the term "deliberative democracy" is a recent coinage, its central ideas can be extended to Rousseau and Kant, philosophers of the Enlightenment. From their rationalistic conception of political order, we can discern the idea that democracy is capable of producing rational decisions. Kant's answer to the question 'What is Enlightenment?' is to free oneself from 'self-incurred minority' by making use of rational agents' public use of reason (Kant 1996: 17). This prescription resonates with today's deliberative democracy movement which views democracy as the exercise of practical and *public* reason among free and equal citizens to determine collectively their shared lives (Habermas 1996; Rawls 1997).

Immanuel Kant's critical projects were to answer the following three questions about reason: 'What can I know?', 'What should I do?' and 'What may I hope?' (Kant 1998: 677, A805/B833). Applying these questions to the context of this paper, I will argue that we can know that deliberative democracy is fundamentally about practical reasoning among free and equal citizens for collectively determining what they ought to do. What they ought to do is a function of robust public deliberation where ideas, perspectives and opinions are traded in civil society as well as the formal institutions of the state. What we may hope is that democracy is capable of producing rational decisions that are acceptable to all citizens.

As we stand at the beginning of the twenty-first century, Jürgen Habermas is one of the leading deliberative democrats. Unlike his critical theory predecessors Horkeimer and Adorno, who had a quite pessimistic view of the progress of reason (Horkeimer and Adorno 1982), Habermas is emphatic that society can be rational and just. The progress of reason, Habermas argues, is now embedded in communicative rationality and action, an interpersonal dialogue among rational agents modeled after the rules of the 'ideal speech situation' (Habermas 1996: 322–323). Habermas's theory of communicative action takes on a full form in his discourse theory of law and democracy (Habermas 1996). This theory is powerful but is subject to some well-known difficulties. One relevant to this essay is that Habermas's democratic theory commits him to the idea that democratic or legal problems admit of a single correct (or valid) answer, but that is problematic (Bohman 1996; McCarthy 1998). I argue that this difficulty found in Habermas's doctrine can be mitigated by appealing to John Dewey's pragmatism and his contemporary followers. Dewey's (or the Deweyan) version of deliberative democracy provides a more attractive view of the rationality of political process which he views as capable of solving complex social problems through intelligent enquiry.

This essay is organised into five sections. The first section uses Hilary Putnam's articulation of the three Enlightenments in *Pragmatism and Enlightenment* to explain why deliberative democrats are the heirs of the Enlightenment. The central issues arising out of the political aspects of the Enlightenment, or what Hilary Putnam calls the commitment to democracy, were the questions of legitimacy or justice of government and the rationality of the political process. Legitimacy and rationality are central issues in democratic theory and they come together more naturally and symbiotically in deliberative democracy, though the concepts have evolved through history. The second section articulates deliberative democracy in some general terms before moving onto discussing deliberative democracy as articulated by Jürgen Habermas (in Section 3) and John Dewey (in Section 4). The final section, Section 5, considers the issues of practicality and the feasibility of deliberative democracy as a means of furthering the 'unfinished project of modernity'.

Section 1: Three phases of enlightenment

The philosopher Hilary Putnam is his Spinoza Lectures in 2001 argues that the Enlightenment is characterised by 'reflective transcendence'. By this Putnam means 'standing back from conventional opinion, on the one hand, and the authority of Revelation on the other, and asking "Why?"' (Putnam 2001: 13). There are two senses of reflective transcendence. The first sense is to transcend the parochial interests of an individual and to reflect on matters of justice and wisdom. The second sense is that of 'criticism of criticisms'. Criticism of criticisms not only criticises 'received ideas, but higher level criticism, the "standing back" and criticising even the ways in which we are accustomed to criticise ideas, the criticism of our ways of criticisms' (Putnam 2001: 18). This questioning and critical attitude towards conventional opinion and the authority of Divine Revelation, the Enlightenment in the sense of reflective transcendence, can be characterised as having three phases.

The "first" Enlightenment began with Socrates and Plato. In Plato's dialogue *Euthyphro*, Socrates asks the question, 'Is the pious loved by the gods because it is pious, or is it pious because it is loved by the gods?' (Plato 1981: 10a). This famous question strikes at the core of two central issues in Western philosophical tradition: the aspiration for justice and the aspiration for rationality (or what Putnam calls critical thinking). The *Euthyphro*'s dilemma brings up the issue of justice because Socrates wants to know the nature of justice as a virtue. This question also strikes at the rational conception of morality because it asks, Is there a standard for the moral rightness claims or is morality based on brute power or the interest of the advantaged? According to Plato, we can discover the truth about morality through the use of reason and come to know what the correct moral standard is. It is clear that Socrates opts for the first horn of the dilemma: god loves piety because it is pious. The philosopher-king needs to be educated to know the Form of the Good in order to be able know the moral truths. Hence, two defining features of the Enlightenment were determined by Socrates and Plato: the issues of justice and rationality.

The "second" Enlightenment began in the seventeenth and eighteenth centuries as a general reaction against Aristotelian philosophy, Medieval scholasticism, and Romanticism. The defining features of the second Enlightenment, according to Putnam, are optimism of progress in newly discovered science and scientific method and the idea of social contract and natural rights. This optimism of progress is captured by the Marquis de Condorcet who wrote of 'joining together indissolubly the progress of knowledge and that of liberty, virtue and the respect for the natural rights of man' (Condorcet 1795). The proliferation of scientific discoveries (including Galileo's discovery that the Earth is not at the centre of the universe) has shown humanity that science could give us complete knowledge about human nature and the universe. Enlightenment social reformers, such as Condorcet, were quite optimistic that social problems and ills could be solved through the use of scientific method. The other defining feature of the second Enlightenment is the idea of social contract and natural rights. Reacting against the monarchical form of government that was dominant through Medieval times, the newly found freedom of men was captured through the idea of social contract. The central question that social contract theorists were trying to answer was 'What justifies the exercise of coercive political power?' We will briefly examine liberal and republican answers to that question.

A liberal response is that the governed must consent to the use of political power. This question is answered differently by modern liberal political thinkers. John Locke, for example, argues that the exercise of political power must be approved by the people by transferring one's natural rights (as prescribed by the laws of nature) to the democratic majority. Although Locke thinks that 'all men by nature are equal,' men nevertheless subject their will to the authority of others: 'being the equal right that every man hath to his natural freedom, without being subjected to the will or authority of any other man' (Locke 1960: 289). This means that the correct use of political power derives its validity from the *consent* of the governed. In other words, the *legitimacy* of government comes from the consent of the governed. People voluntarily agree to form a government outside the state of nature for the purposes of protecting their property; according to Locke, people reason that there is a greater chance that their lives and properties can be protected if everyone were to form a government.

On the other hand, a civic republican response grounds legitimacy in participatory self-governance. According to this tradition, political association is the highest good and it is necessary for the actualisation of humanity. Jean-Jacques Rousseau, for example, argues that the General Will is always right and always tends to the common good (Rousseau 1968: 72–74). The General Will is different from the will of all. While the will of all pays attention to the private interests of individuals and it is a summation of all the individual wills, the General Will is directed only towards shaping the common good (Rousseau 1968: 72). Though Rousseau does not seem to specify how the General Will is formed, it is clear that the General Will is the embodiment of 'the constant will of all the members of the state' (Rousseau 1968: 153). For Rousseau, the General Will is revealed through the voting process. In other words, the decision reached by the majority is the indicator of the General Will. Whatever decision is produced by the majority must be followed because it is produced by the General Will. Rousseau, however, thinks that while the General Will is 'always rightful […] it does not follow that the decisions of the people are always equally right' (Rousseau 1968: 72). This means that the General Will cannot err, but the people's decisions might not always be right. In fact, if someone in the minority disagrees with the decision reached by the majority (but not a simple majority), they must think that they have made a mistake. Rousseau is unequivocal about this point: 'when, therefore, the opinion contrary to my own prevails, this proves only that I have made a mistake and that what I believed to be the General Will was not so' (Rousseau 1968: 153).

This brief discussion of liberal and republican solutions to the question 'What justifies coercive political power?' demonstrates two points of emphasis in this essay. First, the issue of legitimacy of government looms large. For Locke, it comes from the consent of the governed. People voluntarily agree to form a government outside the state of nature for the purposes of protecting their property. For Rousseau, it comes from participatory self-governance within a political community. Second, the issue of the rationality of political process is also prominent, especially in Rousseau's thinking. Rousseau thinks that the General Will is always right; so whatever the majority decides and if the decision accords with the General Will, then the decision is not only legitimate but rightful.

We are on the verge of the "third" Enlightenment. According to Putnam, the third Enlightenment could be traced to the pragmatists and in particular to his philosophical hero, John Dewey. Like the previous two Enlightenments, the third Enlightenment takes on the familiar themes of rationality and legitimacy. But the concepts evolve into a different understanding for Dewey. He understands rationality (or reason) differently than Kant does, for example. According to Kant, reason is the faculty of the mind that organises and synthesises manifold experience. Dewey's understanding of reason is that it is a cognitive faculty to solve problematic situations. The term that he uses is "intelligence", which is predicated on his pragmatic philosophy that is fallibilistic, anti-metaphysical, yet anti-sceptical (Putnam 2001: 25). Dewey believes that human knowledge is fallible, meaning that knowledge does not require a degree of certainty; indeed, he eschews the modern 'quest for certainty'. In addition, Dewey eschews the metaphysics of modernity that tries to discover the first principles of nature and morals. Instead he bases his philosophical method on scientific method, which is fallibilistic and experimental. Nevertheless, he believes that knowledge of truths and morals is possible. This anti-sceptical stance is fully actualised in his hopeful optimism that intelligent conduct in morals and politics is possible. Through public deliberation (or what Dewey calls the 'dramatic rehearsal of problematic situations') the public can devise solutions to their collective problems.

The issue of legitimacy comes up in Dewey. He believes that the policies and decisions must be justified to its citizens. According to Putnam, Dewey does not deny that the legitimacy of a political power depends on the consent of the governed. In this way, Putnam thinks Dewey agrees with the modern social contract theorists, including Locke, Rousseau, and Kant. But this basis derives not from a hypothetical social contract, but from the intention to 'justify the claim that morally decent communities should be democratically organized' (Putnam 2001: 24). Indeed, Dewey had great faith in democratic politics and its way of life.

For the remainder of this essay, I argue that Habermas and Dewey embody the ideals of deliberative democracy as the heirs of the "third" Enlightenment. In particular, I examine how the democratic goals of achieving a legitimate political order and the rationality of political process are played out through the lens of two leading democratic theorists in the deliberative paradigm: Jürgen Habermas, who is a leading proponent of deliberative democracy, and John Dewey (cf. Westbrook 1991; Putnam 2001), whose radical democratic ideals have been employed by contemporary deliberative democrats. It is necessary, first, to have some background on deliberative democratic theory.

Section 2: Deliberative democracy and enlightenment

Though deliberative democracy began as a reaction against liberal interpretations of democracy, it now occupies a central place in all of democratic theory.[2] Until the 1980s, the dominant theories of democracy interpreted democracy along the lines of bargaining and negotiating, driven by strategic coalition-formation and the simple aggregation of preferences. Joseph Schumpeter, for example, doubted that anything like the will of the people could be formed; hence, he thought that democracy is a power struggle among the elites who compete for votes from the citizens, the consumers of politics (Schumpeter 1950). Deliberative democrats reacted against such reductive theories of democracy because of the observation that the behaviour appropriate in a forum is different from the behaviour appropriate in a market (Elster 1997). Moreover, reductive theories of democracy assume that preferences are fixed and rigid. This assumption may hold in economics, but it does not hold in deliberative politics, where preferences can be transformed through deliberation (Elster 1997: 11).

By contrast, deliberative democracy is an approach to democratic theory that emphasises deliberation over voting as the primary political activity. Deliberative democratic theorists argue that the point of political process is to promote deliberation among free and equal citizens, to produce outcomes that all the affected could endorse on the basis of good public reasons. Deliberation occurs in reason-giving; it is an exercise of practical reasoning, the process of offering reasons for why one endorses one policy, law or outcome instead of another. But the reasons deliberators offer are not merely self-interested reasons, but reasons acceptable to all affected citizens. That is, deliberation is concerned with the *kinds* of reasons presented to justify one's endorsing one outcome rather than another. Because deliberation occurs in reason-giving, deliberation is a rational process where citizens ought to be responsive to reasons, evidence, truths and facts. Indeed, the motto is that deliberation should admit only 'the forceless force of the better reason' (Habermas 1999: 937).

Legitimacy is one of the central normative concepts for deliberative democracy because of the fundamental belief that any laws or policies must be mutually justifiable to all (Chambers 2003; Thompson 2008). Laws are coercive and they demand compliance. On what moral basis is the state permitted to exercise coercion upon its citizens? Deliberative democrats answer this question in the following way: legitimate decisions are those that survive a robust deliberative process. Bernard Manin, in his classic article on democratic legitimacy, argues that '[T]he result from deliberation is legitimate because everyone had chance of participating in a deliberation, freely chosen after deliberation [...] it has been able to win the approval of the majority at the conclusion of a process of free confrontation among various points of view' (Manin 1987: 359). Laws resulting from a robust deliberation in which everyone had the chance to participate are *justifiable* to all those living under them (Chambers 2003).

Legitimacy of laws – that is, what is mutually agreeable to everyone on the basis of reasons that all can accept – depends, in part, on the rational quality of deliberation (Habermas 1996; Mansbridge et al. 2012). That is, if legitimacy is a function of robust deliberation and if deliberation is a rational process, then it follows that legitimacy is dependent on the rational quality of deliberation (Manin 1987). Therefore, Cristina Lafont writes. 'According to the deliberative approach, the quality of deliberation has a direct impact on the legitimacy of deliberative outcomes. This is why improving the quality of deliberation is a non-negotiable aim for the realization of deliberative democracy' (Lafont 2015: 46).

If Lafont is right, then there are at least two tasks for deliberative democrats: first, we have to articulate the conception of reason and rationality operative in deliberation and second, we have to understand reason's connection to legitimacy. In what follows, I will accomplish these two tasks through the lens of Habermas and Dewey.

To preview, I trace the lineage of faith in reason and rationality in Habermas and Dewey. For Habermas, as I mentioned earlier, has faith in the progress of reason. Unlike his predecessors who have witnessed the destructive power of instrumental reason through wars and the Holocaust, Habermas maintains his faith in the progress of reason. Reason is not a mentalist reason of an individual rational agent. Rather, reason is embedded in communication between free and equal participants in an ideal discourse. Dewey also valourises reason, though we must note that his conception of reason is neither the Kantian rationality nor instrumental reason. The Kantian rationality is the faculty of the mind that systemises manifold experience. Dewey associates such reason with the 'quest for certainty', which he rejects (Dewey 1984). He also rejects instrumental reason which underlies the logic of bourgeois market activity and technocratic top-down state planning. Dewey instead reconceptualizes the concept of reason as a kind of intelligence to recognise and solve problematic situations. This faith in intelligence allows him to say that ordinary people have expertise in at least one domain of life, knowing how one's shoe pinches, whose expertise must be taken into consideration in the collective deliberation and decision-making.

Second, for Habermas and Dewey, the issue of legitimacy is not disconnected from the aspiration of the rational quality of deliberation. For Habermas, 'laws are legitimate insofar as they are enacted according to a procedure whose inclusive and discursive properties warrant the presumption that its outcomes are reasonable for all citizens to accept' (Rehg 2012: 712). In other words, legitimate laws are internally connected with the rational quality of deliberation. Section 3 examines how Habermas articulates the concepts of legitimacy and rationality. For Dewey, the legitimacy of laws is also internally connected to the rational quality of deliberation, because the legitimate order is a product of intelligent enquiry into problematic situations of how to deal with coercive laws and governments. Section 4 examines how Dewey conceives of this relationship.

Section 3: Habermas's discourse theory of deliberative democracy

Jürgen Habermas is a radical democrat who believes that popular sovereignty is a means of social transformation. However, 'Radical democracy may no longer be the only means to social transformation, though it is clear that it remains the "unfinished project of modernity": realizing and transforming democracy is still a genuine goal even for complex and globalizing societies' (Bohman and Rehg 2011). Habermas's project of deliberative democracy is to reconcile radical democracy with the social facts of complexity and globalisation. In what follows, I will focus on how Habermas understands the concepts of legitimacy and rationality of political process.

Central to Habermas's defence of democracy is the discourse principle (D): 'Just those action norms are valid to which all those affected by decisions could agree as participants in rational discourses' (Habermas 1996: 107). By rational discourse Habermas means 'discourse is [...] supposed to be public and inclusive, to grant equal communication rights for participants, to require sincerity and to diffuse any kind of force other than the forceless force of the better argument. This communicative structure is expected to create a deliberative space for the mobilization of the best available contributions for the most relevant topics' (Habermas 1999: 937). In an 'ideal speech situation', participants are supposed to tell the truth, not use strategic reason to manipulate other participants, and to accept the norms of inclusion and equality (Habermas 1996: 322–323).

Habermas argues that the legitimacy of legal decisions must ultimately be traceable to the robust public discourse influencing the formal decision-making bodies of the state. He argues that (D) should establish a procedure of legitimate lawmaking: 'The democratic principle states that only those statutes may claim legitimacy that can meet with the assent of all citizens in a discursive process of legislation that in turn has been legally constituted' (Habermas 1996: 110). Habermas thinks that (D) can be proceduralized through the two-track conceptions of politics. Borrowing from Nancy Fraser, Habermas makes a distinction between weak and strong publics. The weak public, on the one hand, forms its opinions discursively. According to Habermas, 'This weak public is the vehicle of public opinion [...]. The opinion-formation uncoupled from the decisions is effected in an open and inclusive network of overlapping, subcultural publics having fluid temporal, social, and substantive boundaries [...]. Taken together, they form a "wild" complex that resists organization as a whole [...]. [The weak public] has the advantage of a medium of unrestricted communication' (Habermas 1996: 307–308). On the other hand, the strong public takes up opinions formed in the weak public, crystallised by discursive opinion formation. The strong public is 'decisional' because it is the final arbiter of decisions. The relationship between strong and weak publics is as follows: the strong public takes up input 'provided by a procedurally unregulated public sphere that is borne by the general public of citizens' (Habermas 1996: 307). In other words, the weak public sets the agenda that the strong public must receive and consider in its decision-making process. The boundaries between the weak and strong publics should be 'porous' so that the public opinion is taken up by the strong public.

There are at least two striking points about the weak public. First, the discursive opinion formation in the weak public forms a 'wild' complex that resists organisation. Because of the wild and unregulated nature of the informal public sphere, any idea or perspective can be considered in discourse. In other words, an unpopular or unorthodox solution to a problem is not marginalized or silenced but is given due consideration. Second, the discursive opinion formation wherein citizens in the weak public aim at a rationally motivated consensus on truth, moral rightness, or fair bargaining reveals a very strong cognitive component of Habermas's deliberative democracy. Habermas thinks that democratic decisions have the strong presumption of rationality. Democratic lawmaking is a complex process of opinion and will-formation aiming for a rationally motivated consensus among all reasonable citizens. For this reason, Habermas believes that deliberation still has truth-tracking potential because proceduralized opinion and will-formation have the presumption of rational outcomes (Habermas 2006). Therefore, (D) presupposes that there is a *single right answer* to legal questions and that the right answer is what all those affected could agree to for the same reasons in discursive opinion and will formation.

In response to the strong cognitive demand of (D), we may raise at least two difficulties. First, some have argued that the supposition that there is a single right answer is highly cognitive (Bohman 1996; McCarthy 1999; Bohman and Rehg 2007). The reason is the social fact of diversity and pluralism. Because modern society is fraught with diversity and pluralism, democratic citizens often have incommensurable ends and values. People not only have incommensurable ends, they often disagree. Hence, it is inevitable that there will be moral conflicts and disagreement in politics. If pluralism is a social fact and there is a good reason to think that we should tolerate other people's views and perspectives, then it seems implausible that citizens agree on a single valid answer for the same reasons. Second, even if we suppose that citizens could agree on a single valid answer for the same reasons, it seems implausible to say that what is valid or true is what people could agree to. The reason is that what *is* valid or true is different from whether people believe this to be true or valid. Cristina Lafont, for example, argues that there is a difference between p being true because people believe p is true and p being true because p is true. The former, Lafont argues, rests on an implausible theory of truth, namely the consensus theory of truth: this theory basically says that truth is what we can agree to in an ideal situation. But some have argued that that the consensus theory of truth is implausible because we believe that the proposition 'torturing an innocent baby' is morally wrong because it is wrong to torture innocent babies, not because participants in ideal discourse could agree that 'torturing an innocent baby' is wrong (Chambers 1996: pp. 141–144; Ingram 2010). The consensus theory of truth takes the latter to be what makes a morally right statement true.

Habermas has responded to such criticisms by stating that although the democratic principle (D) sets a very high standard for legitimacy of laws – legitimacy requires the consensus or assent of all citizens – the outcome of a deliberative process has the presumption of reasonableness. That is, the deliberative outcome can be reasonably accepted by citizens even if they disagree with the outcome.

Whatever we think about Habermas's reply to criticisms, it is clear that he is optimistic about democracy's rational capacity to self-organise the logic of the modern state. But it is also clear that Habermas's conception of reason is not monological; that is, an individual's reasoning about valid moral norms on the basis of his or her own practical reason. Rather Habermas's communicative rationality is fundamentally social, intersubjective and dialogical. Indeed, Honneth writes that Habermas's project regards democracy 'as the procedure with whose help society attempts to solve political problems rationally in a legitimate manner' (Honneth 1998: 763). This idea of the importance of pre-political communication in civil society in 'solving political problems rationally in a legitimate manner' is owed, in part, to John Dewey's thoughts, to which we turn next (Habermas 1996: 304).

Section 4: Dewey's deliberative democracy

John Dewey was a radical democrat whose unyielding faith in democratic politics pervaded all of his philosophy. The social and political conditions of his time, however, made it harder to have faith in democratic politics. Because of the rapid industrialisation and the mechanisation of modern life, the resulting networks of complex economic, social and political structures became harder to regulate. The primary problem of the public is that while it suffers the consequences of social actions, it has no reflexive agency to know that it has been eclipsed by the complex structures of the modern life. The historical situation in which Dewey finds himself was daunting, in similar ways to Habermas though in a different context, but he had hope for a democratic 'way of life'.

Dewey's conception of democracy is not an aggregative conception, where the point of democracy is to aggregate individual preferences through the mechanism of voting. While Dewey does not deny that voting is an essential part of Democracy, he writes that 'Democracy is not a state' (Dewey 1984: 325) and 'it [democracy] never is *merely* majority rule' (Dewey 1984: 365). But rather 'it is a mode of associated living' and the 'idea of community life itself' (Dewey 1984: 328). Democracy, according to a reasonable interpretation of Dewey, is a sort of deliberative democracy (Putnam 2001: 13).

Dewey's 'deliberative democracy' is predicated on thinking of democracy as a form of social enquiry. Social enquiry arises out of his idea of intelligent conduct. Dewey thought that individual agents normally act out of habit until they encounter a problematic situation. When the current experience is incoherent or unsustainable, they will conduct a thought experiment, or in Dewey's term, the dramatic rehearsal of problematic situations. They will lay out possible options, and through the process of elimination, reach the best course of action. For example, when someone is stranded in the woods after an airplane crash, they encounter a serious, problematic situation. There are two options to solve it: they can either walk to the nearest town to seek help or stay at the crash spot for the rescue plane. Let us further suppose that the noise comes from the town. The noise signifies that there is life nearby. That piece of information is useful in solving the problematic situation because it can guide practical action.

The above example highlights Dewey's 'instrumental' theory of knowledge which states that knowledge is closely related to action. Dewey's epistemology can be contrasted with the Rationalist or the Empiricist epistemological traditions of the seventeenth and eighteenth centuries. According to the Rationalists, on the one hand, the subject knows through *a priori* self-evident principles and through deduction from those first principles. The Empiricists, on the other hand, think that the subject knows through experience or sense data. There are vast differences between the Rationalists and the Empiricists on how the subject knows, but they are united in having what Festenstein (2014) calls the 'spectator theory' of knowledge. The spectator theory of knowledge, which is a subject-centered epistemology, is about the third-person objective knowledge of the facts "out there". In other words, the enterprise of epistemology aims at how the subject can obtain knowledge of the external world, God, or morality. Pragmatists, including Dewey, instead subscribe to an instrumental theory of knowledge, which essentially means that knowledge guides actions at a particular time and in a particular place.

The instrumental theory of knowledge finds its culmination in Dewey's democratic theory, which he sees as form of social enquiry. Thinking of democracy as social enquiry is vastly different from the democratic theory of Walter Lippmann, who thinks that democratic citizens are not able to control the interdependence of consequences. Lippmann thinks that the consequences are so enormous and impersonal that there is no hope for citizens to control them. Dewey has a more optimistic view of democracy. Just as experimentation in the natural sciences aims at obtaining useful knowledge about nature, Dewey thinks that democracy is an experimentation process to achieve useful knowledge to guide practical actions. The key idea here is that democracy is an intelligent way of solving problematic situations. The public becomes organised when unintended consequences created by social actors are felt, yet cannot be articulated. When the inchoate public "feels" the consequences, it conducts a social enquiry to determine the cause of the consequences. Through the method of experimentation, it tests, weighs options and revises solutions. It is then, and only then, that it becomes uneclipsed and begins taking control of the interdependent consequences that affects it. In short, Dewey's democratic theory is predicated on the instrumental theory of knowledge, which allows us to move the process of social enquiry forward when there are problematic situations.

This suggests that Deweyan social enquiry is a form of public deliberation among all enquirers to formulate, test and implement collective choices. It is a rational process of public deliberation. This rationality has three distinct features. First, Dewey recognizes that existing social and political norms can be mistaken; the circumstances of politics change, people's preferences and desires can change, and the culture can change. This belief is predicated on the fallibilism of human cognition. Arguing against the modern conception of personhood and nature, Dewey cautions against the modernity's 'quest for certainty'.

Second, Dewey's railing against the 'quest for certainty' implies that there is no final end of humans and government; rather, the ends can be revisable by means of deliberation. Dewey's idea of enquiry as deliberation is a dramatic rehearsal of problematic situations. Dewey is a consummate defender of social enquiry, modeled after the methods of natural science. On an individual level, a problematic situation compels one to conduct an enquiry, testing hypotheses through trial and error to find a solution. On a corporate level, if a problematic situation occurs, the public should engage in a social enquiry, intelligently test various options and come to a solution.

Third, Dewey believed that norms, beliefs and actions have to be continually challenged. The consequences of beliefs and actions are resources for revising our beliefs and actions. This articulates the idea that democracy is an ongoing process of collective problem-solving. Elizabeth Anderson, for instance, argues that one of the constitutive functions of democracy is its dynamic aspects, where democratic decisions can be contested at all three levels of the decision-making process: before the election, during election and after the election. She does not view the decision-making process or the outcomes as fixed and absolute (Anderson 2006). Rather they are subject to revision. This revisable function of democracy gives us a critical tool for evaluating policies, laws and decisions. The pragmatic notion of revisablity of democratic process is useful in thinking of democratic politics as not fixed or absolute. The kind of objectivity or social knowledge that democratic politics needs is not logical truths or phenomenal facts about the world. Instead, the inclusive deliberation should capture the fluid and the dynamic aspects of social processes, various perspectives and viewpoints at play and relations among people. The regular dialogue among citizens creates the culture of dissent and contestation where people are not afraid of speaking their minds about policies and the actions of the state.

This leads to Dewey's belief that policies and decisions must be justified to democratic citizens. According to Putnam, Dewey does not deny that the legitimacy of a political power depends on the consent of the governed. But democratic legitimacy does not derive from a hypothetical social contract, but to 'justify the claim that morally decent communities should be democratically organized' (Putnam 2001: 24). Because Dewey has great hopes for democracy and its citizenry, he is optimistic that the public will triumph, but only under one stringent condition. His proposal is that the public will never come out of eclipse – the inability of the public to realize that it has a problem – unless the Great Society transforms itself into the Great Community. The Great Society, on the one hand, embodies the machinery of democracy, the administrative and bureaucratic functions of complex modern society. The Great Community, on the other hand, is an ideal vision, 'A society in which the ever-expanding and intricately ramifying consequences of associated activities shall be known in the full sense of that word, so that an organized, articulate Public comes into being' (Dewey 1984: 350). It is the radical democratic ideal of the 'free gathering of people, reading uncensored newspapers' on the street corners (Dewey 1988: 227). In short, Dewey puts it succinctly: 'Till the Great Society is converted into a Great Community, the Public will remain in eclipse' (Dewey 1984: 324). In the Great Community, the public recognizes that 'intolerance, abuse, calling of names because of differences of opinion about religion or politics or business, as well as because of differences of race, colour, wealth or degree of culture are treason to the democratic way of life [...]' (Dewey 1988: 227). In the Great Community, democratic citizens should be receptive to differences in opinions and perspectives. Disagreement in democratic discourse is fruitful because it is through disagreement that the democratic culture of dissent and contestation is fostered. The democratic experimentalist process of framing and constructing the problem, the devising of a solution set, making a decision and contesting bad outcomes are part of what Misak calls the 'culture of justification' (Misak 2008: 101). Democratic citizens as participants in the democratic experimentalist process give reasons for endorsing a policy. Our fellow citizens are moral agents who deserve to know why asymmetrical effects occur for some and not others. They should be empowered to provide their perspective and situated knowledge arising out of social roles, occupation and personal life-experiences. As moral agents, they should be empowered to say the law is unjust and unwise. It is an ongoing justification to one another. After all, the collective decisions coerce us all and we all have to live together under a system of laws that binds us all. Indeed, public deliberation is a collective exercise of public reason to influence and determine collective outcomes that are binding and enforceable. This reaffirms the idea that deliberative democracy considers legitimacy to be partially dependent on mutually justifying collective outcomes.

Section 5: Practicality and feasibility of deliberative democracy

One of the main themes in Habermas's and Dewey's political thinking is the issue of the practicality and feasibility of democratic ideals. Dewey, like all pragmatists, subscribes to a pragmatic maxim: any idea, theory or action must be evaluated by its consequences. Democratic theory that prescribes principles and courses of actions without looking at how those things might be implemented Dewey would have taken with great distrust. Habermas also believes that the deliberative process will have 'a justified presumption for reasonable outcomes (mainly in view of the impact of arguments on rational changes in preference)' (Habermas 2006: 413). Habermas's point has received validation in the last decade or so through the empirical research in deliberative democracy, at least under highly institutionalized micro-deliberative settings. The practicality and feasibility of democracy resonates with deliberative democratic movement. Indeed, if the legitimacy of legal-political outcomes is a function of deliberation and if 'improving the quality of deliberation is a non-negotiable aim for the realization of deliberative democracy', then it follows that the legitimacy of democracy ultimately depends on the quality of deliberation being improved (Lafont 2015: 46).

The quality of deliberation is improved by experimentation and the testing of deliberative ideals. This spirit of democratic experimentation is present in deliberative democracy. The past decade or so has seen a tremendous effort in improving the quality of deliberation. The 'coming of age' of deliberative democracy has been given a feasible interpretation through institutional innovations (Bohman 1998: 423). This phase of deliberative democracy is the practical research phase where normative concepts are tested in the real world through various small site deliberative forums, such as planning cells, citizen juries, participatory budgeting, consensus conference and deliberative polling. These institutional sites, the halfway-house between the state and the informal public sphere, are designed to approximate or mirror the deliberative ideals, such as those discussed in Section 2 (above). Because of the difficulty of scaling up – for financial, practical and other considerations – deliberation has been confined to small sites. The proliferations of micro-deliberative sites like minipublics, where decisions are legitimized through face-to-face deliberation, speak to that effort. Indeed, if one of the requirements of the legitimacy of decisions is that citizens' reasons are sufficiently articulated through deliberation before collectives outcomes are reached, then minipublics are a good start.

Minipublics which 'convene citizens, in the dozens or hundreds or thousands [...] in self-consciously organized public deliberations [...] are the best promise up to date of actualizing public deliberation as a workable idea' (Fung 2003:

338–339). Minipublics are sites of deliberation that occur episodically over a particular issue or set of issues and for a relatively short duration. They are an effective means of improving citizen participation and public deliberation. When they empower citizens to influence decisions, they satisfy those ideals, albeit on a smaller scale. This process of public deliberation adds to legitimacy because those affected by decisions are included in an authentic deliberation.

In addition to serving the legitimising function of deliberative outcomes, minipublics also serve the instrumental functions of engendering social learning and mutual understanding. Social learning and mutual understanding occur when citizens deliberate with each other, hear expert testimonies and weigh evidence and reasons. One of the most famous examples of minipublics is deliberative polling. The deliberative polling model was invented by the political scientist James Fishkin (Fishkin 2009; Fishkin and Ackerman 2002). It is a mechanism by which participants' public opinion undergoes transformation through deliberation. Unlike the traditional opinion polling which surveys people's unconsidered judgement, deliberative polling measures people's considered judgement. In deliberative polling, people are randomly selected to come to a deliberative forum to talk about weighty and consequential issues like constitutional reforms (Lafont 2015: 54–55). There is a measurable effect of the transformation of preferences after a round of deliberation. It has been documented that participants learn something, appreciate political participation more, etc. The importance of the forum is that it allows ordinary citizens to discuss political matters at length and this mirrors the deliberative ideals of 'having as much time to speak as they wish'. For this reason, among others, Jane Mansbridge touts deliberative polling as the 'gold standard' of deliberation (Mansbridge 2010: 55).

While minipublics are a promising way to make the project of deliberative democracy more practical, they occur in highly institutionalised settings and sometimes disconnected from other parts of the civil society. This deficiency can be overcome by proxy mechanisms. One such example is trust proxies: minipublics serve as a proxy where the deliberative outcomes and learning serve as trusted information that is propagated to the rest of the population (MacKenzie and Warren 2012). These empirical innovations are important for at least two reasons. First, they fulfil the original vision of democracy: that it is a complete theory of democracy, with normative and empirical aspects working together. Second, if deliberative democracy will survive as a lasting alternative to reductive theories of democracy – whether viewing politics as a consumer choice or rule by the elites – it will have to answer to the challenge that it could work on a mass or a global scale.

Conclusion

This essay argues that deliberative democrats are the heirs of the "third" Enlightenment that 'hasn't happened yet, or hasn't at any rate fully happened, but one that I hope will happen, and one worth struggling for' (Putnam 2001: 17). It modestly contributes to thinking about deliberative democrats' self-conception as heirs of the Enlightenment. Habermas famously wrote that democracy is 'the unfinished project of modernity' (Habermas 1997: 35). Commenting on Habermas's deliberative democracy, Bohman and Rehg (2011) write that 'Radical democracy may no longer be the only means to social transformation, though it is clear that it remains the "unfinished project of modernity": realizing and transforming democracy is still a genuine goal even for complex and globalizing societies.' In my view, Habermas and Dewey articulate the road that deliberative democrats ought to walk down. We, as a society, must choose to go down the road towards one world rather than down another, just as gods must choose to create one world rather than another. It is my hope, in concert with Habermas, Dewey and Putnam, that we will continue with the project of deliberative democracy for the emancipation and freedom of all people.

Notes

1   The author thanks Minghe Li and Jim McCollum for helpful comments and discussions on the previous draft of this paper. The author also thanks Martin Davies for excellent editorial suggestions, which improved this paper as a result. Ideas in this essay are owed to Putnam 2001 and Bohman 2005. See Brandom 2004 for an argument that American Pragmatism is a second stage of Enlightenment. In particular, I am indebted to Putnam 2001 for the idea that pragmatism is a third wave of Enlightenment. This essay addresses only the *democratic* strain of the Enlightenment, leaving the discussion of other aspects of Enlightenment to other contributions in this edited volume.
2   Deliberative democracy has a huge literature by now and it will be very difficult to generalise about the field. Nonetheless, I hope to give an overview of deliberative democracy that most deliberative democrats could agree to. For helpful overviews see Chambers 2003 and Thompson 2008. For useful essays in edited volumes see Bohman and Rehg 1997 and Mansbridge and Parkinson 2012.

References

Anderson, E. 2006. 'The Epistemology of Democracy', *Episteme* 3: 9–23.
Bohman J. 1996. *Public Deliberation*. Cambridge, MA: MIT Press.
—. 1998. 'The Coming of Age of Deliberative Democracy', *Journal of Political Philosophy* 4: 418–443.
—. 2005. 'We, Heirs of Enlightenment: Critical Theory, Democracy and Social Science', *International Journal of Philosophical Studies* 13(3): 353–377.
Bohman, J. and Rehg, W. 1997. *Deliberative Democracy: Essays on Reason and Politics*. Cambridge, MA: MIT Press.
—. 2011. 'Jürgen Habermas', *The Stanford Encyclopedia of Philosophy* (Winter 2011 Edition), edited by Edward N. Zalta,. http://plato.stanford.edu/archives/win2011/entries/habermas/ (accessed 11 May 2015).
Brandom, R. 2004. 'The Pragmatist Enlightenment (and Its Problematic Semantics)', *European Journal of Philosophy* 12(1): 1–16.
Chamber, S. 1996. *Reasonable Democracy*. Cornell, NY: Cornell University Press.
—. 2003. 'Deliberative Democratic Theory', *Annual Review of Political Science* 6: 307–326.
Condorcet, M. 1795. *Outlines of an Historical View of the Progress of the Human Mind*. http://oll.libertyfund.org/titles/1669 (accessed 11 May 2015).

Dewey, J. 1984. *The Public and Its Problems: The Later Works*, 1925–1953, vol. 2, edited by J. A. Boydston. Carbondale, IL: Southern Illinois University Press.
—. 1988. 'Creative Democracy: The Task Before Us', in *The Later Works*, 1925–1953, vol. 14, edited by J. A. Boydston. Carbondale, IL: Southern Illinois University Press, pp. 224–230.
Dryzek, J. 2010. *Foundations and Frontiers of Deliberative Governance*. Oxford: Oxford University Press.
Elster, J. 1997. 'The Market and the Forum: Three Varieties of Political Theory', in *Deliberative Democracy: Essays on Reason and Politics*, edited by J. Bohman and W. Rehg. Cambridge, MA: MIT Press, pp. 3–33.
Festenstein, M. 2014. 'Dewey's Political Philosophy', *The Stanford Encyclopedia of Philosophy* (Spring 2014 Edition), edited by Edward N. Zalta (ed.), http://plato.stanford.edu/archives/spr2014/entries/dewey-political/ (accessed 11 May 2015).
Fishkin, James S. 2009. *When the People Speak*. Oxford: Oxford University Press.
Fishkin, J. and Ackerman, B. 2002. 'Deliberation Day', *The Journal of Political Philosophy* 10(2): 129–152.
Fung, A. 2003. 'Survey Article: Recipes for Public Spheres: Eight Institutional Design Choices and Their Consequences', *The Journal of Political Philosophy* 11(3): 338–367.
Habermas, J. 1996. *Between Facts and Norms: Contributions to a Discourse Theory of Law and Democracy*, translated by W. Rehg. Cambridge, MA: MIT Press.
—. 1997. 'Modernity: An Unfinished Project', in *Habermas And the Unfinished Project of Modernity: Critical Essays on The Philosophical Discourse of Modernity*, edited by S. Benhabib and M. P. d'Entrèves. Cambridge, MA: MIT Press, pp. 38–55.
—. 1999. 'Between Facts and Norms: An Author's Reflections', *Denver University Law Review* 76: 937–940.
—. 2006. 'Political Communication in Media Society: Does Democracy Still Enjoy an Epistemic Dimension? The Impact of Normative Theory on Empirical Research', *Communication Theory* 16(4): 411–426.
Honneth, A. 1998. 'Democracy as Reflexive Cooperation: John Dewey and the Theory of Democracy Today', *Political Theory* 26: 763–783.
Horkheimer, M. and Adorno, T. 1982. *The Dialectic of Enlightenment*. New York: Seabury.
Ingram, D. 2010. *Habermas: Introduction and Analysis*. Ithaca, NY: Cornell University Press.
Kant. I. 1996. 'An Answer to the Question: What Is Enlightenment?', in *Practical Philosophy*, edited by M. J. Gregor. Cambridge: Cambridge University Press, pp. 7–22.
—. 1998. *Critique of Pure Reason*, in *The Cambridge Edition of the Works of Immanuel Kant*, translated by P. Guyer and A. W. Wood. Cambridge: Cambridge University Press, pp. 127–702.
Lafont, C. 2004. 'Moral Objectivity and Reasonable Agreement: Can Realism Be Reconciled with Kantian Constructivism?', *Ratio Juris* 17(1): 27–51.
—. 2015. 'Deliberation, Participation, and Democratic Legitimacy: Should Deliberative Mini-publics Shape Public Policy', *Journal of Political Philosophy* 23(1): 40–63.
Locke, J. 1960. *Second Treatise of Government*, in *Two Treatises of Government*, edited by P. Laslett. Cambridge: Cambridge University Press, pp. 285–446.
MacKenzie, M. and Warren, M. 2012. 'Two Sources of Trusted Proxies', in *Deliberative Systems: Deliberative Democracy on Large Scale*, edited by J. Mansbridge and J. Parkinson. Cambridge: Cambridge University Press, pp. 95–124.
Manin, B. 1987. 'On Legitimacy and Political Deliberation', *Political Theory* 15: 338–368.
Mansbridge, J. 2010. 'Deliberative Polling as the Gold Standard', *The Good Society* 19(1): 55–62.
Mansbridge, J. et al. 2012. 'Systemic Approach to Deliberative Democracy', in *Deliberative Systems: Deliberative Democracy on Large Scale*, edited by J. Mansbridge and J. Parkinson. Cambridge: Cambridge University Press, pp. 1–26.

McCarthy, T. 1998. 'Legitimacy and Diversity: Dialectical Reflections on Analytical Distinctions', in *Habermas on Law and Democracy: Critical Exchanges*, edited by A. Arato and M. Rosenfeld. Los Angeles: University of California Press, pp. 115–153.

Misak, C. 2008. 'A Culture of Justification: The Pragmatists' Epistemic Argument for Democracy', *Episteme* 5(1): 94–105.

Plato. 1981. *Euthyphro*. Indianapolis, IN: Hackett Publishing Company.

Putnam, H. 2001. *Enlightenment and Pragmatism*. Amsterdam: Van Gorcum.

Rawls, J. 1997. 'The Idea of Public Reason Revisited', *University of Chicago Law Review* 64 (3): 765–807.

Rehg, W. 2012. 'Discourse Theory', in *The Routledge Companion to Social and Political Philosophy*, edited by G. Gaus and F. d'Agostino. London: Routledge, pp. 706–717.

Rousseau, J.-J. 1968. *The Social Contract*. Harmondsworth, Middlesex: Penguin.

Schumpeter, J. A. 1950. *Capitalism, Socialism, and Democracy*. New York: Harper.

Thompson, D. 2008. 'Deliberative Democratic Theory and Empirical Political Science', *Annual Review of Political Science* 11: 497–520.

Westbook, R. B. 1991. *John Dewey and American Democracy*. Ithaca, NY: Cornell University Press.

PART III
Thinking about Enlightenment and religion

5

CHRISTIANITY AND ENLIGHTENMENT: TWO HERMENEUTICAL APPROACHES TO THEIR RELATIONSHIP

Salvatore Muscolino

Introduction

Generally speaking, up until the Second Vatican Council (1962–1965), the relationship between the Catholic Church and both Enlightenment and modernity was rather conflicted. If one takes into consideration documents of the Magisterium like *Miraris Vos* (1832), *Sillabo* (1864) or *Pascendi dominici gregis* (1907), it would appear that there is no room for constructive dialogue in respect of the queries posed by modern culture.

With the Council, the Roman Catholic Church opened itself up to modernity abandoning *de facto* its previous condemnatory approach. In spite of its undeniable opening up to democracy and its principles of "freedom", the Church's dialogue with modernity, (especially with the Enlightenment, which represents its central moment), is far from being completely resolved; to such an extent that the dispute between conservative and progressive souls within the Catholic Church is still strongly present. It is evident that from the period of the Council to the present day this internal tension has not been overcome.

In this essay, I compare the different hermeneutical models of the relationship between Enlightenment and Christianity of the two of the most prominent Catholic theologians of our age: Johann Baptist Metz and Joseph Ratzinger (later Benedict XVI). In this way, I will confine my field of research to the Catholic sphere, thus excluding the Protestant, Anglican and Orthodox ones. Furthermore, by using two theological models which represent almost two opposite extremes, their comparison should show the above mentioned tension as having a paradigmatic character.

In contrast, I think that it is possible to shine a light on the reasons behind the Catholic Church's attitude over the last thirty years which derives, in great measure, from the theological approach of Ratzinger, who was Prefect of the Sacred Congregation for the Doctrine of the Faith from 1981 to 2005 and later pope until

2013 (it is too early for a considered judgement on the actions of the current pope, Francis). As I said before, Metz's approach can be considered as one of the most remarkable alternative theological conceptions to Ratzinger's, both regarding the general vision of Christianity and the relationship between the Church and the world.

For both of them, the relationship with the Enlightenment is a central theoretical turning point and, even though they are theologians, I argue that the comparison of the two can be very constructive from a philosophical point of view as well. That's why there is a strong relationship between theology and philosophy, especially in the Catholic tradition. In fact, the origin of theological discourse is the historical event of revelation, but its concrete and conceptual articulation was derived from philosophical reflection. Therefore, as I will show in this essay, the differences between Ratzinger's and Metz's theological approaches originate from their respective philosophical options: that in favour of a classical philosophical model (Ratzinger) and that in favour of a modern one (Metz). The theoretical and practical consequences of these different choices explain why these two theologians have a different attitude towards Enlightenment and diverse ways of conceiving Christianity.

More specifically, the differences between these two theological models derive from their diverse attitude towards two crucial turning points: the nominalistic turn in attitude at the beginning of modernity and the relationship between theory and praxis. This different standpoint gives, in turn, rise to a number of consequences regarding the way of conceiving human freedom, the role of religion in the public sphere and, *last but not least*, the function of the Church both in democratic society and in the global world.

Joseph Ratzinger and the primacy of Λόγος

Ratzinger's interpretation of Enlightenment is the logical consequence of his theological vision; I therefore consider it worthwhile to begin by explaining the load-bearing axis of this vision.

During a famous interview with the Italian journalist Vittorio Messori, answering the question about the reasons for his separation from the theological journal *Concilium*, of which he was one of the founders at the time of the Second Vatican Council, Ratzinger said: 'It is not I who have changed, but others' (Ratzinger and Messori 1987: 18). I think that this answer more or less symbolises Ratzinger's theological perspective based on an idea of Truth, a given fact, which human reason must aim at recognising and defending but not at creating. This is the *Leitmotiv* of all Ratzingerian theological reflection in the various fields of ecclesiology and sacramental and systematic theology.

Ratzinger's vision of the rapport between Christianity and Enlightenment also conveys this conception of the link Truth/reason which inserts itself into a particular tradition that classical Augustinian and Bonaventurian reason must be enlightened by faith in order to access Truth. These theoretical roots explain the peculiar character of Ratzinger's theology: 'a preferring of the humility of faith over the pride of philosophy; a defense of the "city of God" over the powers of the "earthly city"; and a recognition of the duality that lies deep within human beings who, even when desiring the good, cannot embrace it' (Corkery 2009: 25).

At this point, Ratzinger's doubts about the most important document of the Second Vatican regarding the relationship between the Church and the world, i.e., *Gaudium et spes*, appear evident. It is well known that this document, like the others, is affected by some terminological and conceptual variations that have given rise to a real "conflict of interpretation"; a conflict which has been characterising the post-conciliar history of the Catholic Church. In the particular case of *Gaudium et spes*, the questions to be answered are: Should this opening-up towards the world, as indicated in this document, be interpreted as the Church's recognition that there is a certain positivity in modern culture and, if so, could it legitimately be possible to speak of a "concession" in favour of a secular mentality? Or, should this opening-up be considered merely a different way of sending the world a message which goes beyond history and contingency and, therefore, it would be improper to speak of a "concession"?

Ratzinger has always defended this second interpretative option regarding not only *Gaudium et spes* but also all the Council, as shown by his commitment, once he had became pope, to oppose the so-called interpretation of discontinuity defended by the 'Bologna School' headed by the Italian historian Giuseppe Alberigo (Ratzinger/ Benedict XVI: 2005). During the above mentioned interview with Messori, Ratzinger strongly argued this point: 'There is no "pre-" or "post-" conciliar Church: there is but one, unique Church that walks the path toward the Lord, ever deepening and even better understanding the treasure of faith that He himself has entrusted to her. There are no leaps in this history, there are no fractures, and there is no break in continuity. In no wise did the Council intend to introduce a temporal dichotomy in the Church' (Ratzinger and Messori 1987: 35).

I wish to stress that, as far as Ratzinger's doubts are concerned regarding the opening-up of the conciliar Church to modernity, a certain variation in judgement can be seen. On the one hand, Ratzinger seems to attribute the 'limits' ascribed to the Council not to its documents, i.e., its 'lettera', but rather to a certain post-conciliar theology which, due to both irresponsibility and ingenuousness, has ended up by giving a distorted vision of historical truth as though the Council had represented a 'new beginning' in the history of Church (Ratzinger and Messori 1985: 28).

However, on the other hand, Ratzinger manifested several doubts about the historical movement of the Council itself. It is a judgement which takes cognizance of the fact that the Council was perceived by its contemporary observers as being an exception as regards the previous councils, and therefore Ratzinger wonders if the Second Vatican wasn't, in a certain sense, an event compromised *ab origine*:

> approval came above all from those who do not take part in the life of, or believe in, the Church, while the faithful who partook in the life of the Church instead felt condemned. The world seemed to approve the movement of the Council, because in thus doing it itself felt upheld, while the

response within the Church was both of hesitation and bewilderment. This circumstance, which concerns the nucleus of the particular historical configuration of the last Council, doubtlessly raises serious questions, like those made by the so-called conservatives – was the movement of the Council legitimate and, if so, what did it actually mean?

(Ratzinger 1984: 306)

The "interpretation of continuity" represents one of the main elements that constitute the theoretical framework for considering all the positions assumed by Ratzinger on modernity. These can be grouped together under some conceptual themes: the relationships between Truth and liberty, religion and politics, the Church and the world.

The decisive point of Ratzinger's doubts regarding his judgement of the Council lies in his personal historical and philosophical vision of modernity. This term, as is common knowledge, is the subject of great discussion in sociological, historical, philosophical, literary and artistic fields, also not least because it needs to be redefined due to the emergence of categories such as postmodern or late modern. To complicate matters more there is also the question of the relationship between modernity and Christianity scholars are still debating today (cf. Taylor 2007: 711–776).

Also from the Augustinian viewpoint, upheld by Ratzinger, the modern tendency to consider human reason absolute is the main mistake to be opposed. This theoretical attitude reveals that Ratzinger's Augustinian approach resembles that of postmodern thinkers since he shares their critique of the grand narrative of modernity as a linear process of emancipation and the triumph of human reason (cf. Milbank 1991: 311–333). In my opinion, the main element he and postmodern theorists have in common concerns the foundation of human reason as not that neutral, absolute and independent faculty affirmed by the Enlightenment but as something that develops through dialogue with the 'Other'. Therefore, theology and postmodernism should not be perceived as opposing each other provided that the nihilist tendency of a certain post-Nietzschian philosophy is rejected (cf. Schreiter 2003: 373–388).

For his part, Ratzinger again tries to propose God as the human being's dialogical Otherness. In other words, the 'Other' is that Truth which, historically incarnated in Jesus Christ, has to be received by human beings in order to make their nature perfect. Following the recognition of this fact, several important consequences arise regarding the nature of liberty and the limits of a certain kind of Enlightenment.

Therefore, Ratzinger's theological starting-point is the Incarnation of Λόγος and its priority over praxis, i.e., over concrete human freedom. This presupposition sheds light on his doubts regarding the historical and cultural path of modernity. The modern human being has expected to distance him- or herself progressively from God, or rather from the Otherness on which he or she is ontologically founded and to gain salvation autonomously by means of reason. Therefore, the mistake of modernity is an anthropological one because reason was seen as an autonomous power in need of emancipation from religion and God. As a consequence, the motto of the Enlightenment's rationale, at least in its majority tendency, was the Kantian *Sapere Aude* (Kant 1996: 11).

It is not surprising at this point that Ratzinger's negative opinion of the Enlightenment applies also to Kant, who was one of the shrewdest advocates of that period. It is no exaggeration to say that, from Ratzinger's perspective, all the mistakes of modernity are present in Kant's works because the Kantian critique of metaphysics has paved the way to relativism and an instrumental conception of reason which are the meaningful elements of European society, the successor to French and German Enlightenment.

It is true that during the Enlightenment and, more generally in the modern day and age, important aims have been achieved both in the political and social fields, by the triumph of liberal-democratic principles, and in scientific fields, by the progress of our astronomical and medical knowledge. Nevertheless, as presented in *Dialectics of Enlightenment* (2002) by Horkheimer and Adorno to which Ratzinger explicitly refers, the history of human reason is not at all a linear process without risks (Ratzinger 1998: 153). On the contrary, it is necessary to speak of a blatant 'pathology' into which reason can collapse when it is made an absolute – as the tragic examples of Totalitarianism undoubtedly showed in the twentieth century (Habermas and Ratzinger 2006: 77).

Therefore, Ratzinger defends a classical conception in line with Augustinian tradition according to which reason, in order to operate positively, must be enlightened by faith. In Ratzinger's interpretation, Kant makes the same mistake of Nominalism which, at the beginning of modernity, anticipated the successive rejection of metaphysics by rejecting the existence of universals. Thus, the possibility of giving a rational, or objective, foundation to knowledge was lost and in the twentieth century this tendency was further radicalised by the 'linguistic turn'. Ratzinger observes that human knowledge cannot be trapped in a never-ending game of interpretation without having the possibility to obtain the truth in itself (Ratzinger 2004: 189–190). This is the outcome of a certain modern and contemporary philosophical culture which, progressively reducing the problem of truth to a mere factual dimension, makes it coincide with what positivist science is able to control.

Besides the legitimacy of his historical and philosophical reconstruction, the main thing here is that if the possibility of metaphysical knowledge (i.e., knowledge open to transcendence) is denied, Ratzinger believes that the chance of finding objective criteria for normatively guiding praxis is also denied. At this point it becomes clear why, by taking advantage of Horkheimer and Adorno's thesis, Ratzinger considers the history of modernity as being condemned to give rise to the cult of techne and relativism. Indeed, as pope, in his famous and controversial lecture in Regensburg, Ratzinger again insisted that the foundations of the modern crisis issued from its theoretical starting point, i.e., the nominalistic and volontaristic turn at the debut of modern age (Ratzinger/Benedict XVI 2006).

To argue the impossibility of any objective knowledge of reality also implies, as its logical consequence, the impossibility of recognising the intrinsic rationality of the world. If in the Judaic-Christian theological tradition the thesis of creation demonstrates this rationality, then, when this option is *a priori* refused, our reason is condemned to fall into a kind of self-referring abyss. In Ratzinger's view, the modern history of liberty is indeed affected by this kind of paradox. If, in fact, on the basis of the "nominalistic turn", metaphysical knowledge appears impossible, then the practice of liberty can no longer be founded upon an objective truth, external and, therefore, always valid for all. As regards morality which in the past was conceived as starting from a Λόγος, an order or a normative request external to the human being, it now becomes merely a subjective choice, if not even an irrational option (Ratzinger 1998: 209). According to Ratzinger, after Bacon the history of modern reason was progressively founded on the categories of utility and techne: 'it is only quantitative reason, the reason of calculation and experiment, that is seen as reason at all, and all the rest as the non-rational that must slowly be overcome and at the same time brought over into the field of "exact" knowledge' (Ratzinger 1998: 209).

In Ratzinger's view, the way in which the issue of liberty is treated in contemporary democratic societies has evidently revealed a dangerous tendency. Above and beyond the unquestionable advantages of democratic socio-political organisations over theocratic ones, which represent a real distortion of the same religious announcement, the main problem is the nature of liberty. If, in accordance with the Enlightenment motto, this means 'liberation from the power of tradition to lay down norms', then only consensus (i.e., majority rule) can regulate it from a social point of view (Ratzinger 1998: 185). But the danger of this conception is that liberty, deprived of a reference to truth, risks going around in circles thus becoming an instrument of the strongest (Eggemeir 2012: 455–458).

To all intents and purposes, contemporary political and juridical philosophy is full of proposals which systematically try to develop this idea of negative liberty. The main models undoubtedly are John Rawls's and Jürgen Habermas's proceduralistic and deliberative ones, which explicitly wish to be non-metaphysical and post-metaphysical, respectively (Rawls 1971, 1993; Habermas 1984, 1996). Nevertheless, Ratzinger poses some queries: 'Can it [the democratic system] declare anything it likes to be law that then is binding on everyone, or does reason stand above the majority so that something that is directed against reason cannot really become law? But who is to say what is reason? Must one simply presuppose that the majority also incorporates more reason?' (Ratzinger 1998: 188).

The crucial point lies in that theoretical and practical paradox on which the German legal philosopher Böckenförde insisted by arguing that the modern State lives on premises that it cannot itself guarantee (Böckenförde 1976: 60). This means that democracies need values or principles which are presupposed by the system and not elaborated on the basis of a mere factual consensus which could, at any given moment, be subordinated to specific interests either economical or of a different nature.

To put it differently, the risk here is that merely formal reason like that defended by Rawls and Habermas during a particular period of their careers could, in the end, show itself as being insufficient to guarantee the sustainability of that same democratic society. In their later work, both Rawls and Habermas reconsidered the role of religions in post-secular societies to guarantee democratic ideals against the crisis that has hit the present-day Western world (cf. Rawls 1997; Habermas 2008, 2011). This fact seems to make Ratzinger's objections to the Enlightenment vision, which considers religion as an obstacle or even a danger to democratic society, look right, at least in part.

We must not forget that several times Ratzinger tried to show how both modernity and Enlightenment are not, in principle, antagonistic towards Christianity: on the contrary, in his view, the modern idea of freedom must be intended as 'a legitimate product of the Christian environment' (Ratzinger 1998: 162).

This attempt to make modernity compatible with Christianity has been criticised by scholars who, even today, consider the Enlightenment as a movement which developed in radical opposition to the Christian religion (Ferrone 2013). But, in my opinion, the limit of Ratzinger's view lies elsewhere.

It would seem that Ratzinger's polemic is aimed only at those immanent tendencies of modernity which want to eliminate both religion and tradition because human reason in itself is self-sufficient. However, he argues that, in this way, the fundamental contribution made by the Judeo-Christian tradition to the genesis of modernity would be underappreciated. In his works regarding European identity, Ratzinger often returns to the historical and cultural mistake made by those who want to dismiss Europe's Judeo-Christian matrix because they risk making the European Union project, and more generally that of the Western world, a failure. Tracy Rowland well summarises this point by considering that, in Ratzinger's view, 'the suicide of the West began when people stopped believing in the Christian account of creation and started to sever the intrinsic relationship of faith and reason' (Rowland 2008: 122).

In other words, in Ratzinger's view the aspiration of the Enlightenment is compatible with Christianity because they share the same interest in law and freedom as instruments for the defence of the human being. However, paradoxically, the modern will to cut the bond with God and religion has generated a dangerous tendency, whereby the human being, on the road to freedom, ends up being nullified by superior and anonymous forces like History (Hegel), Class (Marx), or the Economy (Capitalism).

Despite partially recognising the validity of the Enlightenment, Ratzinger also repeatedly expresses negative opinions regarding the genesis of modernity itself; these fundamentally derive from the fracture caused by nominalism. In my opinion the question now becomes, If, as said before, modernity begins with the nominalistic turn, then is it potentially legitimate or is it condemned *ab origine*? If so, does Ratzinger judge elements of modernity positively because they are fundamentally anti-modern, because, as in the case of liberal-democratic freedom, they themselves in fact result from Christianity (Ratzinger 1998: 215)?

The Ratzingerian option for a classical conception of reason seems to me to be proof of the latter hypothesis, so I would now argue that there is undoubtedly unresolved tension on this point. Indeed, it seems inescapable that the rehabilitation of a realistic and metaphysical perspective desired by Ratzinger is somewhat problematic as regards the demands of modernity and the Enlightenment, especially where the issues of rights and the laity are concerned.

Another topic very close to the Enlightenment issue of emancipation is that of secularisation: how controversial the exact historical and sociological meaning of this term is, is well known. Ratzinger positively values some recent reflections on this matter made by the philosopher Jürgen Habermas. During a famous conference held in 2004, Ratzinger accepts Habermas's proposal to abandon the old model of secularisation that meant abandoning or overcoming religion by reason, in favour of a dialectical vision of modernity as a process involving both dialogue and reciprocal learning between secular and religious thought (Habermas and Ratzinger 2006: 73–77). Ratzinger also agrees with the critique Habermas shares with many trends of contemporary philosophy of the old concept of nature in natural law as unsuitable for giving a rational and universal foundation to ethics (Habermas and Ratzinger 2006: 69).

Nevertheless, and maybe with more scepticism than Habermas, Ratzinger denies that there could be a globally valid, merely rational foundation of ethics (Habermas and Ratzinger 2006: 76). As an Augustinian, he believes that human reason by itself cannot achieve that aim unless it is open to faith. For example, he argues that the occidental view of modernity as a necessary stage in the history of mankind is not universal at all. The critiques which non-Western societies have always moved against European modernity is that it has conceived secularisation as the necessary process of estrangement from God. But, the perspective of comparative history or sociology of religion reveals that this vision of secularisation has made Europe an exception in respect of the rest of the world (the United States included), where religions continue to play an important public role. Even the fact of becoming an exception, in Ratzinger's view, is the heritage of a certain Enlightenment mentality which it would be time to abandon or, at least, to reflect upon critically (Habermas and Ratzinger 2006: 76).

According to Ratzinger, one of the main theoretical degenerations of a modernity that has claimed to eliminate God is represented by the Hegelian-Marxist tradition (useful for the discussion of Metz (below)). The Hegelian-Marxist is one of the theoretical traditions generated by the Enlightenment which, in response to the critique of metaphysics, has progressively subordinated Truth to praxis. Hegel conceived the history of mankind as the history of liberty, while Marx developed this idea in the light of his historical materialism. But, for Ratzinger, the latter conception in particular ends up nullifying human liberty within a theoretical framework in which "necessity" drives historical progress towards the communist society without classes.

Ratzinger's hostility towards Marxist tradition could be explained both by its exponents' explicit atheism and by the influence that its ideas have on important trends in twentieth-century theology which risks, in his view, not being fully orthodox. I especially refer to the proposal of a New Political Theology made by Johann Baptist Metz, about which I will speak later, that anticipated several Theologies of

Liberation at the end of the 1960s to which Ratzinger has always shown a negative attitude (Ratzinger 1998: 255–275). In Ratzinger's vision, by taking on Marxist categories theology risks subordinating Truth to praxis since then the contradictions mentioned above between two different levels, the ecclesiological and the ethical-political, would return.

Regarding ecclesiology, the belief that subordinates Truth to praxis, that is to the consensus of social actors, risks modifying the Church's self-awareness because even the *depositum fidei* could end up being considered as something where majority rule counts. Conversely, Ratzinger argues that 'Truth therefore remains essentially independent of the Church and the Church is orientated towards it as a means' (Ratzinger 1998: 160).

If, for their part, Theologies of Liberation conveying Marxist influence clamour for more democracy in the management of the Church, Ratzinger defends in response an ecclesiological vision incompatible with the democratic model. That's why, as I said before, the Catholic Church exists in order to preserve and to spread a higher Truth that nobody can modify. For Ratzinger, if a democratic government based on majority-rule were applied to the Church, it would *de facto* risk betraying the mission Jesus gave it.

In Ratzinger's view, behind these demands, apparently in line with our age, there hides that dangerous tendency of modernity towards an absolutely formal concept of liberty defined just by consensus. This kind of liberty is negative and Ratzinger opposes it with a positive conception: liberty, seen as self-perfection, realises itself only by respecting the transcendent Truth that the Church, on behalf of Jesus, must announce (Skinner 2002: 239; Ratzinger 1998: 182).

It is evident that this hierarchical ecclesiology has influenced all Ratzinger's thought both as theologian and as pope on delicate issues like the relationship between the magisterium and theological science, the liturgical reform in 2007, the dialogue between the Vatican and the local churches and, *last but not least*, that with the traditionalist movement founded by Marcel Lefevbre (Rowland 2008: 123–143; Corkery 2009: 81–92; Miccoli 2011).

On an ethical and political level, the tensions deriving from the subordination of theory to praxis consist, as I have already said, in the reduction of truth to consensus and utility. Therefore, that Ratzinger refuses this subordination excludes any compromise with the Marxist tradition and, as a consequence, risks creating tension on both a theoretical and practical level with modern culture *tout court*. The defense of a positive conception of liberty based on a rational knowledge of Truth is not fully compatible with the pluralistic nature of contemporary society. One of the *Leitmotive* of Benedict XVI's political activity was, not by accident, the struggle with relativism considered as the evil of contemporary society, the theoretical roots of which I have already indicated: relativism comes from the refusal to recognise that reason can be guided to Truth by faith.

In conclusion: for Ratzinger/Benedict XVI the Church's role today is to defend the truth of Christianity in a world where the Christian religion is no longer in the majority as happened in the Medieval and Modern ages in Europe. Now the

Church has to struggle for its own place within an always more pluralistic global society. Hence, the crucial question: Is Ratzinger's theological attitude, which may be called conservative, uniquely able to preserve the *proprium* of Christianity when confronted by the complexity of present society? Or is it possible to think about other interpretations and paths which differently conceive the Church's relationship with modernity? And, on this question, I proceed to analyse Johann Baptist Metz's theological proposal.

Johann Baptist Metz and 'anamnestic reason'

In contrast to Ratzinger's pretty linear intellectual path, Metz's approach has been characterised by some shifts which, in my opinion, can be conceived as variations on a theme – the relationship between Christianity and modernity (Ashley 1998; Ruz et al. 2008, 2009; Marsden 2012). His first systematic publication bears the influence of his teacher Karl Rahner's transcendental approach, and Metz proposed an interpretation of Aquinas as the first philosopher who tried to treat Christianity in an anthropocentric way (Metz 1962). In 1969 with the publication of *Theology of the World* Metz's perspective offered a 'political theology' which, unlike Neo-Scholastic and transcendental approaches, faced the central question posed by modernity, the question of time and of the future in particular. In the following years, Metz's political theology has increasingly focused on memory within a more problematic viewpoint of human progress presented by recent reflections on the dialectic of Enlightenment from the authors of the Frankfurt School.

Let us leave aside his transcendental works: analysing the two theoretical steps that articulate Metz's proposal of a New Political Theology is a more useful starting point.

The perspective outlined in *Theology of the World* is based on the crucial hypothesis that the main character of the modern age, unlike the previous one, is the perception of the openness of our future experience on both an individual and collective level. To take Reinhardt Koselleck's historiographical categories: the tension between the 'space of experience' and the 'horizon of expectation', the *Spannung* situated around the 1750s, inverts in favour of the latter (Koselleck 2004: 255–275). According to Koselleck, modern culture is exactly characterised by this new perception of temporality where the future has primacy over the past and this, in Metz's view, is one of the central aspects of secularisation in general (Metz 1973: 84–85).

Metz argues that reflecting on these characteristics of modernity is necessary in order to elaborate theological knowledge capable of resisting the modern critique of religion and in particular the Marxist critique which considers Christianity unable to satisfy future demands. Therefore, in the Marxist view the liquidation of religion as superstructure is committed to material and cultural progress situated in the future (Metz 1973: 85–86). Consequently, a theology that wishes to take on this challenge from modernity, and in particular from the Enlightenment, must deal with the problem of the future primarily conceived as a political problem because it concerns the general relationship between the Church and the world. By developing some implications of the Second Vatican, Metz wonders if the Church ought to be thought of as a different entity or, conversely, if it is part of this world and its complex dynamics.

Metz refuses a dualistic model of the Augustinian matrix which sees modernity in terms of decadence, as with Ratzinger, because he believes that this way of thinking jeopardises the real meaning of the event of Incarnation. Those who refuse the process of secularisation risk not comprehending that 'the "spirit" of Christianity is permanently embedded in the "flesh" of world history and must maintain and prove itself in the irreversible course of the latter' (Metz 1973: 16).

The role of the Church in the history of mankind should be to exercise a critique of all the tendencies and situations that prevent a real humanization of the world: 'An eschatologically oriented theology must place itself in communication with the prevailing political, social and technical utopias and with the contemporary maturing promises of a universal peace and justice' (Metz 1973: 96)

With respect to this first systematic formulation of theology as social criticism, Metz later develops more radically his approach, confronting the post-Enlightenment demands of Marxism, in particular dialoguing with the authors of the Frankfurt School. If in *Theology of the World* his most remarkable theoretical reference was to the unorthodox Marxism of Ernest Bloch which focused on the category of future, in the 1970s Metz's interlocutors were above all W. Benjamin and T. W. Adorno (cf. Bloch 2000). In respect to his previous work, for Metz the role of theology becomes more explicitly that of 'working through the Enlightenment itself, a radical enlightening of the Enlightenment, a political-theological Enlightenment concerning the real processes at work in modernity' (Metz 2007: 43)

Like Ratzinger, but with different aims and attitudes, Metz tries to catch the contradictions of Western post-Enlightenment history. On one hand, the post-Enlightenment legacy of Marxism subverts the pretence of "pure" human knowledge, knowledge that independently influences praxis. As a consequence, by definitively accepting its 'impure' character, theology must become political theology (Metz 2007: 53–54). But, on the other hand, Metz also criticises a particular way of interpreting the Enlightenment, and he argues that the theological point of view could shine a light in helping to overcome it.

Therefore, rethinking Enlightenment absolutely does not mean possibly refusing it, that is, persisting with theology as though it had never happened. The crucial turning point on which Metz reflects from the 1970s onwards thus becomes the vision of the historical evolution that triumphs in the post-Enlightenment world and which can be attributed to two main models.

The first one is the logical-evolutionist model that comes from both the Enlightenment and bourgeois culture. It considers human rationality as a self-legitimating faculty able to drive the history of mankind and scientific progress. In this theoretical framework where the individual person is increasingly absorbed by the typical, impersonal and anonymous social processes of modern technological rationality, religion is pushed into the private sphere (Metz 1980: 34–35). This model, in Metz's view, has transformed Christianity into a bourgeois religion, a religion focused just on interiority. Until today the critique of this bourgeois model for the sake of recovering a more genuine Christianity represents one of the main themes of Metz's thought (Metz 2000: 147–159).

The second model is that represented by historical-dialectical materialism, which is characterised by the will to accept the liberation offered by the Enlightenment which, in the first model, would seem to have been lost under the input of technological rationality

Nevertheless, historical-dialectical materialism also comes down to a sort of anonymous evolutionary logic because it ends up defending a teleology of liberty situated inside matter or nature (Bloch 2000). Religion in this second model is considered in a Marxist lexicon as a superstructure the function of which would be conducted by emancipatory reason (Metz 1980: 3–7). From Metz's point of view, 'a history of emancipation without a history of redemption exposes the historical subject to new irrational pressures in the face of the concrete histories of suffering: either the pressure to suspend transcendentally his or her own historical responsibility, to live in continual enmity, or finally to negate him or herself as a subject' (Metz 1980: 112f).

Both of the models described above are figments of the Enlightenment, but their limit, as suggested by the Frankfurt School thinkers, is that the path towards emancipation "forgets" the losers and the dead, that it regards them as mere accidents on the way towards the goal of liberty. Theological reflection aims to call into question these two models in which, for Metz, the Dialectic of Enlightenment described by Horkheimer and Adorno realised itself.

Now I will try to demonstrate that the New Political Theology, created by Metz to defend a vision of religion that contrasts with this "Dialectic", proposes a means of recovering the original message of Christianity which does not involve mere contemplation or pure theory but rather concrete praxis: following Jesus Christ. First, from a linguistic and conceptual point of view, the expression 'New Political Theology' is not intended as a specific application of theological knowledge but rather as the core of theology itself: theological knowledge is 'political' *tout court*. This approach has two consequences. The first one involves rejecting the critiques of those scholars who claim that Metz's proposal is close to Carl Schmitt's political theology. This latter derives from the juridical field, while Metz's program is exclusively theological and incompatible with Schmitt's work (Metz 1992: 1261–1262). The second consequence is that theology, being practical reflection, must critically confront all the conceptual couples born with the Enlightenment: private/public, theory/praxis, religion/society, internal/external and, finally, mystical/political (Metz 1980: 49). Therefore, the programme of a New Political Theology evinces the intention to develop the Enlightenment legacy so that it gives a foundation to theological science that neither makes the mistakes of the Neo-Scholastic, transcendental and metaphysical approaches nor identifies the relationship between religion and society as the starting point of its analysis.

Even if it shares Ratzinger's critique of instrumental reason conceived as a legacy of the Dialectics of Enlightenment, Metz's proposal diverges from it through the diagnosis of the problem and the solutions it offers. While Ratzinger bases the decline of modernity on the nominalistic turn that happened at the end of the Middle Ages and wishes to return to Augustinian metaphysical reason, Metz considers nominalism differently and insists on recovering the Jewish legacy lost in the Western Christian tradition. Metz interprets nominalism in a more articulate way compared both to Ratzinger and to typical conservative theology

Ockham's nominalistic turn did not really mean to cause problems to human rationality by contrasting it with the absolute voluntarism of God. Rather, rethinking reason involved overturning the relationship between the general and the particular. In other words, Nominalism opened the path to modern subjectivity as opposed to the primacy of metaphysical generalities. It thus recovered an authentic requirement of Biblical tradition as described in the Book of Job: Job's meaningless suffering is the symbol of a discourse the Greek metaphysical paradigm adopted by Christian theology finds difficult to accept (Metz, 2000: 147–159).

Metz also thinks that today, together with this first nominalist turn, theology has to take charge of a second one arising from two topics emerging in the twentieth century which it must fully consider in order to reconfigure the role of the Church in the world: the Auschwitz tragedy and cultural and religious pluralism. Both of these elements oppose their singularity to the abstract primacy of the general in the metaphysical tradition of Western theology. To respond to these challenges, Metz argues that it is necessary to reappraise the Judaic relationship with time which, in the metaphysical approach of Christian theological and philosophical thought, tends to disappear in favour of the primacy of contemplation (Metz, 2000: 147–150).

For Metz, the refusal by human reason to recognise its constitutive relation with memory originates in the Dialectics of Enlightenment: that is the anamnestic rationality he wishes to recover. It represents 'the dowry of the Jewish spirit' from which metaphysical Christianity has progressively been distancing itself (Metz and Wiesel 1999: 15). From his point of view, the loss of the Judaic legacy arises ultimately from the centrality accorded to the Greek concept of Λόγος within Christian theology. Its neglect of the question of time, an historical characteristic of Greek metaphysics, would have made it lose the original, temporal character of the human relationship with God that permeates the Judaic tradition (Metz, 1996: 3–7).

Confirming the connection between Reason and Memory were two main factors: the tragedy of Auschwitz already mentioned and the theoretical dialogue with Benjamin and Adorno, that is, with those who made negativity the starting point of their intellectual task (Metz and Wiesel 1999: 23–24). The memory Metz refers to is not a general recollection but rather the precise memory of past innocent suffering. Influenced on this point by Benjamin, Metz thinks he has found a way to criticise the Enlightenment's vision of reason but without losing its positive legacy, that is the priority of praxis (Ruz et al. 2009: 397–420). His proposal assumes the 'suffering of others' as the universal moral authority which must guide our praxis on both a political and social level.

The limit of Enlightenment reason was its breaking its constitutive link with memory by falling again into myth, as shown by Horkheimer and Adorno. Therefore, all the procedural and deliberative forms of rationality elaborated by contemporary philosophers suffer from a fundamental prejudice coming from the Enlightenment: the prejudice against memory (Metz 1989: 733–738). This prejudice arises from the fact that memory or recollection was always perceived with reference to the concept of "tradition", which often produced conflicts or even arguments for refusing the potentiality of critical Enlightenment reason (Habermas 1971: 45–56). Being well aware of the Enlightenment's prejudices against the common notion of memory, Metz proposes considering a particular form of it, the memory of suffering or *memoria passionis*.

To avoid misunderstandings it is necessary to stress that Metz does not mean just the memory of one's own, personal suffering because it risks inciting both conflict and the spirit of revenge. Rather Metz means the 'suffering of others', the memory of which has to shape the public use of our reason. Here Metz's reference to Adorno is explicit: 'The need to lend a voice to suffering is a condition of all truth' (Adorno 2004:17). That's why the memory Metz speaks about is 'Dangerous Memory' (Metz 1989a: 733–738). Consequently, the history of mankind must be conceived as a history of passion in the sense that truth comes to light in the negative form of suffering. On this Enlightenment as critique must base itself even in the pluralistic, present age. Indeed, human suffering, as a critical-negative moment, seems to be the only way of overcoming contemporary pluralism for a universalism that undoubtedly avoids all the proceduralist and deliberative visions of human reason (Metz 1989a: 733–738; Ashley 1998: 27–58).

Conclusion

The contemporary political philosophy that has wished to pursue the Enlightenment project of emancipation has defended a proceduralist or deliberative form of human rationality. So, scholars like Habermas or Rawls have connected the concept of truth to consensus or discourse. As recent developments of global capitalism have shown, these forms of rationality suffer from a certain weakness when containing the pressures of strategic-instrumental rationality, and Habermas, as I mentioned above, is among those who have, partially, recognised this possibly constitutive inadequacy of formal rationality, even in its communicative form.

What contribution could Christianity make in increasing critical reflection upon the path of modernity having taken cognizance of the Dialectics of Enlightenment? After discussing Ratzinger's and Metz's propositions, I now intend to show that the two theological models they presuppose have quite different practical consequences.

If, in Ratzinger's view, the way to heal the Dialectics of Enlightenment is to go back to a classical, Augustinian conception in which reason has opened itself to faith, then the role of religion and the Catholic Church become evident: the Church, as Christ's mystical body, is separated from and higher than the world because it is the guardian of a Truth we have to recognise. In this approach, the reference to praxis is secondary because reason's work is of a contemplative nature: the Truth ought to be just welcomed!

The risk of Ratzinger's approach is that, in a historical age characterised by what John Rawls calls the 'fact of pluralism', such a vision of the relationship between Church and world could devalue both modernity and democracy if they did not conform to the Truth announced by the Church (Rawls 1971: XIV). As a matter of fact, the general tendency of the Catholic Church in the last thirty years was characterised by both John Paul II's severe judgements on democracy and Benedict XVI's efforts against the danger of relativism (John Paul II, 1993, § 101; Ratzinger/Benedict XVI 2007: 229). The attitude shown by these two popes towards issues like pluralism, the nature of liberty, and the autonomy of modernity can be explained by their basically classical, metaphysical approach. But this approach runs into always more difficulties in defending Christianity in a world where the old categories of centre/periphery, liberty/authority, Truth/pluralism no longer offer any resistance, whether inside or outside the Church. The model of a centralist, hierarchical and Euro-centric Church promoted by John Paul II and Benedict XVI also comes significantly from the theological and philosophical model I described in the first section.

With Metz's New Political Theology it is possible to find, at least this is my thesis, some elements that possibly avoid the risks of the previous model. First, the intention to move within modernity and recognise the primacy of praxis over theory imposes a vision of religion quite different from the first model. Attending to the suffering of the Other becomes the prior duty of Christian praxis, which is directly modeled on Christ's praxis. From the first formulations of a New Political Theology, Metz has stressed the public character of Christ's care for the weak, the suffering and the socially excluded. So conceived, religion is not something that can only be lived privately (as in the case of bourgeois religion) but has necessarily a public function.

A further, related aspect concerns inter-religious dialogue which, in Metz's view, can be fruitful just by being based on the care all the great religions traditionally show towards the immensity of suffering. A serious reflection on the social pathologies imposed on us by instrumental reason within the present process of globalisation can just through inter-religious dialogue find the room and normative resources interested in bringing the *Humanum* back to the centre (Metz 1989b: 337–342).

To summarise: today both the individual Christian and the Church ought to see their task as pleading for human suffering whatever form it assumes. This task thus maintains a critical attitude towards myth, especially the myth of science and of the market, into which modernity has relapsed. If the Church's mission is to announce the message Christ gave it, then some of Metz's proposals can surely help to imagine a Church which is not 'against' the world but rather takes charge of it with all its contradictions and crises.

References

Adorno, T. W. 2004. *Negative Dialectics*. London and New York: Routledge.
Ashley, J. M. 1998. *Interruptions: Mysticism, Politics, and Theology in the Work of Johann Baptist Metz*. Notre Dame: Notre Dame University Press.

Bloch, E. 2000. *The Spirit of Utopia*. Stanford: Stanford University Press.
Böckenförde, E.-W. 1991. *State, Society, and Liberty: Studies in Political Theory and Constitutional Law*. New York: Berg.
Corkery, J. 2009. *Joseph Ratzinger's Theological Ideas: Wise Cautions & Legitimate Hopes*. New York: Paulist Press.
Eggemeir, M.T. 2012. 'A Post-Secular and Modernity? Jürgen Habermas, Joseph Ratzinger, and Johann Baptist Metz on Religion, Reason, and Politics'. *Heythrop Journal*, 53 (3): 453–466.
Ferrone, V. 2013. *Lo strano Illuminismo di Joseph Ratzinger. Chiesa, modernità e diritti dell'uomo*. Roma/Bari: Laterza.
Habermas, J. 1971. Zu Gadamers 'Wahrheit und Methode', in *Hermeneutik und Ideologieskritik*, edited by K. A. Otto. Frankfurt a. M: Suhrkamp, pp. 45–56.
—. 1984. *The Theory of Communicative Action: Reason and the Rationalization of Society*. Boston: Beacon Press.
—. 1996. *Between Facts and Norms: Contribution to a Discourse Theory of Law and Democracy*. Boston: MIT Press.
—. 2008. *Between Naturalism and Religion*. Malden, MA: Polity Press.
—. 2011. 'The "Political": The Rational Meaning of a Questionable Inheritance of Political Theology', in Butler, J. and Habermas, J. et al. *The Power of Religion in the Public Sphere*. New York: Columbia University Press, pp. 5–33.
Habermas, J. and Ratzinger, J. 2006. *Dialectics of Secularization*. San Francisco: Ignatius.
Horkheimer, M. and Adorno T. W. 2002. *Dialectics of Enlightenment*. Stanford: Stanford University Press.
John Paul II. 1993. *Veritatis splendor*, http://w2.vatican.va/content/john-paul-ii/en/encyclicals/documents/hf_jp-ii_enc_06081993_veritatis-splendor.html (accessed 15 April 2015).
—. (1998) *Fides et Ratio*, http://w2.vatican.va/content/john-paul-ii/en/encyclicals/documents/hf_jp-ii_enc_14091998_fides-et-ratio.html (accessed 15 April 2015).
Kant, I. 1996. 'An Answer to the Question: What Is Enlightenment?,' in *Practical Philosophy*, edited by M. J. Gregor, introduction by A. W. Wood. Cambridge: Cambridge University Press, pp. 11–22.
Koselleck, R. 2004. '"Space of Experience" and "Horizon of Expectation": Two Historical Categories', in *Futures Past: On the Semantics of Historical Time*. New York: Columbia University Press, pp. 255–275.
Marsden, J. 2012. 'The Political Theology of Johann Baptist Metz', *Heythrop Journal* 53(3): 440–452.
Metz, J. B. 1962. *Christliche Anthropozentrik. Über Denkformen des Thomas von Aquin*. München: Kösel.
—. 1973. *Theology of the World*, translated by W. Glen-Doepel, New York: Herder and Herder.
—. 1980. *Jenseits bürgerlicher Religion: Reden über die Zukunft des Christentums*. Mainz/München: Kaiser.
—. 1989a. 'Anamnetische Vernunft', in *Zwischenbetrachtungen im Prozeß der Aufklärung. Festschrift Jürgen Habermas*, edited by A. Honneth et al. Frankfurt: Suhrkamp, pp. 733–738.
—. 1989b. 'Vielfalt: Probleme und Perspektiven der Inkulturation', *Concilium* 25: 337–342.
—. 1996. 'Im Eingedenken fremden Leids. Zu einer Basiskategorie christlicher Gottesrede', in *Gottesrede*, edited by J. B. Metz et al. Münster: LIT.
—. 2000. 'Gott und Zeit: Theologie und Metaphysik und den Grenzen der Moderne', in *Stimmen der Zeit 125*: 147–159.
—. 2007. *Faith in History and Society: Toward a Practical Fundamental Theology*. New York: Paulist Press.

Metz, J. B. and Kroh, W. 1992. 'Politische Theologie', in *Evangelisches Kirchenlexicon III*, Göttingen: Vandenhöck & Ruprecht, pp. 1261–1265.
Metz, J. B. and Wiesel, E. 1999. *Hope against Hope: Johann Baptist Metz and Elie Wiesel Speak Out on the Holocaust*, translated by J. M. Ashley. New York: Paulist Press.
Miccoli, G. 2011. *La Chiesa dell'anticoncilio. I tradizionalisti alla riconquista di Roma*. Roma, Bari: Laterza.
Milbank, J. 1991. 'Post-Modern Critical Augustinianism: A Short Summa in Forty-Two Responses to Unasked Questions', *Modern Theology* 7(3): 311–333.
Ratzinger, J. 1984. *Das neue Volk Gottes: Entwürfe zur Ekklesiologie*. Dussedorlf: Patmos-Verlag.
—. 1998. *Church, Ecumenism and Politics: New Essays in Ecclesiology*, translated by R. Nowell. New York: Crossroad.
—. 2004. *Truth and Tolerance: Christian Belief and World Religions*. San Francisco: Ignatius.
Ratzinger J. / Benedict XVI. 2005. *Address of His Holiness Benedict XVI to the Roman Curia offering Them His Christmas Greetings*, http://www.vatican.va/holy_father/benedict_xvi/speeches/2005/december/documents/hf_ben_xvi_spe_20051222_roman-curia_en.html (accessed 28 May 2014).
—. 2006. *Faith, Reason and the University Memories and Reflections*, http://www.vatican.va/holy_father/benedict_xvi/speeches/2006/september/documents/hf_ben_xvi_spe_20060912_university-regensburg_en.html (accessed 1 May 2014).
—. 2007. *The Essential Pope Benedict XVI: His Central Writings and Speeches*, edited by J. F. Thornton and S. B. Varenne. New York: Harper Collins.
Ratzinger, J. and Messori, V. 1987. *The Ratzinger Report: An Exclusive Interview on the State of the Church*, translated by S. Attanasio and G. Harrison. San Francisco: Ignatius.
Rawls, J. 1971. *A Theory of Justice*. Cambridge, MA: Harvard University Press.
—. 1993. *Political Liberalism*. New York: Columbia University Press.
—. 1997. 'The Idea of Public Reason Revisited', *Chicago Law Review* 64(3): 765–807.
Rowland, T. 2008. *Ratzinger's Faith: The Theology of Pope Benedict XVI*. Oxford: Oxford University Press.
Ruz, M. O. et al. 2008. 'Razón anamnética, sufrimiento ajeno y teodicea.: Claves de lectura, logros y límites de la obra de Johann Baptist Metz', *Teología y Vida 49*: 575–603.
—. 2009. 'La fuerza subversiva del sufrimiento evocado: Recepción de Walter Benjamin en la teología de Johann Baptist Metz', in *Teología* XVLI: 397–420.
Schreiter, R. 2003. 'La teologia postmoderna e oltre in una Chiesa mondiale', in *Prospettive teologiche per il XXI secolo*, edited by R. Gibellini. Brescia: Queriniana, pp. 373–388.
Skinner, Q. 2002. 'A Third Concept of Liberty', *Proceedings of British Academy 117*: 237–268.
Taylor, C. 2007. *The Secular Age*. Cambridge, MA: Harvard University Press.

6
THE ENLIGHTENMENT LEGACY AND EUROPEAN IDENTITY: REFLECTIONS ON THE CARTOON CONTROVERSY

Carsten Meiner

At the end of the twentieth century the Enlightenment and some of its key concepts enjoyed a return in European intellectual debates, in political life, in the media and also in philosophical contexts. Many were, of course, the reasons that motivated this return as they were used to describe and understand the consequences of many diverse and new European phenomena: the dangers of a globalised world threatening European identity, financial crises, the pressure of religious minorities, what came to be called post-secular Europe. They were also used as a rational precaution for the future after the postmodernist paradigm and its possible irrationalism, to avoid the atrocities of the European wars of the twentieth century, and basically as something that still could unite Europe. It seemed as though a will to find a way back to European values and identity suddenly had gathered force after a century of deceptions and atrocities and that this road to identity ended in the Enlightenment. European identity was delimited by way of necessary, because shared, Enlightenment categories, values, and ideals such as rationality, liberty, equality, toleration, etc. Despite what some rightfully would call the fluffiness of such big-picture descriptions of the return of the Enlightenment, these explanations seem to hold some sort of truth, relative as it may be. What should be noted is that the return of the Enlightenment was not primarily led by eighteenth-century specialists but by a series of prominent thinkers and intellectuals whom one would not readily label Enlightenment-oriented. In *Europe – An Unfinished Adventure* (2004) Zygmunt Bauman argues by way of Kantian cosmopolitanism in favour of the values of universality that have come to define Europeanism. In *L'Esprit des Lumières* (2006) Tzvetan Todorov argues that after the end of utopias and grand narratives the values of the Enlightenment are the only ones to build on. In his diary-like *Lumières Aveuglantes* (2006) Régis Debray discusses the legacy of the Enlightenment and stresses that the eighteenth century, especially in dire times, seems to hold a place of unquestionable and therefore uninteresting cultural and political worth:

'you don't like the Enlightenment? Interesting, neither did Goebbels' (Debray 2006: 13). Debray, however, also claims the real Enlightenment legacy is formal: criticising the historical concepts of the Enlightenment is a gesture emanating right out of the very same period. One could mention other prominent thinkers who have re-used Enlightenment concepts and Enlightenment "stands" in their writings at the turn of the twenty-first century. Ulrich Beck elaborately uses the Enlightenment in his sociological development of a "second modernity" (Beck 1991); in 2000 Pierre Bourdieu operated a violent critique of neo-capitalism significantly entitled 'Für eine neue Aufklärung' (Bourdieu 2010); and yet other texts by such different thinkers as Neil Postman (1999), Bassam Tibi (1998), Richard Rorty (2003) and Anthony Pagden (2013) explicitly invoke the importance of the Enlightenment legacy and (an evaluative consolidation of) its concepts for twenty-first-century Europe. Added to this series of prominent intellectuals should be the series of eighteenth-century specialists like, for instance, Daniel Gordon (2001), Stephen Eric Bronner (2004), Kevin L. Cope and Rüdiger Ahrens (Cope and Ahrens 2002), who also have published books on the relevance of the eighteenth century for philosophy, politics and sociology in the twenty-first century.

More explanatory light is shed on this 'return of the Enlightenment' when it is considered in relation to specific political contexts and "cases" and not just as reactions to structural, financial, demographic and religious changes with their subsequent intellectual discomfort. The first decade of the new millennium was marked by a series of events and tragedies that all in different ways challenged and maybe also altered European identity: terrorist actions in Madrid and London, the extraordinary and irregular rendition of ghost detainees, the Islamic scarf controversy, the problem of abortion in catholic Europe, renewed focus on "women's rights", the killings of Theo van Gogh and Pim Fortuyn in the Netherlands and finally the cartoon controversy in Denmark, then in France, and later elsewhere in Europe.

The interesting thing in our context about all these events and dramas is less their causes than the rhetorical and intellectual analysis and critique that they generated. In their ensuing interventions many intellectuals, journalists and politicians had in fact explicit recourse to the Enlightenment and to what is normally deemed its weightiest concepts and values – the right to one's own body, freedom of expression, separation of church and state, religious tolerance – but terms such as "cultural progress" or "negligence of the separation of powers" also came to the fore. To what extent these are actually Enlightenment concepts, and, if so, what phenomena they allow us to identify and coordinate, is not the question right now. What should be stressed is the fact that they were called upon with explicit reference to the Enlightenment and, together with the intellectual and academic recourse to the Enlightenment just described, a new Enlightenment discourse seemed to have been born. There was an apparent need for the legitimacy of the Enlightenment in these serious issues. But that need for explaining and for legitimate self-positioning showed not only a move beyond postmodernism, a reasonable anti-capitalist or pro-third-world stance, but also, more interestingly, that the Enlightenment made its return in a way both manifest and problematic:

manifest because of its frequency as it was invoked in and during all the events mentioned before; problematic because it came to legitimise quite different and even contradictory points of view. If the intellectual and political return of the Enlightenment thus seems to be a discursive fact, a problem was implied in this return: the Enlightenment was used to legitimise not only different kinds of intellectual positions and claims, but also positions and stands in contradiction with each other. The return of the Enlightenment was as manifest as it was problematic: these positions relativised each other, and maybe they even invalidated each other or at least the legitimacy of the return of the Enlightenment that their claims were founded upon. The Enlightenment might have been called upon in the twenty-first century, it seems, as a rational way of regaining composure after postmodernism's blind alleys and neo-capitalism's dead ends, as a response to the financial crisis, to religious fanatics or to cultural oppression, but also because Europe today experiences problems analogous to those that determined the very thought patterns of, for instance, Voltaire, Kant or Hume.

In what follows I shall exemplify this problematic return of the Enlightenment through a reading of what came to be known as the "cartoon controversy" in 2005 in Denmark and later in most of the Western world. During this controversy concepts such as "liberty of expression" and "tolerance" were invoked as Enlightenment concepts and, as such, impossible to ignore when sorting out the legitimacy, or lack of it, in publishing satirical cartoons. These concepts and their legitimacy, however, also clashed and seemed to formally exclude each other in the eyes of the participants in the controversy, even if they agreed that they clearly were a precious heritage from the Enlightenment. As the background to this analysis, I shall set forth a structural hypothesis about the legacy of the Enlightenment and its role in understanding problems pertaining to questions of European identity in the twenty-first century. More precisely, I shall conclude from this reading that the Enlightenment legacy is one, not simply of values, concepts and institutions but rather of tensions, problems and contradictions and I shall propose a way of exploring this claim methodologically and theoretically.

The cartoon controversy

If one wishes to investigate the reasons for the return of the Enlightenment by paying special attention to a particular case, "the cartoon controversy", it is of course necessary to describe it in some detail.

In September 2005, the Danish newspaper *Jyllands-Posten* published 12 editorial cartoons representing the Prophet Mohammed in order to explore the actual state of the freedom of expression and the possible self-censorship relative to the depiction of Mohammed. The editor of culture at the newspaper, Flemming Rose, wrote in his editorial: 'Modern secular society is rejected by some Muslims. They demand a special position, insisting on special consideration of their own religious feelings'. He stated that this position was 'incompatible with contemporary democracy and freedom of speech', and that one had to be 'ready to put up with insults, mockery and ridicule'. He conceded that it was 'not always attractive and nice to look at' and that religious feelings should not 'be made fun of at any price'. But what he feared most was being on 'a slippery slope where no-one can tell how the self-censorship will end'. For this reason *Jyllands-Posten* had 'invited members of the Danish editorial cartoonists union to draw Muhammad as they see him' (Engelbrecht Larsen and Seidenfaden 2006: 322). Shortly after the publication of the controversial issue of the newspaper, ambassadors from 11 Muslim countries sent a letter to the Danish Prime Minister of Denmark at the time, Anders Fogh Rasmussen, in which they asked him to distance himself from the cartoons, a possibility he firmly rejected. A couple of days later more than 3,000 persons demonstrated peacefully in Copenhagen against the cartoons and a number of Muslim organisations filed a complaint with the Danish police, claiming that *Jyllands-Posten* had committed an offence under sections 140 and 266b of the Danish Criminal Code. Section 140 of the Danish Criminal Code provides that any person who, in public, mocks or scorns the religious doctrines or acts of worship of any lawfully existing religious community in this country shall be liable to imprisonment for any term not exceeding four months. Under section 266 of the Danish Criminal Code any person who, publicly or with the intention of wider dissemination, makes a statement or imparts other information by which a group of people are threatened, scorned or degraded on account of their race, colour, national or ethnic origin, religion or sexual inclination shall be liable to a fine or to imprisonment for any term not exceeding two years. On the background of these formulations the complaint of the Muslim organisations was understandable, but as both of these legal sections comprise limits to the right to freedom of expression (it is formulated in the Danish constitution and also in the European Convention on Human rights), they have always been interpreted narrowly. The Regional Public Prosecutor had already decided that there was no foundation for criminal proceedings against the newspaper in January 2006 and this was confirmed by Director of Public Prosecution on 15 March 2006. The Director's decision was based on the fact that informal and unswerving debate was and is usual in Denmark and that offensive expressions are widely accepted also concerning religious matters. Also, drawings of Mohammed have always existed, while the religious writings of Islam contain an absolute and clear prohibition against depiction of the prophet, and so the cartoons could not be said to be contrary to religious doctrines or acts of worship. The director also concluded that none of the drawings could be said to refer to Muslims in general, which was what was required to instigate criminal proceedings. If the Muslim organisations which had filed the complaint lost the case, they did a kind of rehabilitation. The Director of Public Prosecution distanced himself from the passage in the editorial in *Jyllands-Posten*, where Flemming Rose had stated that 'it is incompatible with the right to freedom of expression to demand special consideration for religious feelings [. . .] one has to be ready to put up with scorn, mockery and ridicule' (Engelbrecht Larsen and Seidenfaden 2006: 322). In a concluding remark the Director underlined that if there was no basis for criminal action against the newspaper there were indeed restrictions to the right to freedom of expression – also other ones than the ones invoked by the Muslim organisations and that consequently the right to express opinions on religious matters in Denmark is not unlimited.

The Danish Prime Minister had also refused to meet the ambassadors, a fact that many commentators saw as a serious diplomatic *faux-pas* on his part. A delegation of Danish Imams travelled to Egypt to meet and inform representatives of the Arab League and the Egyptian authorities of the situation, thereby making another *faux-pas*, that of having included a picture of the Prophet for the authorities which came not from *Jyllands-Posten* but from a pig-contest in Normandy, France. They also demanded international denunciation of the cartoons, some of which were at the time being printed in Norwegian, French, German and Bosnian papers. As the matter received extensive media attention in many Islamic countries, Muslims held demonstrations across the world in February 2006, some of which spiralled into violence resulting in more than 200 reported deaths, attacks on a number of Danish and other European diplomatic missions, on churches and Christians, and a major international boycott. The cartoon controversy was brought before the UN by Islamic organisations (I shall return to the documents later), and a Danish diplomatic delegation was eventually well received in Egypt.

Return of the Enlightenment as discourse

It is difficult to say when or if the controversy stopped. If the immediate political pressure was dealt with quite early on in the process, many events were to follow which showed that the controversy was far from over. One of the cartoonists, Kurt Westergaard, who had depicted Muhammed with a bomb in his turban, was in 2010 attacked with an axe in his home by a Somali fanatic; and Chechnyan-Belgian terrorist Lors Doukaiev planned the same year to bomb the seat of *Jyllands-Posten* but was injured in his hotel before he got to carry out the plan. Lines could be drawn from these events right up to the attacks in Paris in January 2015 and in Copenhagen in February the same year. Many more incidents and diplomatic exchanges could be cited, but the most interesting aspect in our context to consider is the specific way in which the the cartoons were discussed in the Danish and European media and in political or intellectual debates. What I would like to stress in this account of the controversy is thus neither the clash between Danish and Muslim authorities nor the clash between two "cultures" or civilisations. Instead, I would like to draw attention to the double *European* reaction to the cartoons and in this way highlight a slight twist in the conceptual framework of the debate. Those in favour of the cartoons had recourse to the notion of "liberty of expression", deeming the publication necessary as an experiment in self-censorship and making the possible provocation of a religious and cultural minority secondary. If the cartoons were an experiment in self-censorship, it was because it was necessary to clarify the cartoonists' will to publish what could be considered dangerous material as part of a larger project, that of protecting journalistic and artistic value number one: liberty of speech. In fact it was interesting to notice that "liberty of speech" and "freedom of expression" were notions invoked again and again in the debate but that they did not seem to suffice in themselves when met by their opponents with charges either of blasphemy or of fanatical devotion, a stupid 'duty' of expression, according to some detractors. Against such charges many Danish pro-cartoon commentators and intellectuals took another argumentative step based on the historical fact that freedom of expression was the crown in the Enlightenment legacy. As such it was indispensable for modern European society and impossible to dismiss regardless of the degree of provocation that any utterance may have. Liberty of speech was justified as the cornerstone of "our" Enlightenment heritage and so no further arguments seemed necessary to sustain the point of the necessity of the cartoon experiment. However necessary this point might be, it would probably not be very academically interesting had it not been for the fact that the opponents of the publication of the cartoons and thus the opponents of the "liberty of speech stand" actually made up a similar set of arguments: first the cartoons were deemed childish from a commonsense point of view; then they were considered belligerent and dangerous; then the cartoons were said to constitute a moral violation of the notion of religious and cultural tolerance; and lastly this concept of tolerance was referred to as the principal Enlightenment value. Tolerance is the cornerstone of our Enlightenment legacy and it is only historical ignorance that keeps us from understanding the real damage that the cartoons did or could have occasioned. At times justifying their claim by way of Locke and Voltaire, the opponents to the cartoons managed by the same token to distance themselves from any kind of postmodernist or constructivist "multiculturalism" that was much criticised in Denmark at the time. These two factions, whose members were mixed up in surprising political constellations, exchanged an infinite series of blows both on the intellectual and the political scene and only agreed on one thing: justification by reference to the Enlightenment.

The cartoon controversy is exemplary because of the clear-cut antagonistic and confrontational character of the Enlightenment concepts it invoked. An easy way to cut through this paradox would be to claim that the two adversaries used the concept of the Enlightenment only in an insubstantial way, for political purposes in the Danish public sphere; the controversy on the Enlightenment went no further than the rhetorical level. Of course political agendas governed the legitimatisation of both camps' claim to the Enlightenment but the paradox does not entirely go away by stressing the rhetorical aspects of either of the factions' interventions. The publication of the cartoons elsewhere in the world triggered the same recourse to the Enlightenment as in Denmark. The reactions in France to the publication of the cartoons in the satirical weekly *Charlie Hebdo* (Charlie Hebdo: 2006) triggered the same paradoxical reactions; 'Au secours, Voltaire', *France Soir* famously entitled a front page in 2006 showing pictures of Muslims burning Danish flags (France Soir: 2006). On the other hand several politicians, even as they endorsed liberty of speech, demanded that any journalist think twice before publishing provocative material. After the publication in *Charlie Hebdo* on 18 September 2012 (Charlie Hebdo: 2012) of new caricatures, Prime Minister Jean-Marc Ayrault stated in an official communiqué: 'that the freedom of expression is one of the fundamental principles of our Republic', and also that 'the values of tolerance and respect for religious convictions, is at the heart of our Republican pact. And this is why, in the current context, the Prime Minister is keen to express his disapproval of any excesses. He urges everyone to demonstrate a spirit of responsibility'(Ayrault 2012). And more interestingly, other dramatic or infamous events, the invasion of Iraq for instance, were surrounded by the same kind of justification by the Enlightenment. For instance, the invasion of Iraq and the critique of the invasion were both largely justified by the same ideological-rhetorical paradox. In ths connection let us give two quotations whose clash is as eloquent as it is spectacular: Victor Davis Hanson, in the *Wall Street Journal* on 26 November 2006 claimed: 'We are not fighting for George Bush or Wal-Mart alone, but also for the very notion of the Enlightenment' (Hanson 2006); whereas Ken Sanders, in *The Dissident Voice* on 25 March 2005, on the contrary claims: 'The dimming of the Enlightenment ideals upon which the U.S. was founded is spearheaded by Bush and the Republicans, who profess to be conservatives but behave like zealots' (Sanders 2005). The point to be made is simply that the paradox of the Enlightenment and its discursive rebirth cannot entirely be dismissed as a question of the rhetoric of Danish politics but could be said to have something general about it. It is a question of global discursive power just as much as local political rhetoric.

The best indication of this claim is the wording of the diplomatic documents that were integral to the controversy and, some have claimed, were constitutive of its escalation. In his editorial in *Jyllands-Posten* Flemming Rose had talked about 'democracy and freedom of speech' (Engelbrecht Larsen and Seidenfaden 2006: 322). As already mentioned, 11 ambassadors of Muslim countries consequently wrote to the Danish Prime Minister at the time, Anders Fogh Jensen, on 12 October 2005, and their choice of wording should be stressed: 'We strongly feel that casting aspersions on Islam as a religion and publishing demeaning caricatures of Holy Prophet Muhammed (PHUB) goes against the spirit of Danish values of tolerance and civil society. This is on the whole a very discriminatory tendency and does not bode well with the high human rights standards of Denmark [. . .]. The Danish press should not be allowed to abuse Islam in the name of democracy, freedom of expression and human rights, the values that we all share' (Engelbrecht Larsen and Seidenfaden 2006: 326). Liberty of expression and democracy are universal values but they should not be misused to explain or legitimise inappropriate and condescending behaviour; instead the Danish Press and the Danish prime minister should stick to the spirit of Danish values with its two cornerstones: tolerance and human rights. If this letter uses the notions of tolerance and human rights to reveal that the use of the notions of democracy and liberty of expression is just a moral cover for depreciative behaviour, the reply given by the Danish Prime minister to the 11 ambassadors of 12 October remains within the conceptual framework: 'Thank you very much for your letter. Danish society is based on respect for the freedom of expression, on religious tolerance and on equal standards for all religions. Freedom of expression is the very foundation of Danish democracy. Freedom of expression has a wide scope and the Danish government has no means of influencing the press' (Engelbrecht Larsen and Seidenfaden 2006: 329).

Many important eighteenth-century values pop up in this diplomatic epistolary exchange: equality, democracy, freedom of expression, tolerance, human rights. All these concepts are invoked as cornerstones in the Danish 'spirit' and 'system'. They are not explained but referred to as immutable and foundational values that are threatened but cannot be questioned. Tolerance is threatened by the liberty of expression which, in its secular and radical Western version, is at odds with a notion of tolerance, whose necessity is deemed important but inferior to that of the liberty of expression. The secretary-general of the organisation of the Islamic conference, Ekmeleddin Ihsanoglu, on 15 October, repeats to Anders Fogh Jensen the necessity of reconsidering the lack of tolerance in Danish society: 'We understand that the Muslim Danish citizens are considerably alarmed and feel threatened in the face of this ever increasing trend of intolerance and degrading discrimination against them, in which every Muslim is treated as a potential terrorist and criminal' (Engelbrecht Larsen and Seidenfaden 2006: 328).

The most eloquent version of this clash of values between tolerance and liberty of expression within Danish society is found in the Annex to the letter to the secretary-general of the UN from the permanent representative of Egypt, signed by the Egyptian Minister for Foreign Affairs Ahmed Aboul Gheit. After having described the events in Denmark the letter concludes:

'I am bringing this gross behaviour to your attention in the context of the provisions of General Assembly resolution 56/5, entitled "Global Agenda for Dialogue among Civilisations", which embodies the collective will of the international community and its determination to enhance and maintain this dialogue. Resolution 56/5 recalls "The United Nations Millenium Declaration of 8 September 2000", which considers, *inter alia*, that tolerance is one of the fundamental values essential to international relations in the twenty-first century [. . .]. We do not expect any country to take punitive or disciplinary action against a newspaper as we fully know that the right to the freedom of expression is incorporated in article 19 of the "Universal Declaration of Human Rights" and in article 19 of the "International Covenant on Civil and Political Rights", adopted by the General Assembly in 1948 and 1966, respectively' (Engelbrecht Larsen and Seidenfaden 2006: 330).

This letter clear-sightedly places the two values, tolerance and liberty of expression, in their historical-legislative context, a fact which also points directly to inherent problems in solving the matter juridically. The two values each have their history, their legitimacy, and role in modern Europe, which however does not mean that their actual, lived co-existence is given by the same token. On the contrary, the events in Denmark showed not only that both still are important in European self-understanding but also that they actually co-exist in a confrontational mode. Living side by side in peaceful solemnity in the charters and declarations of international institutions, it is the event which dramatises the problematic coexistence of the two values.

Isaiah Berlin and colliding values

In the light of what has been said about the cartoon controversy I would like to propose a series of reflections on the Enlightenment legacy. The eighteenth century is important not so much because we inherited important concepts and values (freedom, humanism, equality, democracy and so forth) from it; the Enlightenment is important because we inherited a series of conceptual "battlegrounds", tensions or conflicts from it. The relevance of the Enlightenment today is not one founded on a conceptual legacy according to which, e.g., democracy, liberty or toleration were handed over as untouchable and unalterable gems from the past. We inherited a series of conceptual problems, conflicts and tensions from the eighteenth century. The cartoon controversy is exemplary in that tolerance and liberty of speech here are articulated as both precious conceptual Enlightenment legacies *and* contradictory concepts. Yet other tensions or conflicts born or strongly thematized in the eighteenth century could be singled out. It suffices to think of the many designations the eighteenth century has been given to become aware of all the possible tensions lying herein: the century of reason, the century of sensibility, the century of happiness, the century of the modern state, the century of individualism, the century of rights, the century of progress, the century of cosmopolitanism, the century of contingency, the century of freedom, of luxury, commerce, universalism, cultural relativism etc. It is clear that these appellations form a cluster of partial truths which do, however, not form a coherent whole, with many of them being in direct opposition, some in productive exchange. The historical and discursive complexity of the eighteenth century has in some cases been the motor of significant scientific distinctions (a tension such as the one between reason and sensibility leading to the distinction between reason and aesthetics); the tension between eighteenth-century ideas of self-interest on the one hand and ideas of sympathy and solidarity on the other (as seen in Mandeville and Smith), *both* necessary for a reasonable and prosperous society; 'sympathy versus self-interest' is exactly a tension and not necessarily a contradiction or collision between incompatible concepts and theories. The same, but again differently, goes for the tension between state security and individual rights, the latter being universal and at the same time necessary to control and even survey in the name of public security. The discovery of cultural pluralism (Vico, Herder or Montesquieu) is, in an analogous way, in tension with the idea of cosmopolitanism or universal anthropology.

One way of conceptualising this problematic co-existence could be by way of Isaiah Berlin's idea of essential collisions of values. In a famous passage from the essay 'The Pursuit of the Ideal', Berlin states:

> What is clear is that values can clash – that is why civilisations are incompatible. They can be incompatible between cultures, or groups in the same culture, or between you and me. [. . .] Values may easily clash within the breast of a single individual; and it does not follow that, if they do, some must be true and others false. [. . .] Both liberty and equality are among the primary goals

pursued by human beings through many centuries; [. . .] total liberty of the powerful, the gifted, is not compatible with the rights to a decent existence of the weak and the less gifted. Equality may demand the restraint of the liberty of those who wish to dominate. [. . .] These collisions of values are of the essence of what they are and what we are (Berlin 1990: 12).

Berlin's notion of colliding values and his theory of pluralism are seminal to any thinking on paradoxical European identity. In our context of European Enlightenment it should furthermore be noted that many of his ideas on the pluralism of values come exactly from reading eighteenth-century thinkers such as Vico and Herder. However, and even if the essentialism of Berlin's value-pluralism has its historical dimension, three critical remarks could be made in terms of its eighteenth-century context: the power inscribed in values as hierarchically ordered, the possibility of a complex historical whole of several colliding values and finally the relation between colliding values and historical events. This will lead to a final reflection on the essence of the colliding values with which Berlin concluded. As Berlin often notices, it is clear that these tensions do not come out of the blue in the eighteenth century. They have a long pre-history, but it could be claimed that in the eighteenth century they move into a certain kind of conceptual equilibrium where the tensions between the two terms seem to be more or less of equal importance. Which is more important? Toleration or liberty of speech? Self-interest or sympathy? Individual rights or the state? Reason or sensibility? The two terms in the different relations liberate themselves from their hierarchical positions and are no longer subordinated one to the other. "State" had been dominating "individual right", "reason" had been dominating "sensibility" and "us" had been dominating "them"; but in the eighteenth century these relations are opened up and investigated. The cultures of Europe's Others are for the first time taken seriously on a relativist note not only in Vico and Herder but also in literary texts, e.g., in Montesquieu's *Lettres persanes* (1721) or in Voltaire's *L'Ingénu* (1767), and on a universal note in Diderot's *Supplément au voyage de Bougainville* (1772). And it is also in the eighteenth century that the relationship between state and individual becomes dynamic. The ruler is no longer god-given and synonymous with the state, since he, even if still absolute, is also enlightened by other realms than religious ones. The state governs and disciplines the individuals through institutions and laws but the individuals also begin to demand rights from the state with intellectual resistance and revolutions as "measures of retaliation". The possibility of changing hierarchies is stressed and feared by the authorities continously, just as the individual understands and appreciates the civil security provided by the state. It is a way of confronting, challenging or experimenting with European identity and if it is deemed fundamentally reasonable to do so, the analysis of conceptual and historical hierarchies is also fully legitimate in itself as intellectual endeavour.

European identity and the Enlightenment

Having claimed that this argument concerns European identity without having specified what is meant by 'European' and 'identity', it seems fruitful at this point to make a theoretical detour. Berlin's notion of colliding values can in fact be supplemented by some of the key thoughts and arguments from Edgar Morin's *Penser l'Europe*. It can be argued that the historical balancing of these relations, their dynamic and precarious equilibrium, does form not only a series of binary conceptual antagonisms but also *together* a *European continuum*. What is European identity? We know that the question is asked more and more frequently in relation to discussions on the financial crisis, drafts for a European constitution, national referenda, and also in connection with phenomena such as globalisation and migration. The frequency of the question as it is asked in the media, in academic circles and in politics has revealed a simple but fundamental problem: that it is extremely difficult to define a European identity. The difficulty is seen in the very long and diverse series of answers: *genetic* definitions have analysed the rise of Europe, often with focus on specific historical circumstances (Christianity, the Renaissance, industrialisation, nation-building); the *analytical* definitions, according to Anthony Pagden's introductory essay in *The Idea of Europe*, have tried inductively to define the fundamental elements such as institutions, language and geography which together form European identity (Pagden 2002: 1–32); the *essentialist* definitions have insisted on specific characteristics of a European identity and thus presupposed a sort of metaphysics of European identity (Bauman 2004); *pluralist* definitions stress that European identity should always be defined in the plural because of a fundamental regional heterogeneity (Goddard 1996). Other definitions emphasise *contingency* as the key element in the definition of European identity, as Europe was a product of more or less random historical and political events. In the wake of Benedict Anderson's influential and much debated *Imagined Communities* (Anderson 1983), some theories stress the *constructivist* dimension of European identity as mental representations of narratives, myths and symbols; still other *minimalist* or *negativist* theories define European identity with recourse to simple but irrefutable common denominators, for instance the lack of death penalty. Morin starts his book by asking what European identity is and answers in a way that ressembles Berlin's definition of colliding values: 'Si l'on croit dévoiler son attribut authentique, alors on occulte un attribut contraire, non moins européen. Ainsi, si l'Europe c'est le droit, c'est aussi la force; si c'est la démocratie, c'est aussi l'oppression; si c'est la spiritualité, c'est aussi la matérialité; si c'est la mesure, c'est aussi l'*ubris*, la démesure; si c'est la raison, c'est aussi le mythe, y compris à l'intérieur de l'idée de raison' ['If one thinks one is revealing its authentic attribute, one occludes a contrary attribute, no less European. In that way Europe is rights but also power, if it is democracy, it is also oppression; if it is spirituality, it is also materiality; if it is moderation, it is also *ubris*, excess; if it is reason it is also myth, including the myth inherent in the idea of reason'] (Morin 1987: 33).

So far not much distinguishes Berlin from Morin, especially when the latter programmatically states: 'Il s'agit de donc d'interroger l'idée d'Europe justement dans ce qu'elle a d'incertain, de flou, de contradictoire, pour essayer d'en dégager l'identité complexe' ['the idea of Europe should be interrogated especially in its uncertain, hazy and contradictory dimension in order to understand its complex identity'] (Morin 1987: 33). But when he sustains this claim he uses the example of Christianity, and a first difference between him and Berlin emerges. Christianity is of course an important component in European identity but it has nevertheless been caught in a series of conflicts: with Islam (Tours 732, the Crusades, the fall of Granada in 1492); with philosophy and science (Bruno, the scientific revolutions of the seventeenth century, Spinoza, the Enlightenment, Nietzsche); with capitalism, with the nation-state, with homosexuality and maybe first and foremost with itself: the Great Schism in 395, Arianism, Catharism, the Inquisition, the Reformation. The point is not simply that Christianity has had many conflicts but, as Morin points out, that Christianity had many conflicts on many levels of reality: with foreign states, with primitive peoples, with science, with academic insitutions, with art, and with doctrinal conflicts within itself. Christianity is one out of many examples which allows Morin to define European identity not only as a conflictual identity but as a *complex* conflictual identity. The complexity resides exactly in the idea of a European historical continuum of wars, doctrines, states, anthropology, values and concepts. These are of diverse levels of reality and they interact and amalgate, which is the reason why Morin, throughout his work, by the way, insists on the term "complexity", *in casu* the constitutive complexity of the tensions in European history, and not just on colliding values. The tensions can be separated only on an analytical level but in their historical evolution they have actually been influencing and determining each other. Their interdependancy could, following Morin's main thesis, in fact be called a specific European phenomenon because the tensions, taken separately, can be found in many other major cultures. Their constant social, military, intellectual and cultural connectedness forms what Morin calls a historical continuum which is uniquely European. A quick return to the cartoon controversy exemplifies this: when the concepts or values of tolerance and liberty of expression were invoked and hypostatized both State, individual, riots, security, Christianity, rights and pluralism were engaged. The fact that they depend on and influence each other is exactly what Morin calls Europe.

It is clear that "self-interest" should be identified on a whole other level than that of "democracy". The differentiation of the tensions and relations according to social, political, conceptual and psychological levels is of course necessary from the point of view of any historical analysis. Another way of looking at it, however, should be suggested in this context. One thing is to claim that some tensions are clearly historically born and transmitted and that others clearly belong to the inner life of human beings as concepts and values. How exactly the transmission and intermingling of the relations occurs between the different realms is extremely difficult to explain. This might, however, be so because some of the tensions belong to neither. If they rightly were born out of historical conflictual circumstances and then became values, one might argue that the tensions and conflicts also came to *naturalise* themselves as moulds of thought rather than as hypostatized values. They internalised themselves as shared and thus objective forms of "European" thinking. They became fundamental ways of perceiving and understanding reality, and if they are moulds and only formal, they were hypostatized because of their shared European naturalness. They are incomplete but fundamental forms of the condition of European thinking and sensibility. Tolerance and freedom of expression, state and individual, us and them, self-interest and sympathy are today not so much values as they are moulds or diagrams which structure our ideas of reality antagonistically. More than valuable referents, ideals, for "European" thinking, they have become structuring forms for the very way we perceive, identify and coordinate the problems of reality. The tensions could, in this version, be thought of as rudimentary forms of intelligibility, or historical schematisms, as Ernst Cassirer could have said: sorts of simple forms of intelligibility of the European mind. During the cartoon controversy, tolerance and liberty of expression came to be the way we Europeans reacted to the cartoons, the way we identified them as objects of thought and feeling. This claim calls for a final argumentative act: if the tensions naturalised and internalised themselves as moulds of thought, they also became partly empty abstractions. If tolerance and freedom of expression today are less objects of thought or clear-cut values than diagrams which structure our understanding of "European" reality antagonistically, they consequently need problematic events for them to be activated: they need problems for them to start thinking in order both to leave their status as partly empty abstractions and to prevent themselves from becoming simple ideals. They need events which articulate them or provoke them to activate their antagonism. Their mode of existence could be thought of not as real nor as conceptual but as virtual, being in need of a problem forcing them to think. The cartoons were actually 'designed' to do this: they forced a debate and animated a battleground anew; they actualized the internalised thought patterns in a new, complex European configuration.

Much can and has indeed been said about the cartoon controversy. But one thing which was important but less highlighted than other aspects of the conflict was the fact that they made us remember that once you take the Enlightenment legacy for granted, as a historically accomplished fact, a European achievement hypostatized as an ideal, you can be sure that you will be forced to think again. And that is probably the real Enlightenment legacy. Once you idealise the content of the Enlightenment you also lose it, because you refuse to think, because you refuse to admit that for thinking to be reasonable it has to question the very content transmitted, the relation between reality and the patterns of thought actualizing and identifying the very aspects of the reality that made us think in the first place. That might be the real legacy of the Enlightenment.

References

(Unless otherwise indicated, translations are my own.)
Anderson, B. 1983. *Imagined Communities*. London and New York: Verso.
Ayrault, J.-M. 2012. 'Freedom of Expression', Communiqué issued by M. Jean-Marc Ayrault, Prime Minister, on 18 September in Paris, http://www.ambafrance-uk.org/France-backs-freedom-of-expression (accessed 30 May 2015).
Bauman, Z. 2004. *Europe: An Unfinished Adventure*. Cambridge: Polity Press.
Beck, U. 1991. *Ecological Enlightenment: Essays on the Politics of the Risk Society*. Amherst, NY: Prometheus Books.

—. 1992. 'From Industrial Society to the Risk Society: Questions of Survival, Social Structure and Ecological Enlightenment', in *Theory, Culture and Society* 9(2): 97–123.
Berlin, I. 1991. 'The pursuit of the ideal' in *The Crooked Timber of Humanity*. London: Fontana, pp. 1–19.
Bourdieu, P. and Ehalt, H. C. 2010. *Für eine europäische Aufklärung*. Wien: Picus Verlag.
Bronner, S. E. 2004. *Reclaiming the Enlightenment. Toward a Politics of Radical Engagement*. New York: Columbia University Press.
Charlie Hebdo, 2006. 8 February.
Charlie Hebdo, 2012. 18 September.
Cope, K. L. and Ahrens, R. (eds.). 2002. *Talking Forward, Talking Back: Critical Dialogues with the Enlightenment*. New York: AMS.
Debray, R. 2006. *Lumières Aveuglantes*. Paris: Gallimard.
Engelbrecht Larsen, R. and Seidenfaden, T. 2006. *Karikaturkrisen. En undersøgelse af baggrund og ansvar*. Copenhagen: Gyldendal.
France Soir, 2006. 1 February.
Goddard, V. A. et al. (eds.). 1996. *The Anthropology of Europe: Identities and Boundaries in Conflict*. Oxford: Berg Publishers.
Gordon, D. 2001. (ed.). *Postmodernism and the Enlightenment: New Perspectives in Eighteenth-Century French Intellectual History*. London: Routledge.
Himmelfarb, G. 2005. *The Roads to Modernity: The British, French and American Enlightenments*. New York: Alfred A. Knopf.
Hanson, V. D. 2006. 'Free Speech Doesn't Come without a Cost', in *Wall Street Journal*, 29 November, pp. 12–14.
Morin, E. 1987. *Penser l'Europe*. Paris: Gallimard.
Pagden, A. 2002. 'Introduction' in *The Idea of Europe: From Antiquity to the European Union*, edited by A. Pagden. Cambridge: Cambridge University Press, pp. 1–32.
—. 2013. *The Enlightenment: And Why It Still Matters*. New York: Random House.
Postman, N. 1999. *Building a Bridge to the Eighteenth Century: How the Past Can Improve Our Future*. New York: Vintage Books.
Rorty, R. 2003. 'Humiliation or Solidarity', in *Dissent Magazine*, Fall 2003, pp. 23–26.
Sanders, K. 2005. 'Turning Out the Lights on the Enlightenment', in *Dissident Voice*, 25 March.
Tibi, B. 1998. *Europa ohne Identität? Leitkultur oder Wertebeliebigkeit*. München: Siedler.
Todorov, T. 2006. *L'Esprit des Lumières*. Paris: Robert Laffont.

PART IV
Thinking about Enlightenment and gender

7

BETWEEN SHADOW AND LIGHT: WOMEN'S EDUCATION

Christophe Regina

If the education of European noblewomen is fairly well known, much less is known about women from other backgrounds (Grell 2005: 7–9). The historiography of women's education under the Ancien Régime still needs to be considered and enriched, especially regarding the issue of ordinary women's access to knowledge in urban or rural areas (Sonnet 1987: 17; Duby 1993: 132–137). Questioning women's education during the Enlightenment must therefore consider several aspects (Clinton 1975: 283–299). Consequently, the diversity of philosophical ideals and oppositions that could crystallise in the issue of women's education and their assessment remains central in a time of intellectual progress.

If the Enlightenment philosophers believed in the ideal of progress driven by reason, not all of them promoted this in the same way for women and their role in society. From behind the philosophical debates in the eighteenth century emerge all the stereotypes affecting women, representations influencing the ideals for female education and what they implied. The issue of education can be seen as just a hidden argument of power related to knowledge (Foucault 1969: 75). By restricting and supervising women's intellectual potential, men for the sake of their misogynist and essentialist prejudices denied women the plural potential of their intellect and genius. This hypocrisy was obviously and regularly the object of denunciations, perceptible in the heated debates that fuelled the *Querelle des femmes* from the late Middle Ages to the early twentieth century (Viennot 2012: 7–9). The *Querelle des femmes* was probably one of the most intense debates on the role and place of gender equity in European society. The issue of women's education is, therefore, one facet of a much broader debate on the social role of women. Studying the *Querelle* allows for a better understanding and sense of the issues linked to educating women. After finding the diverse and varied arguments made for or against women's access to knowledge, the question arises regarding the reasons for wanting to keep women away from such knowledge. The progression of women's education relates more broadly to changing the perception of women in the society to which they belong. Finally, it is necessary to ask if the progress of reason is synonymous with a recognition by society of a feminine desire for access to education or if it indicates an awareness of women about their condition. The issue of women's internalisation of gender inequality is largely responsible for the egalitarian nature of access to knowledge. Indeed, the cultural construction of a standard related to gender roles could convince men and women that their place in society was natural. There is, therefore, within knowledge a powerful force: women can ask for education as the expression of a form of agency, as a space for developing their capacity for action (Montenach 2012: 7–10). Between the supposed leadership of women and the reality of its expression, there obviously exists a multitude of nuances that the historian must consider. Assessing through the work of Enlightenment thinkers the relationship of eighteenth-century philosophy to the issue of women's education seems relevant since it raises doubts about the notion of progress itself.

In this essay we will pay attention to the place granted to the education of women in the eighteenth century, seek to show that it takes more the form of instruction, and so detect the convergences and ruptures of discourses intrinsically linking women and knowledge. The limited scope of this present chapter cannot exhaust the plurality of these discourses, but it still can follow those that were dominant along with their evolution and query the notion of progress too often associated with the Enlightenment that seems, on the issue of women, less brilliant than the political and economic advances the philosophers encouraged. The issue of women's education cannot be restricted only to philosophical debate, but, instead, must be entered through the prism of a society that strictly defines gender roles relayed by the throne, the altar and their representations of women.

As we suggest, the education of women under the Ancien Régime is hardly a vector of modernity in as much as knowledge was meant to allow women to govern their households better in order to make them the last temples of virtue. The famous treatise by Fénelon, *De l'éducation des filles*, repeatedly reprinted throughout the eighteenth century, promotes the teaching of women not with the intention of making them intellectuals but rather models that should inspire both children and husbands, the disorders of the latter being explicable only by the dissolute life of their foolish wives (Fénelon 1687). But if the education of women has certainly not been thought of as a source of empowerment, it prepared the way towards it by allowing women to access knowledge they had too long been denied. According to Fénelon, education should not push girls from a modest background to extract themselves from their condition; education in no way intended to facilitate the social promotion of one social order to another (Touboul 2004: 325–329). One of the major ambitions of the Enlightenment is to reform society by means of education which should allow the formation of a new man; but would it matter if there were a new woman?

An old debate partly inherited from the *Querelle des femmes*

The unequal access of the sexes to knowledge is heir to an ancient intellectual tradition. Already in *The Republic*, Plato wondered if 'woman is able to share all the work of the male sex', implying that a woman would be nothing more than a failed man, an attitude that perfectly reproduces the way in which the Greek philosophers theorised the inferiority of women (Gould 1980: 9–14). This inferiority was then taken over by Roman law which institutionalised the subordination of women (Desclos 2010: 306). The Aristotelian heritage recovered by the Church Fathers reinforced the subordinate position of women in the West, helping to forge the idea of a natural inferiority that could not allow women to enjoy the same rights and the same duties as men (Moller Okin 1979: 99–105).

Not all the issues raised by the question of women's education appear under the Ancien Régime or specifically during the Enlightenment; they are much older and largely derived from the Ancient and Medieval intellectual heritage. This simple observation is, however, not useless. It marks the eighteenth century as neither more nor less than a passionate and exciting step in the vast field of debates on the place of women in society then agitating the West. From the Middle Ages, Vincent of Beauvais, William of Tournai, and Pierre Dubois reflected in a more or less modern manner on the education of women (Lett 2013: 17). In the last third of the fourteenth century, the well-known Geoffroy de La Tour-Landry wrote a didactic treatise for his daughters, *Livre pour l'enseignement de ses filles* (cf. Montaiglon 1854; De Gendt 2003). His treatise had no other purpose than to make his daughters good Christians, guided by virtue and decency, as expected by Medieval society (Mulder Baker 2004: 11). For centuries centred on faith, household, and morality, this triptych – good Christian, virtue, decency – formed the keystone of a system for women's education that focussed on rudimentary rather than on academic knowledge (Fiévet 2006: 47). The famous *Querelle des femmes* which troubled Europe from the Middle Ages to the twentieth century (and even to this day) did not just discuss ideas, but also offered a wide range of intellectual experiences defining the role and the place of the sexes. Hence, as a matrix of sexual roles education offered a principal line of defence both for women and for their critics. In this controversy, the weight of the Church was obviously important, since it helped to connect women's dangerous relationship to education with Eve and the knowledge she initiated. The few works cited here were addressed to women of the nobility and the elite, not to women in general.

'If it was the custom of sending girls to school and methodically teaching them science, as is done for boys, they would learn and understand the difficulties of the arts and the sciences as well as boys do': this observation made by Christine de Pisan on the cause of gender inequality recognises that the access of men and women to knowledge is largely unequal (Viennot 1996: 27). Between the beginning of the fifteenth century and the Enlightenment, was the progress on the issue of women's education remarkable? The Tridentine reform undoubtedly contributed to the development of school structures as a way of thwarting both the progress of the

Reformation and its emphasis on education, one of its spearheads (Astoul 1996: 37–61). Since the Holy Word was inaccessible in Latin and, therefore incomprehensible to the majority of the faithful, it was then in the vernacular put within their reach to be known and lived. Learning to read then had an eminently spiritual purpose. Unable to leave access to the Scriptures to the Protestants, Rome reformed Catholic education. Girls' access to small schools, free or paid, for a period of two to three years, assured only very rudimentary learning based primarily on religious instruction: reading, sometimes a little arithmatic, and obviously training for needlework in order to guarantee and ensure competence in a respectable profession. The schools were in many respects an extension of the Tridentine decisions condemning idleness. The instruction given in small schools was thus shaping a good Christian and future wife conscious of her role and responsibilities.

Only the most wealthy families had the means to send their daughters to study in convents which in theory were intended simply to ensure preparation for communion, preparation backed up by mastery of reading. 'When a mother put her daughters in the convent, she gave them a writing master, a dancing master, a music master, she believes she acted prudently; she no longer worries how they are brought up' (Puzin de La Martinière Benoist, 2002: 111). To complete a very rich education for girls, families could supply at their own expense masters of writing, dancing, etc.

Enlightenment thinkers almost unanimously condemned sending girls to the convent: 'From the paternal home our girls are transported into convents with their character already formed because the heart is formed before the head. This transplantation which is often at birth is one of the greatest misfortunes with which families' lax attitudes have afflicted society. Here the first evils follow them, without any of the first pleasures: No paternal kiss, no dear hand will wipe away their tears. Forced to seek consolation in a foreign friendship, they will break these natural chains whose links their parents first broke' (Bernardin de Saint-Pierre 1811: 89). Bernardin de Saint-Pierre, for example, considers convents directly responsible for the poor education of women. He argues that, as the heart's intelligence is formed before the mind's, the rupture in the family threatened its formation. Distinctive among the female orders vested in education were the Visitandines with their convent schools and the Ursulines that without mixing the girls attending them provided a boarding-school as well as a free day school (Lux-Sterritt 2005: 28; Annaert 1992: 113–115; Duret 1996: 13–18). But were these structures conducive to the intellectual development of girls?

To educate or to instruct women?

Throughout the eighteenth century, beyond the few places that provided a quality education, discussions about the education of women emerged in various forms, particularly in the competitions organised by the Academies. As such, the subject proposed by the Chalon-sur-Marne Academy on 25 August 1783 invited participants to discuss 'ways of improving the education of women in France', which reveals the interest that the subject evoked (Choderlos de Laclos 2009: 23–27). Choderlos de Laclos won the award that year, with a quote from Seneca that brilliantly summarised his position opening his reflection on the issue: 'Evil is no remedy when vices are changed into morals' (Choderlos de Laclos 2009: 23). For Laclos, the education given to women was an education in name only. The question posed by the competition shows the many reflections that arose concerning education, but we must admit that most of them concerned the training of boys. This growing interest in education can be understood in at least two ways: first, as evidence of an increased concern for education in general, required for the formation of a new man; second, as a way reinforcing the centuries-old positions assigned to women. Under the guise of modernity, the contents of education recommended for either sex reflects their social expectations and men's and women's respective roles in society.

The contents of these treatises reveals the limits that weighed heavily on women. One of the best examples concerns the debates that formed around the question of genius which, for Voltaire like Rousseau, could only be masculine. Are women capable of genius (Krief 2012: 61; Darling and Van de Pijpekamp 1994: 115–132)? This issue encompasses the whole debate on the education of women. Some Enlightenment philosophers distinguish between the brilliance of mind they deny to women and knowledge that is practical, or even pragmatic. For Rousseau, this distinction is not surprising in the more general context of his vision of the sexes: woman must be at the service of man to make his daily life pleasant; it is best for her not to discuss major subjects since she risks becoming conceited and thus not fulfilling her "functions" (Magnier 1977: 59–78). Although he attaches great importance to the question of women and the family in his political reflections, Rousseau relies on the natural inferiority of women to develop, as in *Émile*, Book V, dedicated to Sophie's education. He develops a training tailored to women's physiology since this, according to Rousseau, determines her intellectual capacity (Rousseau 1969: 529; Lange 2002: 26). Associated with the notion of self-love, involving love of equality (reciprocity, equal recognition), it is unlikely that this view is paternalistic. Contradiction arises because self-love is an emotional source of the love of equality, shared by men and women, and of a distinctive desire.

Where is the social difference between men and women? It is in the manipulation, dictated by men's self-esteem rather than women's, that ensures men's domination. This leaves Rousseau with a problem: how to situate women so that they avoid excesses of self-love yet not becoming estranged from themselves. His solution is not to leave them dominated by masculine laws, but to reposition them in their very nature. From the perspective of the Enlightenment we have inherited, hence from the standpoint of public opinion, what Rousseau proposes as "anti-feminist". But from the standpoint of nature it is "feminist" in a certain sense claimed both by revolutionary women in their quest for autonomy and by contemporary feminism, albeit in part and with many nuances. In Montesquieu's work there is also the idea of female inferiority, explained not by women's lack of education but by their nature (Montesquieu 1990: 348). Voltaire and Diderot are in turn more cautious on the issue, the first admiring Émilie du Châtelet, the second deploring the situation of women while admitting they lack principles and reasoning (Voltaire 1736; Diderot 1821: 450). Enlightenment reformers take up quite extensively the educational programmes offered by Fénelon and Fleury, supporting or strengthening them without losing sight that the main goal was to produce good Christian women, wives, and mothers (Fleury 1687: 27).

The idea of a different nature developed and this difference arose from distinguishing between the intellectual faculties of men and women, a difference created first in nature and then in culture. Rousseau did not see the establishment of a 'feminine empire' within households as derogatory, but as an extension of a gender complementarity that originated in nature. This claim of a condition formed *by* and *in* nature should have resolved the issue of gender roles in the Ancien Régime, but the evidence for it was not there (Magnier 1977: 59–78). For Fleury, any training involving the faculties of abstraction is wasted on women: rhetoric, mathematics, philosophy, ancient languages have no usefulness in everyday life (Fleury 1781: 117–120). The many editions of the works of Fénelon testify to the pervasiveness of his ideas and the influence they continued to exert in the eighteenth century.

Legal incapacity reinforces the idea of women's inabilities outside the private sphere. However, Ancien Régime legislation was not as unequal as generally presumed, offering more than one way and the legal means to oppose men. But did an elementary education allow women access to justice? The research I have conducted on women in Marseilles in the eighteenth century shows that, while most of them could not write, they knew their rights very well and the possibilities that justice permitted them. The indignation of the Enlightenment intelligentsia with a poorly educated populace is tempered somewhat by the forms of practical intelligence women could develop in order to negotiate everyday life, which reveals women's great resilience (Regina 2012: 8). Women faced real barriers, such as not having the legitimacy as litigants to confront in court a third party of higher status. But until 1792 it was possible for women to obtain a legal separation as well as have property divided and the freedom to live away from their husbands though without the possibility of having their marriage dissolved.

The existence of a judicial culture forged not by education but by the reappropriation of collective knowledge allows us to reconsider the creation of intellectual equality (Regina 2014: 11–16). The desire of philosophers to prove the victory of reason over centuries of lies and ignorance is, therefore, illusory, and even contemptuous of all the forms of practical genius that enabled women to participate in society even without the weapons of education advocated by the Enlightenment. But was this education, largely designed to make women good wives and good mothers, essential to the advancement of the status of women? In the second half of the eighteenth century, intellectuals also questioned the place of women's education, the most famous probably being the Countess of Miremont, the Marquise d'Epinay and Countess de Genlis (Charrier-Vozel 2010: 294; Cavanaugh 2007: 13–18; Gougeaud-Arnaudeau 2000: 7–8). Madam d'Epinay early on defended the idea that men and women are of 'the same nature and constitution', but found that in practice this equality was hardly expressed (Dulac 1994: 33). The educational mission assigned to women by the Enlightenment was taken very seriously by Louise d'Epinay, who in her childhood had suffered too superficial an education for her taste. As a mother, she put to good use her own experience to create an education for her granddaughter so as to avoid the pitfalls of her own education. Madame de Genlis, like Louise d'Epinay or Madame de Miremont, encouraged a pedagogy based on the pleasure of knowledge and not an education based on severity, coercion and punishment (Cherrad 2007: 93–95). They also recommended exercise, to make the female body stronger. Training for the mind and body, love of learning: they seem to have adopted the ideas of Rousseau they considered relevant by modernising them and restoring women to a place that was not second or inferior to men.

Therefore, during the Enlightenment a certain hypocrisy surrounds the subject of female genius. Exceptional women, such as Émilie du Châtelet, Marie Agnezi and Anna Morandi Manzolini, to mention only a few, are presented as outside their nature. Consequently their condition cannot be a model for all women, since their exceptional background is not 'natural' (Sartori 2006: 102). The myriad books dedicated to famous women who flourished during the Ancien Régime did not celebrate women but genius which through narration and narrative was closer to fiction than to reality. The emergence of these quasi-hagiographic biographies is old. In Plutarch we can find stories featuring the excellence, courage, magnanimity and unique character of famous women. We find in such writers as Boccaccio, Plutarch and Brantôme stories like this republished many times, but also among women to whom we owe *Les dames illustres, où par bonnes et fortes raisons il se prouve que le sexe féminin surpasse en toutes sortes de genres le sexe masculin* (Guillaume 1665; Regina 2011: 69). These feminine exceptions that contradict the absence of genius among women did not aim to promote education for women. This continued to be limited to the acquisition of practical and mechanical knowledge in order to make good wives, the goal of feminine existence in the eighteenth century. Paradoxically, at the same time as Enlightenment thought was promoting intellectual emancipation from the pervasive obscurantism built by the Church, some philosophers were still appropriating the clichés and stereotypes associated with femininity.

An education adapted to the destiny of women to become wives and mothers

The first thing that a mother should teach her daughter is virtue.

—Bernardin de Saint-Pierre, 1811

Even if they did not all agree on the goals of women's education, Enlightenment thinkers widely condemned the education provided in convents. Voltaire's position sums up the position of eighteenth-century intellectuals who were interested in the question. In one of his essays, entitled *Éducation des filles* (1761) (Voltaire 1829: 71–72), he speaks in the name of those who criticise and condemn convent education and promote maternal education (Goodman 2007: 33–36). He denounces primarily the role of governesses who were entrusted with the education of young girls as they returned from their wet nurse. Rousseau too strongly criticised convents, which he saw as temples of coquetry. According to him, Protestant countries without such structures produced better wives. The most fundamental criticism against convents mainly concerned the outdated and inappropriate nature of knowledge provided there, as emphasised by Voltaire through the voice of Sophronie, the heroine of his essay. If the fulfillment of every woman's destiny is to become a wife and a mother, it seems paradoxical that the education of girls is entrusted to those who have known neither marriage nor motherhood. It has been a long time since society encouraged virginity and celibacy as ideals. Voltaire's position that deemed reading as being edifying for girls was not unanimously shared, since women's education was first and foremost about making good wives (Bérenguier 2007: 23–32). Poulain de la Barre denounced the theory of women's natural inferiority long ago. He shifted the issue of gender inequality from a question of nature to that of culture (Poulain de la Barre 1671, 1673, 1675). Evidently inequalities affecting the sexes are due only to the different educations provided for each sex. In the eighteenth century, Helvetius and d'Alembert take the position that gender inequality is not natural but cultural (Helvétius 1989: 55; d'Alembert 1759: 450). Madame de Miremont, Madame de Genlis and Louise d'Epinay proposed expanding the knowledge traditionally accepted for women to include history, geography, literature, physics, chemistry, natural history and even modern languages, deemed more useful than Classical languages (Miremont 1779–1789: 289).

Faced with the reality of an education system ineffective for reforming society, a scathing critique of the convents, and doubts about the value of knowledge provided at home, philosophers called for state intervention to improve access to knowledge. Even within the Church, an awareness occurs, particularly in the writings of the abbot of Saint-Pierre, who wants the organisation of convents modeled on that of the Royal House of Saint-Cyr founded by Madame de Maintenon in 1686 (Castel Saint-Pierre 1728: 82; Jacquemin 2007: 10–11; Picco 1993: 23). The ambitious project of the abbot turned out to be hardly innovative. Indeed, the courses offered at Saint-Cyr were not among the most modern in the eighteenth century. Remarks against and critiques of religious orders are, in turn, still relevant. Baron d'Holbach supported convent education, not for the same reasons as the abbot Reyre, for example, but because retirement (he said) is conducive to study. Thus, he proposed to transform fundamentally these institutions by renewing the training of religious orders to make them more effective in their teaching mission (Roche 1978: 3–6). The debates regarding the education of girls dealt mostly with the upper classs, the education of the masses being viewed with suspicion. Indeed, apart from Rousseau, who early on asserted his republican ideas, Enlightenment thinkers did not support major social upheavals and and were conscious of preserving the social hierarchy (Foisneau 2007: 463–479). Diderot, however, thought that the education of the masses through the implementation of free and compulsory education for all was a necessity, since he saw ignorance as the source of the social evils of the Ancien Régime: superstition, crimes and public disorder (Dolle 1973: 7–9).

The education of women as Rousseau conceived it had no other purpose than to prepare women to consent to submission. The exaltation of motherhood through the figure of Julie Wolmar has no other purpose than to commend her ability to educate girls into submission by developing gentleness, virtue and modesty (Brouard-Arens 1991: 265–275). Rousseau's vision of women was well received by Enlightenment thinkers because it was presented as enshrined in a continuity imposed by nature. We find this influence in Bernardin de Saint-Pierre, who defines women's education in terms of making men better. Here the position of women is once again magnified as a source for achieving excellence, but not as a direct source of excellence: her education concerns men. For Bernardin de Saint-Pierre, a good man is a happy man, and this happiness must be nourished by a devoted wife. This education for subordination is even more strongly advocated by Restif de la Bretonne:

> Both sexes are not equal; equalizing them means to denature them. Yet this is the great axiom of our century. Listen to our Bachelors, and the flibbertigibbets they whistled at : women ought to have the same education as men, to apply themselves to the sciences; women have as much capacity, more delicacy, and a thousand other trifles. So untrue is it that there should be physical equality between the sexes and that their moral equality should be established, that the deference, even the most distinguished, displayed by men merely announces our inferiority; rather it shows respect, the moderation of the strong in respect of the weak.
>
> Restif de la Bretonne 1988: 41

Education, therefore, often has the appearance of practical knowledge that does not need to resort to abstraction, conceptualisation, or theorisation. The domestic economy remains the priority of women, which is what Enlightenment society stipulates (Chatenet, 2009: 21–34). Basic female education rested upon, as we have said, the formation of a good Christian, reading and mathematics being provided later. Learning some arts, such as dance or music, was promoted only with the idea of pleasing the husband. Again, it is not a question of seeking another form of recognition. For Rousseau, women should learn and know only what is suitable and beneficial to them (Rousseau 1969: 538). They must also have a strong body, shaped by exercise, in order to bring forth vigorous offspring. Rousseau points out that this may be one of the advantages of convents: here physical exercises were planned, whereas education practiced at home was hardly conscious of concerns related to the body. He especially criticised the softness associated with women, because the daughter of idleness had to be fought. The Philosophes were inspired by references to antiquity, to the famous Spartans for their strength, but also by the writings of Plutarch who marveled at the robustness of the Germans (Plutarch 2002: 46–47).

'The soul of women cannot be of another nature than that of man. But all understanding where our ideas & the principles of our actions derive from, residing in the soul alone, why would women's souls be less able than men's to indulge in the sciences, arts, philosophy, and to distinguish themselves there with the greatest success?' (Riballier 1779: 3). In 1779 Riballier, author of a treatise on the physical and moral education of women, protested against Rousseau's positions, stressing that the only difference that exists between the sexes is women's frailty due to lack of exercise. He equally encouraged women to become erudite. Partisan of an identical education for both sexes, Riballier supported the study of philosophy, mathematics and metaphysics, which up to that point was the prerogative of men. If spiritual lessons are still the basic education for both sexes, Riballier also proposed physical exercise as a necessary practice, including the use of weapons (Riballier 1779: 80–81). He used famous historical examples, citing Joan of Arc or the Countess of Montfort, stressing that the use of arms is not incompatible with being a woman and that certain women had proved themselves capable of using them. Unfortunately the revolutionary pretenses of this pedagogy are not as cutting-edge as they seem. It is above all, once again, to form good mothers, reiterating the idea that a new society will be brought forth only through women, 'these women to whom, in the order of nature, belongs the work of pregnancies & childbirth, nourishing and caring for children, which occupies at least the most active third of their life. They are, moreover, by a completely natural general convention, the origin of which dates back probably to the early ages of the world, responsible for all the details within the household' (Riballier 1779: 7). We cannot separate education from motherhood, since the idea of autonomous education independent from procreation was completely unthinkable at the time. This is probably where the main source of inequality between men and women lies, the former being forced to become direct players in a life under state control, a dynamic over which women have no control.

The contents of education "programmes" for girls further highlight the place given to women in the Ancien Régime. Most educational treatises were for elite women; the "programmes" for ordinary girls were in turn considered less and can be summed up most of the time by the contents of the regulations of the different organisations open to them. Nevertheless, all girls shared the same destiny: to become a wife and mother. The girls sent to convents also became wives, the chaste wives of Jesus, but were also conditioned by their education to submit to authority. They lived in a century in which education had to prepare them to accept a subordinate position removed from the world. This submission to a natural order returned once again to the question of the nature of women (Hoffman 1995: 388–395). In small schools, girls and boys received the same education in contrast to the convent, where knowledge dispensed through coeducation was unthinkable (Carter 2008: 417–423). This coeducation, however, does not provide evidence of gender equality.

Conclusion

If the Enlightenment undoubtedly upset European intellectual life, by fighting prejudice and superstition, by fighting against injustice and despotism, and by promoting individual freedom, it is clear that it was not very forward-thinking on the issue and the status of women in society. Confirming Kant's conclusion that we live not 'in an enlightened age', but in an 'age of enlightenment' (Kant 1985: 215), the issue of female education vividly shows the limits of the Enlightenment. On this subject, it largely reinforced the natural or naturalised vision of the role of women, reducing them to their maternal functions. The issue of gender inequality, inherited from the ancients, prevented in many respects a revolution of thought and a reorganisation of society. The arrival of the French Revolution emphasised even more the biased nature of the social changes envisaged, since after the closure of female political clubs in 1793 it relegated women to their homes (Godineau 2009: 143–166). Condorcet's proposal to establish a similar education for girls and boys, beyond being unheeded, indicates that the European Enlightenment was not yet ready radically to renew the foundations of a society where gender would no longer have roles in the name of natural ideals. Although not largely considered from this perspective, Ancien Régime judicial archives allow us to approach the issue of women's education differently, on the one hand, by assessing those who knew how to write, and, on the other hand, by considering the rhetorical strategies successfully deployed by women in the courts. The goal of such an approach should be to highlight female resilience and women's ability to adapt to a given situation – to overcome a lack of education through the development of practical knowledge, imposed by everyday life and required for living together.

References

(All translations of works cited are my own unless indicated otherwise.)

Annaert, P. 1992. *Les Collèges au féminin : les Ursulines, enseignement et vie consacrée aux XVIIe et XVIIIe siècle*. Namur: Vie consacrée.

Astoul, G. 1996. 'L'instruction des enfants protestants et catholiques en pays aquitains du milieu du XVIe siècle à la révocation de l'Édit de Nantes', *Histoire de l'éducation* 69: 37–61.

Bérenguier, N. 2007. 'Mères, gouvernantes et livres de conduite : guerre ou alliance?', in *Femmes éducatrices au siècle des Lumières*, edited by I. Brouard-Arends and M.-E. Plagnol-Diéval. Interférences. Rennes: Presses Universitaires de Rennes, pp. 23–32.

Bernardin de Saint-Pierre, J.-H. 1811. *Œuvres complètes*, edited by L. Aimé-Martin. Bruxelles: Auguste Wahlen.

Bolufer Peruga, M. and Morant Deusa, I. 1998. 'On Women's Reason, Education and Love: Women and Men of the Enlightenment in Spain and France,' *Gender & History* 10(2): 183–216.

Brouard-Arens, I. 1991. *Vies et images maternelles dans la littérature française du XVIIIe siècle*. Oxford: Voltaire Foundation.

Carter, K. E. 2008. '"Les garçons et les filles sont pêle-mêle dans l'école": Gender and Primary Education in Early Modern France', *French Historical Studies* 31(3): 417–443.

Castel de Saint-Pierre, I. 1728. *Projet pour perfectionner l'éducation, par M. l'abbé de Saint-Pierre*. Paris: Briasson.

Cavanaugh, A. (ed.). 2007. *Performing the 'Everyday': The Culture of Genre in the Eighteenth Century*. Newark: University of Delaware Press.
Charrier-Vozel, M. 2010. 'Dialogues sur l'éducation des femmes : Mme d'Épinay, Galiani, Thomas, Diderot', in P. Pasteur et al., *Genre et éducation : former / se former / être formée au féminin*. Rouen/Havre : Presses Universitaires de Rouen et du Havre, pp. 289–298.
Chatenet, A. 2009. 'La femme, maîtresse de maison ? Rôle et place des femmes dans les ouvrages d'économie domestique au XVIIIe siècle', *Histoire, économie & société*, 28e année, no. 4, pp. 21–34.
Cherrad, S. 2007. 'De l'éducation des mères à une possible éducation publique : Mesdames d'Épinay et de Miremont', in *Femmes éducatrices au siècle des Lumières*, edited by I. Brouard-Arends and M.-E. Plagnol-Diéval. Interférences, Rennes: Presse Universitaire de Rennes, pp. 93–102.
Choderlos de Laclos, P. 2009. *Traité sur l'éducation des femmes*. Paris: Agora.
Clinton, K. B. 1975. 'Femme et Philosophe: Enlightenment Origins of Feminism', *Eighteenth Century Studies* 8(3): 283–299.
Darling, J. and Van de Pijpekamp, M. 1994. 'Rousseau on the Education, Domination and Violation of Women', *British Journal of Educational Studies* 42(2): 115–132.
De Gendt, A.-M. 2003. *L'art d'éduquer les nobles damoiselles : le 'Livre du Chevalier de la Tour Landry'*. Paris: H. Champion.
Desclos, M.-L. 2000. *Le rire des Grecs: anthropologie du rire en Grèce ancienne*. Grenoble: Jérôme Millon.
Diderot, D. 1966. *Mémoires pour Catherine II*, edited by P. Vernière. Paris: Garnier Frères, pp. 130–138.
Dolle, J.-M. 1973. *Diderot, politique et éducation*. Paris:Vrin.
Duby, G. and Perrot, M. (eds.). 1993. *A History of Women in the West: Renaissance and Enlightenment Paradoxes*. Cambridge, MA: Belknap.
Dulac, G. and Maggetti, D. (eds.). 1994. 'Lettre de Mme d'Épinay à Galiani du 14 mars 1772', *Correspondance*. Paris: Desjonquères, vol. 3, p. 33.
Duret, A. 2006. *Les communautés religieuses enseignantes et missionnaires de Luçon aux XVIIe-XVIIIe siècles*. Unpublished PhD thesis, Université de Poitiers.
Ehrenpreis, S. (ed.). 2007. *Frühneuzeitliche Bildungsgeschichte der Reformierten in konfessionsvergleichender Perspektive : Schulwesen, Lesekultur und Wissenschaft*. Berlin: Duncker & Humblot.
Fénelon, (de) F. 1687. *De l'éducation des filles*, Paris: P. Aubouin.
Fiévet, M. 2006. *L'invention de l'école des filles : des Amazones de Dieu aux XVIIe et XVIIIe siècles*. Paris: Éditions Imago.
Fleury, C. 1687, *Traité du choix et de la méthode des études*. Paris: P. Aubouin, P. Émery et C. Clousier.
—. 1780–1781. *Traité du choix et de la méthode des études* [1687]. Opuscules, Nîmes: P. Beaume.
Foisneau, L. 2007. 'Gouverner selon la volonté générale: la souveraineté selon Rousseau et les théories de la raison d'Etat', *Les Études philosophiques* 83: 463–479.
Foucault, M. 1969. *L'Archéologie du savoir*. Bibliothèque des sciences humaines, Paris: Gallimard.
Godineau, D., et al. (eds.). 2009. 'Femmes, genre, révolution', in *Annales historiques de la Révolution française*. Paris: Armand Colin, n°358.
Goodman, D. 2007. 'Le rôle des mères dans l'éducation des pensionnaires au XVIIIe siècle', in *Femmes éducatrices au siècle des Lumières*, edited by I. Brouard-Arends and M.-E. Plagnol-Diéval. Interférences. Rennes: Presses Universitaires de Rennes, pp. 33–44.
Gougeaud-Arnaudeau, S. 2000. *Entre gouvernants et gouvernés : le pédagogue au XVIIIe siècle*. Villeneuve-d'Ascq: Presses Universitaires du Septentrion.
Gould, C. C. and Wartosfsky, M. W. (eds.). 1980. *Women and Philosophy: Toward a Theory of Liberation*. New York: Perigee.

Grell, C. (ed.). 2004. *L'éducation des jeunes filles nobles en Europe: XVIIe-XVIIIe siècles*. Paris: Presses de l'Université Paris-Sorbonne.
Guillaume, J. 1665. *Les dames illustres, où par bonnes et fortes raisons il se prouve que le sexe féminin surpasse en toutes sortes de genres le sexe masculin*. Paris: T. Jolly.
Helvétius, C.-A. 1989. *De l'Homme, de ses facultés intellectuelles et de son éducation* [1772]. Corpus des œuvres de philosophie en langue française. Paris: Fayard.
Hoffman, P. 1995. *La femme dans la pensée des lumières*. Genève: Slatkine.
Jacquemin, H. 2007. *Livres et jeunes filles nobles à Saint-Cyr (1686–1793)*. Angers: Presses Universitaires d'Angers.
Kant E. 1985. 'Réponse à la question : qu'est ce que les lumières?', in *Œuvres Philosophiques*, translated by H. Wismann. Paris: Gallimard, t. II.
Krief, H. 2012. 'Le génie féminin. Propos et contre-propos au XVIIIe siècle', in *Revisiter la "querelle des femmes". Discours sur l'égalité des sexes, de 1750 aux lendemains de la Révolution*, edited by É. Viennot and N. Pellegrin. Saint-Étienne: Publications de l'Université de Saint-Étienne, pp. 61–76.
Lange, L. (ed.). 2002. *Feminist Interpretations of Jean-Jacques Rousseau*. University Park: Pennsylvania State University Press.
Le Rond d'Alembert, J. 1821. 'Lettre à Jean-Jacques Rousseau, citoyen de Genève, [1759]', *Œuvres Complètes*. Paris: A. Belin, vol. 4, p. 450.
Lett, D. 2013. *Hommes et femmes au Moyen Âge: Histoire du genre XIIe-XVe siècle*. Paris: Armand Colin.
Lux-Sterritt, L. 2005. 'Redefining Female Religious Life: French Ursulines and English Ladies in Seventeenth-Century Catholicism' in *Catholic Christendom, 1300–1700*. Aldershot: Ashgate Publishing Limited.
Magnier, M. 1977. 'Locke, Rousseau, et deux éducateurs britanniques au XVIIIe siècle', in *Bulletin de la société d'études anglo-américaines des XVIIe et XVIIIe siècles*, no. 5, pp. 59–78.
Miremont, (de) A. 1779–1789. *Traité de l'éducation des femmes et cours complet d'instruction*. Paris: P.-D. Pierres.
Moller Okin, S. 1979, *Women in Western Political Thought*. Princeton, NJ: Princeton University Press.
Montaiglon, (de) A. 1854. *Le livre du Chevalier de la Tour-Landry pour l'enseignement de ses filles*. Paris: P. Jannet.
Montenach, A. (ed.). 2012. 'Agency : un concept opératoire dans les études de genre?', *Rives Méditerranéennes*, no. 41, Aix-en-Provence: Telemme.
Montesquieu. 1990. *De l'esprit des lois*, in *Œuvres complètes*, edited by R. Caillois. Paris: Gallimard/Pléiade, vol. 2.
Mulder-Baker, B. 2004. *Seeing and Knowing: Women and Learning in Medieval Europe, 1200–1550*. Turnhout: Brepols.
Picco, D. 1993. *Les Demoiselles de Saint-Cyr (1686–1793)*. Paris: Université de Paris I Panthéon-Sorbonne. 3 vol.
Plutarque. 2002. 'Conduites méritoires des femmes', in *Œuvres morales*, edited by R. Flacelière. Paris: Les Belles Lettres, tome 4, pp. 46–47.
Poulain de la Barre, F. 1671. *De l'éducation des dames pour la conduite de l'esprit dans les sciences et dans les mœurs*. Paris: J. Dupuis.
—. 1673. *De l'égalité des deux sexes: Discours physique et moral où l'on voit l'importance de se défaire des préjugés*. Paris: J. Dupuis.
—. 1675. *De l'excellence des hommes contre l'égalité des sexes*. Paris: J. Dupuis.
Puzin de La Martinière Benoist, F.-A. 2002. *Célianne, ou, les amants séduits par leurs vertus* [1766]. Saint-Étienne: Université de Saint-Étienne.
Regina, C. 2011. *La violence des femmes: Histoire d'un tabou social*. L'inconnu, Paris : Max Milo.

—. 2012. *Femmes, violence(s) et société, face au tribunal de la sénéchaussée de Marseille (1750–1789)*, unpublished PhD thesis, Université d'Aix-en-Provence.

Regina, C., et al. (eds.). 2014. *La culture judiciaire des origines à nos jours*. Histoires Dijon: Presses Universitaires de Dijon.

Restif de la Bretonne, N.-E. 1988. *Les gynographes ou Idées de deux honnêtes femmes sur un projet de règlement proposé à toute l'Europe pour mettre les femmes à leur place et opérer le bonheur des deux sexes* [1777]. Geneva and Paris: Slatkine Reprints.

Riballier, 1779. *De l'éducation physique et morale des femmes : avec une notice alphabétique de celles qui se sont distinguées dans les différentes carrières des sciences & des beaux-arts, ou par des talens & des actions mémorables*, Bruxelles, Paris: chez les frères Estienne.

Roche, D. 1978. 'Éducation et société dans la France du XVIIIe siècle : l'exemple de la maison royale de Saint-Cyr', *Cahiers d'Histoire* 23(1): 3–24.

Rogers, R. 2007. 'L'éducation des filles: un siècle et demi d'historiographie', *Histoire de l'éducation* 115–116: 37–79.

Rousseau, J.-J. 1969. *Émile ou de l'éducation* [1762]. Paris: Gallimard.

Sartori, E. 2006. *Histoire des femmes scientifiques de l'Antiquité au XXe siècle*. Paris: Plon.

Sonnet, M. 1987. *L'éducation des filles au temps des Lumières*. Paris: Cerf.

Timmermans, L. 2005. *L'accès des femmes à la culture sous l'Ancien Régime*. Champion classiques Essai, Paris: Honoré Champion.

Touboul, P. 2004. 'Le statut des femmes: nature et condition sociale dans le traité "De L'Education des filles de Fénelon"', *Revue d'histoire littéraire de la France* 104(2): 325–342.

Turcot, L. 2013. *L'ordinaire parisien des Lumières: Édition critique de trois textes du for privé*. Paris: Hermann.

Viennot, E. and Pellegrin, N. 2012. *Revisiter la « querelle des femmes: Discours sur l'égalité des sexes, de 1750 aux lendemains de la Révolution*. Saint-Étienne: Publications de l'Université de Saint-Étienne.

Voltaire. 1736. 'Épître à Madame du Châtelet'. *Alzire*, Paris: J.-B.-C. Bauche.

—. 1829. 'L'éducation des filles (1761)' in *Oeuvres complètes de Voltaire*, avec notes, préfaces, avertissements. Paris: Armand Aubrée, vol. XXIX, pp. 70–72.

Whitehead, B. J. (ed.). 1999. *Women's Education in Early Modern Europe: A History, 1500-1800*. New York: Garland.

8
"RACE", "SEX", AND "GENDER": INTERSECTIONS, NATURALISTIC FALLACIES, AND THE AGE OF REASON

Carina Pape

Introduction

The terms "race" and "sex/gender" have a specific relation to the Age of Enlightenment. Both were relevant for the new discourses of anthropology or the 'nature of men'. Both have 'naturalistic' and social aspects that *intersect*, as the double-termed idea of "sex/gender" shows explicitly. The idea of "race" is no less complex. Both terms were topics of *theoretical* anthropology, but were nevertheless charged with *pragmatic implications* which lead to *naturalistic fallacies*: the equation of physical features and character traits or mental skills (Stiening 2012: 20; Lutterbeck 2012: 112; cf. Moore 1993). Therefore, even today there is a complex intersection between *both terms*.

Recently, there has been a growing interest in these and other intersections, especially in disciplines which deal with equality issues, like gender studies or the social sciences. The phenomenon of *intersectionality* was first analysed in its social and legal implications by Kimberlé Crenshaw, professor of law at UCLA School of Law (Los Angeles) and Columbia Law School (New York) in the 1980s (Crenshaw 1989). The relationship between 'sex/gender' and 'race' has been investigated by many researchers since then, first of all in *critical race theory* and *feminist theory* (Dines and Humez 2015; Goswami 2014; Rolandsen Agustín 2013; Michlin 2013). *Intersectionality* became its own academic discipline, one which analyses the intersections between different forms of discrimination (linked to gender, 'race', class, disability, etc.). The intersection of natural and cultural aspects in the terms themselves was analysed as well, especially in the case of the double-term "sex/gender". For example, Donna Haraway pointed out that 'nature and culture as well as sex and gender mutually construct each other, so that one pole of each dualism cannot exist without the other' (Salih 2007: 98; Haraway 1991: 12). And Guy Harrison wrote that 'race' is 'the intersection of difference and meaning', therefore, it 'cannot be discovered by examining human differences, since all people are different' (Harrison 2010: 9).

However, these studies concentrate on *current* issues of intersections. Although there are a few studies dealing with the *history* of sexism and racism, almost none of them deals with their *historical relation* (Janz and Schönpflug 2014; Vertovec 2015; Zinsser 2005; Bancel 2014; Bethencourt 2013).[1] I will show that the connection between them goes back to the roots of the terms and first appeared with a special significance in the anthropological discourses of the Enlightenment. To describe this connection I will use Bernard Williams's *history of ideas*. He believed the history of ideas focusses on the *contemporary context* of a text and the changes parallel to the changing context, while the history of philosophy focusses on the meaning a historical text might have *today* (Williams 2005: 9–11). Using this history of ideas first I will go back to a time before 'races' were invented and 'gender' became scientifically relevant. How did these categories of the *other* (from the European perspective) historically develop? What is or was their function? What kinds of (unconscious) intersections were there? I will then provide an overview of the use of the term "race" and its etymology. I will then reconstruct the development of the term "sex/gender". Why, in which way and by whom were they used? And how did the terms intersect from the beginning and thereby reinforce the confusion of 'naturalistic', scientific, social and other aspects (*naturalistic fallacy*)?

I will focus on these questions. In so doing we can better understand the Enlightenment's negative legacy and the sexisms and racisms of today. What is left of the 'anti-enlightenment conceptions, especially the concept of "race", endemic to the eighteenth-century European Enlightenment' (Eze 2002: 287)? The main cause of prejudice and discrimination may be the fact that we are afraid of what we do not know or understand. Therefore, it is called xeno*phobia* or homo*phobia*. The Enlightenment might be an inspiration for more self-critical questioning, even though or *because* of the Enlightenment's own blind spots.

The other I: a negative definition of "us"?

The other was always something to fear and to be fascinated with at the same time. In general we need another person in order to perceive ourselves as an individual. I perceive myself as a person only because I can set myself apart from another person. Otherwise this feeling of an "I" would evanesce; I 'would have to be everything and therefore would be nothing', as the Russian phenomenologist Simon Frank put it (Frank 2012: 355).[2] The others are important for groups of people, as well. They were essential for the "self" of civilisations like the Greek or the Roman, the Chinese empire or the colonial powers: 'The Barbarian or the Gentile was, indeed, the "other" against which, respectively, the Medieval […] civilization defined itself' (Eze 2002: 282).

Nevertheless, *how* these others were defined changed. The Greek concept of the barbarian referred to all non-Greeks. It was adopted in Medieval times, but towards the end of the Middle Ages the barbarian became more ambivalent. The 'savage' of the Renaissance was 'a category parallel to, yet different from the "Barbarian" or

"Gentile" prevalent in preceding medieval centuries' (Eze 2002: 282). The idea of the other was still functional for European identity. But somehow this European identity *as a unit* needed new others besides the old hereditary enemies inside Europe. These others were not a strictly negative example anymore, for example, in the Baroque dramas written by Daniel Caspar von Lohenstein (1635–1683) or in the case of Jean-Jacques Rousseau's idealised 'savage'. Suddenly they 'were rendered the subject of Europe's positive and negative projections' and they received the opportunity to be a positive role model once in a while (Jacques 1997: 201).

Lohenstein's novel about the Germanic field-commander Hermann (*Großmütiger Feldherr Arminius*, 1689–1690) gives an impressive picture of the new ambiguity. A first *intersection* of gender issues and xenophobic ideas can be traced here, as well. His description of Germanic women as 'natural' beauties, modest, chaste and virtuous, in contrast to the manipulating Italian woman Sentia (actually a critique of French customs, judged as decadent and artificial, influencing the German aristocracy) or the female Orientals: the lascivious priestess Ada from Thrace (Bulgaria today), ambitious for power, and her maidservant Eriphyle, depicted with extraordinarily detailed and exotic (sexualized) features (Borgstedt 1992: 392). This seems quite misogynic and racist. But at the same time, Lohenstein declared himself against xenophobic attitudes (Wucherpfennig 1973: 223) and gave examples of ideal foreign females, like the Armenian princess Erato, who is depicted as being as virtuous as the Germanic princess Thußnelda.

In the Renaissance the "savage" had already become a *possible* positive counter-example to the decadent, corrupt European societies. The idea was, for example, used by the French Humanist Michel de Montaigne (1533–1592) in his cultural criticism. In his essay *On cannibals* he argued that it is less barbarous to eat an enemy when he is dead than to torture him alive under the pretext of faith (Montaigne 1953: 121): 'One calls "barbarism" whatever one is not accustomed to' (ibid: 117). He reminded his contemporaries of their own 'barbarous' attitudes, like spitting or sneezing into a fine cloth and carrying this cloth – and the snot – with them all day (Montaigne 1967: 38). Montaigne gives a good example of a humoristic (self-) awareness of what is now called *Eurocentrism*: a non-objective perspective analysed by post-colonial studies. But, his savage was just *not worse* than the Europeans.

The term "*noble* savage", wrongly attributed to Jean-Jacques Rousseau, gave a model for a person, good or virtuous by nature and not corrupted by civilisation (Gay 2009). The term became popular in English in the seventeenth century because of John Dryden's play *The Conquest of Granada* (1672). Since the eighteenth century it has been associated with Native Americans. A prominent example of this is Alexander Pope's *Essay on Man* from 1734. Though the "noble savage" was meant to show the "other" as not inferior, it became a stereotype, no less racist: a noble savage is still a savage. And the noble idea itself did not protect "indigenous" peoples from all over the world from being shown in the highly degrading and racist "human zoos" during ethnological expositions, especially during the New Imperialism period from the 1870s until the early twentieth century.

The categories from the other at the end of the eighteenth century were much more multifaceted and ambiguous than the formally Greek/non-Greek or Christian/non-Christian division. The attitude toward these new and various others reminds me of a statement by the Neo-Kantian Hermann Cohen: It is the other, about whom 'the [Romantic, C. P.] poet says: The one I love and do not know; one understands: do not want to know' (Cohen 1904: 240). How does this attitude and complexity have an impact on the concepts of "race" and "sex/gender"?

The other II: A history of naturalistic fallacies and intersections

There were precursors of racisms and sexisms before "race" and "sex/gender" appeared as (scientific) categories in the eighteenth century, for example, in the Indian caste system (Geiss 1993: 49 f.). Also, anti-Judaic content can be found in sermons and other cultural artefacts of Medieval Christianity (Chazan 1997). However, Medieval anti-Judaism or anti-Semitism was *religious* in nature, whereas the anti-Semitism of the Enlightenment and the post-Enlightenment in Europe was part of a process of *scientification* and *naturalisation*. These laid the groundwork for the racial anti-Semitism which led to the Nazism of the twentieth century. This form of anti-Semitism as a *scientific racism* is based on nationalism, Social Darwinism and related concepts since the eighteenth century. The term "anti-Semitism" even became *popular* in Germany in the late nineteenth century, because it sounded more '*scientific*' than "Jew-hatred" (Laqueur 2006: 21; Chanes 2004: 150). I will now examine the changes which led to such a development.

An (ongoing) process of naturalisation can be traced back to radical social and political changes from the late Middle Ages on. The Medieval estate-based society was founded on religiously justified hierarchies. The church had strong secular powers. The kings were kings by the grace of God. Religious and social aspects were deeply *intersected*. The 'others' were other tribes or ethnic groups of people, but also the 'other sex', for God made Adam *first*. There are a lot of studies on how women were marginalized or demonized for centuries in Christian society: 'The discourse of misogyny runs like a rich vein throughout the breadth of medieval literature' (Bloch 1987: 1; cf. Cooper 2013).

From the thirteenth to the sixteenth century things changed. At the very latest, with the discovery of America by Christopher Columbus in 1492, the church lost its authority over the explanation of the world. Columbus was honored as a 'new Tiphys', the mythological helmsman of the Argonauts, and thereby became a quasi-religious hero himself (Bruno 1969: 74). Not only knowledge about the shape of the world and its continents changed extraordinarily, so, too, did knowledge about their inhabitants. There are two relevant aspects for the conception of human "races" here. I have already mentioned the meaning that borders have for individual identity and self-consciousness as well as for the identity of a group or nation. These psycho-physical borders were shattered even more when the Europeans crossed the physical frontiers of the formally known world. Self-consciousness became even more vulnerable with the crossing of the borders of former limits of knowledge.

Former 'truth' was no longer valid. Thereby new categories of the other came up in this context of the *scientific revolution*, introducing new forms of empirical and natural sciences, and of *European imperialism* and colonisation, bringing new objects to study – including people (Marks 2008: 28).

First and foremost it was the denial of the traditional Christian conception of the world, associated with the Enlightenment, that provoked a new definition of the human being in a new *order of nature* that had to be justified scientifically (Oehler-Klein 2012: 140; 145). That was the birth of "race". The formally confused or ambiguous categories of the other became seemingly more distinct. Discrete racial categories did not exist for the Greeks or the Medieval Christians. Their barbarians were those who were not organised in a special social and legal system or who did not believe (in their God). Phenotypical features were not that relevant (Oehler-Klein 2012: 136; Hannaford 1996: 43–57). The focus was on the social order aspect instead. One could even become a non-barbarian. Those religious and social aspects were (seemingly) replaced by a new order: 'In addition to the impact of travels [...] nature was still conceptualized as a hierarchical system (the Chain of Being), in which every being, from humans down to flora and fauna, had a "naturally" assigned position and status' (Eze 2002: 284–285).

The former intersection of religious and social aspects transferred to the new order of nature and science. Those who 'replaced the authority of religion with that of reason' also tried to replace God by nature and belief by fact (Eze 2002: 284). In this process of *naturalisation*, still theologically influenced, coloured skin was named for the first time as an 'indicator of a disease' or the 'result of contamination' by the environment (Bernasconi 2012: 206; Harris 2001: 86). This was a transformation of the idea that dark skin was the punishment for an *original sin*. Black Africans were thought to be the descendants of the Biblical Ham, son of Noah, and therefore called "Hamites", just as the supposed descendants of the other sons, S(h)em and Japhet, were called "Semites" and "Japhetites". According to the book of Genesis, Ham was not of dark skin colour, but probably this belief was established through folk etymology and the misnomer "ham" = "dark" or "brown" (Goldenberg 1997: 24–25). In the Babylonian Talmud of the sixth century we find the statement that the descendants of Ham are punished by 'being Black' for their ancestor's sin (Sanders 1969: 521–522). This explanation of black skin was used by Arabian slave traders and later was adopted by Europeans in the eighteenth and nineteenth centuries to justify slavery (Swift and Mammoser 2009: 3; Goldenberg 2003: 170; Braude 1997). What is new in the argument of *scientific* racism that saw black skin colour as a *disease* was simply the point that not God (or Noah) was supposed to be the punisher anymore, but *nature*: climate, environment, and 'natural disposition' or germs (which later became genes).

However, the alien or the other was named 'race', ordered hierarchically on an empirical basis and thereby 'naturalised', just like the other sex (Honegger 1991). Seemingly 'natural' aspects were questioned, especially in the twentieth century, like the "sex"-category, and accompanied by social aspects, the "gender"-category (see, among others: West and Zimmerman 1987: 136). These categories were questioned again, for example in the critique of the distinction between "sex" and "gender" by Judith Butler and others (Butler 1990: 7). Though the concepts of "race" and "sex/gender" have been exposed as a naturalistic fallacy, as mentioned before, even today new 'modes of biological naturalization have again re-emerged, and concepts such as the "sexed brain", "sociopathy" as defined by the neurosciences, or the re-emergence of the concept of race are just some indicators of this process' (Lettow 2013: 118; see also: Gilman 2010; Karafyllis 2008).

Therefore, to understand the development of the concepts of "sex/gender" and "race" together with their ethical and ideological implications, to 'understand both the stability and the discontinuities', we need to look closer at the time when they first appeared in anthropological discourses which were themselves emerging between theology, natural sciences, travelogues, anatomy, politics and philosophy (Lettow 2013: 118; Hoßfeld 2005, 56–57; Daston and Park 2001).

The history of "race" within the history of ideas: Intersections of values

"Race" is an abstract concept of order or a *taxonomic rank*, based on a *subjective* classification, and more or less obsolete today. Since the time when it was first used to divide human variety into groups it also became a *social* and *ideological* concept, as I will show. It may even be described as a key concept of anthropology and, therefore, as important for the development of the humanities, as Eze argued: 'The modern idea of humanity – ambiguous and questioned as in Rousseau, or unequivocally endorsed as in Kant – is irrevocably linked to a theory of race' (Eze 2002: 286). The interdisciplinary question of "human nature" was paradigmatic for the Enlightenment with its pursuit of new forms of knowledge and secularisation, before anthropology became its own academic discipline in the nineteenth century.

The term became popular in English ("race") and German ("Rasse") as a word loaned from the French "race". Its origin is not clear, but it might be the Latin word "radix", conjugated as "radic-". "Radix" means "*root*" and is still common in the German word "Radies(chen)", English "radish". Another origin might be the Arabic "ras" that possibly came to Europe as the Spanish "raza" or the Italian "razza". It means "head" and may refer to the (male) *head of the family* and thereby to the *origin* of the family or the tribe. All possible etymologies, therefore, refer to an origin.

A sporadic use of the word "race" can be found in Romance languages since the thirteenth century (Conze and Sommer 2004: 137). Since the fifteenth century, it was used more frequently, mainly to refer to different French noble families disputing rights and possessions (Geulen 2007: 13 f.), and later also to refer to religious groups, the "Christian race", or to humankind, the "human race" (Geulen 2007: 36 f). The French physician François Bernier (1625–1688) first used the term "race" to describe the *phenotypic* variation of humans, like the color of their skin, eyes, or hair, in an anthropological taxonomy called *Nouvelle division de la terre par les différents espèces ou races qui l'habitent* [*New division of the earth by means of the different species or races living on it*] (1684). He was followed by the Swedish botanist, physician and zoologist Carl Linnaeus (1707–1778, known as the father of modern biological taxonomy), the German physician, physiologist and anthropologist Johann Friedrich Blumenbach (1752–1840) and others. In his own work *Systema Naturae* (1735) Linnaeus added to Bernier's ideas the supposition that the different phenotypes were caused by climate (Hoßfeld 2005: 60). Thereby he initiated a controversy on the origin of the different human "races" – equated with the (possible) cause of different phenotypes – with two parties: *monogenists*, who assumed one ancestry for all human varieties, and *polygenists*, who assumed different roots. The Dutch anatomist Petrus Camper linked the question on skin colour explicitly to the question of origin in his speech *On the origin and colour of blacks* in 1764 (Meijer 1999: 183–192).

The purpose of these early taxonomic models was the *scientific* and *objective* classification of given, mostly visible phenomena. These models are inextricably linked with an ideology of "race", with prejudices and discrimination. Its strongest form, racism, is based on an understanding of "race" not as an abstract and subjective concept, but as an objective reality or fact (Mayr 1997: 36 f.). The question is still controversial: How *real* is "race" and *what* does "real" mean? 'While it is now widely accepted that races do not share robust, biobehavioral essences, opinions differ over what, if anything, race is (Mallon 2006: 525; cf. Harrison 2010; Mukhopadhyay, Henze and Moses 2007; Sarich 2005). Most academics today reject a biological foundation of the concept of race: 'The billions of humans alive today simply do not fit into neat and tidy biological boxes called races. Science has proven this conclusively. The concept of race [...] is not scientific and goes against what is known about our ever-changing and complex biological diversity' (Harrison 2010: 21 f.). Most of the classifications were associated with racist hierarchies. The French naturalist and mathematician Georges-Louis Leclerc, Comte de Buffon (1707–1788), declared white Europeans to be superior to the other "races". Others' positions, like Immanuel Kant's (1724–1804) or Georg Forster's (1754–1794), were less clearly racist. In his writings about the human races, in 1775 and 1785, Kant points out that the description of four races and especially the 'white' and 'black' variants are just an *auxiliary* to the scientific description of an *eternal* variety of human beings, not an *ideological statement* of hierarchy (AA, II: 433; AA, VIII: 103). His definition of 'races' assumed the *possibility* of the descent from one couple for all human variations – that is monogenesis (AA, VIII: 102). Therefore, this thesis belongs to the realm of *natural history* [*Naturgeschichte*], which has a notional, speculative or teleological method. Natural history does not aim to provide the definite and true existence of two, four or even twelve races. It describes a *possible* development of human culture and nature, while the empirical *description of nature* or physiography describes the varieties that can be observed (ibid.: 93): 'Natural description only sees varieties, differences. Natural history sees the unity behind that variety and makes it possible to identify the different races' (Bernasconi 2012: 195). The one focusses on nature, the other on culture. Nevertheless, the statements of both merged in what became *scientific racism*, because one cannot divide nature and culture when the question is about human beings. As Kant pointed out in his *Pedagogy*, we are 'nothing more than what education makes of us' (AA. IX: 443).

Anyway, Kant (more or less unintentionally) 'drew on pro-slavery sources' (Bernasconi 2012: 207; Bernasconi 2002). In his lectures on *Physical Geography* (1802) he makes a clear statement about the superiority of the whites (AA, IX: 316), though the blacks also 'may' have virtuous and good qualities (AA, IX: 408; 410ff.). Eze points out that such an irrational irresponsibility 'shadows Enlightenment's ahistorical (Hume's) and transcendental (Kant's) conceptions of the Negro' (Eze 2002: 286). The anatomist Samuel Thomas Soemmerring (1755–1830) claims that the blacks are not 'less human' than the 'most beautiful Greek women', but he also declared black people less intelligent than whites in general (Sömmerring 1785: XX; Oehler-Klein 2012: 149). Kant's opponent Georg Forster, who travelled the world together with James Cook and who claimed to use an empirical method in his ethnological research, first took a position characterised by respect toward foreign ethnic groups. Then, influenced by the anatomical postulates of Soemmerring, he too changed to a statement of the superiority of the whites, for example, in his essay *Über Leckereyen* [*On delicacies*] (1788) (Forster 1991: 167). Later he argued again that physical and cultural diversity needed to be respected (Oehler-Klein 2012: 161).

Linnaeus, for example, described four 'races' in his *Systema Naturae*, differentiating among them by their skin colour and continent (white Europeans; red Americans; brown, later yellow, Asians; and black Africans). He also created a 'wastebasket taxon' named *monstrosus* to fill taxonomic gaps, including '"Troglodytes", "Satyrs" and "Pygmies", as well as six monstrous varieties of Homo sapiens' – one of them later turned out to be an ape (Park and Daston 1981: 54; Linnaeus 1758: 22–25). Linnaeus succeeded in turning the formerly metaphysical explanation of the origins of humanity into a scientific explanation, but at the same time he linked the description of phenotypes and habitat with the classical ideas of four temperaments: sanguine, melancholic, choleric and phlegmatic (Hoßfeld 2005: 58; Keevak 2011: 52–53; Marks 2010: 265). This example shows how ancient ideas which many people believed had been left behind – and the prejudices wedded to them – did not simply vanish, but were transformed and merged with new ideas: the idea that *all* blacks are phlegmatic or *all* whites are melancholic replaced the astrological idea that *all* Pisces are phlegmatic or *all* Capricorns are melancholic.

The *Eurocentrism* mentioned earlier had increasing influence on scientific discourses. All anthropological taxonomies named define the European, linked to a more or less white skin, as the standard, the origin or the superior form of the suspected races. For example, Buffon stated that 'everyone's "true colour" was White' (Bernasconi 2012: 202), and Kant stated that the original couple we all are supposed to have descended from was white (AA, II: 521; Lutterbeck 2012: 108). Only few of the scientists were aware of this egocentric point of view. Forster, for example, wrote that we all see the world differently as through personal 'coloured glass' (Forster 1982: 13). Blumenbach wrote that the white "Caucasian race" is the best example of a beautiful skull and face within 'the European understanding of beauty' (Blumenbach 1803: 66). Others did not seem to be as aware of this, like

Soemmerring, whose belief in the superiority of his own "race" might have led him to the postulate that black Africans are *less* intelligent, because they have *stronger* nerves (Oehler-Klein 2012: 149). This naturalistic fallacy, an invalid analogical conclusion between biological or empirical facts and abstract ideas or mental capacities, is typical of the Enlightenment, *because* of its approach to scientification (turning religious explanations to scientific ones).

The history of "gender" within the history of ideas: Even more intersections

The origin of the term "gender" might be the Latin word "genus", that means "kind", "type", or "sort" in the most general sense. There is also a link to different words like the Latin "gens" or the Arabic "genat", which have a relation to the area of birth ("pregnant"), descent ("genes", "genesis"), and family ("generation"). What is important here is that these words can *synonymously* refer to a clan or stock; they can mean "people" – and even "race". One example is the word "genocide", referring to the murder of a larger group of people belonging to one ethnicity, tribe or "race". Therefore, originally both terms, "gender" and "race", referred to a descent or to roots – in a more or less physical way. Blood is thicker than water. Both were equally used to make a clear distinction between "us" and "them". This *etymological intersection* between "race", "sex" and "gender" has survived in many words still in use today.

While English knows the two terms "gender" and "sex", German ("Geschlecht") and French ("sexe") still have only one term. All these terms are related to the concept of the other, as manifested in the term "race" during the Enlightenment. In German, "Geschlecht" (sex/gender) and "Rasse" (race) refer equally to an origin or ancestry, as in the words "Menschen*rasse*" and "Menschen*geschlecht*", both meaning "humankind". Especially Kant often used words referring to "gender" or "race" synonymously: 'zwei Menschen*gattungen*' ['two human sexes'] (AA, II: 228) beside 'Charakter der Menschen*gattung*' ['character of the human race/humankind'] (AA, VII: 321) or 'das menschliche *Geschlecht*' ['humankind'] (AA, VIII: 307) beside 'das weibliche *Geschlecht*' ['the female sex/gender'] (AA, VII: 305). This overlap can be found in the word "Menschengeschlecht" (humankind, humanity), which is still commonly used, while "Geschlecht" today is used only for "sex" or "gender". The French "race" was used to distinguish between different noble families in the beginning and since the eighteenth century has distinctly differentiated between "human races". The French word "gens" still means "people" in general. The different sexes are named by "sexe". Only in German and French academic discourse – influenced by the feminist theory – is "gender" used, borrowed from the English.

However, there is not only an intersection of the terms "gender/sex" and "race", there is also an intersection between social and biological, ideological and physical aspects in the double-term "sex/gender". Originally "gender" referred to femininity or masculinity, though mostly in the sense of grammatical gender: feminine, masculine and neuter. In 1926 Henry Watson Fowler even declared "gender" to be 'a grammatical term only', its reference to a person he judged to be 'a blunder' (Fowler 1926: 211). Of course there are examples of references to the femininity or masculinity of a person in history which use 'gender', from William Congreve (1670–1729) to Laurence Sterne (1713–1768) (Congreve 1967: 467; Sterne 1968: 31), and in Ambrose Bierce's (1842–1914) *The Cynic's Word Book* (1906):

> GENDER, n. The sex of words.
> A masculine wooed a feminine noun,
> But his courting didn't suit her,
> So he begged a verb his wishes to crown,
> But the verb replied, with a frigid frown:
> 'What object have I? I'm neuter.'
> (Bierce 1967: 111)

The intersection of biological and social aspects in the double-term "sex/gender" leads and led to naturalistic fallacies, as well – as in the case of 'race'. Though one might think that their cause, the process of naturalisation during the scientific revolution, has been overcome, new 'modes of biological naturalization have again re-emerged', as mentioned above (Lettow 2013). Since the sexologist John Money introduced its terminological *distinction* from the biological sex in 1955, "gender" has been used to describe *social roles* based on the sex of a person. In his theory, the gender of a person could differ from his or her sex, but it was also somehow still defined by biological features. The concepts *gender role* and *gender identity* have both been adopted and criticised by feminist theory since then.[3] There is another similarity to "race": the academic controversy on the sex-gender distinction continues. What is 'gender', how real is it and what does that mean (Mikkola 2008, 2012; Miller 2012)?

Academics and activists had already questioned *gender roles* in the eighteenth century, especially in the context of the social and political upheavals which led to the French Revolution. Famous female activists, such as Olympe de Gouges (1748–1793) or Mary Wollstonecraft (1759–1797), Anne Louise Germaine de Staël (1766–1817) and Jeanne-Marie Roland de La Platière (1754–1793), fought for equal rights for men and women. Olympe de Gouges not only fought against the exclusion of women, but also against the exclusion of other "races" from human rights, and against slavery. She published her famous *Declaration of the Rights of Woman and the Female Citizen* in 1791, in 1784 she had already written a play, *Zamore and Mirza*, criticising slavery. At the same time there were reactionary tendencies, as in every case of progressive development: de Gouges was executed by the guillotine in 1793; but three days before her anti-slavery play was first performed in 1789 she had already been threatened with death in an anonymous letter (Geier 2012: 321).

The source of conservative reactions to women activists was similar to those of the opponents of slavery, mainly economic and power interests. But if my thesis is right and fear is an important cause of prejudices and even hate, the conservative reaction is not only about material interests. The boundaries of self-construction which had been conditioned by the other (as barbarian) were challenged by expeditions of discovery and led to the need for a new definition of the other itself. This need was justified by the seemingly scientific and taxonomic category of "race". Just like the concept of the other as barbarian, gender roles, a concept of social order, did not seem to be as stable as they were before.

For Martin Luther the distinction between men and women was given by God. His *Sermon on the Estate of Marriage* (1519) begins with a definition of humankind as 'divided by God into two pieces', with reference to the Book of Genesis (Luther 1991a: 284). Therefore, he claims, it neither is in our power to make a man a women nor otherwise (ibid.). For Luther a woman is inferior to her husband just as man is inferior to God (Luther 1991b: 92). It is an asymmetrical relationship, but characterised by love. Around 250 years later, we find Immanuel Kant writing similarly, for example: 'I hardly believe that the fair sex is capable of principles' (AA, II: 232). Yet there are also sentences in Kant which seem to be from a totally different person, for example, when Kant describes the 'most perfect woman' ['vollkommenste Frau'] as prudent, wise, reasonable, and 'wacker' [upright or brave in a down-to-earth manner] in a side note in his *Observations on the Beautiful and the Sublime* (AA. xx: 179) – the same text the first quotation is from. What should we make of that?

In the eighteenth century it was quite common to describe women as the beautiful or fair(er) sex and men as the strong or rational one; this classification still retains much of its 'appeal' (Mays 2012: 277). *The Lady's Magazine*, a British fashion magazine (1770–1837), was also known as an *Entertaining Companion for the Fair Sex, Appropriated Solely to Their Use and Amusement*. From 1693 on *The Ladies' Mercury*, a spin-off from *The Athenian Mercury*, aimed to answer questions sent 'by the fair sex' (Turner 2002: 65), concerning 'love, marriage, behaviour, dress and humour of the female sex, whether virgins, wives, or widows' (Keeble 2005: 13). These three categories of women reflect their social and legal status. They seem to *have* a status only as the (virgin) children of their parents or in their relationship to a husband – dead or alive.

Kant also opens his statements on the beautiful and the sublime as a topic of gender issues with the remark that the one who first understood women to be the fair or beautiful sex was right (AA, II: 228). Of course, his description of this fair sex is ambivalent from a modern perspective. He tells us what women can or should not do. As mentioned above, women *are* hardly capable of principles, *should* not go to war or defend themselves in court, according to Kant (AA, VII: 209). At the same time he describes women as custodians of and encouraging for culture and for the moral improvement of humanity (ibid.: 306; cf. Jauch 1989: 92; Heinz 2002). This ambiguity is typical of the Enlightenment. Is John Zammito right? Was Kant simply 'not enlightened enough'? (Zammito 2012: 230).

Just like Luther, Kant begins his *Conjectural Beginning of Human History* (1786) with the same reference to Genesis (AA, VIII: 109 f.). And in his *Observations* he makes a remark about the 'charming difference' between the beautiful (female) and the sublime (male) sex, quite similar to Luther's: 'It is most important that a man becomes the most perfect as a man and a woman as a woman, that is […] to make the one even more sublime and the other's features even more beautiful' (AA, II: 242). But in 'default of those principles' one might take over the merits of the opposite sex, now and then (ibid.). Though Kant talks of human *nature* and the *nature* of the two sexes, this is just a metaphor. In fact he describes ideal-typical male and female characteristics which have to be cultivated (Jauch 1989: 23). His gender difference in fact is a *gender* difference, not a God-given or a biologically distinct division (both essentialist positions). And his view on women was not that negative. He does not criticise women as *coquettes per se* (which would be an essentialist position); otherwise, he would have changed his mind from one page to the next when he describes the perfect woman as prudent, upright and reasonable.[4] Instead, he criticises *coquetry* as a misfortune, for men and women – equally. For Kant, the wish to attract corresponds to the feminine ideal (related to beauty). And the coquette caricatures this attitude just like her male pendant, the '*petit maître*' (AA, xx: 3). A female '*prude*' (a prim person) caricatures the opposite masculine ideal (related to duty) as well as the '*rauhe pedant*' (rough pedant or rule-monger) (ibid.).[5] For Kant both sexes should have feminine and masculine aspects, but such that for a woman all positive aspects should increase and accentuate the female character as the fairer one (AA, II: 228). The idea of the feminine (beautiful, sensitive, subtle) is thought to mirror the masculine (noble, sublime, strong) and they are supposed to complement each other in harmony (cf. Kersting 2012: 188–191, 194–197).

The half social, half (pseudo-) scientific concept of *gender difference*, as in the already mentioned sexed brain, was originally developed in the context of social restructuring after the disintegration of the estates of the realm (Mikkola 2011: 106; Kersting 2012: 183–184). Therefore, it has a *socio-cultural* context that differs from the more *science-oriented* context of the invention of a category like "race". Kant's definition of the two sexes and/or genders is *not* primarily based on *science-oriented*, *empirical findings*, but on pragmatic hypotheses. Nevertheless, the tendency of naturalisation, leading to naturalistic fallacies, sexism, and racism, has an impact on the gender category, as well. There were theories in the eighteenth century which coupled explicitly the *physiognomy and phenotype* of women to character and intelligence (Pearl 2010; Hiller 2009), as in the case of the Swiss philosopher and theologian Johann Caspar Lavater (1741–1801). Thereby, the *social* roles "mother", "wife" and "housewife" were justified by *physical* or biological traits, and the socially and legally inferior position of women was justified by their weaker physical constitution (*naturalistic fallacy*).

Kant's aim was the reciprocal and thereby self-neutralising interdependence of men and women which generates 'equality from the difference' (Kersting 2012: 196; cf. Geier 2012: 308–313). However, it gave rise to stronger gender-based discrimination and heteronormativity in the nineteenth century.

Conclusion

What Kant described were gender roles. As Simone de Beauvoir put it: 'One is not born a woman, but made a woman' (Beauvoir 2012: 334). Around 150 years before Beauvoir, Kant asked himself, in a side note again, if 'femininity is just education or a natural disposition?' (AA, XV: 642). His remarks on the *coquette* and the *petit maître*, the *prude* and the *pedant* give his answer, as well as his statement in the lectures on *Pedagogy*. According to this, humans are 'nothing more than what education makes of them' (AA, IX: 443).

The two main reasons for the development of the naturalisation of the two sexes were the new hunger for scientific truth and categorisation in the Enlightenment and the need for categories of social order. These led to the intersection of social and biological aspects and a mixture of different forms of social order: religious, socio-cultural and (seemingly) biologically founded ones. A very impressive example of the intersection of the terms of social order today are the people of Amarete in Bolivia (cf. Rösing 2001). They make social distinctions between ten genders in regard to the biological sex, but also in regard to the 'gender' of the profession or the post one has, the land the person lives on, etc., because everything has its gender and has an impact on people. The more male one is, the higher a person's social status is.

The same hunger for categorisation and order caused the concept of "race" to become one used to discriminate, even though some of its inventors might have had good intentions. Etymologically rooted in a longing for an *individual descent* one could depend on and a *distinct other* one could distinguish oneself from as an individual, both "race" and "gender" intersected from the very beginning. They were the two new main categories of the rising anthropological discourses of the Enlightenment. Still we have to deal with the negative legacy of all three of them. Though the term "race" has more or less vanished from the science-orientated anthropological discourse today, the social sciences have to deal with it in the form of racism, just like sexism.

When the Enlightenment is understood as a never-ending work in progress, the aim is not to find *the* answer to one question, like 'What is man?', but to take one more step in this process by answering and provoking new questions. That might tell us more about what it means to be human than, for example, can be done by anatomy or, currently, neuroscience.

Notes

1 One exception is a work by Brigitte Fuchs (Fuchs 2003). Yet Fuchs examines only anthropological discourses in Austria from the nineteenth to the twentieth century.
2 All English translations of German quotations are mine.
3 Feminists especially criticized Money's heteronormativity, for he did not see anything other than a feminine or masculine sex, as in the concrete case of David Reimer. Reimer had a sex reassignment as a child, partly based on Money's recommendation, and later committed suicide.
4 In the eighteenth century a coquette was a woman playing with her charms, flirting or trying to get attention or admiration, often without a serious ambition. In the nineteenth century the connotations became more negative, from vanity to prostitution.
5 A French variant of a dandy or fashionmonger which acquired a negative connotation in the later eighteenth century as artificial, old-fashioned, superficial or amoral.

References

Bancel, N. (ed.) 2014. *The Invention of Race: Scientific and Popular Representations*. Routledge Studies in Cultural History, 28. New York: Routledge.

Beauvoir, S. de. 2012. *Das andere Geschlecht: Sitte u. Sexus d. Frau*. Reinbek bei Hamburg: Rowohlt.

Bernasconi, R. 2002. 'Kant as an Unfamiliar Source of Racism', in *Philosophers on Race: Critical Essays*, edited by J. K. Ward. Oxford: Blackwell, pp. 154–158.

——. 2012). 'True Colors: Kant's Distinction Between Nature and Artifice in Context', in *Klopffechtereien – Missverständnisse – Widersprüche? Methodische und methodologische Perspektiven auf die Kant-Forster-Kontroverse*, edited by R. Godel and G. Stiening. Laboratorium Aufklärung, 10, Paderborn: Fink, pp. 191–210.

Bethencourt, F. 2013. *Racisms: From the Crusades to the Twentieth Century*. Princeton: Princeton University Press.

Bierce, A. 1967. *The Enlarged Devil's Dictionary: With 851 Newly Discovered Words and Definitions Added to the Previous Thousand-Word Collection*, edited by E. J. Hopkins, preface by J. Myers. Garden City, NY: Doubleday & Comp.

Bloch, R. H. 1987. 'Medieval Misogyny', *Representations* 20: 1–24.

Borgstedt, T. 1992. *Reichsidee und Liebesethik*. Studien zur deutschen Literatur, 121. Tübingen, Frankfurt (Main): Niemeyer.

Braude, B. 1997. 'The Sons of Noah and the Construction of Ethnic and Geographical Identities in the Medieval and Early Modern Periods', *William and Mary Quarterly* LIV: 103–142.

Bruno, G. 1969. *Das Aschermittwochsmahl*, translated by F. Fellmann. Frankfurt am Main: Insel-Verlag.

Chanes, J. A. 2004. *Antisemitism: A Reference Handbook*. Santa Barbara, CA: ABC-CLIO.

Cohen, H. 1904. *Ethik des reinen Willens*. Berlin: B. Cassirer.

Congreve, W. 1967. *The Complete Plays*, edited by H. Davis. Chicago: University of Chicago Press.

Conze, W. and Sommer, A. 2004. 'Rasse', in *Geschichtliche Grundbegriffe: Historisches Lexikon zur politisch-sozialen Sprache in Deutschland*, edited by O. Brunner et al. Stuttgart: Klett-Cotta, vol. 5, 135–178.

Cooper, K. 2013. *Band of Angels: The Forgotten World of Early Christian Women*. London: Atlantic Books.

Daston, L. and Park, K. 2001. *Wonders and the Order of Nature: 1150–1750*. New York: Zone Books.

Dines, G. and Humez, J. M. (eds.) 2015. *Gender, Race and Class in Media: A Critical Reader*. 4th edn. Thousand Oaks: Sage.

Forster, G. 1982. *Reise um die Welt: Teil 1* [1778], in *Georg Forsters Werke: Sämtliche Schriften, Tagebücher, Briefe*. Berlin: Akademie-Verlag.

——. 1991. 'Über Leckereyen' [1788], in *Kleine Schriften zu Philosophie und Zeitgeschichte*, edited by S. Scheibe. 2nd edn. Berlin: Akademie-Verlag, pp. 164–181.

Fowler, H. W. 1926. *A Dictionary of Modern English Usage*. Oxford, London: Clarendon Press; Humphrey Milford.

Fuchs, B. 2003. *"Rasse", "Volk", Geschlecht: Anthropologische Diskurse in Österreich 1850–1960*. Frankfurt/Main: Campus-Verlag.

Gay, P. 2009. 'Breeding Is Fundamental: Jenny Davidson Reflects on Enlightenment Ideas about Human Perfectibility: Review', *Book Forum* 2009 (April/May), http://www.bookforum.com/inprint/016_01/3519 (accessed 19 May 2015).

Geier, M. 2012. *Aufklärung: Das europäische Projekt*. Reinbek bei Hamburg: Rowohlt.

Geiss, I. 1993. *Geschichte des Rassismus*. Frankfurt am Main: Suhrkamp.
Geulen, C. 2007. *Geschichte des Rassismus*. München: Beck.
Gilman, S. L. 2010. *Disease and Diagnoses: The Second Age of Biology*. New York: Transaction.
Goldenberg, D. M. 1997. 'The Curse of Ham: A Case of Rabbinic Racism?', in *Struggles in the Promised Land: Toward a History of Black-Jewish Relations in the United States*, edited by J. Salzman. New York: Oxford University Press.
—. 2003. *The Curse of Ham: Race and Slavery in Early Judaism, Christianity, and Islam*. Princeton, NJ: Princeton University Press.
Goswami, N. 2014. *Why Race and Gender Still Matter: An Intersectional Approach*. London: Pickering & Chatto.
Haraway, D. J. 1991. *Simians, Cyborgs, and Women: The Reinvention of Nature*. New York: Routledge.
Harris, M. 2001. *The Rise of Anthropological Theory: A History of Theories of Culture*. Walnut Creek, CA: AltaMira Press.
Harrison, G. 2010. *Race and Reality: What Everyone Should Know about Our Biological Diversity*. Amherst, NY: Prometheus Books.
Heinz, M. 2002. 'Das Gegenverhältnis der Geschlechter: Immanuel Kant', in *Philosophische Geschlechtertheorien: Ausgewählte Texte von der Antike bis zur Gegenwart*, edited by M. Heinz and S. Doyé. Stuttgart: Reclam, pp. 191–198.
Hiller, J. R. 2009. *Bodies that Tell: Physiognomy, Criminology, Race and Gender in Late Nineteenth- and Early Twentieth-Century Italian Literature and Opera*. Unpublished PhD dissertation: University of California.
Hoßfeld, U. 2005. *Geschichte der biologischen Anthropologie in Deutschland: Von den Anfängen bis in die Nachkriegszeit*. Stuttgart: Steiner.
Jacques, T. C. 1997. 'From Savages and Barbarians to Primitives: Africa, Social Typologies, and History in Eighteenth-Century French Philosophy', *History and Theory* 36(2): 190–215.
Janz, O. and Schönpflug, D. (eds.). 2014. *Gender History in a Transnational Perspective: Networks, Biographies, Gender Orders*. New York: Berghahn Books.
Jauch, U. P. 1989. *Immanuel Kant zur Geschlechterdifferenz: Aufklärerische Vorurteilskritik und bürgerliche Geschlechtsvormundschaft*. Wien: Passagen Verlag.
Kant, I. (1910–1917; 1923 ff.) *Gesammelte Schriften*. Herausgegeben von der Preußischen Akademie der Wissenschaften. 29 vols., Berlin: Reimer; de Gruyter:
- AA. II (Beobachtungen über das Gefühl des Schönen u. Erhabenen, 1764). 1905/1912.
- AA. II (Bemerkungen über die Beob. ü. d. Gefühl d. Schönen u. Erhabenen). 1942.
- AA. VII (Anthropologie in pragmatischer Hinsicht, 1798). 1907/1917.
- AA. VIII (Muthmaßlicher Anfang der Menschengeschichte, 1786). 1923.
- AA. IX (Pädagogik, 1800). 1923.
- AA. XV (Reflexionen). 1923.
- AA. XX. (Aus dem Nachlaß). 1942.
Karafyllis, N. C. 2008. *Sexualized Brains: Scientific Modeling of Emotional Intelligence from a Cultural Perspective*. Cambridge, MA: MIT Press.
Keeble, R. 2005. *Print Journalism: A Critical Introduction*. Abingdon: Routledge.
Keevak, M. 2011. *Becoming Yellow: A Short History of Racial Thinking*. Princeton: Princeton University Press.
Kersting, W. 2012. 'Immanuel Kant: Vom ästhetischen Gegenverhältnis der Geschlechter zum rechtlichen Besitzverhältnis in der Ehe', in *Geschlechterordnung und Staat: Legitimationsfiguren der politischen Philosophie (1600–1850)*, edited by M. Heinz and F. Kuster. Berlin: Akademie-Verlag.
Laqueur, W. 2006. *The Changing Face of Antisemitism: From Ancient Times to the Present Day*. Oxford: Oxford University Press.

Lettow, S. 2013. 'Modes of Naturalization: Race, Sex and Biology in Kant, Schelling and Hegel', *Philosophy & Social Criticism* 39(2): 117–131.
Linnaeus, C. 1758. *Systema Naturae Per Regna Tria Naturæ, Secundum Classes, Ordines, Genera, Species, Cum Characteribus, Differentiis, Synonymis, Locis*. Holmiae, Stockholm: Salvius.
Luther, M. 1991a. 'Vom ehelichen Leben', in *Luther deutsch: Die Werke Martin Luthers in neuer Auswahl für die Gegenwart*, edited by K. Berlin: Evang. Verl.-Anst. vol. 7, 284–411.
—. 1991b. 'Erste Vorlesung über die Psalmen', in *Luther deutsch: Die Werke Martin Luthers in neuer Auswahl für die Gegenwart*, edited by K. Aland. Berlin: Evang. Verl.-Anst. vol. 1, pp. 19–434.
Lutterbeck, K.-G. 2012. 'Normativität des Faktischen? Integrale Wissenschaft vom Menschen und ihre Folgen', in *Klopffechtereien – Missverständnisse – Widersprüche?: Methodische und methodologische Perspektiven auf die Kant-Forster-Kontroverse*, edited by R. Godel and G. Stiening. Laboratorium Aufklärung, 10, Paderborn: Fink, pp. 97–118.
Mallon, R. 2006. '"Race": Normative, Not Metaphysical or Semantic', *Ethics* 116: 525–551.
Marks, J. 2008. 'Race: Past, Present and Future', in *Revisiting Race in a Genomic Age*, edited by B. A. Koenig. New Brunswick, NJ: Rutgers University Press.
—. 2010. 'Ten Facts about Human Variation', in *Human Evolutionary Biology*, edited by M. P. Muehlenbein. Cambridge: Cambridge University Press, pp. 265–276.
Mayr, E. 1997. *Evolution and the Diversity of Life: Selected Essays*. Cambridge, MA: Belknap.
Mays, A. 2012. 'Determinanten traditionell-sexistischer Einstellungen in Deutschland: Eine Analyse mit Allbus-Daten', *Kölner Zeitschrift für Soziologie und Sozialpsychologie* 64: 277–302.
Meijer, M. C. 1999. *Race and Aesthetics in the Anthropology of Petrus Camper: 1722–1789*. Studies in the History of Ideas in the Low Countries, 4. Amsterdam: Rodopi.
Michlin, M. 2013. *Black Intersectionalities: A Critique for the 21st Century*. Liverpool: Liverpool University Press.
Mikkola, M. 2012. *Feminist Perspectives on Sex and Gender*. Stanford Encyclopedia of Philosophy. (Fall 2012 edition), edited by Edward N. Zalta. http://plato.stanford.edu/archives/fall2012/entries/feminism-gender/ (accessed 24 May 2105).
—. 2011. 'Kant on Moral Agency and Women's Nature', *Kantian Review* 1: 89–111.
—. 2012. 'Der Begriff der Entmenschlichung in der Philosophie', in *Philosophie und die Potenziale der Gender Studies: Peripherie und Zentrum im Feld der Theorie*, edited by H. Landweer et al. Bielefeld: Transcript-Verl, pp. 87–115.
Miller, S. 2012. 'Der Streit um die feministische Utopie', in *Philosophie und die Potenziale der Gender Studies: Peripherie und Zentrum im Feld der Theorie*, edited by H. Landweer et al. Bielefeld: Transcript-Verl., pp. 118–139.
Montaigne, M. E. De. 1953. *Die Essais*. Leipzig: Dieterich.
—. 1967. *Essays*, edited by J. Bode et al. Leipzig: Reclam.
Moore, G. E. 1993. *Principia ethica*. With the preface to the second edition & other papers. Cambridge, MA: Cambridge University Press.
Mukhopadhyay, C. C. et al. 2007. *How Real Is Race? A Sourcebook on Race, Culture, and Biology*. Lanham, MD: Rowman & Littlefield Education.
Park, K. and Daston, L. J. 1981. 'Unnatural Conceptions: The Study of Monsters in Sixteenth- and Seventeenth-Century France and England', *Past & Present* 92: 20–54.
Pearl, S. 2010. *About Faces: Physiognomy in Nineteenth-Century Britain*. Cambridge, MA: Harvard University Press.
Rösing, I. 2001. *Religion, Ritual und Alltag in den Anden: Mundo Ankari/zweiter Ankari-Zyklus; Kollektivrituale der Kallawaya-Region in den Anden Boliviens*. Frankfurt am Main: Zweitausendeins.
Salih, S. 2007. 'Filling Up the Space Between Mankind and Ape: Racism, Speciesism and the Androphilic Ape', *ARIEL* 38(1): 95–111.

Sanders, E. R. 1969. 'The Hamitic Hypothesis: Its Origin and Functions in Time Perspective', *Journal of African History* 10: 521–532.
Sarich, V. 2005. *Race: The Reality of Human Differences*. Boulder: Westview Press.
Sömmerring, S. T. 1785. *Über die körperliche Verschiedenheit des Negers vom Europäer*. Frankfurt; Mainz: Varrentrapp Sohn und Wenner.
Sterne, L. 1968. *A Sentimental Journey through France and Italy by Mister Yorick: To Which Are Added the Journal to Eliza and A political Romance*, edited by I. Jack. London: Oxford University Press.
Stiening, G. 2012. '[E]s gibt gar keine verschiedenen Arten von Menschen', in *Klopffechtereien – Missverständnisse – Widersprüche? Methodische und methodologische Perspektiven auf die Kant-Forster-Kontroverse*, edited by R. Godel and G. Stiening. (Laboratorium Aufklärung, 10) Paderborn: Fink, pp. 19–54.
Swift, J. N. and Mammoser, G. 2009. 'Out of the Realm of Superstition: Chesnutt's 'Dave's Neckliss' and the Curse of Ham', *American Literary Realism* 42(1): 1–12.
Turner, D. M. 2002. *Fashioning Adultery: Gender, Sex and Civility in England, 1660–1740*. Cambridge: Cambridge University Press.
Vertovec, S. (ed.). 2015. *Routledge International Handbook of Diversity Studies*. London: Routledge.
West, C. and Zimmerman, D. H. 1987. 'Doing Gender', *Gender & Society: Official Publication of Sociologists for Women in Society* 1: 125–151.
Williams, B. A. 2005. *Descartes: The Project of Pure Enquiry*. New York: Routledge.
Wucherpfennig, W. 1973. *Klugheit und Weltordnung. Das Problem politischen Handelns in Lohensteins 'Arminius'*. Freiburg i. Br: Universitätsverl. Becksmann.
Zammito, J. H. 2012. 'The Forster-Kant-Controversy: The Provocations of Interdisciplinarity', in *Klopffechtereien – Missverständnisse – Widersprüche? Methodische und methodologische Perspektiven auf die Kant-Forster-Kontroverse*, edited by R. Godel and G. Stiening. (Laboratorium Aufklärung, 10) Paderborn: Fink, pp. 225–244.
Zinsser, J. P. 2005. *Men, Women, and the Birthing of Modern Science*. DeKalb: Northern Illinois University Press.

PART V
Thinking about Enlightenment and its limits

9

ADOPTION AS A LIMIT-CASE FOR ENLIGHTENMENT: LESSING'S *NATHAN DER WEISE* AND KLEIST'S *DER FINDLING*

David D. Kim

In Vicente Franco and Gail Dolgin's controversial documentary *Daughter from Danang* (2002), Heidi Bub, a middle-aged woman from the U.S. state of South Carolina, returns to Vietnam to meet her long-lost biological mother. Bub had been adopted by an American woman some 22 years before, but, having struggled to find her place in a predominantly white society, she decided to reconnect with the maternal world from which she had violently been uprooted. The historical backdrop against which her emotionally charged story of transnational adoption and roots trip unfolds is the infamous, yet hardly remembered Operation Babylift. In April 1975, as the Vietnam War was winding down, a handful of Western governments headed by President Gerald Ford's administration collaborated with Christian organisations to evacuate some 3,300 interethnic children from South Vietnam and place them in adoptive homes around the globe. The premise of this internationally coordinated humanitarian operation was that the communist regime would execute these children for having been fathered by enemy soldiers. Bub, too, was the child of an unknown American soldier and, as she would remember this day, it was the most traumatic event in her painfully split life.

To illustrate the complexity of this top-down humanitarian intervention in the Second Indochina War, the documentary weaves together Bub's profound sense of dislocation and a public scandal of internationalism. Rather than celebrate the much-anticipated reunion between Bub and her biological mother, it exposes the trauma that comes from being suddenly torn from the arms of a frightened and misinformed mother. At the same time, it captures the onset of a second related trauma as Bub struggles to cope with feelings of guilt and discrepant expectations back in Vietnam. On her simultaneously self-reflective and naively judgmental journey, she feels nauseous going back and forth between American consumerism and Third World poverty, U.S. provincialism and Vietnamese filial piety, biological origin and cultural upbringing. After more than two decades of split identity, she fails to acquire any more unified sense of self after all.

As Margaret Homans has pointed out, stories of transnational adoption illuminate 'the problem of the unknowability of origins and the common tendency to address that problem with fiction making' (Homans 2006: 5). Even when adopted children meet their biological parents, this reconnection exemplifies the crossroads whose trajectory diverges from a teleological narrative of identity, nation and history. Caught between cultural norms, political crises and social hardships, they come with many cultural, moral, legal and political challenges in giving homes to orphaned children across international borders. As *Daughter from Danang* illustrates, mother and daughter are emotionally further apart despite their physical proximity, and the subsequent breakdown in communication represents an impasse both for cross-cultural exchange at an interpersonal level and for international humanitarianism at a larger scale.

I do not wish to delve any further into the politics of transnational adoption, as it is examined today; nor is it my intention to make sweeping claims about adoption at large.[1] It goes without saying that innumerable parents adopt children both domestically and internationally for all the right reasons. I have begun this essay with a brief analysis of *Daughter from Danang* because the documentary serves as a provocative point of departure for thinking critically about the relevance of Enlightenment texts for contemporary concerns with adoption, origin, translation and identity. Frauke Berndt and Daniel Fulda (2012), David Harvey (2009), Jonathan Israel (2001, 2006, 2010), Anthony Pagden (2013), and Tzvetan Todorov (2009) have lately argued that Enlightenment principles such as religious freedom and moral autonomy demand ongoing reflection, if not faithful preservation. They contend that the interesting question now is not whether we are for or against Enlightenment, but what our Enlightenment is in the twenty-first century. The following interpretation takes its cue from this proposition, thus renewing the Enlightenment ever so subtly as an inexhaustible legacy for the living. In the following pages, I wish to raise what I believe are unresolved questions about adoptive relationships, biological kinships, affective bondings and moral virtues in modern society. How is it that the idea of biological origin remains a measure for cultural production even after two centuries? What values do we assign blood relations, and why do we continue to place culture and nature in false dichotomies? Or are roots and routes as interchangeable as scholars deem them to be? And what binds children to parents beyond naïve comparisons between nature and nurture? It is beyond the scope of this essay to answer each of these questions in a comprehensive manner, but I want to address them through the stigmatized lens of adoption and explore the Enlightenment as a seminal point of orientation for the present moment.

To pursue this study of cultural assessment, philosophical rumination and historical legacy, I concentrate on adoption as the principal figure of Enlightenment, and I do so by reading two canonical German Enlightenment texts as literary foundations for this enquiry: Lessing's *Nathan der Weise* [*Nathan the Wise*] (1779) and Heinrich von Kleist's *Der Findling* [*The Foundling*] (1811). As I argue, they represent the rise and the fall of Enlightenment pedagogy around 1800. Lessing explores the cultural, moral and philosophical promises of adoption whereby the father raises his child without grounding his paternal authority in genealogical origin. Nathan embodies the enlightened father figure *par excellence*. Less than half a century later, Kleist draws upon this play not to uphold the same principles, but to depict the perils of adoption whereby an initially loving adoptive father-child relationship transmogrifies into an antagonistic tragedy. Lessing's work of cultural tradition and universal order collapses in this post-Kantian representation of the world. Read side by side, then, *Nathan der Weise* and *Der Findling* conceive of adoption as a limit-case for the Enlightenment.

According to Karl-Josef Kuschel, the countless interpretations that exist of *Nathan der Weise* mostly fall into one of two categories. Either they consider the play to be the only German-speaking literature offering 'das Modell einer Versöhnbarkeit von Juden, Christen und Muslimen' [the model of a reconcilability between Jews, Christians and Muslims] after an interreligious conflict, or it is interpreted as a literary illustration of the 'Konflikt zwischen der Forderung der pädagogischen Vernunft und den Prägungen der Herkunft' [conflict between the demand of pedagogical reason and the imprints of origin] (Kuschel 2004: 102, 103).[2] That is, the play stages the possibility of a reconciliation between world religions in struggle, or it lays bare the irreducible gap that exists between 'die geistige Erziehungsfamilie' [the spiritual pedagogical family] bound in adoption and 'die Blutsfamilie' [blood family] trapped in unreason (Kuschel 2004: 103). However, I think that both lines of enquiry fail to take into consideration the traumatic context within which adoptive relationships are set up as testing grounds for Enlightenment pedagogy. By abstracting adoption as an allegorical figure of *Bildung* beyond cultural difference and biological descent, they ignore the darkness from which Nathan emerges in adopting Recha. The same goes for Antonio Piachi in *Der Findling*.

Adoption constitutes a vital way out of losing a child. It enables the parent who has painfully lost his or her biological offspring to cope with this particular trauma. This substitution is discernible in the old German expression for adoption: *die Annahme an Kindes Statt* [the adoption or the assumption in place of the child] (Adelung 1990: 172). Lessing clearly gives voice to this expression when Nathan in his conversation with the friar recollects the tense moment of adoption. It happened soon after the brutal murder of his family by Christian crusaders.

> Nathan   Doch nun kam die Vernunft allmählig wieder.
> Sie sprach mit sanfter Stimm': „und doch ist Gott!
> Doch war auch Gottes Ratschluß das! Wohlan!
> Komm! übe, was du längst begriffen hast;
> Was sicherlich zu üben schwerer nicht,
> Als zu begreifen ist, wenn du nur willst.
> Steh auf!" – Ich stand! und rief zu Gott: ich will!
> Willst du nur, dass ich will! – Indem stiegt Ihr
> Vom Pferd', und überreichtet mir das Kind.

                    In Euern Mantel eingehüllt. – Was Ihr
                    Mir damals sagtet; was ich Euch: hab' ich
                    Vergessen. So viel weiß ich nur; ich nahm
                    Das Kind, trugs auf mein Lager, küßt' es, warf
                    Mich auf die Knie' und schluchzte: Gott! auf Sieben
                    Doch nun schon Eines wieder!
[Nathan   But gradually my reason returned.
                    With gentle voice it spoke: 'And yet is God!'
                    That too was God's decree! Up then!
                    Come! practice what you have long understood;
                    What is scarcely harder to perform
                    Than just to comprehend, if you only will.
                    'Arise!' – I stood and cried to God: I will!
                    If Thou wilt, I will! – Then you dismounted
                    From the house, and handed me the child
                    Wrapped in your cloak. – What you
                    Then said to me; or I to you: I have
                    Forgotten. Only this I know: I took
                    The child, I bore it to my encampment, kissed it, threw
                    myself upon my knees, and sobbed: O God! for seven
                    Already one again!]

(Lessing 1993: 596–597)

Just as Nathan was recovering from the shock of losing his seven children, he remembers that he was unexpectedly given an opportunity to adopt Recha and realign his will with that of God. Although Recha was born Christian and Nathan was Jewish by faith, this unforeseen gift allowed him to cope with the pain of mourning the violent death of his family. It encouraged him, as he suggests, to make use of reason at a time when hopelessness, madness and fury threatened to gain control of his broken life. It set in motion a deliberate action – 'Tat' [deed] – toward personal healing and religious reconciliation (Lessing 1993: 597).

Reading adoption as a post-traumatic solution to losing the biological child invokes once again Foucault's controversial definition of Enlightenment. In an essay titled 'Qu'est-ce que les Lumières?' ['What Is Enlightenment?'], the French philosopher seems to think of nothing other than Lessing's play while at the same time examining Kant's famous definition of this concept. Foucault describes the obligatory and courageous use of reason as "a *limit-attitude*" with which individual subjects transition from a state of immaturity, or *Unmündigkeit*, to historical awareness (Foucault 1984: 45). Caught between Kant and Mendelssohn who – as we know – serves as a historical model for Lessing's Nathan, Foucault defines what Enlightenment is by splitting the answer into a self-critical reflection on history and an ever-renewable enquiry into the present moment. Enlightenment, he writes, means searching for 'an *Ausgang*, an "exit", a "way out";' to the extent that "a difference" is produced between past and present. 'What difference does today introduce with respect to yesterday?' he asks (Foucault 1984: 45). This means that the Enlightenment cannot be wished away. Enlightenment thinking shapes the ways in which we perceive the world vis-à-vis change: 'We must free ourselves from the intellectual blackmail of being for or against the Enlightenment' (Foucault 1984: 45).

If the violent death of Nathan's family constitutes a most traumatic and senseless event, adoption provides him with the crucial opportunity for working through this horror and staying committed to moral universalism. By substituting Recha for one of his murdered children, he manages to rise from the ashes and listen to his inner voice rather than declare war on God or on Christianity. This decision not only follows the will of the divine *Vernunftsvater* [father of reason], but it also enables him to introduce a present difference to the past. By embracing his new life as an adoptive father, he lifts himself up both physically and spiritually and serves as a paternal example for Recha.

Of course, scholars have investigated the central role that adoption plays in *Nathan der Weise*. Friedrich Kittler explains that adoption constitutes 'ein diskursives Ereignis' [a discursive event] in which the construction of an interreligious family makes possible an 'aufklärerische Gleichsetzung von Natur und Vernunft' [an Enlightenment equivalence between nature and reason], as the family of procreation is substituted by that of generation (Kittler 1977: 121, 124). As Nathan successfully protects his name as Recha's legitimate father, adoption functions as 'eine Semiotechnik' [a semiotic technique] for engendering 'ein Produkt und eine Produktionsstätte der Kultur' [a cultural product and a site of cultural production] (Kittler 1977: 111, 121). An ideal embodiment of Lessing's 'Erzieher aller übrigen Völker' [pedagogue of all other peoples], the Jewish merchant places *Natur* and *Vernunft* on equal footing, such that the true father is not merely someone who claims the status of parenthood on the basis of kinship, but he is a thoughtful person who raises his child both in love and with reason (Lessing 2001: 78). David Wellbery concurs with Kittler's interpretation when he asserts that fatherhood in Lessing's play amounts to 'eine diskursive Instanz' [a discursive instance] in which paternal authority is culturally produced as opposed to being naturally given (Wellbery 2002: 21).

I am not in disagreement with this interpretation, but it neglects the traumatic context within which Nathan adopts Recha. In other words, what Kittler and Wellbery suggest at a discursive level seems to be as applicable to Nathan as it is to Saladin, who in his early conversation with Recha expresses his desire for being her adoptive father as well. 'Aber macht denn nur das Blut/Den Vater? nur das Blut?' [But is blood all that makes/The father?], Recha asks before the Muslim ruler without knowing that he is actually her uncle (Lessing 1993: 619). Saladin's response is 'Ja wohl: das Blut, das Blut allein/Macht lange noch den Vater nicht! macht kaum/Den Vater eines Tieres! gibt zum höchsten/Das erste Recht, sich diesen Namen zu/Erwerben!' [Indeed: blood, blood alone/Is far from all that makes the father! Scarce/Can make the father of a beast! At most confers/The first right to acquire this name!] (Lessing 1993: 620). Saladin's statement extends fatherhood beyond biological reproduction and places the emphasis on *Geist* and *Vernunft* as vital postnatal nourishments for the child. Without knowing at this point that he is biologically related to Recha, he believes that he can also be one of her *Vernunftsväter*: 'Ich will ein guter Vater,/ Recht guter Vater sein!' [I want to be a good father/a right good father!] (Lessing 1993: 620).

It is true that both Nathan and Saladin know the pain of losing a close family member, but there is surely a difference in the fact that only for the former adoption offers a morally uplifting solution to the bottomless pain of being suddenly childless. For Saladin, becoming Recha's adoptive father is a way of showing moral goodness primarily based on choice, but for Nathan adopting Recha amounts to an obligatory and courageous attempt to survive the violent death of his family in Enlightenment. This crucial difference explains why Recha never responds to Saladin's wish or why Saladin and Nathan remain apart even in the closing scene. As the blood family gathers together to embrace itself, Nathan stands apart from this reunion, distinguishing himself from the biologically determined bonding.

It helps to approach the same exchange between Saladin and Recha from a slightly different angle. Instead of locating the name of the father in the biological progenitor, both characters define fatherhood in a variety of terms, including parental intimacy, moral individuality and rational upbringing. Their conversation suggests that multiple fathers are not just possible in a reasonable world, but are necessary if the need arises. And yet, things are very different in the closing scene. Nathan conceives of kinship in adoptive terms, and he refers to the Templar who is Recha's biological brother as his adopted son if and only if the latter welcomes this status: 'O meine Kinder! Meine Kinder! –/Denn meiner Tochter Bruder wär mein Kind/Nicht auch, – sobald er will?' [O children mine! My children! –/For shouldn't my daughter's brother be my child/As well, – Soon as he will?] (Lessing 1993: 626). By contrast, Saladin insists upon his fatherhood on the basis of their blood relationship. For him, this relationship is not subject to choice. In front of the Templar, he cries out: 'Mein Sohn! mein Assad! meines Assads Sohn!' [My son! my Assad! my Assad's son!]. And later again: 'Nun mußt du doch wohl, Trotzkopf, mußt mich lieben!/*zu Recha:*/Nun bin ich doch, wozu ich mich erbot?/Magst wollen, oder nicht!' [Now, you headstrong boy, you will have to love me!/*To Recha:*/And now I am what I proposed to be?/Whether you will or not!] (Lessing 1993: 627). Whereas Nathan considers the possibility of extending the family beyond father and daughter only with the Templar's consent, Saladin considers his newly acquired paternal status as a matter of biological determination and thus beyond negotiation. In the meantime, Recha associates parenthood with 'den Samen der Vernunft' [the seeds of reason], which is to say, with the kind of education free of the authoritarianism of blood (Saladin) and church (Daja) (Lessing 1993: 542). The Templar likewise equates the biological father to a slave who is driven by physical desire, whereas the adoptive father embodies a divine artist: 'Ach! Rechas wahrer Vater/Bleibt, Trotz dem Christen, der sie zeugte – bleibt/

In Ewigkeit der Jude' [Ah! Recha's true father remains despite the Christian who begot her/Now and forever the Jew] (Lessing 1993: 604).

Helmut Schneider has contended that the difference that remains in the closing scene stands for Nathan's Jewish alterity in a fundamentally discriminatory Enlightenment: 'Nathans Judesein ist letztlich der Makel, der Fleck der irreduziblen Körperlichkeit schlechthin, die in keiner Universalität aufgehen kann. Es ist der blinde Fleck der Aufklärung' [Nathan's Jewishness is ultimately the blemish, the stain of the irreducible embodiment par excellence, which cannot be absorbed in any universality. It is the blind spot of the Enlightenment] (Schneider 1995: 104). Whereas Christians and Muslims belong together in natural kinship, the Jew has nowhere to go but to stand apart on stage. It seems to me that this reading echoes Lessing's own commentary on the play. As he writes in the preface, his fellow Germans at the end of the eighteenth century are not yet ready for the play: 'Noch kenne ich keinen Ort in Deutschland, wo dieses Stück schon jetzt aufgeführt werden könnte. Aber Heil und Glück dem, wo es zuerst aufgeführt wird' [I do not know of any place in Germany where the piece could be staged now. But happiness and fortune to the city that puts it on first] (Lessing 1993: 666).

My argument diverges from Schneider's interpretation insofar as adoption functions as a figure of Enlightenment within the context of a traumatic loss, perhaps the greatest one that can happen to any human being, since Nathan embodies the highest ideal, namely Kant's call for self-revelation from rage to reason and from enmity to reconciliation in universal reason. It is possible that Nathan stands apart from the biological family because of his Jewishness, but I contend that this isolation is indicative more than anything else of a future-oriented idealism and a common universal destiny.

The following exchange between Nathan and the friar who meet again after decades of their first encounter supports this interpretation. The latter describes the former's goodness or impartial love of neighbours by invoking the Christian religion. 'Nathan! Nathan!', says the friar, 'Ihr seid ein Christ! – Bei Gott, Ihr seid ein Christ!/Ein bessrer Christ war nie!' [Nathan! Nathan! You are a Christian! – By God, you are a Christian!/A better Christian never lived!' (Lessing 1993: 597). 'Wohl uns!' [Well for us!] Nathan says in response: 'Denn was/Mich Euch zum Christen macht, das macht Euch mir/Zum Juden!' [For what/makes me a Christian for you makes you for me/a Jew!] (Lessing 1993: 597). Although the friar's outburst of admiration collapses Christian and Jew with one another, Nathan does not consent to this equation because for him the Christian does not embody a universal figure of absolute goodness. He gives an alternative statement, which reads in paraphrase: all good men are x, x being members of one's own faith. What this dialogue reveals is the disjunction between the friar's statement of standardisation – basically, that the most faithful Christian serves as a universal measure of absolute goodness – and Nathan's alternative formulation of universal morality: that is, the most faithful believer of one of the three monotheistic religions qualifies for such a measurement. Without this nominal or denominational interchangeability, Christians, Jews and Muslims remain worlds apart.

Another passage in which this idealism is expressed entails the ring parable. In resonance with the closing scene, the outcome of this parable defers the unity of world religions to the future. When Saladin asks Nathan what the single true religion is, the latter tells the story of three sons, all of whom claim to be in possession of the father's original ring. Without any evidence, the judge declares the following: 'Der echte Ring/Vermutlich ging verloren' [The original ring/presumably got lost] (Lessing 1993: 559). He goes on to say:

> Geht nur! – Mein Rat ist aber der: der nehmt
> Die Sache völlig wie sie liegt. Hat von
> Euch jeder seinen Ring von seinem Vater:
> So glaube jeder sicher seinen Ring echten.
> [...]
> Es eifre jeder seiner unbestochnen
> Von Vorurteilen freien Liebe nach!
> Es strebe von euch jeder um die Wette,
> Die Kraft des Steins in seinem Ring' an Tag
> Zu legen!
> [Go! – But my counsel is this: Accept
> The matter wholly as it stands. If each one has
> His ring from the father
> Then let each one believe his ring to be the true one.
> [...]
> Let each aspire to emulate his father's
> Unbeguiled affection free of affection!
> Let each strive to match the rest
> In bringing to the fore the magic of the ring!]
>
> (Lessing 1993: 559)

The sons are to believe in the authenticity of their reproduced rings and, with this belief, they should demonstrate the power of their likely replicated ring by earning everyone's favour. Since the original seems to have been lost, there is no other way of verifying the authenticity of the three copies unless the sons act upon their conviction not just individually, but with a moral impact on subsequent generations.

> Und wenn sich dann der Steine Kräfte
> Bei euern Kindes-Kindeskindern äußern:
> So lad' ich über tausend tausend Jahre,
> Sie wiederum vor diesen Stuhl. Da wird
> Ein weisrer Mann auf diesem Stuhle sitzen,
> Als ich; und sprechen.
> [And when the magic powers of the stones

Reveal themselves in children's children's children:
I invite you in a thousand thousand years
Before this seat. For then
A wiser man than I will sit as judge upon
This seat and speak]

(Lessing 1993: 559)

The judge rules that the truth will reveal itself in a multigenerational act of goodness, as the reproductions are brought as closely as possible to the original and this approximation takes shape in moral action. The 'Tyrannei des Einen Rings' [The tyranny of that one ring], as Nathan suggests, will end in noble deeds as opposed to familial disputes (559). Homologous to Nathan's adoption case, the parable presents a revelatory story: *eine Offenbarungsgeschichte*. It defers the promise of unity or authenticity to a distant future.

In the beginning of the nineteenth century, Enlightenment texts shift their focus from configuring genealogical connections to deconstructing familial kinships (Weigel 2005: 110). Critical of the universal order in which the welfare of common humanity is not secured after all, writers and thinkers register the limits of Enlightenment philosophy. This line of enquiry includes the study of family, *Bildung*, inheritance and origin. Published some three decades after *Nathan der Weise*, Kleist's novella *Der Findling* exemplifies such a poignant response to a contemporary historical problem. Here, too, adoption marks an instance of moral uplifting, but it does not stop there. If Lessing stages a delicately split interreligious family held together by faith in universal reason, Kleist introduces an element to this Enlightenment model whereby adoption, despite good intentions and repeated resolutions, leads to moral downfall.

Similar to *Nathan der Weise*, *Der Findling* tells a story of personal trauma, which comes from losing the biological child. It begins with a journey that Antonio Piachi, a wealthy merchant from Rome, and his young son Paolo take from Ragusa back to Rome when a cholera-like epidemic wreaks havoc and puts travelers on alert. At this precarious moment, the Piachis meet Nicolo, whose parents have already succumbed to the disease. Without anyone to take care of him, he is destined to die, so Antonio, as kindhearted as he is, takes upon himself this responsibility, although he understands how dangerous it is for his own family. As the novella reads, sympathy – 'Mitleid' – takes over the merchant.

Dabei faßte er [Nicolo] des Alten [Antonio Piachi] Hand, drückte und küßte sie und weinte darauf nieder. Piachi wollte in der ersten Regung des Entsetzens, den Jungen weit von sich schleudern; doch da dieser, in eben diesem Augenblick, seine veränderte und ohnmächtig auf den Boden niedersank, so regte sich des guten Alten Mitleid: er stieg mit seinem Sohn aus, legte den Jungen in den Wagen, und fuhr mit ihm fort, obschon er auf der Welt nicht wußte, was er mit demselben anfangen sollte

(Kleist 2001: 199)

[And, catching the old man's hand, he squeezed and kissed it and bathed it with tears. Piachi, in a first reaction of horror, was about to fling the boy from him; but when the latter changed color at this very instant and sank to the ground in a dead faint, the kind old man's pity was aroused; he and his son got out, lifted the boy into the carriage, and drove on, although he did not have the faintest notion what he was going to do with him]

(Kleist 1973: 232)

In an act that is symbolic of adoption, Antonio lifts up Nicolo onto the wagon and takes him to the nearest hospital. Yet, the price he pays for this selfless act is as high as it gets. For Paolo falls ill soon thereafter, and before they reach Rome, he dies, whereas Nicolo recovers from his illness.

Similar to Nathan, Antonio struggles to cope with Paolo's death, and it is once again in this traumatic moment that Antonio accepts Nicolo 'an seines Sohnes Statt' [in lieu of his son].

Piachi beugte sich aus dem Schlage heraus und fragte ihn, mit einer von heftigem Schluchzen unterbrochenen Stimme: ob er mit ihm reisen wollte? Der Junge, sobald er den Alten nur verstanden hatte, nickte und sprach: o ja! sehr gern; und da die Vorsteher des Krankenhauses, auf die Frage des Güterhändlers: ob es dem Jungen wohl erlaubt wäre, einzusteigen? lächelten und versicherten: daß er Gottes Sohn wäre und niemand ihn vermissen würde; so hob ihn Piachi, in einer großen Bewegung, in den Wagen, und nahm ihn, an seines Sohnes Statt, mit sich nach Rom

(Kleist 2001: 200)

[Piachi leaned out of the coach door and asked him, in a voice interrupted by violent sobs, if he would like to come along with him. As soon as the boy understood the old man's question, he nodded his head and said, 'Oh yes, very much'; and as the wardens of the hospitals, upon the broker's asking whether the lad was free to get in, smiled and assured him that Nicolo was a son of God whom nobody would miss, Piachi swung the boy up into the carriage in one motion and took him along to Rome in his son's place]

(Kleist 1973: 232–233)

As this quintessential paragraph makes clear, the similarity between Nathan's situation and Antonio's decision is unmistakable. Nicolo not only occupies the void that Paolo leaves behind in death, but the head of the local hospital also describes the former as a son of God. In both stories of adoption, traumatised fathers work through their loss by adopting a child. Similar to Nathan's thanksgiving to God for Recha, Piachi's acceptance of Nicolo as his adopted son seems to affirm divine intervention in human suffering. Of course, the crucial difference between these cases is that Antonio loses his son as a tragic consequence of his goodwill, whereas Nathan's painful loss happens more or less coincidentally in times of war. Instead of simply adopting Lessing's story, Kleist creates a narrative that probes the very wisdom of someone who risks his own life and that of his son to come to aid of an orphaned child in need.

Another similarity between the two stories resonates with Schneider's topographic analysis of Kleist's oeuvres. As Schneider explains, 'standing upright, rising to one's feet in order to confront the world and face one's fellow humans, distinguished man from animal and symbolized his moral autonomy' and Kleist willfully invoked this bodily gesture to illustrate the rise and fall of an enlightened person (Schneider 2000: 504). In the first passage that I have quoted, adoption signifies this upward mobility. Just as Nathan lifts up Recha in his arms, Antonio raises Nicolo onto the wagon, where Paolo is already sitting. Hence, the biological son and the temporarily adopted child are equal in social standing.

Adoption takes an official turn in the novella when Piachi bestows his wealth onto Nicolo after the latter has shown signs of maturity and responsibility. Antonio takes this final and utmost step by transferring most of his property to Nicolo's name.

> Kurz, als Piachi sein sechzigstes Jahr erreicht hatte, tat er das Letzte und Äußerste, was er für ihn [Nicolo] tun konnte: er überließ ihm, auf gerichtliche Weise, mit Ausnahme eines kleinen Kapitals, das er sich vorbehielt, das ganze Vermögen, das seinem Güterhandel zum Grunde lag, und zog sich, mit seiner treuen, trefflichen Elvire, die wenige Wünsche in der Welt hatte, in den Ruhestand zurück
>
> (Kleist 2001: 202)

> [And when Piachi reached his sixtieth birthday, he did the utmost he could do for Nicolo: he legally made over to him all the property which was the foundation of his real-estate business, keeping back only a small fund for himself, and with his faithful wife Elvire, whose worldly wants were few, withdrew into retirement]
>
> (Kleist 1973: 234)

With his wife Elvire who, too, has looked after Nicolo with motherly love, Antonio goes into retirement. Kleist's emphasis on the legal procedure of this inheritance is crucial; for Nicolo becomes the *pater familias* in replacement of his adoptive father. It is before the law that Nicolo assumes Paolo's filial place, as well as Antonio's paternal authority. It is also important to add that the church, which approves of this wealth transfer, is deeply corrupt. The monks in the local Carmelite monastery conspire with the bishop to legitimise Nicolo's inheritance and benefit from it, and the bishop's concubine Xaviera Tartini plays an essential role in Nicolo's moral downfall, including his betrayal of wife Constanze (Kleist 2001: 201).

The plot centres on Elvire's tragic secret involving a young Genoese patriarch named Colino and, along with it, Nicolo's 'satanischen' [satanic] attempt to disguise himself in his image and make love to his adoptive mother (Kleist 2001: 212). The details of this perverse breach of trust and love need not concern us here, but Kleist describes the feelings Nicolo has for Elvire as 'seine unnatürlichen Hoffnungen' [his unnatural hopes] and 'schändlichen Freude' [shameful joy] (Kleist 2001: 211). It is again pivotal to see how Kleist adopts certain parts of Lessing's play to illustrate a very different outcome of adoption. In *Nathan der Weise*, Daja, the Christian servant in Nathan's home, describes the young Templar who rescues Recha from the burning house and later turns out to be her biological brother as follows:

> Er kam, und niemand weiß woher.
> Er ging, und niemand weiß wohin. – Ohn' alle
> Des Hauses Kundschaft, nur von seinem Ohr
> Geleitet, drang, mit vorgespreiztem Mantel,
> Er kühn durch Flamm' und Rauch der Stimme nach,
> Die uns um Hülfe rief.
> [He came, and no one knows from whence.
> He went, and no one knows where to. – Devoid
> Of knowledge about the house, only by his ear
> Guided, spreading out his cloak in front,
> He boldly pressed through flame and smoke toward
> The voice that cried for help]
>
> (Lessing 1993: 488)

In *Der Findling*, Colino appeared similarly from nowhere and saved Elvire from the burning house:

> Schon wollte sie [Elvire] sich allen Heiligen empfehlen und unter zwei Übeln das kleinere wählen, in die Fluten hinabspringen; als plötzlich ein junger Genueser, vom Geschlecht der Patrizier, am Eingang erschien, seinen Mantel über den Balken warf, sie umfaßte, und sich, mit eben so viel Mut als Gewandtheit, an einem der feuchten Tücher, die von dem Balken niederhingen, in die See mit ihr herabließ
>
> (Kleist 2001: 201)

> [She was about to commend herself to the saints and, choosing the lesser of the evils, jump into the water, when all of a sudden a young Genoese from a patrician family appeared at the entrance, flung his cloak across the beam, took her in his arms, and with as much courage as skill slid down one of the lengths of wet cloth hanging from the beam into the water]
>
> (Kleist 1973: 235)

Kleist's gestural language adopts much of Lessing's play, but instead of recreating the original as an allegorical representation of the *Menschheitsfamilie*, Kleist shows how an act as benevolent as adoption leads to personal tragedy. In *Nathan der Weise*, the Templar safely saves the life of his sister without being aware of it, but in *Der Findling* the young man dies from the injury he sustains while rescuing Elvire. After three agonising years of medical treatment following a devastating blow to his head by a falling stone in the burning house, he succumbs to this injury. This tragedy is followed by Antonio's merciful adoption of Nicolo, but it, too, leads to the death of his biological son and the rape of his faithful wife.

At the end of the novella, Antonio's profound sense of betrayal, hatred and injustice culminates in nothing less than murder. He kills Nicolo in revenge. Antonio also refuses to accept the absolution of a corrupt church before execution. He says: 'Ich will nicht selig sein. Ich will in den untersten Grund der Hölle hinabfahren. Ich will den Nicolo, der nicht im Himmel sein wird, wiederfinden, und meine Rache, die ich hier nur unvollständig befriedigen konnte, wieder aufnehmen!' (Kleist 2001: 214–215); [I don't want to be saved. I want to go down to the lowest pit of hell. I want to find Nicolo again, who won't be in heaven, and take up my revenge again, which I could only satisfy partly here!] (Kleist 1973: 247).

To descend into hell and complete the unfinished work of retribution, Antonio rejects the possibility of having his sin be forgiven. He turns away from any resolution to reject the validity of an enlightened commonwealth or a universal ethics. Rational deliberation, legal compensation or religious faith do not suffice to put to rest his fury over Nicolo's vile action.

It is not difficult to see the currency of adoption in postindustrial society, not least because legally verified orphans and children illegally stolen from their biological parents in poor parts of the globe are sold to benevolent, yet uninformed couples in more affluent countries. The moral, ethical, legal and political challenges are obvious in these terrible cases. On second glance, however, the long history of adoption tells a story that calls into question our ability to see these problems clearly. The potential of this ancient social practice for undermining discriminatory or oppressive values has repeatedly been lost to the world. For instance, ancient Greek and Roman laws allowed adult male citizens to adopt non-biological sons in order to secure the future of traditional rites after death. Adoption established and at times even expanded the patriarch's sociopolitical power. And as the child was transplanted from the domain of one *paterfamilias* to that of another, the laws declared this transfer to be a cultural imitation of nature whereby the adopted son was raised to a higher legal status, namely that of a natural offspring.

Enlightenment thinkers were deeply familiar with adoptive practices and they, too, showed a wide range of sensibilities. Rousseau was raised by relatives, after his mother had died shortly after giving birth and the father had abandoned him in Geneva. He himself gave up his five children whom he had fathered with Marie-Thérèse Levasseur at a Parisian orphanage. Lessing adopted Eva Körner's two children after their belated wedding and her premature death two years before writing *Nathan der Weise*. In this essay, I have deliberately refrained from hypothesizing about possible connections between authorial lives and life writings to concentrate instead on adoption as an ambiguous trope of Enlightenment whereby the act of taking a child in or becoming an adoptive father exposes certain limits to modern discourses on origin, identity, reason, passion and morality.

In *Nathan der Weise* and *Der Findling*, adoption constitutes a limit-figure of Enlightenment, and its discursive configuration serves the purpose of raising critical questions about reason, passion and morality. More specifically, Lessing stages an ideal instance of Enlightenment pedagogy wherein an adoptive parent replaces the biological father, and the authority of *Herkunft* [origin] recedes to the background, as *Vernunft* [reason] takes center stage. Kleist, too, conceives of adoption as a *Denkfigur* [figure of thought] for Enlightenment philosophy, but he does so to turn Lessing's universal pedagogy on its head. Rather than equate *Vernunft* and *Herkunft* at a symbolic level, he explores adoption as an extreme case study in which Enlightenment thinking rises and falls in the wake of institutional corruption, individual sin or historical coincidence.

Around 1800, these semiotic drifts proliferate father-child relationships to the extent that the hierarchy of biological procreation and cultural reproduction undergoes critical revaluation. They open up the paradigm of natural kinships and universal orders to an alternative conceptual field of evaluating Enlightenment principles. In this sense, the study of adoption resonates with what Albrecht Koschorke (1999), Joseph Vogl (1999) and Dirk Oschmann (2007) have variously suggested about the poetics of knowledge around 1800. Both Lessing and Kleist reconstitute modern subjectivity by producing *Sprachbewegungen* [language movements], which push anthropology, history, literature, philosophy, psychology and rhetoric to hotspots, discard old knowledges and acquire new ones (Koschorke 1999: 20).

Notes

1 For more information about contemporary transnational adoption, see David Eng (2003), Sally Haslanger and Charlotte Witt (2005), Margaret Homans (2006) and Marianne Novy (2001, 2005).
2 All translations are mine unless otherwise stated.

References

Adelung, J. C. 1990. *Grammatisch-kritisches Wörterbuch der Hochdeutschen Mundart*, 2nd ed., edited by Helmut Henne. Hildesheim: Georg Olms Verlag.
Berndt, F. and Fulda, D. 2012. *Die Sachen der Aufklärung*. Hamburg: Felix Meiner Verlag.
Dolgin, G. and Franco, V. 2002. *Daughter from Danang*. Waltham: Balcony Releasing.
Eng, D. L. 2003. 'Transnational Adoption and Queer Diasporas', *Social Text* 76: 1–37.
Foucault, M. 1984. *The Foucault Reader*, edited by P. Rabinow, translated by C. Porter. New York: Pantheon Books.
Harvey, D. 2009. *Cosmopolitanism and the Geographies of Freedom*. New York: Columbia University Press.
Haslanger, S. and Witt, C. (eds.). 2005. *Adoption Matters: Philosophical and Feminist Essays*. Ithaca: Cornell University Press.
Homans, M. 2006. 'Adoption Narratives, Trauma, and Origins', *Narrative* 14(1): 4–26.

Israel, J. 2010. *A Revolution of the Mind: Radical Enlightenment and the Intellectual Origins of Modern Democracy*. Princeton: Princeton University Press.
—. 2006. *Enlightenment Contested: Philosophy, Modernity, and the Emancipation of Man, 1670–1752*. Oxford: Oxford University Press.
—. 2001. *Radical Enlightenment: Philosophy and the Making of Modernity, 1650–1750*. Oxford: Oxford University Press.
Kittler, F. A. 1977. '"Erziehung ist Offenbarung": Zur Struktur der Familie in Lessings Dramen', *Jahrbuch der Deutschen Schillergesellschaft* 21: 111–137.
Kleist, H. v. 2001. *Sämtliche Werke und Briefe*, edited by H. Sembdner, vol. 2. München: Deutscher Taschenbuch Verlag.
—. 1973. *The Marquise of O and Other Stories*, translated by M. Greenberg. New York: Frederick Ungar.
Koschorke, A. 1999. 'Wissenschaften des Arbiträren: Die Revolutionierung der Sinnesphysiologie un die Entstehung der modernen Hermeneutik um 1800', *Poetologien des Wissens um 1800*, edited by J. Vogl. München: Wilhelm Fink Verlag, pp. 19–52.
Kuschel, K.-J. 2004. *"Jud, Christ und Muselmann vereinigt"? Lessings "Nathan der Weise"*. Düsseldorf: Patmos.
Lessing, G. E. 1993. *Werke und Briefe*, edited by K. Bohnen and A. Schilson, vol. 9. Frankfurt am Main: Deutscher Klassiker Verlag.
—. 2001. *Werke und Briefe*, edited by A. Schilson and A. Schmitt, vol. 10. Frankfurt am Main: Deutscher Klassiker Verlag.
Novy, M. 2005. *Reading Adoption: Family and Difference in Fiction and Drama*. Ann Arbor: University of Michigan Press.
—. (ed.). 2001. *Imagining Adoption: Essays on Literature and Culture*. Ann Arbor: University of Michigan Press.
Oschmann, D. 2007. *Bewegliche Dichtung: Sprachtheorie und Poetik bei Lessing, Schiller und Kleist*. München: Filhelm Fink Verlag.
Pagden, A. 2013. *The Enlightenment: And Why It Still Matters*. New York: Oxford University Press.
Schneider, H. J. 2000. 'Standing and Falling in Heinrich von Kleist', *MLN* 115(3): 502–518.
—. 1995. 'Der Zufall der Geburt: Lessings *Nathan der Weise* und der imaginäre Körper der Geschichtsphilosophie', *Körper/Kultur: Kalifornische Studien zur deutschen Moderne*, edited by T. W. Kniesche. Würzburg: Königshausen & Neumann, pp. 100–124.
Todorov, T. 2009. *In Defence of the Enlightenment*. London: Atlantic Books.
Vogl, J. 1999. "Einleitung," in *Poetologien des Wissens um 1800*, edited by J. Vogel. München: Wilhelm Fink.
Weigel, S. 2005. 'Zur Dialektik von Geschlecht und Generation um 1800: Stifters Narrenburg als Schauplatz von Umbrüchen im genealogischen Denken', in *Generation: Zur Genealogie des Konzepts – Konzepte von Genealogie*, edited by S. Weigel et al. Munich: Wilhelm Fink, pp. 109–124.
Wellbery, D. E. 2002. 'Kunst-Zeugung-Geburt: Überlegungen zu einer anthropologischen Grundfigur', in *Kunst-Zeugung-Geburt: Theorien und Metaphern ästhetischer Produktion in der Neuzeit*, edited by C. Begemann and D. E. Wellbery. Freiburg im Breisgau: Rombach, pp. 9–36.

10
FROM UNSOCIAL SOCIABILITY TO ANTAGONISTIC SOCIETY (AND BACK AGAIN): THE HISTORICAL ROLE AND SOCIAL-SCIENTIFIC PRESENCE OF AN ANTHROPOLOGICAL TROPE

Tilman Reitz

General anthropological statements have two historical conditions of success. They should, of course, not sound dated, but express something we can still recognise as fundamentally true, and they should look as though they could have always been accepted as such basic truth. Both of these classical conditions are, ironically, often met by animal images of human nature and conduct. Sheep or wolves, doves or snakes, foxes and lions are well-known examples. The essentially human creature central to my topic is the porcupine. As Schopenhauer explained, under the stress of cold weather (at least metaphorically part of the human condition), a group of these creatures will be driven by two contrary impulses: seeking for warmth, they will move close to their fellow-beings; feeling the others' quills, they will strive away from each other (Schopenhauer 1974: 621). A general concept for this paradigmatic situation had been formulated by Schopenhauer's intellectual authority, Kant: unsocial sociability. In the following, I want to examine the role of this trope in the formation of social thought in the age of Enlightenment, and trace some of its repercussions in the modern social sciences.

My general idea is that, contrary to the appearance of timeless truth, the anthropological teaching in question had a rather short time of full validity, between the early eighteenth and the middle nineteenth century. Before that time, leading notions of human coexistence were different; afterwards, the assumed property of human nature had to be understood less as a cause, but as an effect of specific social relations. Thus unsocial sociability can be seen as performing a specific role in the exploration or even "invention" of society, as the problematic whole of practical interrelations. On the one hand, it helped to overcome older notions of sociability, which saw human nature integrated into pre-determined communities – the family, the church, the state. But on the other hand, it also impeded the exploration of social mechanisms as such. Instead of investigating contingent formations of living together, Enlightenment thinkers still were in search of a human nature (or reason, or moral capacity) on the basis of which they could identify some of these formations as universal and good. An ironic aspect, however, may be that their effort is not simply historical, but has an ongoing afterlife. I will try to demonstrate that a recurrent tendency to naturalise methodological abstractions in the social sciences – namely *homo oeconomicus*, or generally utility-maximising rational agents – can be understood only in the light of the Enlightenment experiments with non-traditional human sociability. The simple alternative would be to identify the antagonistic *conditions* under which humans only unwillingly enter into their most important social relations. But as we will see, this is still less than established knowledge.

I will proceed in three steps. *Firstly*, I will take Kant's concise presentation of 'unsocial sociability' as a point of departure in order to trace the early modern roots of the concept: in new experiences of market socialisation, but also non-religious statehood, aristocratic or urban civilised conduct and class formation. In my *second* step I will assemble exemplary post-revolutionary arguments which dissolve the anthropology of unsocial sociability into newly conceived social relations. While conservative critics of the French Revolution and modern market society saw the atomisation of traditional order as the underlying process, socialist critics explored antagonistic relations which are irreducible to questions of political citizenship. The *third* and last step will be to show how the liberal tradition grew immune to such criticisms. Its proponents often displaced substantial conceptions of human nature by methodological assumptions on which the social sciences could build calculable models of interaction – but almost as often these assumptions are re-naturalised. My contention will be that even without this last move, a social science which is based on unexplained human dispositions falls back into patterns of thinking which had already been rightly criticised in the aftermath of Enlightenment.

Before I start, I should explain in a few words why I take the anthropology of unsocial sociability to be historical in this strong sense. A general (and even Enlightenment-style) argument of John Dewey's on the status of anthropological principles in social science is crucial here. In *The Public and Its Problems*, he compares the idea of political or sociable human instincts

> with the notorious potency of opium to put men to sleep because of its dormitive power. [...] The instincts, whether named gregariousness, or sympathy, [...] at best account for everything in general and nothing in particular. And at worst, the alleged instinct and natural endowment [...] represent themselves physiological tendencies which have previously been shaped into habits of action and expectation by the very social conditions they are supposed to explain
>
> (Dewey 1984: 242)

A few years later, in the context of ethical theory, he translates the argument to the opposite kind of impulses: 'A very considerable portion of what is regarded as the inherent selfishness of mankind is the product of an inequitable distribution of power' (Dewey and Tufts 1989: 189). In short, specific conditions of social coexistence determine both our so-called sociability and our unsocial drives. If this is still valid, it will be good to gain reflective distance from Enlightenment anthropology.

Kant's concept and its socio-historical roots

An interesting feature of human 'sociability', in ancient as well as in modern accounts, is that it tends to transcend the classical ultimate frame of social relations, the political community. As diverse reflections show, the register of forms of human coexistence is less structured and more extensive than this community. While the ancient polities give household economies, friendships, education, often also cultic practice a fixed place, some forms of contractual association, philosophical or religious group building, or elementary duties among strangers reach well beyond it (for references see Riedel 1975: 805–806). This also affects the conceptual situation in the high Middle Ages. When Thomas Aquinas lists different 'societates' aiming at different ends, he not only adopts Aristotle's types of human communities or *koinoniai*, governed by the *koinonia politike*, but also defends the legitimacy of Christian worshipping, teaching and community building beneath and beyond any government (Aquinas 1970: 65f). For stoics and neo-stoics, the decisive frame of reference is not the city or state, but humanity or cosmic order, anyway. Yet however trans-political human sociability may be conceived, it classically involves direct orientation towards some general good and integration into some kind of community. From late antiquity to early modernity, sociability is therefore not only given, but also a duty. Nature has made us 'sociabilis', says Seneca, so let us behave as members of a great body, 'in commune' (Seneca 1962: vol. III, 90 [letter 95]). Like the concept of society, that of sociability for the longest time does not depart from ideas of community. One could also say: the unsociable factor is missing.

When this changes between the end of the seventeenth and the middle of the eighteenth century, at least three contexts of experience and reflection are involved: civilised intercourse in the upper classes, market exchange and market-oriented production, and the formation and articulation of pre- or proto-political social distinctions under monarchist rule. The negative impulse to discover a new unsocial sociability in these fields is mainly given by the centralised state and its theory. It is against arbitrary, demoralised political power that human needs for refined intercourse, productive cooperation, solidarity and distinction are developed – but it is also in close exchange with political theory that they assume their typical traits of deception, egoism and mutual impairment. A closer understanding of this double dynamic can be derived from an analysis of the dense high Enlightenment concept of unsocial sociability in Kant, which will in turn be historicised and contextualised.

The goal to develop a general theory is obvious even in the more political parts of Kant's writing. While Scottish and French philosophers offer various conjectural histories, his *Idea for a Universal History with a Cosmopolitan Aim* (1784) is designed as a systematic discussion and paradigmatic execution of the genre. A central element is the anthropological principle which Kant calls 'unsocial sociability' [*ungesellige*

Geselligkeit]. His account uses earlier debates in order to reconstruct unintended, even widely unperceived progress. This affords generalisation. Diverse forms of social orientation are drawn together in the dense sample of 'ambition, tyranny and greed' [*Ehrsucht, Herrschsucht, Habsucht*]; their various mechanisms are reduced to a competitive 'antagonism' (Kant 2007: 111). Specified in this basic way, the bipolar inclination 'to become socialized' and 'to individualize' can explain two general tendencies of human history: the continual development of human capacities or 'predispositions' [*Anlagen*], and the evolution of a 'lawful order' or 'civil society' (Kant 2007: 111). Only competition gives people incentives to do all they can, only conflict makes collective rule attractive to every single agent. Thus 'nature' reaches her aims with the human race not because of good intentions of individuals, but rather through their conflicting interests. It is clear that this account is influenced both by early modern state theory and by motives of the Scottish and French Enlightenment, and the innovative core of the whole complex should be equally obvious: the 'bad', antisocial side of human nature is taken as the very basis of social order. Kant's merit is mainly to point out this paradoxical strategy.

The background story behind each of his three characteristics is more complicated. As I will argue, it includes a bundle of new theories of collective life. The best point of departure (and return) may be ambition, or the will to dominate. There is reason to let unsocial sociability begin with Hobbes, whose rationally self-interested agents have to be convinced and forced to accept social order at all (cf., among others, Hont 1994: 60–72). Authors working within or at the margins of the natural law discourse answered with new versions of a positive sociability or will to live in society (Gordon 1994: 54–65). However, one important piece of argument is missing in these answers as well as in Hobbes's account itself: the mechanisms which bind selfish individuals to collective life from the outset, prior to and beyond their intentions. The discovery of such mechanisms can be traced in the shifting terminological field of 'society', of the 'social' and 'sociability' since the late seventeenth century – and in each case well-known examples show how social context is reduced to anthropological principles between this time and the classical Enlightenment.

Civilised intercourse. The various theories of the courtier and what follows (cf. Luhmann 1980) – mainly French moralism – may count as the first genre to reflect unsocial sociability. Probably this context (and the retreat from it) was already crucial to Montaigne, who coined the phrase that 'there is nothing so unsociable and so sociable as man' (cit. in Schneewind 2009: 94). But the set of contextual features is obviously enriched by the late seventeenth-century moralists, who often rather speak of *société* when they analyse micro-social dynamics (for references, see Baker 1994: 98f; 118f). Whether in the court, in the city, in provincial aristocratic or Christian societies, people learn that they have to conquer and defend their position in the eyes of their peers and superiors. While the end is thus egoistic, the standards of success are purely social. The case of La Rochefoucauld shows how this tension becomes dramatic vis à vis the absolutist ruler. The king, so the aristocracy has reason to complain after the defeat of the *Fronde*, makes people valuable just at will, like pieces of money – but not at their real price (La Rochefoucauld 1992: 150). But even the most cultivated voluntary *société* of country aristocrats is characterised by the will of each to find pleasure and success at the cost of others. So all one can do – for the sake of society *and* of one's own good – is to hide one's inclination: 'Il faudrait du moins savoir cacher ce désir de préférence' [It would be necessary at least to conceal this desire for preference] (La Rochefoucauld 1992: 185). Put in a more aggressive way, we have to cheat and be cheated: 'Les hommes ne vivraient pas longtemps en société s'ils n'étaient dupes les uns des autres' [Men would not live for long in society if they were not duped by each other] (La Rochefoucauld 1992: 26). Numerous eighteenth-century theories of urban civility and salon sociability work on mitigating this harshness, or simply redefine polite behaviour as an expression of goodwill towards others (cf. Lilti 2005: 211–217). But the core of La Rochefoucauld's unsocial version is preserved in criticisms of the new civility. A century later, Rousseau only has to change judgements and add a natural alternative in order to arrive at his *amour propre*, which then explains and judges a comprehensive range of phenomena by *one* essentially social human drive: 'Amour-propre is only a relative sentiment, artificial and born in society, that inclines every individual to set greater store by himself than by anyone else, inspires in men all the evils they do to one another, and is the genuine source of honor' (Rousseau 1997, 218).

Market socialisation. It has been argued (by Hirschman 1977 and Luhmann 1980, among others) that the blessings of economic self-interest were also discovered in the context just described. Indeed the very concept of interest was worked out in moralist teachings and its way can be traced from there to market theory. One important mediating figure is Pierre Nicole, with his idea that economic indifference will serve civil peace better than passionate attachment to doctrines and people (cf. Keohane 1974). Yet the full force of the argument unfolds only when prosperity comes in – and that is, after a series of marginal remarks in social contract theory, with Mandeville. Together with his long list of publicly beneficial vices, he also develops a notorious minimal anthropology in which the drive of pure self-love engenders all valued human dispositions. In sum, he wants to show 'that the sociableness of man arises only from these two things, viz. the multiplicity of his desires, and the continual opposition he meets with in his endeavour to gratify them' (Mandeville 1989: 347). Mandeville obviously starts with the problems of the consumer: scarce means and insatiable hunger for more. This enables him to include noble prodigality and monarchic pomp, but weakens his account as a contribution to work ethics. So when the Scottish philosophers correct his picture, they not only defend Shaftesbury's moral teachings but also promote a more productive modernisation. To do so, they simply have to re-translate evil into indifferent human drives – namely into the famous 'desire of bettering our condition, a desire which, though generally calm and dispassionate, comes with us from the womb, and never leaves us till we go into the grave' (Smith 1976a: I, 341).

Group distinctions. The combination of Mandeville and Smith can also be used to exemplify how group differences are articulated in terms of unsocial sociability.

Retrospectively, different classes look more like social or historical formations than anthropological facts, and it was exactly not the Enlightenment project to justify inherited social hierarchies. But the desires for group-forming, belonging and distinction were also often located deep within human nature. In Mandeville, the basic mechanisms are crude and simple: because people will not work voluntarily, wealthy nations need 'a multitude of Laborious Poor' (Mandeville 1989: 294), and since simple material needs will soon be fulfilled, competition between ranks and orders of wealthy consumers is needed as well (Mandeville 1989: 148–158). Both ideas are at best partly anthropological, the other part being quasi-functional devices to increase social wealth. Smith succeeds in avoiding this aspect of artificial inequality and strategic planning by adding a piece of social psychology. As he famously explains, our sympathy with others favours positive identification. We want to share joy rather than pain with our fellow-beings. Thus we take sides with those who are well-off in any respect – and '[u]pon this disposition of mankind, to go along with all the passions of the rich and the powerful, is founded the distinction of ranks, and the order of society' (Smith 1976a: 47). One should not be too sceptical about the logic of this deduction. It has the decisive strength to derive social inequality as such from human nature, even if it attributes to this nature an ambivalent disposition which, 'though necessary [. . .], is, at the same time, the great and most universal cause of the corruption of our moral sentiments' (Smith 1976a: 53). Others have found alternative ways to determine the disposition in question. Rousseau, for example, experiments with interested self-love [*amour-propre intéressé*] and with devouring ambition [*ambition dévorante*] in order to explain the initial growth of social inequality (Rousseau 1997: 218; 220). In any case, the pattern of basic drives causing group inequalities remains fertile. A writer as modern as Georg Simmel still postulates that human beings both need to identify with others and to distinguish themselves – so that they have to cultivate class distinctions, for example through fashion (Simmel 1992: 106f).

Taken together, these stories of unsocial sociability constitute a rich pool of early and high Enlightenment social thought. We do not want to honour or praise others, but out of our own desires for recognition and reputation, we have to; we famously do not desire to work for others, but do so in order to satisfy our own restless needs; and while we are all equipped with the same drives for well-being, distinction and identification, their effect is a system of group inequality. As I have argued, all these mechanisms can be spelled out both in terms of social mechanisms and of anthropological principles, and as I have tried to show, the latter become dominant in the course of Enlightenment thought. This is, of course, also the problem I want to discuss. It can be introduced both as a critique of the Kantian account and via Adam Ferguson's attacks on commercial society.

Kant's theory of unsocial sociability, in spite of its merits, has a decisive flaw: it gives up the theoretical advantages over Hobbes that Kant's predecessors had gained, and even the central idea of unintended results. At the end of the essay, the central process is to establish a 'lawful order' or 'civil society' by actions which closely resemble a social contract; all mechanisms behind the backs of the agents have vanished (Kant 2007: 111). This re-introduction of direct intentionality stands behind Kant's famous phrase that even a nation of devils could solve the riddle of rationally living together, and it also enables his hope that at some point we will 'transform a *pathologically* compelled agreement to form a society finally into a *moral* whole' (Kant 2007: 111). Ferguson, who famously denies the intentional creation of human institutions, offers a decisively different account of the phenomena in question. He, too, discusses the dispositions, actions and mechanisms which may be summed up as unsocial sociability – but he sees them not as original causes, but as effects of modern social arrangements. While there has never been a pre-social state of nature, something similar is produced by 'the spirit which reigns in a commercial state': 'It is here indeed, if ever, that man is sometimes found a detached and a solitary being: he has found an object which sets him in competition with his fellow-creatures, and he deals with them as he does with his cattle and his soil, for the sake of the profits they bring' (Ferguson 1995: 24).

Post-revolutionary alternatives

If the intellectual steps which lead to Kant's concepts of unsocial sociability and "antagonism" may be read as a process of encrypting social mechanisms, various decryptions take place in the formative period of sociology in the nineteenth century. Due to changed realities and political strategies, however, social content is not just revealed, but transformed. I want to examine two main results which unfold in two important formations of social thought: Durkheimian sociology and Marxian theory, with their ideas of anomic crises and class struggle. It is not just coincidence that these theories are fed by either socialist or conservative background convictions – as I will try to show later, liberals, rather, remain true to the anthropological principles of unsocial sociability.

Diverse scholars, namely Robert Nisbet (1952, 1993), have offered interesting arguments for anchoring early sociology in conservative critiques of the revolution, of marketization and of eroding tradition in general. When authors from Burke, de Maistre and de Bonald via Hegel to Wilhelm Heinrich Riehl and Frédéric Le Play explain that established social order cannot be changed at (political) will, they refer to phenomena which shortly later engage sociological thinking: rituals, roles, institutions, binding solidarity and social control. And for most of them, these forms of cohesion are not only corroded by abstract principles of Enlightenment philosophy and revolutionary politics, but also by a general social process: atomisation, the dispersion of collective life into individual life-projects. In accounts which often resemble Ferguson's critique of market society, they reconstruct unsocial sociability as result of a multiple corrosion of social unity.

In the beginning, these discussions aim at the tension between established political institutions and the ideas of political Enlightenment; the most extensive discussion may be found in de Maistre, who sees constitutions as a result of countless historical circumstances which cannot and should not be made transparent (de Maistre 1984: 246f). But soon attention shifts to the dynamic between social authorities in general, from the father via the patron to the church – whose power is vanishing – and a strangely abstract new order which is nearly structured only by the 'cash nexus' (as Carlyle famously called it) or 'distinctions of fortune' (Lamennais 1826: 25).

The Catholic writer de Lamennais, a follower of Bonald and de Maistre who later turned to socialism, uses the second formulation in an interesting context. In trying to give an account of the given 'state of society in France' [*État de la société en France*], he first highlights that no substantial distinctions remain. 'Hierarchy', 'classifications' and specific rights have been fully replaced by general law and individual riches. 'Thus France is an assembly of thirty million individuals, among which law acknowledges no other distinction than that of fortune' (Lamennais 1826: 24f, my translation).[1] Lamennais then explains how individuals under these circumstances contribute to the prevailing centrifugal tendencies. Since they can no more rely on collective structures of value, they seek instantaneous selfish fulfilment instead: 'Within the general instability, everyone, feeling that he loses grip of everything, that even family is no more a guarantee of duration, only looks to himself, only thinks of himself. Equally deprived of future and past, [. . .] isolated in time and life, individuals demand of the present day that which, in the bosom of a true society, only centuries yield' (Lamennais 1826: 43).[2] This might be the first instance of a fully formulated, paradigmatic account of modern socialisation: the explosion of unsocial drives in a situation of anomie.

The classical sociological explanation is, of course, given in Durkheim's two basic works on *The Division of Labour in Society* (1893) and on *Suicide* (1897). In the latter book, both 'egoistic suicide' and 'anomic suicide' may be read as symptoms of specifically modern situations which produce unsocial sociability. In the 'egoistic' case, it is even questionable whether 'sociability' is the right term, for here Durkheim mainly traces weakening social control: single persons are more likely to kill themselves than family members, and while communities in the Catholic parts of Europe still have a tight grip on the life of the believers, Protestant areas tend to leave individuals alone – so that, among other things, suicide rates are higher (Durkheim 1951: 152–170). The more interesting case may be anomic suicide, where specific social mechanisms weaken social cohesion. Durkheim's famous example is the notorious ups and downs of financial assets: every strong change, be it *baisse* or *hausse*, shakes the frame of individual orientations, so that the growing number of suicides in *both* situations should be no surprise for sociologists (Durkheim 1951: 241–245). The precise mechanism is that rapidly enriched or impoverished individuals no longer know what they may legitimately expect from life, so that their desires run wild and end in desperation; a specific social setting destroys the necessary collective fixations of needs, desert and gratification.

> Appetites, not being controlled by public opinion become disoriented, no longer recognize the limits proper to them. [. . .] At the very moment when traditional rules have lost their authority, the richer prize offered these

appetites stimulates them and makes them more exigent and impatient of control. The state of de-regulation or anomy is thus further heightened by passions being less disciplined, precisely when they need more disciplining

(Durkheim 1951: 253)

The isolating and disorienting tendencies which had been critically captured by Lamennais are given a quasi-objective, but still crypto-normative shape here. In Durkheim's study on the division of labour, the normative aspect had been even more explicit: modern as well as archaic societies need a structure of basic solidarity, and 'anomie' is a title for its regrettable, destructive absence.

In this context, Durkheim analyses more than mere isolation; his issue is competition and opposition of interests. However, a dynamic of dispersion is still seen as the basic process. In the case of working contracts and conditions which are dictated by power alone, Durkheim mainly sees a lack of communication and normative consensus:

> As the market extends, great industry appears. But it results in changing the relations of employers and employees. [. . .] Machines replace men; manufacturing replaces hand-work. The worker is regimented, separated from his family throughout the day. He always lives apart from his employer, etc. These new conditions of industrial life naturally demand a new organization, but as these changes have been accomplished with extreme rapidity, the interests in conflict have not yet had the time to be equilibrated
>
> (Durkheim 1933: 370)

With these systematisations, the first version of a sociological reconstruction of unsocial sociability can be completed. The paradoxical orientation in question does not result from human nature in general, but rather from a specific situation of the dissolving or incomplete transformation of collective life. It is thus rather a historical accident than a general principle.

The (structurally) conservative account implies the difficult conviction that the new situation cannot last.[3] But since the works of Simmel and Tönnies on money, urban life, community and society, atomisation is increasingly translated (or re-translated) into an individualisation which is the ambivalent, yet stable condition of modernity. A middle position is occupied by socialist theories of class antagonism. While they envisage a more or less contoured horizon of overcoming bourgeois class rule, they also analyse how the given power situation is maintained by conditions of production, state force, law and ideology. Within this political-theoretical framework, the conservative order of the elements of atomisation (or dissolution) and antagonism (or conflict, dominance etc.) is reversed: group antagonism is portrayed as the real basis, general atomisation as an appearance of what was once unsocial sociability. It is helpful to trace the structure of this re-ordering in some central arguments of Marx.

The early, "humanist" Marx obviously adopts more of Enlightenment political ethics than its conservative critics. In a well-known formulation, however, his connection to both sides becomes apparent. At first sight, the phrase sounds mainly like a translation of Kant to the society-aware nineteenth century: 'The critique of religion ends in the doctrine that man is the supreme being for man; thus it ends in the categorical imperative to overthrow all conditions in which man is a debased, enslaved, neglected, contemptible being.' (Marx 1970: 137) The obvious point is that a positive orientation towards others always has to be *regained* from social conditions which deny it, especially from asymmetric power relations. However, words like 'debased' and 'neglected' – '*verlassen*' [abandoned] in the original German text – give a hint to mechanisms beyond oppression which are equally responsible for the inhuman situation of human beings: the atomising forces of the market and privatised existence in general. This trait is confirmed by Marx's text *On the Jewish Question* (1843), where the dominant civil or bourgeois society of egoistic owners is contrasted to a merely 'spiritual' political life, and it is in accord with the impulses of earlier socialists. Charles Fourier, for example, had designed his phalange communities against the scenario of a '*morcellement*', a fragmentation of life and labour into small private units (Fourier 1929: 11).

Part of the important change in the later, 'scientific' Marx is that he includes core values of the Enlightenment in his critique of the fragmented market society. The idea finds its clearest expression in the ironic passage of *Capital* which depicts the sphere of market exchange as 'a very Eden of the innate rights of man'. The argument starts with a list of equations between market structures and rights, before, in an attack on Bentham, Marx exposes the underlying principle of atomisation:

> There alone rule Freedom, Equality, Property and Bentham. Freedom, because both buyer and seller of a commodity, say of labour-power, are constrained only by their own free will. [. . .] Equality, because [. . .] they exchange equivalent for equivalent. Property, because each disposes only of what is his own. And Bentham, because each looks only to himself. The only force that brings them together and puts them in relation with each other, is the selfishness, the gain and the private interests of each. Each looks to himself only [. . .], and just because they do so, do they all, in accordance with the pre-established harmony of things, or under the auspices of an all-shrewd providence, work together to their mutual advantage, for the common weal and in the interest of all
> (Marx 1976: 280)

This also includes a critique of Smith or, most importantly, Kant. The critical aim, however, goes beyond questioning the naïve praise of atomisation. The picture of market exchange is also *misleading*, because it obscures the *antagonism* (and power differential) between the owners of the means of production and those who can only sell their labour force. This opposition of interests (and the practice of exploitation) really lies behind the universal reach of privatised market relations. The argument had already been formulated in the *Communist Manifesto* (1848): 'modern bourgeois private property is the final and most complete expression of the system of producing and appropriating products, that is based on class antagonisms, on the exploitation of the many by the few' (Marx and Engels 1969: 475).

All of this has been heavily criticised and extensively refined. For my argument, the crucial point is that Marx delivers a remarkably full translation of unsocial sociability into concrete social mechanisms: a specific basic *antagonism* of group interests (between employees and employers, and, a fortiori, owners of land and financial assets, state officials etc.) can only be maintained under the conditions general *atomisation* (through market exchange as the generalised medium of productive cooperation) and in the form of *competition* (for goods, buyers, employment, profits etc.). This may explain why so many modern critical followers of the Enlightenment took the Marxian account as super-empirical truth about modern society.

Enlightenment anthropology in individualist social science

The account given so far leaves open a specific and a general question about the further fate of unsocial sociability in modern social science. The specific puzzle has already been mentioned: Is early social thinking essentially communitarian (in either leftist or right varieties), or is there also a genuinely liberal decryption of the Enlightenment trope? The more general problem can be derived from the observation that the very easiness of Marx's translation gives reason to pause. Put in Marxian technical terms: maybe a good sociological reconstruction of the ensemble of relationships and character masks which shape modern subjectivities would lead to patterns which differ markedly from the clean dialectic unity of unsocial drives which produce social order. The answers to both questions can be combined: mainstream liberalism avoids the problem by shifting to methodology, and the triumph of this strategy has heavily limited social scientists' capacities to develop a more complex equivalent to socially produced unsocial sociability. I will spell out the first part of the answer rather shortly, with two more nineteenth-century references, and then use a broader sample of recent social theory to deal with the second part.

Ideas of class antagonism are not strange to nineteenth-century liberalism (if the retrospective ascription of such a tradition is feasible). They figure in Mill, in Constant and others. A less renowned, but conceptually interesting figure is the German liberal Robert von Mohl, who discovered 'society' in the wake of the 1848 Revolutions. In order to see what this new reality meant for the science of the state, he introduces 'communities of interest' [*Interessen-Genossenschaften*], which are located exactly between self-interested individuals and the state. Mohl first characterises these groups by a common end; but after traditional cases like estates or the local community are supplemented by modern classes, the remaining criterion is group interest as such. Von Mohl defines: '*Social* circles of life are all communities, formally organised or not, which develop out of a definite interest; *social* conditions are the consequences such a powerful interest has at first for those who are involved and then indirectly for those not belonging to the community'; and '*society*' itself is the sum of all of these groupings and states in a given context (von Mohl 1855: 101, my translation).[4] So in this account, society is *only* the conflict and combination of interests.

What would have been hard to swallow for other liberals may be not so much this main issue but the talk of common ends and communities. As Ian Hacking noted, in early social science bigger aggregates of people were only partly accepted as units of society – mainly in an East European tradition in which Germany participated, but not in the Western tradition, which treated the individual as the basic unit: 'Mainline western thought was atomistic, individualistic, and liberal. The eastern, in contrast, was holistic, collectivist and conservative' (Hacking 1990: 36f). Even if this opposition might be too schematic, the problem remains for a strong liberal attitude: How is it possible to analyse collective realities without violating the principle that individuals are and ought to be the elements of society? And how to account for the way in which social conditions shape individual orientations?

John Stuart Mill offered the most successful solution. In general, he is well aware of the sociality of the individual. An especially strong formulation is given where he explains moral attitudes in *On Liberty* – significantly with recourse not only to social conditions, but also to anthropological principles, namely self-interest:

> Men's opinions [. . .], on what is laudable and blameable, are affected by all the multifarious causes which influence their wishes in regard to the conduct of others, and which are as numerous as those which determine their wishes on any other subject. Sometimes their reason – at other times their prejudices and superstitions: often their social affections, not seldom their antisocial ones [. . .]: but most commonly, their desires and fears for themselves – their legitimate or illegitimate self-interest
>
> (Mill 1988: 10).

In this impressive bundle of explanatory strategies (which even includes the Enlightenment pairing of sociable and unsociable drives), self-interest clearly wins. However, no structural reason for this dominance is given; it is simply assumed that 'most often' we pursue our own welfare. Mill's famous move in his theory of economic science is to turn this empirical guess into a methodological assumption. In order to have a science of economy at all, one simply has to assume that people act out of a specific form of self-interest, their desire for wealth: 'Political Economy considers mankind as occupied solely in acquiring and consuming wealth; and aims at showing what is the course of action into which mankind, living in a state of society, would be impelled, if that motive [. . .] were absolute ruler of all of their actions' (Mill 2000: 322).

This is a decisive methodological gain. Mill does not rule out non-material, non-selfish motives, and he even defines 'living in a state of *society*' as 'forming a part of a body or aggregation of human beings, systematically co-operating for common purposes' (Mill 2000: 319). But since no specific social science can do everything, economic science should follow the attitudes which are really prevailing in its thematic realm. There might be even a chance for some meta-economic theory to explain why this kind of attitude has gained such importance.

There is, however, a problem of scientific practice which comes with Mill's solution. What is introduced as a mere methodological device always tends to be re-naturalised as a basic or even as the dominant human drive – especially when its social constitution is not continually questioned. This tendency can be shown in highly self-reflective texts of the socio-economic tradition.

In one respect, economists of the late twentieth century are even more methodological than Mill: they refuse to restrict their economic analysis to fixed motives such as wealth, gain or selfish pleasure. As Gary S. Becker makes clear, one should not only keep in mind that economic thought 'is a *method* of analysis, not an assumption about particular motivations'. He also postulates an absolute openness about goals which may be rationally pursued: 'The analysis assumes that individuals maximize welfare *as they conceive it*, whether they be selfish, altruistic, loyal, spiteful, or masochistic. Their behavior is forward-looking, and it is also consistent over time. [. . .] Forward-looking behavior, however, may still be rooted in the past, for the past can exert a long shadow on attitudes and values' (Becker 1992: 38). Implied in such an assumption is that 'economic' analysis can easily be extended to every aspect of (social) life. In Becker's own intellectual career, which is summarised in his Nobel Lecture, racist and sexist discrimination, crime, education and family life have been theorised in economic terms. In the light of Becker's principal openness, nothing seems to be problematic about this extension – but this amounts to the same as asking: What is its point? The Nobel Lecture suggests two answers, to which a third can be added.

Firstly (and quite explicitly), the pairing of costs and benefits becomes a universal analytical tool of analysing 'rational' human behaviour, or (where rational choice theory prevails) human action in general. Criminals, who have no strong values of keeping the law, weigh material benefits against the potential costs of punishment; in the sphere of education, costs (including opportunity costs) are rational in so far as knowledge is valued and enhanced 'human capital' increases wages; parents bear the costs of bringing up children in order eventually to receive the benefits of care in their old age etc. To many sociologists, such an approach should not be scandalous; Weber's definition of means-end-rationality says nothing radically different. In Becker's examples, however, a certain priority of narrowly economic goals catches the eye. Clear, more or less quantifiable material or monetary gains and costs prevail over the assumed relevance to 'ethical and moral considerations', 'altruism within families' and the like (Becker 1992: 41f.; 48).

This is the second, less explicit and more complex point: in spite of all general openness, the economic frame of analysis focuses attention on narrowly economic features of action – and adequately so, because the calculation of potential losses and gains makes most sense in such aspects. If I really try to weigh the costs of betraying my ethical principles against the benefits of getting money or pleasure in some situations (which may well be the case), calculations become difficult, and ascriptions of rationality almost arbitrary. As a result, Becker tends to find calculations of 'real' economic profit wherever possible and in an almost Mandevillean manner reconstructs other orientations as a result: 'For example, parents worried about old-age support may try to instill in their children feelings of guilt, obligation, duty, and filial love that indirectly, but still very effectively, can "commit" children to helping them out' (Becker 1992: 49f.). Arguments of this kind not only show a certain imperialism of economic attitudes, they also closely resemble the most radical accounts of unsocial sociability. Even the love of the ones close to us is not primitive, but has to be reconstructed as a result of strategically acting self-interest.

The possible third point is only half supported by the example just quoted: in the explanatory setting, individual preferences always seem to vary at will. While children are programmed to feel obligation and act accordingly, their parents seem to be free to follow either egoistic or altruistic motives. This latent incoherence may be resolved by the assumption that people *always* form their goals in collective contexts instead of freely choosing (or simply having) them – but then it would be hard to explain why they are not equally restrained in the choice of means, and the whole pattern of preferences and rational calculation would break down. The opposite possibility is explicitly to deny any collective determination of ends and means. An important consequence becomes visible in Mancur Olson's analysis of collective action, which strongly resembles Becker's account, but leaves out factors of education and collective habits. The result is that in any larger social context, unforced solidarity becomes unthinkable, because it would be individually irrational:

> Even if the member of a large group were to neglect his own interests entirely, he still would not rationally contribute toward the provision of any collective or public good, since his own contribution would not be perceptible. A farmer who placed the interests of other farmers above his own would not necessarily restrict his production to raise farm prices, since he would not know that his sacrifice would not bring a noticeable benefit to anyone
>
> (Olson 1965: 64)

This is correct as long as one takes unsocial individuals as units of social analysis, and it is best illustrated with market examples where anticipatory solidarity would be really irrational. But it strangely leaves out other possible conditions. Social settings where people have simply learned to act in certain ways (which, for example, support the cohesion of an aristocracy) or where solidarity is incited by collective symbols, rituals and exemplary practice (as in modern social movements) are either left out or translated into market language by Olson.

So far, the inheritance of Enlightenment anthropology seems to be a problem for economists. Sociological theory may offer resources of correction – from Durkheim's notion of solidarity to Parsons's argument that social order is conceivable only when action takes places within a shared normative horizon.[5] But contemporary social theory and research increasingly accept the economic frame of analysis. A field in which the tendency is obvious is the sociology of education, specifically of the way in which education mediates the transmission of social status from parents to children. While two paradigms have long dominated the field, the individualist one seems to be winning. For Pierre Bourdieu and his followers, the decisive factor in status transmission was collectively trained ways of acting, perceiving and judging – the *habitus* – acquired in families and class socialisation, and effective in educational practice and choices. Raymond Boudon (1974), in contrast, focuses on individual resources and choice, the latter following rational calculations of costs and benefits. Most important contemporary analyses are based on Boudon.

This theory choice often results from tacit practical considerations; factors like the economic resources, job position, and educational status of parents can be easily captured with Boudon's categories, while complex and problematic measures are needed really to trace a class habitus. But sometimes explicit justifications are also attempted. In the important research of John Goldthorpe, they run as follows:

> In trying to explain the persistence of class differentials in educational attainment, I shall invoke only [...] basic or 'constitutive' features of class – i.e. those that derive directly from employment relations – rather than ones of a more contingent kind. In particular, I shall avoid reference to distinctive class values, norms, [...] or other supposed aspects of class cultures or subcultures. For this would [...] be to imply that class formation was at a level at which a 'capacity for socialization' [...] was present
>
> (Goldthorpe 1996: 487).

It is not easy to get the argument here (and in the following explanations), but one thing seems to be clear: the attempt to trace a (socially varying) collective pre-structuring of individual attitudes would be too risky, while easier, individualist means can also explain the phenomena. The price is to assume an unexplained human drive of bettering one's condition that never leaves us until we close the sociological textbook.

The picture becomes more complete when one looks at Bourdieu himself. Even if he is proud to explain individual attitudes by social context, he also pursues his own program of tacitly universalising competitive orientations. The tension lies in the relationship between his *habitus* analysis and his other main set of concepts: economic, cultural, social and symbolic capital, for all of which everyone seems to compete, regardless of origins and acquired attitudes. The ambivalent point of Bourdieu's diverse 'forms of capital' is not far from the economists' extension of cost-benefit calculations to every conceivable practical goal – he tries to do the same for the factors which constitute social inequality. The idea is once more to avoid a narrowly economic point of view: 'It is in fact impossible to account for the structure and functioning of the social world unless one reintroduces capital in all its forms and not solely in the one form recognized by economic theory' (Bourdieu 1986: 241).

Class power does not rest merely on wealth, but also on education, networks of social connections, and general reputation. In calling all of this 'capital', however, Bourdieu produces new restrictions in two respects – he misses the dynamics of exploitation which is central to Marxist authors (for the 'other forms of capital' highlight only the work of the privileged strata themselves), and he introduces a general competition for positions in all important spheres of social life. Where I could see myself as keeping in touch with my friends or extending my solidarities, as sharpening my cultural judgement or sensibility, Bourdieu's sociological reconstruction would always be that I try to enhance my social and cultural capital. His super-category of symbolic capital or reputation for success in general even leads back to the writings of the French moralists: in the last analysis, we always strive to improve our appearance in the eyes of others.

It is not improbable that a universal competition for positions really characterises modern and contemporary society. It is even possible that such a motive is inherent in any kind of society, or that assuming it helps to analyse differences between historical and cultural formations. But the distinction between such possibilities – universal or modern and western, ontological or methodological? – would presuppose clarity about the theoretical status of competitive human orientations or dimensions of socialisation. As in high Enlightenment thought, in the case of Bourdieu their quasi-transcendental status prevents further analysis.

Conclusion

The trope of unsocial sociability remains problematic in interesting ways; the short history which has been presented here contains numbers of unresolved questions. A first aspect has been the long and difficult exploration of 'society', a whole of human relations whose order typically reproduces itself behind the backs of individual agents (and organised collectivities). But 'unsocial sociability' also discloses more specific mechanisms of Enlightenment and later modern socialisation: the norms of universal civility, the centrality of markets, the existence of classes in a society with egalitarian principles – as well as the erosion of traditions, the weakening of social ties and a growing awareness of competitive and conflicting interests. In contrast to notions such as alienation, the Enlightenment ideas of unsocial sociability help to see the ambivalence of these processes, or even to analyse them in non-partisan ways. An adequate social psychology which would allow us to understand the relationship between the social developments and individual orientations in question has yet to be written. My text should have shown that this is not only methodically difficult (instruments derived from Adorno's account of Enlightenment or post-structuralist theories of subjectivation might help), but also politically problematic. The orientations which helped to gain distance from the Enlightenment trope were conservative or socialist, and thus not really compatible with the liberal-Western mainstream. The general situation might change into something less liberal – but then even ambivalent aspects of Enlightenment social thought could turn out as far too optimistic.

Notes

1 'Parmi nous, nulle hiérarchie, nulle classification sociale, nuls droits reconnus que ceux acquis à tous par la loi commune. [. . .] Ainsi la France est un assemblage de trente millions d'individus, entre lesquels la loi ne reconnoît nulle autre distinction que celle de la fortune.' (Lamennais 1826: 24f).

2 'Dans l'instabilité générale, chacun, sentant que tout lui échappe, que la famille même n'a plus de garantie de durée, ne regardera que soi, ne pensera qu'à soi. Également privés d'avenir et de passé, [. . .] isolés dans le temps que dans la vie, les hommes demanderont au jour présent ce qu'au sein d'une vraie société les siècles seules accordent' (Lamennais 1826: 43).
3 Durkheim is of course not politically conservative – but he still inherits central motives of the conservative tradition. Put in more general terms: 'The paradox of sociology [. . .] lies in the fact that although it falls, in its objectives and in the political and scientific values of its principal figures, in the mainstream of modernism, its essential concepts and its implicit perspectives place it much closer, generally speaking, to political conservatism' (Nisbet 1993: 17).
4 'Gesellschaftliche Lebenskreise sind also die [. . .] aus einem bestimmten Interesse sich entwickelnden natürlichen Genossenschaften, gleichgültig ob förmlich geordnet oder nicht; gesellschaftliche Zustände sind die Folgen, welche ein solches mächtiges Interesse zunächst für die Theilnehmer, dann aber auch mittelbar für Nichtgenossen hat' (von Mohl 1855: 101).
5 Cf. his first book, *The Theory of Social Action* (Parsons 1937). In my critiques of Becker and Olson, I borrow from Parsons's argument against the 'utilitarian' concept of action, which is characterised exactly by the feature that goals or ends vary at random.

References

Aquinas, Thomas of. 1970. 'Contra impugnantes Dei cultus et religionem', in *Opera Omnia* 41. Rome: Ad Sanctae Sabinae.
Baker, K.M. 1994. 'Enlightenment and the Institution of Society: Notes for a Conceptual History', in *Main Trends in Cultural History. Ten Essays*, edited by W. Melching and W. Velema. Amsterdam and Atlanta, GA: Rodopi, pp. 95–120.
Becker, G. S. 1992. 'The Economic Way of Looking at Life. Nobel Lecture', http://www.nobelprize.org/nobel_prizes/economic-sciences/laureates/1992/becker-lecture.pdf (accessed 25 January 2015).
Boudon, R. 1974. *Education, Opportunity, and Social Inequality: Changing Prospects in Western Society*. New York: Wiley.
Bourdieu, P. 1986. 'The Forms of Capital', in *Handbook of Theory and Research for the Sociology of Education*, edited by J. Richardson. New York: Greenwood, pp. 241–258.
Dewey, J. 1984. 'The Public and Its Problems' [1926], in *The Later Works*, vol. 2, edited by J. A. Boydston. Carbondale: Southern Illinois University Press, pp. 235–404.
Dewey, J. and Tufts, J.H. 1989. *Ethics* [1932], *The Later Works*, vol. 7, edited by J. A. Boydston. Carbondale: Southern Illinois University Press.
Durkheim, E. 1933. *The Division of Labor in Society* [1893]. New York and London: Collier Macmillan.
—. 1951. *Suicide: A Study in Sociology* [1897]. New York: Free Press.
Ferguson, A. 1995. *A History of Civil Society* [1767]. Cambridge: Cambridge University Press.
Fourier, C. 1929. *Le nouveau monde industriel et sociétaire: Ou Invention du procédé d'industrie attrayante et naturelle, distribuée en séries passionnées* [1828]. Paris: Bossange.
Goldthorpe, J.H. 1996. 'Class Analysis and the Reorientation of Class Theory: The Case of Persisting Differentials in Educational Attainment', *British Journal of Sociology* 47(3): 481–505.
Gordon, D. 1994. *Citizens without Sovereignty: Equality and Sociability in French Thought, 1670–1789*. Princeton, NJ: Princeton University Press.
Hacking, I. 1990. *The Taming of Chance*. Cambridge: Cambridge University Press.

Hirschman, A. O. 1977. *The Passions and the Interests: Political Arguments for Capitalism before Its Triumph*, Princeton, NJ: Princeton University Press.

Hont, I. 1987. 'The Language of Sociability and Commerce: Samuel Pufendorf and the Theoretical Foundations of the "Four-Stages-Theory"', in *The Languages of Political Theory in Early Modern Europe*, edited by A. Pagden. Cambridge: Cambridge University Press, pp. 253–276.

—. 1994. 'Commercial Society and Political Theory in the Eighteenth Century: The Problem of Authority in David Hume and Adam Smith', in *Main Trends in Cultural History. Ten Essays*, edited by W. Melching and W. Velema. Amsterdam and Atlanta, GA: Rodopi, pp. 54–94.

Kant, I. 2007. 'Idea for a Universal History with a Cosmopolitan Aim' [1784], in *The Cambridge Edition of the Works of Immanuel Kant in Translation. Anthropology, History, and Education*, edited by G. Zöller. Cambridge: Cambridge University Press, pp. 107–120.

Keohane, N. O. 1974. 'Nonconformist Absolutism in Louis XIV's France: Pierre Nicole and Denis Veiras', *Journal of the History of Ideas* 35, no. 4 (Oct.–Dec.): 579–596.

Lamennais, F. R. de. 1826. *De la Religion. Considérée dans ses rapports avec l'ordre politique et civil*, 3rd ed. Paris: Bureau du mémorial catholique.

Lilti, A. 2005. *Le monde des salons. Sociabilité et mondanité à Paris au XVIIIe siècle*. Paris: Fayard.

Luhmann, N. 1980. 'Interaktion in Oberschichten. Zur Transformation ihrer Semantik im 17. und 18. Jahrhundert', in *Gesellschaftsstruktur und Semantik: Studien zur Wissenssoziologie der modernen Gesellschaft*, vol. 1. Frankfurt a. M.: Suhrkamp, pp. 72–161.

Maistre, J. de. 1984. 'Essai sur le principe générateur des constitutions politiques' [1809], in *Œuvres complètes*, Lyon 1884, repr. Hildesheim: Olms, pp. 1–184.

Mandeville, B. 1989. *The Fable of the Bees. Or Private Vice, Publick Benefits. With an Essay on Charity and Charity Schools, and A Search into the Nature of Society* [1724], edited by P. Harth. London: Penguin Classics.

Marx, K. 1957. 'Zur Judenfrage' [1843], in *Marx Engels Werke*, edited by Institut für Marxismus-Leninismus beim ZK der SED, vol. 1. Berlin, GDR: Dietz, pp. 347–370.

—. 1970. 'Towards a Critique of the Hegelian Philosophy of Right. Introduction' [1844], in *Critique of Hegel's 'Philosophy of Right'*, edited by J. O'Malley. Cambridge: Cambridge University Press, pp. 131–142.

—. 1976. *Capital, Volume I* [1867], translated by B. Fowkes. London: Penguin Books.

Marx, K., and Engels, F. 1888. *Manifesto of the Communist Party* [1848], translated by S. Moore. Chicago: Charles H. Kerr.

Mill, J. St. 1988. *On Liberty* [1859], in *On Liberty and Other Writings*, edited by J. Gray. Oxford: Oxford University Press, pp. 5–128.

—. 2000. 'On the Definition of Political Economy; and on the Method of Investigation Proper to It' [1844], in *Essays on Economics and Society*, edited by J. Robson. Toronto: University of Toronto Press, pp. 309–339.

Mohl, R. v. 1855. *Die Geschichte und Literatur der Staatswissenschaften. In Monographien dargestellt*, vol. 1, Erlangen: Enke.

Nisbet, R. A. 1952. 'Conservatism and Sociology', *American Journal of Sociology* 58: 167–175.

Nisbet, R. A. 1993. *The Sociological Tradition*. New Brunswick: Transaction Publishers.

Olson, M. 1965. *The Logic of Collective Action: Public Goods and the Theory of Groups*. Cambridge, MA and London: Harvard University Press.

Parsons, T. 1937. *The Structure of Social Action: A Study of Social Theory with Special Reference to a Group of Recent European Writers*. New York: McGraw Hill.

Riedel, M. 1975. 'Gesellschaft, Gemeinschaft', in *Geschichtliche Grundbegriffe*, vol. 2, edited by O. Brunner, W. Conze and R. Koselleck. Stuttgart: Klett Cotta, pp. 801–862.

Rochefoucauld, F. de La. 1992. *Maximes, suivies des réflexions diverses, du portrait de La Rochefoucauld par lui-même*, edited by F. Truchet. Paris: Bordas.

Rousseau, J.J. 1997. *Discourse on the Origin and the Foundations of Inequality among Men* [1755], in *The 'Discourses' and Other Early Political Writings*, translated by V. Gourevitch. Cambridge: Cambridge University Press, pp. 111–222.

Schneewind, J. B. 2009. 'Good out of Evil: Kant and the Idea of Unsocial Sociability', in *Kant's Idea for a Universal History with a Cosmopolitan Aim. A Critical Guide*, edited by A. Oksenberg Rorty and J. Schmidt. Cambridge: Cambridge University Press, pp. 94–111.

Schopenhauer, A. 1974. *Parerga and Paralipomena: Short Philosophical Writings* [1851], translated by E. J. F. Payne. Oxford: Oxford University Press.

Seneca., L. A. 1962. *Ad Lucilium epistulae morales*, edited by R. M. Gummere, 3 vols. London: Heinemann.

Simmel, G. 1992.'Zur Psychologie der Mode: Sociologische Studie' [1895], in *Gesamtausgabe*, edited by O. Rammstedt, vol. 5, Frankfurt a. M.: Suhrkamp, pp. 105–114.

Smith, A. 1976a. *The Theory of Moral Sentiments* [1759], edited by D. D. Raphael and A. L. Macfie, The Glasgow edition of the works and correspondence of Adam Smith, vol. 1. Oxford: Oxford University Press, 1976.

—. 1976b. *An Inquiry into the Nature and Causes of the Wealth of Nations* [1776], edited by R. H. Champell and A. S. Skinner, The Glasgow Edition of the Works and Correspondence of Adam Smith, vols 2.1 and 2.2. Oxford: Oxford University Press.

PART VI
Postscripts: Thinking about Enlightenment thinking

11
MULTIPLE COUNTER-ENLIGHTENMENTS: THE GENEALOGY OF A POLEMICS FROM THE EIGHTEENTH CENTURY TO THE PRESENT

Theo Jung

Current debates about the enduring relevance of the Enlightenment to the present regularly revolve around a conceptual opposition between Enlightenment and Counter-Enlightenment. The former being commonly understood as (for better or worse) the origin of the modern era, the latter is conceived as its anti-modern counterpart. From this point of view, the narrative of Western history since the eighteenth century is written in terms of a double helix of two opposing spiritual forces: as the Enlightenment tradition gradually established itself as the major intellectual force in the West, a counter-tradition emerged on its margins, criticising its philosophical deficiencies as well as its socio-political consequences. As these mirroring traditions are seen to have been engaged in a continuous struggle for dominance over the character of the modern era, intellectual movements, individual thinkers and even entire periods are framed as belonging either to the Enlightenment or the Counter-Enlightenment, and judged according to the normative values ascribed to these categories.

As recent historical research has shown, the roots of this interpretative framework lie in the eighteenth century itself. The publication of the first tomes of the *Encyclopédie* in the 1750s sparked a highly charged public debate in which the terms "Enlightenment" and "Counter-Enlightenment" were used as designations of literary factions on the one hand and of intellectual positions on the other. Cultural actors identifying themselves with what increasingly came to be called *lumières* and their contemporary rivals both understood themselves to be involved in a historical struggle between *philosophie* and *anti-philosophie*. In these debates, conflicting interpretations of the character of the present tied in with derogatory descriptions of the respective counter-positions. In consequence, a binary framework of understanding gradually emerged which has since become all but inescapable, continuing to inform our own understanding of the present.

But does this dualist model, reducing our reflexion about the relationship between the Enlightenment and the present to a simple pro/contra alternative, do justice to the complexities of the modern era and its modes of (self-)reflexion? And if it doesn't, what would allow us to escape its black-and-white alternative? In this chapter, we draw on the method of historical semantics to outline the genealogy of the Enlightenment/Counter-Enlightenment divide. The analysis of the semantic and rhetoric dimensions of these counter-concepts since the eighteenth century provides a more precise understanding of the processes of emergence of "the Enlightenment" and its counterpart. At the same time, it enables us to gain some analytical distance from this overly schematic opposition. Although sifting through the layers of semantic sediment that make up the ground on which we stand today cannot suspend the gravity that binds us to it, it may help us better to understand our historical position, informing our movements in a space that we only marginally control.

The double helix of modernity

Especially in the Anglo-Saxon world, the paradigmatic origin of most current debates about the relationship between Enlightenment and Counter-Enlightenment is to be found in the work of Isaiah Berlin (cf. Berlin 1980; Crowder and Hardy 2007). In his view, the concept of Counter-Enlightenment designated a tradition of thinkers turning, for various reasons, against the Enlightenment understood as the essence of the present era. In a number of books and essays, Berlin analysed the work of these intellectual outsiders as they attempted to counter the Enlightenment's rationalism and universalism with a complex mixture of historicism, particularism and irrationalism. From its earliest origins in the work of Vico, Herder and Hamann through various counter-revolutionaries and Romantics up to Nietzsche and – finally – postmodernism, Berlin traced an intellectual tradition with a profound impact on modern thought.

The current influence of Berlin's concept reaches from philosophy and intellectual history to sociology and literary studies (cf., e.g., Pippin 1991; Gray 1997; Compagnon 2005; Jedlicki 2007; Sommerer and Zaganiaris 2010). Its most prominent representative in contemporary research is the political scientist Graeme Garrard, who in a number or works both expanded upon and systematised the line of research introduced by Berlin, culminating in a wide-ranging overview over the plurality of *Counter-Enlightenments: From the Eighteenth Century to the Present* (Garrard 2006). But even beyond academic discourse, a host of similarly aligned narratives can be found, building upon chronologically extended and philosophically focussed concepts of the Enlightenment and its rival, the Counter-Enlightenment. To be sure, neither Berlin nor most of these current authors go as far as Jochen Schmidt, an emeritus professor of German literature at Freiburg University, who advocated their use as 'anthropological' categories, applicable to the whole of human history (Schmidt 1989; cf. also Lilla 2003). Nor, however, do they confine their use to the description of particular historical constellations within the limits of a specifically defined time period. Rather, Enlightenment and Counter-Enlightenment are conceptualised as two intellectual positions, that, although they have emerged during a specific period (the eighteenth century), have since remained viable – and will remain so, for as long as the modern period endures. Accordingly, these concepts are marked by a deliberate tension between their abstract and concrete dimensions. What is understood in abstract terms as two philosophical *positions*, becomes part of a concrete historical narrative through the image of a struggle between two *traditions*: distinct and continuous series of thinkers. Building on this image, Berlin and his successors are able to move beyond the purely philosophical (and timeless) descriptions of the Enlightenment and Counter-Enlightenment toward their pluralisation, identifying a multiplicity of historical Enlightenments and Counter-Enlightenments from the eighteenth century to the present.

Two analytical concepts of Counter-Enlightenment

On being asked who coined the word "Counter-Enlightenment", Berlin once answered that he didn't know. 'Could it be myself?' he wondered. But it wasn't. In a series of posts on his blog *Persistent Enlightenment*, the Boston historian of ideas James Schmidt has shown that when Berlin first used the term in a dictionary entry published in 1973, it had been circulating in academia for at least a few decades (Berlin 1973: 100; Mali and Wokler 2003: vii; James Schmidt 2013–2014). As difficult as it has proved to be to trace the direct lines of influence leading up to Berlin's popularisation in the 1970s and '80s, it is nevertheless clear that the binary framework of interpretation that provided its conceptual basis reaches back a lot further. In fact, the understanding of Enlightenment and Counter-Enlightenment as two opposing currents, battling over the spiritual composition of the modern age, had been around since the Age of Enlightenment itself, where it originated in contemporary debates about the Enlightenment in the phase of its constitution as a powerful force in the literary world.

In stark contrast to the vast academic and non-academic literature on the Enlightenment – Robert Darnton's quip against the 'Enlightenment industry' comes to mind – their contemporary adversaries had until recently received relatively little attention (Darnton 2003: 3; Tietz 1998: 95; Albrecht and Weiß 1999: 8). In part, this may be explained by the fact that in terms of new methodologies, theoretical perspectives and research questions, Counter-Enlightenment research lagged far behind. Whereas Enlightenment research was revitalised from the 1970s onwards by its extension beyond the limits of the history of philosophy, progressively taking into account the social, economic and cultural factors as well as the media, networks and institutions that determined its establishment in the context of eighteenth-century literary and political life, the study of the Counter-Enlightenment long remained confined to minute interpretations of the philosophical works of a limited number of thinkers. Since the turn of the century, however, a new approach to the study of the Counter-Enlightenment has been establishing itself. This new wave of interest was triggered by the publication of two books by authors who (although they do not seem to have taken notice of each other before publication) on the basis of similar material reach a number of analogous conclusions – and even similar book titles: Didier Masseau's *Les ennemis des philosophes* and Darin McMahon's *Enemies of Enlightenment* (Masseau 2000; McMahon 2001).[1]

Masseau and McMahon view the Counter-Enlightenment less in terms of a philosophical tradition than as a concrete network of various types of cultural actors in the eighteenth-century literary world, a more or less loosely knit group, whose main unifying trait lay in their common rejection of what they viewed as the rise and/or dominance of the *philosophes* as a pernicious social and cultural force. Rather than focussing exclusively on these actors' philosophical positions, they trace the process in which the *anti-philosophes* merged into a more or less coherent literary movement after the publication of the first volumes of the *Encyclopédie* in the early 1750s; how in the decades before the French Revolution they gradually lost ground to their *philosophe* enemies in the competition for offices and honours in the republic of letters; how they regained strength during the directorate, the Napoleonic era and the Restoration, establishing themselves as a fixed cultural force on the right of the political spectrum. They take into account the media, institutional and social aspects of group formation, analysing the functioning of their social networks as well as the accompanying mechanisms of admission, patronage and cooperation. Most of all, they describe the bitter conflicts that forged two loose clusters – that initially had overlapped quite significantly – into integrated 'parties' combating their respective adversaries with every tool available, from the literary (criticism, invective, satire) to the political (censorship and persecution) and social (intrigue).[2]

What is crucial to this new approach, is that the concepts of Enlightenment and Counter-Enlightenment are no longer understood to designate homogeneous ideologies, philosophical positions or currents of thought, but rather concrete networks in the literary sphere, whose identity was only gradually established (Masseau 2014: 111–113). For the same reason, one of the central themes of this line of research has been exactly *how* these group identities emerged in the interaction with their respective enemies and – more specifically – how this process was both mirrored in and reinforced by discursive practices of mutual labelling.

Since the early twenty-first century, then, Counter-Enlightenment research has been split into two separate fields, taking their vantage points from different conceptual framings of their subject matter. One part, for which Isaiah Berlin's work is paradigmatic, sketches a quasi-transhistorical tradition revolving around a more or less fixed set of philosophical principles. Its methods are firmly rooted in the history of ideas, identifying moments of original thought as well as tracing complex lineages of influence and diffusion. Another, represented by Masseau and McMahon, is based on a much more restricted perspective on the Enlightenment and their enemies. Drawing on the tools of social and cultural history, its aim is the detailed historical micro-analysis of the structures and dynamics of the eighteenth-century public realm. Beyond the limited number of philosophical giants on which the work on the Counter-Enlightenment *tradition* has focussed, this perspective includes a whole range of contemporary publications and actors, as well as its underlying social and economic structures and media. Consequently, the concept of Counter-Enlightenment in this context refers to a more or less well-defined and continually changing literary faction, composed of militant priests, conservative aristocrats, government and church censors as well as a large number of prolific authors that – even at the time – were often considered to be of "secondary" stature, in short: of all those identifying themselves with what the new philosophy would have called "fanaticism".

Perhaps unsurprisingly, current debates about the relevance of the Enlightenment and the Counter-Enlightenment to the present have primarily referred to their strong, philosophical concepts rather than to the more limited and diffuse concepts used in recent historiography. It may be argued, however, that these new approaches – and specifically the research into the conceptual history of Enlightenment and Counter-Enlightenment in the eighteenth century itself – promise some valuable new insights into the nature of these phenomena and their historical development. A brief overview of some of the central areas of this research shows how this perspective may crucially enrich current debates about the present in its relation to the Enlightenment.

Enlightenment and Counter-Enlightenment in the eighteenth century

Even if their intellectual origins reached much further back, the *lumières* did not gain a definite profile as a literary group until the publication of the first volume of the *Encyclopédie* in 1751. This was a seminal event, uniting a number of like-minded but dispersed authors around a common project with wide cultural appeal. At the same time, it also gave focus to the hitherto fragmented efforts of various other cultural actors *against* the tendencies of a fashionable new type of philosophy that had been gaining momentum for some time, bringing them together in a common campaign of what at the time was called *anti-encyclopedism*. Contemporaries understood this struggle in the familiar terms of a literary *querelle*. 'The encyclopedists', wrote Augustin Simon Irailh in his *Querelles littéraires, ou Mémoires pour servir à l'histoire des révolutions de la république des lettres*, a history of literary disputes from antiquity to the present, 'form a society of literary men, and their adversaries multiple respectable bodies. Magistrates, theologians, clergymen, protestant ministers, many authors, [some] perhaps driven by private animosities, some by a true zeal, made all efforts to prevent the continuation of the work that is announced as the vastest, boldest, most useful that has ever been conceived' (Irailh 1761: 118).[3] In his detailed account, Irailh stressed that the animosity between these two groups was by no means exclusively founded upon philosophical or theological differences. Rather, the competition for scarce resources in the literary field played a major role in their antagonism.

Soon after the publication of the *Encyclopédie*'s first volume, a pamphlet war ensued that would endure well into the next decade, reaching a climax in the context of the work's (temporary) suppression in 1759. Although at least quantitatively, the *encyclopedists* initially had the upper hand, the *anti-encyclopedists* made every effort to keep up. Both sides had their own periodicals, social circles and networks of patronage. The *Journal encyclopédique ou universel*, which was published from 1756 onwards, faced powerful resistance from established journals like the Jesuit *Mémoires de Trévoux* and the Jansenist *Nouvelles ecclésiastiques* (O'Keefe 1974). In addition, a number of new periodicals were founded, with the explicit mission to contradict the *philosophes*. The most influential of these was the *Année littéraire*, edited by Élie Catherine Fréron. Besides his editing and writing activities, Fréron was, as McMahon has shown, something like a "recruiting agent" for the *anti-philosophe* cause (McMahon 1998: 82; Balcou 1975; Lu 2005: 145–234). He sought to attract young literary talent to the campaign, in return offering them assistance in the attainment of positions, pensions and literary assignments. The most zealous of these young authors were often those who had previously tried to gain access to the *philosophe* camp, but had become stranded in its increasingly restrictive mechanisms of exclusion. Their frustration with and personal resentment of the proud *philosophes*, hoarding all the resources of the literary world amongst themselves, imparted their attacks with a particular acidity.

Paradigmatic in this respect was the career of Nicolas-Joseph-Laurent Gilbert. Born in a small town in the Vosges region, he had come to Paris in 1770 with dreams of literary glory and a letter of introduction to Jean le Rond d'Alembert. But the famous philosopher ignored him, and Gilbert's attempts to ingratiate himself with the literary *beau monde* came to nothing. Since in his precarious position literary failure inevitably resulted in financial hardship, he finally decided to join the *anti-philosophe* camp (cf. Sonenscher 2008: 101–109). In his successful satire *Le Dix-huitième siècle*, first published in 1773, (which was dedicated to Fréron) he took literary revenge on the *philosophes*, painting their growing influence in ominous terms: 'A monster grows and strengthens itself in Paris, / Which, clothed in the coat of philosophy, / Or rather, falsely vested in its name, / suffocates the talents and destroys virtue' (Gilbert 1797: 1). His aggressive attacks against the likes of Voltaire, Beaumarchais, Diderot, Marmontel and d'Alembert by no means exclusively targeted their philosophical positions. First and foremost, his rage turned against their exclusive hegemony in the literary world, the fact that as 'tyrants of the Parnassus' they were able to control the distribution of 'honours, riches, employments' (ibid.: 13).

On the other side of the divide, similar career paths were to be found. When in 1758 a young Jean-François de La Harpe – a nineteen-year-old orphan, fresh out of school – first attempted to embark upon a literary career, he started out by publishing *L'Aléthophile, ou l'ami de la vérité*, a forceful counter-strike against Fréron ('le Chef de la cabale, qui s'est formée contre les Encyclopédistes') and the *anti-philosophes*. Even if this early work received only a lukewarm reception by the critics, it was nevertheless successful in that it managed to attract the attention of Voltaire, who subsequently took the young author under his wing and helped him to establish himself as one of the most outspoken voices of the *philosophe* cause (La Harpe 1758: 11; cf. Masseau 2014: 114). For young, talented authors seeking to establish themselves, the *querelle* between the encyclopedists and their enemies offered welcome opportunities to catch the eye of the powerful leaders of their respective networks who held the keys to various forms of patronage. At least some of the rhetorical violence of their mutual attacks was thus predicated upon the social (and financial) necessity to attract attention and cause a stir in the literary world.

On a more elevated social level, analogous battles for resources reached into the highest spheres of the *Ancien Régime*, where both factions tried to attach those in power to their causes. The *Encyclopédie*'s success was not least predicated upon the fact that the position of chancellor, entailing among other things the authority over the censorship office, was held by Guillaume-Chrétien de Lamoignon de Malesherbes, who was well-disposed towards the project. Even at court, their position was prominently represented by the circle around Madame de Pompadour. Conversely, the so-called *parti dévot*, a conservative religious court coterie grouped around the heir apparent, Louis Ferdinand, and his mother, Maria Leszczyńska, did everything in their power to obstruct the *philosophes* and their publications. To the *anti-philosophes*, the crown prince consequently represented hopes of a religious revival after the death of Louis XV and a favourable shift in the balance of power in the literary world. His early death in 1765, however, would foil these.

Taking these factors into account, it is clear that in a certain sense, the *philosophes* and *anti-philosophes* presented two distinct social networks on opposing sides of a battle for social, cultural and economic capital. Nevertheless, their group identities were never simply given or completely distinct. In fact, the overlap between the two camps was much more extensive than any of them would have cared to admit. Conversions like those of Gilbert – for opportunistic reasons or out of conviction – were quite common, and, apart from a relatively small core group of radical partisans, most of those active in the literary field could not be unambiguously identified as belonging to either camp. Although a number of exclusive social spaces in which *philosophes* or *anti-philosophes* remained amongst themselves existed, these remained exceptions. On the contrary, most *salonnières* prided themselves on their ability to bring people of different backgrounds and opinions together in polite conversation. Since – perceived hegemonies notwithstanding – the literary world in fact remained thoroughly divided, the membership of the academies continued to show a similar diversity. Neither side was able to monopolise these institutions which played a vital role in the politics of publication and literary honour.

From a purely formal point of view, the literary products of both camps came increasingly to resemble each other. As is well known, the *philosophes* were masters in the art of publicity. Their writings – often in the form of short essays, dialogues, satires, letters, lexica or philosophical stories – were specifically attuned to a mass audience. To their adversaries, this strategy of popularisation presented an unwelcome break with the mores of the *res publica litteraria* and the gravity of traditional philosophy. Instead of remaining within the 'silent obscurity' of real philosophers, wrote Simon Nicolas Henri Linguet, these so-called new philosophers were driven toward a publishing 'furor' by their ambition for 'vociferous reputation' (Linguet 1764: 9). With their exclusivist claims to the truth, their combative sectarianism, and their direct appeals to a readership well beyond the narrow confines of the scholarly audience, the *philosophes* breached the established codes of conduct of learned debate. Associating the traditional order of the literary world with that of society as a whole, the *anti-philosophes* could point to the dangerous implications of the *philosophes*' revolutionary behaviour in the republic of letters.

Yet at the same time, this type of critique put the *anti-philosophes* into a paradoxical position: to be effective, the defenders of traditional literary conventions were forced to retort to the very tools they so adamantly despised. Thus, in the introduction to his two-volume *Dictionnaire anti-philosophique* – which was conceived as a corrective to Voltaire's popular *Dictionaire philosophique* – Dom Louis-Mayeul Chaudon conceded that '[t]he alphabetical order is today's taste, & one has to yield to it if one wants to have readers' (Chaudon 1771: I, vii; cf. Goldzink 1993). In time, the *anti-philosophes* learned to adapt successfully. As was the case with the *philosophes* themselves, the resonance of their writings even beyond the French borders was significant. Claude-François Nonnotte's *Les Erreurs de Voltaire* of 1762, for example, was published in three Italian, three German and two Spanish editions before the French Revolution. In 1793, a Russian translation followed (Nonnotte 1766; Israel 2009: 88). Only by the use of fashionable genres and a fluid style adapted to the reading habits of modern audiences could these authors bring the point across that these very practices were unworthy and would have vicious effects upon French society. On the other hand, using the enemy's weapons against him encompassed the danger that the *anti-philosophes*' utterances would become indistinguishable from those of their adversaries. As Masseau put it, it put the Counter-Enlightenment at risk – 'to lose its soul' (Masseau 2000: 210).

Finally, group solidarity in both camps was always fragile. In both cases, it involved a delicate coalition based on the struggle against a common enemy. The differences that were deflated in the immediate confrontation could resurface at any time. Thus, the group identity of *philosophes* and *anti-philosophes* had to be continuously reproduced. On both sides, the primary instrument to achieve this goal was the construction of a unified common enemy ominous enough to impart some discipline into the unruly ranks.

When Charles Pallisot's satirical play *Les Philosophes* was first performed in Paris in 1760, it showed Rousseau, Voltaire, Diderot and Helvétius side by side (Rousseau on all fours, primitivistically nibbling on a leaf of lettuce) (Palissot 1777). Of course, this integrated group the audience witnessed on stage had never existed in reality. But in presenting them in this manner, their enemies moulded the *philosophes* into a unity in the public's perception. Although many *anti-philosophe* writings were marked by violent invective, satire proved at least as valuable a weapon in this effort. One of the most prominent examples of this was the quasi-anthropological description of the *philosophes* as a newly discovered tribe, the *Cacouacs*. First introduced by the historian Jacob Nicolas Moreau in a short article in the *Mercure de France* of October 1757, its author quickly capitalised upon its success, publishing a detailed account of more than 100 pages about the character, beliefs, mode of government and peculiar forms of 'magic' of this curious tribe (Moreau 1757a; idem 1757b).

Other *anti-philosophes* soon picked up on this catchy metaphor, like Joseph Giry de Saint Cyr, who published a Cacouac catechism almost entirely composed of quotations from *philosophe* writings, including a speech of the Cacouac 'patriarch' upon the reception of a new 'disciple' (Giry de Saint Cyr 1758; see also Chaudon 1771: vol. I, 65–68). In time, even some of the *philosophes* now began to refer to themselves as *Cacouacs*, showing how they too increasingly perceived themselves as a unified group (Cf. Masseau 2000: 124–129; Stenger (ed.) 2004).

Just as their shared conception of "Enlightenment" was constitutive of the Counter-Enlightenment, the Enlightenment itself owed its group identity in large part to its reaction to the latter's assaults. Thus, in a process described by Jeffrey D. Burson as a 'dialogical evolution', two groups constituted themselves in mutual reaction to one another (Burson 2008: 957, 961).

Mutual name-calling

To attain a better understanding of this process, it is worthwhile to consider in some detail the strategies of mutual designation employed in it. Strikingly, both sides' discursive strategies showed great similarities. In fact, the terms of abuse were often the same. An example of this is the term "fanaticism", probably the most common defamation used in Enlightenment discourse to designate their enemies. Yet in time, the Counter-Enlightenment found ways to appropriate this powerful semantic weapon for themselves. In their struggle against religious fanaticism, Linguet pointed out in a popular pamphlet titled *Le Fanatisme des philosophes*, the *lumières* often showed the very excessive zeal they criticised in others (Linguet 1764: 7). The true fanatics, he concluded gleefully, were those who accused everyone else of fanaticism.

The same reciprocal use could be observed in the concept of "party". In their self-perception, neither the *philosophes* nor their adversaries were parties. Throughout the eighteenth century, this concept had a clear negative connotation. It was associated with bigotry, fanaticism and selfishness and was understood to be the opposite of the common good and general truth. The image of a struggle between opposing parties – which would later become a commonplace of historical research – thus originated less in the respective social realities of these groups than in their mutual perceptions of the other *as* a party or faction. This becomes clear when we trace back the usage of this term to its eighteenth-century origins. The title of Peter Gay's influential two-volume interpretation popularising the idea of the Enlightenment as a 'party of humanity' referred to a quotation from Voltaire's *Lettres philosophiques* (Gay 1966/1999). In a passage on the philosophy of Blaise Pascal, the philosopher had solemnly declared 'to support [*prendre parti pour*] humanity against this sublime misanthrope' (Voltaire 1734: 2). In constructing his title, Gay not only added an article, he also extracted the 'party of humanity' from the standing expression *prendre parti pour quelqu'un*. What to us may seem a minor variation, to contemporaries would have made a world of difference. Whereas it was perfectly respectable to take someone's side, being associated with a party (even of humanity as a whole) was quite another matter. Just how strong these negative connotations were may be gleaned from the fact that throughout the eighteenth century, the expression "*parti de l'humanité*" was exclusively used in combination with mitigating expressions like *prendre/embrasser/tirer parti* (e.g., Linguet 1767: vol. II, 513; Pluquet 1767: vol. II, 337).

Accordingly, when applied to the *philosophes* and *anti-philosophes* the concept of party was exclusively used as a derogatory term (e.g., Palissot 1757: 22; Giraud 1760: 8, 14). Both sides accused each other of being a conspiratorial and narrow-minded *clan, clique, coterie, cabale, ligue* or *parti*. This involved the common ironic designation of Voltaire as a "patriarch" as well as a wide range of military metaphors. Judging from contemporary semantics, an *armée anti-philosophique* stood against a no less combative *armée philosophique*, both with their respective generals, lieutenants, auxiliary forces and tactics (e.g., Morellet 1769: 2–3; Fréron 1778: 207; cf. Ferret 2007: 369–373, 378–385).

Even the contemporary designations of these enemy groups as *philosophes* and *anti-philosophes* had a much more complicated dynamic than the common image of party conflict may lead us to assume. After the contributors to the *Encyclopédie* and their supporters began to lay exclusive claim to the term *philosophe* for themselves, their enemies quickly came to be known as *anti-philosophes* (Cf. Gumbrecht and Reichardt 1985: 24–51, 32–34). Yet what began as a derogatory term in time was appropriated as an honorific title and slogan for the growing campaign against the dissemination of this new current. This becomes apparent in the title of polemic publications like the anti-Diderot *Pensées antiphilosophiques* or the previously mentioned *Dictionnaire anti-philosophique* (Allamand 1751; Chaudon 1771). Still, these self-designations as "counter-philosopher" were invariably accompanied by elaborate justifications, explaining that readers should not misunderstand this term to imply a general renunciation of philosophy, but only of the "so called" philosophy currently fashionable. In this manner, Daniel Le Masson de Granges in his *Le Philosophe moderne, ou L'Incrédule condamné au tribunal de la raison* stressed that he was well aware of the achievements of 'real philosophy'. What he criticised was the 'unreasonable', 'desperate' and 'arrogant' philosophy which opposed Christianity, 'countering legitimate reasoning with nothing but indecent ridicule and gross slander'. Since this new style of thinking had recently become 'the philosophy à la mode', he had had no choice but to become a 'modern anti-philosopher'. Nevertheless, he emphasised that in light of the real concept of philosophy, the actions of these so-called *lumières*, showed themselves to be 'the most anti-philosophical conduct ever' (Le Masson de Granges 1759: xxi, 140, 179, 226–228).

In a closing speech before the Paris Parliament in 1770 against a number of Enlightenment works – in the context of a trial which would lead to their suppression – the prosecution warned the judges that an 'impious and audacious sect has risen among us, she has adorned her false wisdom with the name of Philosophy; under this imposing title, she has pretended to possess all knowledge' (Séguier 1770: 104). Against this insolence, the *anti-philosophes* deemed themselves to be the real philosophers, employing a variety of neologisms to distinguish between philosophy's true nature and its modern, fashionable incarnation. In this fashion, they equated new philosophy to philosophism, fashionable philosophy, unphilosophy or misosophy and modern philosophers with philosophists, philosophaille or philosophasters (see, e.g., Anonymous 1765; Fréron 1772: 291; Rigoley de Juvigny 1787: 385, 463–464, 521–522).

Finally, the metaphors of light and darkness that were at the centre of the *lumières*' self-conception were turned around against them. Whereas the *anti-philosophes* were regularly denounced in *philosophe* discourse as obscurantists and shadow-creatures, they saw themselves as representing the true and eternal light against the deceptive shimmer of will-o'-the-wisps. 'Truncated and superficial ideas of philosophy,' wrote the Parisian priest and theologian Antoine-Adrien Lamourette, 'may well aid an infinity of fickle and vapid persons to remove themselves from faith; but […] mature and solid minds will always be returned towards religion; because only she can fully illuminate us on the origin of things, on the use of our faculties and on the final destination of everything that exists; and that consequently she is the true and perfect philosophy' (Lamourette 1786: 16–17; cf. Albertan-Coppola 1988: 178–179). To emphasise the contrast between the eternal light and the worldly light sources championed by the *philosophes*, the *anti-philosophes* exploited the latter's blinding and potentially destructive metaphorical implications to their rhetorical advantage, such as when the abbé Antoine Sabatier de Castres warned that the supposed *lumières* had in fact proven themselves to be 'burning torches, ready-made to carry fire everywhere' (Sabatier de Castres 1779: vol. I, xcv; cf. Deprun 1973: 717).

Early Enlightenment research was often guided by this very semantic framework first established in the eighteenth century. It conceived of Enlightenment and Counter-Enlightenment in terms of distinct philosophical "parties" or "positions". Consequently, its analyses moved on a terrain stretching between the poles of a number of sharp conceptual dichotomies. Recent research has made an attempt to break away from the 'spirit of simplification and amalgamation' such binary categories entailed. 'Research can start from the moment when we discuss these labels, where we shake up the categories,' wrote Michel Delon, one of the most prominent scholars of the period (Delon 1993: 87–88). Particularly, it can start when we no longer simply take the traditional categories at their word, but instead turn to explore their own semantic and pragmatic dimensions. Using the methods of historical discourse analysis, we are able to describe the complex processes of group formation through mutual defamation without losing sight of the various forms of overlap which continued to exist across the borderlines drawn by contemporary actors. At the same time, the genealogy of these concepts allows us to gain some analytical distance from a framework of interpretation which continues to inform our own confrontation with the eighteenth century.

Anachronisms and guilt by association

Compared to the complex analyses presented above, the sweeping invocations of a manichean struggle over the spirit of Modernity – Enlightenment vs. Counter-Enlightenment – appear flat and overly schematic. Yet it would be a mistake to leave it at that, contrasting the fine-grained analytical concepts of Counter-Enlightenment found in recent historical research with their relatively one-dimensional counterparts in other areas of public discourse and haughtily declaring that the latter have been weighed on the scales and found wanting. If their analytical value is low, this is mainly because their main function was never to provide tools for historical analysis. Rather, their long-lasting popularity is founded on their usefulness for polemical purposes, to which their role as pivots of historical narrative is ultimately subservient. Against the background of the historical analysis presented above, we thus come to realise that in many ways, these concepts continue to function in the same way today as they did when emerging in the eighteenth century.

Rather than providing a superior alternative to the common usage of the concept of Counter-Enlightenment in public debates, historical analysis of the plurality of Counter-Enlightenments from the eighteenth century to the present is more fruitfully thought of as providing a new perspective on them. The genealogy of these concepts and the analysis of their semantical and rhetorical dimensions at the time of their emergence opens a valuable new perspective on their functioning in the present. In conclusion to this chapter, a brief overview over some uses of the concept of Counter-Enlightenment since the second half of the twentieth century may show how this point of view can enrich debates about our historical situation with reference to the Enlightenment.

As the German philosopher Herbert Schnädelbach has pointed out, current debates revolving around the conceptual opposition between Enlightenment and Counter-Enlightenment are hardly symmetrical. Whereas up until the 1980s, the Enlightenment was regularly exposed to profound criticism from various sides – from the neo-conservative reaction to '68' to the postmodern criticism of Enlightenment rationalism – nowadays hardly any critical voices are to be heard (Schnädelbach 2004: 66–68). The few that remain, like the anti-Enlightenment arguments articulated in some forms of Islamic radicalism, are formulated from a position outside Western civilisation rather than from within. In this manner, the concept of Counter-Enlightenment becomes part of a more general critique of the West and its values, losing the reflexive dimension that had so long been at its core. As it no longer presents a form of self-criticism – pointed at a particular tendency in the culture of which the articulating voice is itself a part – it loses much of its original pathos.

Within the Western world, self-descriptions in terms of "Counter-Enlightenment" have become very rare. But of course, even now a few exceptions remain, some of them in unexpected places. One recent example is a speech by the heir to the British throne, Prince Charles. 'I was once accused of being the enemy of the Enlightenment,' he confided to his audience at the annual meeting of his Foundation for the Built Environment in February 2010. 'I felt proud of that. […] I thought, "Hang on a moment". The Enlightenment started over 200 years ago. It might be time to think again and review it and question whether it is really effective in today's conditions'. First and foremost, he was thinking of the impact on the environment resulting from what he understood to be Enlightenment's exploitative attitude to nature. 'We cannot go on like this, just imagining that the principles of the

Enlightenment still apply now. I don't believe they do. But if you challenge people who hold the Enlightenment as the ultimate answer to everything, you do really upset them' (quoted in Low 2010). Significantly, the prince explained his own Counter-Enlightenment identity as originating in a hostile description by an anonymous other. In a climate in which the political right refers to Enlightenment ideals as much as the left, the concept of Counter-Enlightenment has become a derogatory term to denounce opponents. As current debates are increasingly fought between conflicting interpretations of the Enlightenment, the positive value of which is assumed on all sides, "Counter-Enlightenment" has become a term of abuse used against a wide variety of political others – from neo-conservatism to Islamism.

The form these Counter-Counter-Enlightenment arguments take is almost always the same. Typically, they outline a historical lineage, reaching from an ancestor of the Counter-Enlightenment tradition (often Rousseau) to his contemporary descendants. Of course, the names of the particular thinkers and currents of thought listed vary according to particular argumentative needs. What remains identical, however, is the approach of the quasi-pedigree, framing the subject in terms of a current of thought leading from a distinct origin up to the particular present incarnation of Counter-Enlightenment that the argument, ultimately, is designed to undermine (e.g., Johnson 1979; Fetz 2009; Henschel 2010). Motivated by current polemics and centred on the binary framework of interpretation described above, these narratives evoke a centuries-old struggle between the forces of good and evil. From a purely historical point of view, such narratives have many weaknesses. Besides the simplifications necessary to streamline them, they have a tendency to lead to anachronistic interpretations. If Enlightenment and Modernity are used as synonyms, then, logically, the Counter-Enlightenment is outside of Modernity. This means that its interpretation must either reach back to the pre-modern past or out into the future. Sure enough, present instances of Counter-Enlightenment are regularly interpreted as a remnant of the pre-modern era, yet to be overcome in the course of the Enlightenment project. Conversely, the tradition is presented teleologically as a series of precursors to particular contemporary phenomena – serving as a polemical weapon against them. This figure of guilt by association, identifying particular current phenomena with the Counter-Enlightenment tradition and turning its bad reputation against them, is the motivating core behind the success of this interpretative framework.

Paradoxically, this figure of argument has been used to very diverse purposes. Isaiah Berlin himself interpreted the history of the Counter-Enlightenment as the pre-history of the German *Sonderweg*. The German thinkers of *Sturm und Drang* and Romanticism 'rebelled', he wrote, 'against the dead hand of France in the realms of culture, art and philosophy, and avenged themselves by launching the great counter-attack against the Enlightenment.' (Berlin 1990: 196). The teleological nature of his interpretation was hard to miss when he wrote that the dark tenets of the Counter-Enlightenment 'inspired nationalism, imperialism, and finally, in their most violent and pathological form, Fascist and totalitarian doctrines in the twentieth century' (Berlin 1980: 24).

Robert E. Norton, a professor of German studies at the University of Notre Dame, has recently formulated a sharp criticism of this narrative (Norton 2007; cf. also the response in Lestition 2007). Apart from objections to its philological support ('shoddy scholarship'), his critique focused on the origins of the underlying research model. As he pointed out, the idea of a tradition of thought directed against the Enlightenment had been firmly established long before its popularisation by Berlin. The real origin of this 'myth of the Counter-Enlightenment', he argued, lay in the context of the nationalistic German Movement around 1900 and its intellectual counterpart: the German tradition of the history of ideas. In this context, a historical narrative had been established in which "Enlightenment" stood for the depravity of Western civilisation and "Counter-Enlightenment" for the original force of German culture. Later interpreters of the Counter-Enlightenment tradition after the Second World War, ranging from Fritz Stern and Georg Lukács to George Mosse and Isaiah Berlin, unconsciously adopted the very same framework of interpretation – only reversing its normative valuations.

Recent examples of this argument have most often used the Counter-Enlightenment pedigree to discredit postmodernism, identifying its purported irrationalism with a tendency against freedom, democracy, human rights and tolerance (cf. Lübbe 1980; Tallis 1997; Wolin 2004). Yet its versatility was again underlined in a recent book by the Israeli historian of ideas Zeev Sternhell titled *The Anti-Enlightenment Tradition* (Sternhell 2009). Over its first 490 pages, the book presents a fairly typical tirade against the Counter-Enlightenment. Like many others before him, Sternhell presents his object as a unified current of thought finding its nadir in Auschwitz, but reaching into the present. The book's main argument is visualised on the cover of the English edition, on which the words *The*, *Enlightenment*, and *Tradition* are set in a modern, white typeface, while the prefix *Anti* is set in black gothic letters. Still, in the last chapter, the author manages to surprise the reader when he turns the argument of Counter-Enlightenment suspicion against Isaiah Berlin himself. In his effort to analyse the Counter-Enlightenment, Sternhell argues, Berlin had ultimately been infected by it, leading to the paradoxical result that one of the prototypical icons of post-war liberalism had in fact been a secret mouthpiece for anti-liberal thought.

Conclusion

The final example shows how this framework of interpretation, surfacing in various isomorphic versions, eventually carries itself ad absurdum. Its schematic nature constricts the debate about the self-reflexion of the present with regard to its relation to the Enlightenment's current relevance to a reductive black-and-white decision (James Schmidt 2006: 659–660). It forces the interpretation of individual authors and schools of thought into the straitjacket of an unambiguous allocation to one of two possible parties. And finally, it implicitly demands that the reader commit to one side or the other – you're either with us, or against us. Michel Foucault already warned against this type of intellectual 'blackmail' with regard to the Enlightenment.

In his view, doing justice to the Enlightenment and its relevance to the present meant 'that one has to refuse everything which presents itself under the form of a simplistic and authoritarian alternative [...]. We have to try to analyse ourselves qua historically determined beings in part through the Enlightenment.' (Foucault 1994: 571–572). To achieve this goal, Foucault stressed the need for historical research – especially in moving beyond essentialist notions of Enlightenment. As we have seen, current research increasingly satisfies these requirements. Taking into account the complexities of historical language use in the eighteenth century itself, an analytical perspective is established that allows us to reflect upon the semantic and rhetorical dimensions of the concepts of Enlightenment and Counter-Enlightenment not only in the past, but also in the present.

Notes

1 These studies both focus on the French case, but others have extended this research to other European contexts (Sozzi 1992; idem 2001; Albrecht 2005; Mücke 2008).
2 The publication on a dictionary of Counter-Enlightenment has been announced (Masseau [forthcoming]).
3 All translations are my own.

References

Albertan-Coppola, S. 1988. 'L'apologétique catholique française à l'âge des Lumières', *Revue de l'histoire des religions* 205: 151–180.

Albrecht, W. 2005. 'Gegenaufklärung', in *Lexikon zum Aufgeklärten Absolutismus in Europa: Herrscher – Denker – Sachbegriffe*, edited by H. Reinalter. Vienna: Böhlau, pp. 256–259.

Albrecht, W. and Weiß, C. 1999. 'Einleitende Bemerkungen zur Beantwortung der Frage: Was heißt Gegenaufklärung?', in *Von "Obscuranten" und "Eudämonisten": gegenaufklärerische, konservative und antirevolutionäre Publizisten im späten 18. Jahrhundert*, 2nd edn., edited by C. Weiß. St. Ingbert: Röhrig, vol. I., pp. 7–27.

[Allamand, F.] 1751. *Pensées anti-philosophiques*. The Hague: Pierre van Cleef.

[Anonymous] 1765. 'Le Philosophisme: Chanson. Sur l'Air, des Pendus', in [Anonymous], *Lettre du Chevalier M… à Milord K…: Traduite de l'Anglois*, London.

Balcou, J. 1975. *Fréron contre les philosophes*. Geneva: Droz.

Berlin, I. 1973. 'The Counter-Enlightenment', in *Dictionary of the History of Ideas*, vol. II, edited by P. P. Wiener. New York: Charles Scribner's Sons, pp. 100–112.

——. 1980. 'The Counter-Enlightenment', in *Against the Current: Essays in the History of Ideas*. London: Viking Press, pp. 1–24.

——. 1990. 'European Unity and Its Vicissitudes', in *The Crooked Timber of Humantiy*. London: John Murray, pp. 175–206.

Burson, J. D. 2008. 'The Crystallization of Counter-Enlightenment and Philosophe Identities: Theological Controversy and Catholic Enlightenment in Pre-Revolutionary France', *Church History* 77: 955–1002.

Chaudon, L. M. 1771. *Dictionnaire anti-philosophique: Pour servir de Commentaire & de Correctif au Dictionnaire Philosophique, & aux autres Livres qui ont paru de nos jours contre le Christianisme*, 2nd edn., 2 vols. Avignon: Aux dépens de la Société.

Compagnon, A. 2005. *Les antimodernes: De Joseph de Maistre à Roland Barthes*. Paris: Gallimard.

Crowder, G. and Hardy, H. (eds.). 2007. *The One and the Many: Reading Isaiah Berlin*. Amherst, NY: Prometheus.

Darnton, R. 2003. 'The Case for the Enlightenment: George Washington's False Teeth', in R. Darnton, *George Washington's False Teeth: An Unconventional Guide to the Eighteenth Century*. New York: W.W. Norton & Company.

Delon, M. 1993. 'Crise ou tournant des Lumières?', in *Aufklärung als Mission: Akzeptanzprobleme und Kommunikationsdefizite*, edited by W. Schneiders. Marburg: Hitzeroth, pp. 83–90.

Deprun, J. 1973. 'Les Anti-Lumières', in *Histoire de la philosophie*, vol. II, edited by B. Parain and Y. Belaval. Paris: Gallimard, pp. 717–727.

Ferret, O. 2007. *La fureur de nuire: Échanges pamphlétaires entre philosophes et antiphilosophes (1750–1770)*. Oxford: Voltaire Foundation.

Fetz, B. 2009. *Das unmögliche Ganze: Zur literarischen Kritik der Kultur*. München: Fink.

Foucault, M. 1994. 'Qu'est-ce que les Lumières?', in idem, *Dits et écrits, 1954–1988*, vol. IV. Paris: Gallimard, pp. 562–578.

Fréron, É. C. 1772. 'Lettre XIII', *L'Année Littéraire*, no. 2: 289–323.

—— 1778. 'Lettre de M. Palissot à M. de la Harpe, imprimée dans la Gazette de Politique & de Littérature...', *L'Année Littéraire*, no. 4: 204–216.

Garrard, G. 2006. *Counter-Enlightenments: From the Eighteenth Century to the Present*. London: Routledge.

Gay, P. 1966/1969. *The Enlightenment. An Interpretation*, 2 vols. New York: Norton.

Gilbert, N. J. L. 1797. 'Le dix-huitième siècle: Satire à M. Fréron', in N. J. L. Gilbert, *Satires et poësies diverses*. Paris: Des Essarts, pp. 1–16.

[Giraud, C.-M.] 1760. *Épitre du diable, à Monsieur de Voltaire, Comte de Tournay, près Genève*. Aux Délices.

[Giry de Saint Cyr, O. J.] 1758. *Catéchisme et décisions de cas de conscience, à l'usage des Cacouacs*. [Paris].

Goldzink, J. 1993. 'A propos de trois dictionnaires anti-philosophiques', *Les Cahiers de l'ENS Fontenay* 71/2: 97–119.

Gray, J. 1997. *Enlightenment's Wake: Politics and Culture at the Close of the Modern Age*. London: Routledge.

Gumbrecht, H.-U. and Reichardt, R. 1985. 'Philosophe, Philosophie', in *Handbuch politisch-sozialer Grundbegriffe in Frankreich 1680-1820*, vol. III, edited by R. Reichardt et al. München: Oldenbourg.

Henschel, G. 2010. *Menetekel: 3000 Jahre Untergang des Abendlandes*. Frankfurt a. M.: Eichborn.

Irailh, A. S. 1761. 'Les encyclopédistes, et les anti-encyclopédistes', in idem, *Querelles littéraires, ou Mémoires Pour servir à l'Histoire des Révolutions de la Republique des Lettres*, vol. IV. Paris: Durand, pp.118–153.

Israel, J. 2009. 'Les "antiphilosophes" et la diffusion de la philosophie clandestine dans la seconde moitié du XVIIIe siècle', *La Lettre clandestine* 17: 73–88.

Jedlicki, J. 2007. *Die entartete Welt: Die Kritiker der Moderne, ihre Ängste und Urteile*, translated by Jan Conrad. Frankfurt a. M.: Suhrkamp.

Johnson, L. 1979. *The Cultural Critics: From Matthew Arnold to Raymond Williams*. London: Routledge & Kegan Paul.

Lamourette, A. A. 1876. *Pensées sur la philosophie de l'incrédulité, ou Réflexions sur l'esprit et le dessein des philosophes irréligieux de ce siècle*. Paris: chez l'auteur.

Le Masson de Granges, D. 1759. *Le Philosophe moderne, ou L'Incrédule condamné au tribunal de la raison*. Paris: Despilly.

Lestition, S. 2007. 'Countering, Transposing, or Negating the Enlightenment?: A Response to Robert Norton', *Journal of the History of Ideas* 68(4): 659–681.

Lilla, M. 2003. 'What Is Counter-Enlightenment?', in *Isaiah Berlin's Counter-Enlightenment*, edited by J. Mali and R. Wokler. Philadelphia, PA: American Philosophical Society, pp. 1–11.

[Linguet, S. N. H.]. 1764. *Le Fanatisme des philosophes*. London: De Vérité.

—— 1767. *Théorie des loix civiles, ou Principes fondamentaux de la société*, 2 vols. London.

Low, V. 2010. 'Prince Charles declares war on…the Enlightenment', *The Times*, 4 February, http://www.thetimes.co.uk/tto/news/uk/article1946844.ece (accessed 20 November 2014).

Lu, J. 2005. *"Qu'est-ce qu'un philosophe?" Éléments d'un enquête sur l'usage du mot au siècle des Lumières*. Saint-Nicholas: Presses universitaires de l'Université Laval.

Lübbe, H. 1980. 'Aufklärung und Gegenaufklärung', in *Aufklärung heute: Bedingungen unserer Freiheit*, edited by M. Zöller. Zürich: Edition Interfrom.

Mali, J. and Wokler, R. 2003. 'Editors' Preface', in idem (eds.), *Isaiah Berlin's Counter-Enlightenment*. Philadelphia, PA: American Philosophical Society, pp. vii–xi.

Masseau, D. 2000. *Les ennemis des philosophes: L'antiphilosophie au temps des Lumières*. Paris: Albin Michel.

—— 2014. 'Qu'est-ce que les anti-Lumières?', *Dix-huitième siècle* 46: 107–123.

—— (ed.) [forthcoming]. *Dictionnaire des anti-Lumières et des antiphilosophes*. Paris: Champion.

McMahon, D. M. 1998. 'The Counter-Enlightenment and the Low-Life of Literature in Pre-Revolutionary France', *Past and Present* 159: 77–112.

—— 2001. *Enemies of the Enlightenment: The French Counter-Enlightenment and the Making of Modernity*. Oxford: Oxford University Press.

[Moreau, J. N.] 1757a. 'Avis utile, ou Premier mémoire sur les Cacouacs', *Mercure de France*, October: 15–19.

—— 1757b. *Nouveau mémoire pour servir à l'histoire des Cacouacs*. [Paris].

[Morellet, A.] 1769. *Mémoire pour Abraham Chaumeix: Contre les prétendus Philosophes Diderot & d'Alembert*. Amsterdam.

Mücke, U. 2008. *Gegen Aufklärung und Revolution: Die Entstehung konservativen Denkens in der iberischen Welt, 1770–1840*. Köln: Böhlau.

Nonnotte, C. 1766. *Les erreurs de Voltaire*, new edn., 2 vols. Amsterdam: Compagnie des Libraires.

Norton, R. E. 2007. 'The Myth of the Counter-Enlightenment', *Journal of the History of Ideas* 68(4): 635–658.

O'Keefe, C. B. 1974. *Contemporary Reactions to the Enlightenment (1728–1762). A Study of Three Critical Journals: The Jesuit "Journal de Trévoux", the Jansenist "Nouvelles ecclésiastiques", and the secular "Journal des Savants"*. Geneva and Paris: Slatkine.

Palissot, C. 1757. *Petites lettres sur de grands philosophes*. Paris.

—— 1777. 'Les Philosophes', in idem, *Œuvres*. Liège: Clément Plompteux.

Pluquet, F.-A.-A. 1767. *De la sociabilité*, 2 vols. Paris: Barrois.

Pippin, R. B. 1991. *Modernism As a Philosophical Problem: On the Dissatisfactions of European High Culture*, 2nd edn. Malden, MA: Blackwell.

Rigoley de Juvigny, J. 1787. *De la décadence des lettres et des mœurs, depuis les Grecs et les Romains jusqu'à nos jours*, 2nd edn. Paris: Merigot le jeune.

Sabatier de Castres, A. 1779. *Les trois siècles de la littérature françoise, ou Tableau de l'esprit de nos écrivains, depuis François I, jusqu'en 1779*, 4th edn., 4 vols. The Hague: Moutard.

Schmidt, James. 2006. 'What Enlightenment Was, What It Still Might Be, and Why Kant May Have Been Right After All', *American Behavioral Scientist* 49: 647–663.

—— (2013-4) *Fabricating the "Counter-Enlightenment"*, Persistent Enlightenment, http://persistentenlightenment.wordpress.com (accessed 20 November 2014).

Schmidt, Jochen (ed.). 1989. *Aufklärung und Gegenaufklärung in der europäischen Literatur, Philosophie und Politik von der Antike bis zur Gegenwart*. Darmstadt: Wissenschaftliche Buchgesellschaft.

Schnädelbach, H. 2004. 'Die Zukunft der Aufklärung', in idem, *Analytische und postanalytische Philosophie: Vorträge und Abhandlungen 4*. Frankfurt a. M.: Suhrkamp.

Séguier, A.-L. 1770. 'Réquisitoire sur lequel est intervenu l'Arrêt du Parlement du 18 Août 1770, qui condamne à être brûlés différents Livres ou Brochures', in *Avertissement du clergé de France*, edited by Assemblée générale du clergé de France. Lille:Van Constenoble, père.

Sommerer, E. and Zaganiaris, J. (eds.). 2010. *L'obscurantisme: Formes anciennes et nouvelles d'une notion controversée*. Paris: Harmattan.

Sonenscher, M. 2008. *Sans-Culottes: An Eighteenth-Century Emblem in the French Revolution*. Princeton, NJ: Princeton University Press.

Sozzi, L. (ed.). 1992. *Ragioni dell'anti-illuminismo*, Pegaso, vol. II. Alessandria: Edizioni dell'Orso.

—— (ed.). 2001. *Nuove ragioni dell'anti-illuminismo in Francia e in Italia*. Pisa: ETS.

Stenger, G. (ed.). 2004. *L'Affaire des Cacouacs. Trois pamphlets contre les philosophes des Lumières*. Saint-Étienne: Presses de l'Université de Saint-Étienne.

Sternhell, Z. 2009. *The Anti-Enlightenment Tradition*. New Haven, CT: Yale University Press.

Tallis, R. 1997. *Enemies of Hope: A Critique of Contemporary Pessimism, Irrationalism, Anti-Humanism and Counter-Enlightenment*. Basingstoke & London: Macmillan.

Tietz, M. 1998. 'Der Widerstand gegen die Aufklärung in Spanien, Frankreich und Deutschland', in *Europäische Aspekte der Aufklärung: (Deutschland, England, Frankreich, Italien, Spanien)* edited by A. Maler, Á. San Miguel and R. Schwaderer. Frankfurt a. M.: Peter Lang, pp. 93–112.

Voltaire. 1734. *Lettres philosophiques*. Amsterdam: E. Lucas.

Wolin, R. 2004. *The Seduction of Unreason: The Intellectual Romance with Fascism from Nietzsche to Postmodernism*. Princeton, NJ: Princeton University Press.

12
'THE PROPER STUDY OF MANKIND': ENLIGHTENMENT AND TAUTOLOGY

Martin L. Davies

Preamble: Useful knowledge

Enlightenment knowledge was meant to be useful. Diderot sees the purpose of encyclopedias as transmitting the knowledge accumulated by those alive now to those coming afterwards. This way the work of past centuries will not have been 'useless work' for future generations. These latter, 'becoming better informed', will 'become at the same time more virtuous and more happy'. So they, the former, 'will not die without being worthy of mankind' (Diderot 1994a: 363).

Usefulness signifies not a property of knowledge for contemplation. Rather it gauges its responsiveness to the current cognitive situation, its purpose for that situation. Those thinkers orientating the Enlightenment (e.g., Bacon, Descartes, Spinoza, Hobbes) dismissed the dogmatic Aristotelianism of the 'Schools' as ineffective. The reconception of the world by contemporary science (e.g., Newton), political philosophy (e.g., Rousseau) and the theory of knowledge (e.g., Kant) proved what Enlightenment knowledge could do. Knowledge never develops for its own sake. (Ask to what end "better understanding" is "better".) Rather it takes performative re-appraisals, radical paradigm-shifts, and alternative 'thought styles' evinced in different, often conflicting 'thought collectives' that in themselves aim to realise an intention or a function compelled by cultural or political motives – motives that, even if external to them, operate best through them.[1]

But if the Enlightenment advocated useful knowledge, what use is it itself? Actually – in disciplinary terms, from cosmology and the natural sciences to issues of physiology, psychology, medicine, gender and ethnicity – it has been superseded. Subsequent cognitive intentions have historicized it: e.g., psycho-analysis has moved on from exploring tensions between passions and reason; once a human contrivance lands on one, debating comets' superstitious portents is void. It never was reasonable to confine women "naturally" to kids and the kitchen or to de-humanize or patronise "primitive" peoples. For such historicized issues, life-support is inevitably academic.

Still the question remains – though asking about the use of a 'thought-collective' is not like evaluating it, not like asking if its thinking matters. That question is superficial, dependent on arbitrary criteria and preconceived values. It is also an abstraction: the Enlightenment as one matter amongst many other cultural-political matters constituting the general (social) intellect, disseminating the (socially) dominant ideas; the Enlightenment as one mediated matter amongst a plethora of matters. So the question of usefulness turns 'towards the concrete': it 'tries to elucidate the configurations reflexive thinking presupposes as its starting-point and its main support' (Wahl 2004: 13).[2] It remains because usefulness targets an immediate apprehension. Can Enlightenment thinking clarify vital interests in cognitive situations? Apparently there is little doubt. In affirming useful knowledge, the Enlightenment thought-collective also proved its value: unlocking the secrets of nature, challenging religious and secular authority, establishing the basis of morality, disclosing a progressive tendency in the human species. In vindicating the usefulness and value of thinking, it also insisted on its integrity. This comes out in its concern (evinced – *inter alia* – in Arnauld, Descartes, Vico, Spinoza) with improving one's understanding, with disciplinary expertise no distraction from promoting common-sense [*studium bonae mentis*] and universal wisdom [*universalis sapientia*] – hence with 'making the effort to think well' [*travaillons donc à bien penser*] (Descartes 1996: 3 (Règle I); Pascal 1963a: 528). How could knowledge, motivated by the 'audacity to discover for oneself' [*sapere aude*], not be the basis for personal autonomy as a human right (Kant 1982b: 53)? How could it not – fending off dogmatism, licentiousness or fanaticism – support the individual's intellectual and moral self-orientation (Kant 1977a: 281–283)?

Whether or not the Enlightenent "matters" depends on the aims now deemed to matter actually mattering to it; and that depends on Enlightenment discourse – in intellectual histories conventionally condensed into sound-bite paraphrase – being translated into a currently intelligible, cognitively useful idiom. And that question of discursive and cognitive commensurability arises because intellectual history – naturally – pictures the Enlightenment "process" as the categorical-biographical coordination of authors and ideas. By ignoring the question of translatability and commensurability, by defaulting to being yet another subsequent representation – a true likeness, but likeness nevertheless – intellectual history abstracts itself from its object.

Hence the need to turn towards the concrete, to the thought-styles and knowledge-paradigms inherent in discourse that formulate its intentions prior to intellectual history, arrogating them to its own scholastic self-interest. These are immediately available in the Enlightenment's tangible remains: texts, in various different editions, various different formats (in paperback, in expensive scholarly editions, as precious archival documents, as reprographic reprint, or online in virtual reality), some more, some less familiar, depending on research trends and disciplinary fashions. The vitality of the thought-style informing the thought-collective keeps alive texts intellectual history otherwise embalms in prefabricated historical contexts.

So to explore in this material the usefulness of Enlightenment thinking, to turn towards the concrete, to the thought-styles and knowledge-paradigms supporting it means elucidating their 'conceptual field' – i.e., 'the ensemble of synonyms existing at a certain time in a certain language' – within which the Enlightenment thought-collective operated, since 'it is not the fact that a certain concept was paramount in a certain civilization that matters most, but the way in which it was present at various times: the way in which its infuence made itself felt in details. To state a historical truth about a philosophical concept is not enough' (Spitzer 1963: vi, 3). It means tracing the grammatical structure supporting Enlightenment discourse, the *a priori* laws of thought in the mental operations that generate structures of meaning, the logical and grammatical norms that determine what is meaningful (Husserl 2009: 302, 344–345). (This conception of a 'pure grammar' comes from the rationalist (Cartesian, Leibnizian) concept of a 'universal mathematics' [*mathesis universalis*] (Husserl 2009: 344).) Finally, it has recourse to philology, particularly to figures of speech. Though discourse changes, rhetorical figures – structures generated *a priori* by 'pure grammar', mental tropes signifying a cognitive stance – persist.

Enlightenment tautology: The constitution of a conceptual-semantic field

'*Know then thyself*, presume not God to scan; / The proper study of *Mankind* is *Man*': Enlightenment thinking affirms the utility of knowledge – as in this couplet from Pope's often-cited *An Essay on Man* (Pope 1983: 250).[3] Human self-interest is its sole concern. Its powerful motive demands tautological formulation: 'the act of exact and immediate repetition or reiteration' is 'primary to tautology' (Steiner 1997: 353).

Figures of speech: Criteria of intelligibility

Initially Pope's couplet offers a figure of speech: the rhetorical figure *epanalepsis* or *epanados*. Quintilian sees it as a form of *amplificatio*, a means of amplifying a topic, of lending emphasis to a proposition by means of repetition (Quintilian 2001: III, 368–369 (8.3.51); IV, 118–121 (9.3.35,37)). Writing on *Figure* in the *Encyclopédie*, Dumarsais defines it as a form of *epanadiplosis* [*épanadiplose*], as the 'repetition' or 'duplication' of the same word (at the beginning and end of a sentence) that brings a 'feeling of grace [...] to discourse or the disturbance it causes' (Dumarsais 1988, 351–352). In this and subsequent examples the 'rhetoric of grace' disarms resistance to the mental reorientation they propose.

This syntactical organisation is not fortuitous. The crucial word is "proper" – along with its cognates "property" and "propriety". 'Proper study', asserting its self-determined coherence, regards 'scanning God' is an "improper", misconceived pre-occupation. It suggests that knowledge is a property particular to, and adequate for, mankind, not just a species characteristic, but its unique, constantly accumulating possession, that really can be passed on with interest to posterity.[4]

This imperative of human self-interest is formulated tautologically, as a self-evident attitude. Redundancy of meaning justifies absolute affirmation. As Pope's lines confirm, it demonstrates that asserting something as being self-evidently the same – "that it is what it is" – makes the rectitude of its existence indisputable. Tautology, therefore, represents what Bergson calls 'the absolute law of consciousness', Heidegger 'the supreme law of thought': the logical principle of identity (A = A) – for Leibniz 'in propositions the first necessary' for any demonstration of certainty, the basis of 'originary truths' that 'affirm the same about the same' [*idem de se ipso affirmantes*] (Bergson 1982: 156; Heidegger 2002: 9; Leibniz 1960/1961c: 194; 1999a: 1655).

The rhetorical ornament converges with the fundament of Western thought. Reflecting on the 'Great Tautology' – in *Exodus* God's own assertion of isolated omniscience and creative omnipotence: 'I am that I am' – Steiner sees identitary propositions (A = A) as 'generative of reason and of systematic constructs of thought'. In fact, with 'the verb "to be" [...] no inert copula, but [...] maximally dynamic and constructive', such propositions 'inform western criteria of intelligibility' (Steiner 1997: 353, 356). In Parmenides the identity principle proposes that thinking is adequate for determining what exists, that what is thought cannot not be (since no-one can think about what does not in some way or other exist). Its conviction derives from its principle that the 'same thing exists for thinking and for being' (Kirk and Raven 1969: 269). Tautology, therefore, informs three canonical definitions of truth (as set out in Aquinas): not just Augustine's assertions that (i) 'the true is that which is', or that (iii) 'Truth is that whereby what a thing is is shown', but particularly the second proposition whereby (as Isaac Israeli states) (ii) 'Truth is the adequation of thing and intellect'. In a cognitive situation that makes Mankind the 'proper study' of Man and Reason its cognitive instrument, Reason has to be adequate, sufficient, for this task. Aquinas quotes Anselm that 'Truth is rectitude perceptible to mind alone' and comments that 'rectitude' here means 'a certain adequation'. And he proceeds to citing Aristotle to confirm that this definition lends the mind a decisive – reality defining – force that permits no intermediate equivocation: what is true is 'to say what is is, and what is not is not' (Aquinas 1998: 167; Aristotle 1996: 200–201 (1011b25)). In this form – that thinking and being are the same, that intellect has its own adequate rectitude – tautology vindicates Descartes' essential inference. Irrespective of what he thought, be it delusion or veracity, that he was thinking at all meant he must exist. Hence the conclusion: *je pense, donc je suis* (Descartes 1966: 60).

Sameness as cognitive incentive

Repeating words with the same meaning (Mankind / Man) confirms self-interest by affirming self-identity. Style and logic converge in the concept of tautology itself. It comes from the Greek: *autos* = self, my self, oneself. Hence: *to auto* = 'the same'; *tauto-logos* = 'the same word' or 'the same that has been said'. Hence the injunction, reiterated by Pope, *gnothi seauton*, 'know thyself' (the inscription at the Temple of Apollo, Delphi – a maxim with broad credence across the Classical Greek and

Roman world (Pope 1983: 279;Vico 1993: 38–40)). Thus (the tautological principle collapsing historical differences) a Classical intention stimulates Modern thinking: the recourse to origins an incentive to progress. Mankind studying Man 'properly', with 'propriety', thereby coming to know itself, offers a useful principle for systematising knowledge, revealing its comprehensive scope, requiring its encyclopedic organisation, and so guaranteeing its truth, the hallmark of the usefulness it predetermines.

However, tautology as a stylistic figure and identity as a logical principle are predicated on duality, if not duplicity (i.e., A = A; Mankind ↔ Man). Automatically it ensures *a priori* that the ideal is adequate to reality, the abstract to the material, the theoretical to the practical – that transcendental order encapsulates behavioural heterogeneity. Certainly tautology offers conceptual parsimony: a single principle, Man, coordinates everything. But it needs to. Man implies (anthropic) infinity – as another, frequently cited formulation of Mankind's cognitive self-interest (from Terence's comedy *Heautontimoroumenos* [*The Self-Tormentor*]) confirms: '*Homo sum, humani ni a me alienum puto*' [I am human: I think nothing human is foreign to me] (Terence 2001: 186–187).[5] Self-evidently, whatever human beings do is human (and so nothing strange or estranging). This single principle, Man, projects a transcendental standpoint that reads unending diversity as human identity.

If 'Man' is the proper study of 'Mankind', its transcendental self-augmentation is indispensable. Self-sufficient reason sustains it, reason that of itself produces sameness: *tauto-logos*. With the human realm being infinite, human nature would be 'a mystery to Man himself' unless 'illuminated by reason alone' (D'Alembert 2011: 85). The different types of existing specialised knowledge that already constitute human self-knowledge need an organising principle. Hence the recourse to 'a genealogical or encyclopedic tree' to 'assemble them under the **same** point of view' [*sous un même point de vûe*] and, acknowledging their origins, coordinate them. These diverse disciplines arranged by their derivation from the faculties of human understanding (reason, memory and imagination) offer the *philosophe* from his transcendental vantage point above the 'vast labyrinth' of the sciences and the arts a comprehensive overview of all their various interconnections 'at a glance' (D'Alembert 2011: 99, 100, 103; Diderot 1994b: 236–237).

Evidently tautology as a cognitive stance relies on balance or equivalence: diversity of knowledge counterbalanced or matched by comprehensive overview. Connecting matter and mind radically, reductively, through sameness, it offers knowledge a secure, immediately recognisable foundation: that 'in fact all our knowledge can be reduced to sensations which are roughly the *same* in all Men' [*qui sont à peu près les **mêmes** dans tous les hommes*] (D'Alembert 2011: 89). Mobilised by a pervasive thought-style, by a particular grammar of conceptualisation, tautology variously supplies a rhetorical strategy, structures an entire work, or generates a comprehensive knowledge-system (e.g., the *Encyclopédie*, or *An Essay on Man*).

Tautology thus produces a comprehensive semantic field, offering in the contemplation it affords of all knowledge already known an irresistible incentive for human self-knowledge. It defines the cognitive situation for the Enlightenment thought-collective, its *self-identity*, universally identifiable for Mankind. Its guiding identity principle (A = A) offers conceptual schemes of (i) *identity – similitude, sameness, resemblance, likeness, imitation (mimesis), replication*; (ii) *adequacy – equality, equity, equivalence, proportion, reciprocity, balance, coordination, harmony* (i.e., identifiable particular differences calculated to produce meaningful sameness or equivalence). These schemes are coordinated by universal, comprehensive categories immediately implicating human beings in different ways yet automatically operating with their own identitary logic, with their own synchronic and diachronic order: *Providence, Nature, History, Mankind, Reason*. Together these categories of sameness are indispensable instruments of knowledge-management. For the *philosophes* – as knowledge managers – surveying the 'mighty maze', this 'scene of Man', they organise all existing types of knowledge (Pope 1983: 241). They provide a comprehensive "filing system" for them as 'curators' of the existing stock of human self-reflection (Heidegger 1967a: 26, 29). They facilitate their 'administrative gaze' commanding this entire, heterogeneous knowledge culture (Adorno 1979: 122).

Mapping the conceptual field (1): Tautology and its cognates

Tautology offers a thought-style predicated on comprehensive sameness. The identity principle ensures the same comprehensive order for human existence. It, therefore, operates both cognitively and ethically, both theoretically and practically: the rational order and the social order should be the same. This provocative, critical intention sustains its conceptual field – as the following samples show.

Knowledge, self-knowledge, and one's semblables

The injunction "to know oneself" is both theoretical and practical. The point of self-examination is to identify ourselves with others, by definition others like us, our *semblables*.[6] As (e.g.) D'Holbach argues in his *Système social* (1773), the self and others are by definition already the same, coordinated by their sameness. Man inevitably keeps meeting those already resembling him. *Semblable* is, therefore, loaded with both uncompromising ethical propriety and absolute cognitive validity. In ethical terms it makes 'true morality [...] the *same* [*la* **même**] for all the inhabitants of the globe'. Consequently, 'if man is everywhere the *same*, if he has the *same* nature, the *same* inclinations, the *same* desires, by studying man in his constant relationships with others of his species, we easily discover his duties towards himself and towards others'. Physical and cultural differences between human beings accidentally due to climate, government, education nothwithstanding, both 'the primitive and civilized man [...] have the *same* nature' [*L'homme sauvage et l'homme policé* [...] *ont une* **même** *nature*'] (D'Holbach 2004: 38). In cognitive terms it rests on the identity principle: morality based on sameness will be true, capable of being 'as rigorously demonstrated as in arithmetic and geometry', because it is 'based on man *himself*' [*partant de l'homme* **lui-même**], on 'man as he is' (ibid.).

Given this ethical propriety and cognitive validity, self-knowledge automatically supports philosophical reconceptions of morality, society and politics. In *Leviathan* (1651) Hobbes proposes a 'saying not of late understood', '*Nosce te ipsum, Read thyself*' as the basis for understanding human social behaviour. It teaches 'that for the *similitude* of the thoughts, and Passions of one man, to the thoughts, and Passions of another, whosoever looketh into himself, [...] shall thereby read and know, what are the thoughts, and Passions of all other men, upon *like* occasions'. Moreover, it comes with a politically critical point: 'he that is to govern a whole Nation, must read in *himself*, not this or that particular man; but *Man-kind*' (Hobbes 1972: 82–83 (italics in original)).

For Adam Smith in the *Theory of Moral Sentiments* (1759) (citing Edmund Burke), 'the Nature of man, that is always the *same*' forms the basic social bond (Smith 1982: 28). As he observes, 'as we have no immediate experience of what *other men feel*, we can form no idea of the manner in which they are affected, but by conceiving what *we ourselves should feel* in the *like situation*' (Smith 1982: 9). Sameness (as a copula) thus regulates self-identification and social involvement: 'To *approve* of the passions of another, therefore, as suitable to their objects, is *the same thing* as to *observe* that we *entirely sympathize* with them; and *not to approve* of them as such, is *the same thing* as to observe that we do *not entirely sympathize* with them' (Smith 1982:16). As an ideal *semblable*, generating *within the self* the duality that constitutes the identity principle (A = A) requisite for self-knowledge, Smith posits an 'impartial spectator'. This 'great demigod within the breast' provides the only means of 'scrutinizing the propriety of our own conduct': the '*looking-glass*' that is 'the eyes of other people' (Smith 1982: 112, 246–247). This 'impartial spectator' replicates not just the present society of *semblables*, is not just the voice of conscience, but the personification of the universal moral system. It is the same thought-style: just as the *Encyclopédie* acts as a maximally constructive, diachronic copula between humanity past and humanity future (cf. The *Encyclopédie* as copula between precursors and posterity, below), so the 'impartial observer' is a maximally constructive metaphysical copula between humanity and 'the great society of all sensible and intelligent beings, of which God himself is the immediate administrator and director' (Smith 1982: 235). Hence, to act morally (i.e., with the approval of the 'impartial observer') is not just 'necessarily [to] pursue the most effectual means for promoting the happiness of mankind', but also 'in some sense to cooperate with the Deity, and to advance [...] the plan of Providence' (Smith 1982: 166). Thus though in judging vice and virtue Nature follows 'rules fit for her' and Man those 'fit for him', their aim is identical: 'both are calculated to promote the *same* great end, the order of the world, and the perfection and happiness of human nature' (Smith 1982: 168). In Smith's comprehensive survey of diverse ethical attitudes, sameness guarantees what is ethically proper for mankind. Having acquired the supreme virtue of autonomy, of *self*-command, that person 'does not merely affect the sentiments of the impartial spectator. He really adopts them. He almost *identifies himself* with, he almost *becomes himself* that impartial spectator, and scarce even feels but as that great arbiter of his conduct directs him to feel' (Smith 1982: 147).

In these samples cognitive self-evidence (A = A) vouchsafes moral perfection: the harmonious society of *semblables*. But the theoretical reconfiguration of social reality masks the social reality that has been reconfigured. Self-knowledge functions critically not just by affirming a moral ideal, but by magnifying a psychopathic reality – as in the social-psychological journal *Gnothi Seauton oder Magazin zur Erfahrungsseelenkunde* (1783–1793), edited in Berlin by Karl Philipp Moritz (1756–1793), a catalogue of eccentric and deviant behaviour, mental and physical illness, narratives of traumatic memory and suicidal depression, these also an indelible "legacy" of the Age of Enlightenment.

Man: A comprehensive cognitive template

The tautological identity principle guarantees truth since Man defines both the scope and the structure of human knowledge. As suggested already by D'Alembert (cf. Sameness as cognitive incentive, above), human self-knowledge must at a glance be comprehensive. As Vico observes in his lectures *On Humanistic Education* (1699–1707), knowing oneself involves dedicating oneself to acquiring a comprehensive knowledge of the humanities, to learning 'the total accumulation of knowledge that has been discovered and passed on by the most distinguished scholars' (Vico 1993: 51). Further, comprehension is guaranteed because – according to Terence's maxim Vico affirms when defining wisdom in terms of 'knowing with certainty, acting rightly, and speaking with dignity' – nothing human can be 'foreign' to Man (Vico 1993: 129). Terence's maxim makes comprehensiveness self-evidently non-exclusive, non-estranging. According to Dumarsais in the *Encyclopédie*, it supports the *philosophe*'s concern for society as a whole. Unlike important people too distracted for contemplation and 'intolerant to those they cannot recognize as *equals*' [*féroces envers ceux qu'ils ne croyent pas leurs **égaux***] and 'ordinary philosophers' too absorbed in thought for human company, the *philosophe* 'full of humanity' maintains a sense of *proportion* and *balance* (like the *just medium* history affords the philosopher, according to Hume (cf. Historical ratio as cognitive compensation, below)). He 'knows how to divide himself between retirement and human company' [*sait **se partager** entre la retraite & le commerce des hommes*]. Like Terence's character, Chremes, he is aware of himself as a Man, so humanity alone involves him in his neighbour's bad or good fortune: *Homo sum, humani à me nihil alienum puto* (Dumarsais 1743/1765). Further, this maxim vindicates specific cognitive stances in contemporary philosophical discussion – as in the 'Preliminary Discourse' to the *Encyclopédie*, where D'Alembert sees it personified in Bacon who 'could have said, like Terence's old man, that nothing regarding humanity was foreign to him'; or as in the correspondence between Spinoza and Oldenburg where both cite this same maxim to vindicate their differing standpoints (D'Alembert 2011: 121; Spinoza 1925b: 67, 310; §§13, 74).

But the comprehensive scope of human knowledge requires an intelligible structure. This the identity principle automatically predicates on Man. In the *Encyclopédie* the mental faculties constituting human understanding (i.e., memory, reason and imagination) order and interconnect the multifarious knowledge disciplines (cf. Sameness as cognitive incentive, above). Kant's definition of the Enlightenment, that one should 'think for oneself', is articulated in terms of human development from childhood to maturity as a universal and necessary stage in one's life (Kant 1982b: 53; cf. Reed 2015:8). In Pascal, Hume and Herder the development of the human life span articulates the phases of human historical development (cf. Man, the template of historical sense, below). In *Leviathan* human physiology explains the State's internal workings.

Hobbes likens the 'Common-wealth' to an 'Artificiall Man' made by men, thereby affirming its '*resemblance* [...] to a naturall man' – *similes* variously exploitable. So internal conflict, particularly between religious and political authority, that can 'Trouble, and sometimes destroy a Commonwealth', is likened to 'a Disease which not unfitly may be compared to the Epilepsie or Falling-sicknesse [...] in the Body Naturall'. *Likeness* thus preserves the identitary structure especially in crisis (Hobbes 1972: 263, 306, 371ff.). So money – 'some thing of *equal* value' – facilitating commerce is the life-blood of the commonwealth: Gold and Silver being 'a commodious *measure* of the value of all things else between Nations'; money itself 'a sufficient *measure* of the value of all things else, between the Subjects of that Common-wealth'. 'Sanguinification' describes the circulation of money 'Nourishing (as it passeth) every part' of the state: 'For naturall bloud is *in like manner* made of the fruits of the Earth: and circulating, nourisheth by the way, every Member of the Body of Man'. Hence the basic simile extends to describing the state's financial administration: 'And in this also, the Artificiall Man *maintains his resemblance* with the Naturall; whose Veins receiving the Bloud from the severall Parts of the Body, carry it to the Heart; where being made Vitall, the heart by the Arteries sends it out again, to enliven, and enable for motion all the Members *of the same*' (Hobbes 1972: 274ff. 299–301).

Man thus offers a comprehensive template for knowledge of all areas of human activity: intellectual, moral, cultural and political. That this is (actually) *self*-evident – tautological – guarantees its truth.

Human self-equivalence

The tautological basis of the Enlightenment can be affirmative, defining comprehensively things as they are; critical, estimating equivalences to challenge existing cognitive and social orders; revolutionary, producing equality to re-evaluate cognitive and social values. It illustrates the power of knowledge.

The self-identical presence of mind derives from its actual social, political and cultural circumstances: thus Helvétius's empiricist argument in *De l'esprit* (1758). It itself demonstrates the mind's '"proper character" [*le propre de l'esprit*]', which is 'to observe, to generalize its observations, and from them draw results or maxims'. On this basis it explores morally and metaphysically 'man in general' [*l'homme en général*], thereby here too proposing human solidarity in both global (synchronic) and historical (diachronic) terms (Helvétius 1988: 439; 179 (cf. The *Encyclopédie* as copula between precursors and posterity, below)).

Universality – anthropic and historical – is tautological: a form of Mankind's self-recognition. The cognitive intention is to produce conceptual sameness, comprehensive structures of meaning for managing the heterogeneity of the world and its contingencies. Producing new and general ideas derived from observation, sense-perception and its linguistic signs, 'all the mind's operations come down to studying *the resemblances and differences* between diverse things' [*toutes les opérations de l'esprit se réduisent à connoître* **les ressemblances et les différences** *qu'ont entr'eux les objets divers*] (Helvétius 1988: 21–22, 49, 51ff., 442, 523). Sameness specifically guarantees the rectitude of cognitive self-orientation. Beyond the distractions of the 'fashionable mind' [*l'esprit de mode*] contingent on 'changes in the commerce, government, passions, occupations, and prejudices of peoples' (arbitrarily 'enlightening', 'witty', 'tasteful', 'broad', 'balanced' [*juste*], 'common-sense', 'of its century') lies by contrast the 'true mind'. This, the 'most desirable' mind, with its eternal and *inalterable* utility independent of the diversity of customs and governments, 'adheres to the *nature of man himself* [*tient à* **la nature même de l'homme**] (Helvétius 1988: 178; 419ff. cf. 108–109). Further the sameness of mind, defined by its essential equality, is guaranteed by the materialistic premise that its nature is the same as Nature itself, that it is itself a 'gift of nature' (Helvétius 1988: 260, 329). 'All human beings,' he asserts, 'are by nature endowed with an *equally* balanced mind [*un esprit* **également** *juste*]; and, presented with the *same* objects, they would all come to the *same* judgement on them' [*et qu'en leur présentant les* **mêmes** *objets, ils en porteroient tous les* **mêmes** *jugemens*]. Hence, all have the capacity 'to ascend to the highest ideas' ((Helvétius 1988: 260; 387). Mental capacity may seem unequally distributed in society: this does not indicate cognitive inequality but rather the interference of contingent behavioural, social or political influences on personal conduct such as the willingness to be educated, the type of government, the mood of the times (Helvétius 1988: 50, 261, 417). Hence the conclusion: 'we have in us the power to reach the *same judgements* on the *same things*. In other words, *to see things the same*, is to have an *equal capacity* of mind' [*nous avons tous en nous la puissance de porter les* **mêmes jugemens** *sur les* **mêmes choses**. *Or,* **voir de même**, *c'est avoir* **également d'esprit**] (Helvétius 1988: 386–387, cf. 415). By means of the identity principle, the natural convergence of thinking and being, cognitive equality automatically necessitates political egalitarianism.

Sameness functions as a dynamic copula since it aligns the individual's cognitive and political situation. Its political force is indisputable. Tautology drives natural law, based on reason and providence, underpinning civil and religious law. Affirming Man as the proper study of Mankind also means that 'to *man* [...] there is nothing more useful than *man*' [**homini** *igitur nihil* **homine** *utilius*] (Spinoza 1996: 125–126; IV, P18, Schol.; Spinoza 1925a: 223). Man may well 'hold nothing more dear than himself' and study 'to preserve himself', but alone still remains vulnerable. The advantages human life now enjoys result 'from men's mutual assistance': 'There is nothing in this world, save the great and good God Himself, from which greater advantage can come *to man* than *from man* himself' (Pufendorf 1991: 33, 34).

Natural law, therefore, functions on *reciprocity* to ensure the freedom and security essential for both one's own and others' virtuous self-preservation and intellectual self-realisation. Hence, the 'fundamental natural law' requires 'every man [...] to do as much as he can to cultivate and preserve sociality', which means 'joining forces with *men like himself* and so *conducting himself towards them*' so that they 'become willing to preserve and promote his advantages' (Pufendorf 1991: 35). Each individual has, therefore, a duty to contribute usefully to society. This includes: not harming or causing loss to others, since 'the Creator has willed that *all men be bound as men*'; 'each *man valuing* and treating the *other* as naturally his *equal*, or *equally* as a *man*', given that 'human nature [...] belongs *equally to all* and no-one would or could gladly associate with anyone who does not value *him as a man as well as himself* and a partner in *the same nature*', given too that *equality* means 'that he who wants to use the services of others to his own advantage must be ready to make himself useful to them *in return*'; and 'everyone [being] useful to others, so far as he conveniently can', thus recognising a '*kinship* among men', established by nature, for giving and sharing 'such things as will encourage mutual goodwill' (Pufendorf 1991: 56, 61–62, 64).

This production of sameness at least in *thought* confronts *existing* political and economic differences. And, at least in thought, it can – quite provocatively – collapse them, even if in reality retaining them. So the wealthy who distribute their surplus to the poor actually "even out" metaphysical imbalances in nature: 'They are led by an invisible hand to make *nearly the same* distribution of the necessities of life, which would have been made, had the earth been divided into *equal* portions among all its inhabitants, and thus without intending it [...] advance the interests of society, and afford means to the multiplication of the species'. Equally, sameness predicated on the 'real happiness of human life' collapses vast existing differences in social position and material well-being: 'In ease of body and peace of mind, all the different ranks of life are *nearly upon a level*, and the beggar, who suns himself by the side of the highway, possesses that security which kings are fighting for' (Smith 1982: 184–185).

On the other hand, natural equality and reciprocal self-recognition can give rise to conflict it takes a further tautological structure – the state – to resolve. 'Nature hath made men so *equall*, in the faculties of body, and mind,' Hobbes asserts, that 'when all is reckoned together, the difference between *man*, and *man*, is not so considerable, as that *one man* can thereupon claim to himselfe any benefit, to which *another* may not pretend as well, as he'. Equity erases difference, a 'Precept of the Law of Nature' to which 'a Sovereign is as much subject, as any of the meanest of his people': securing public safety requires 'that Justice be *equally* administered to all degrees of People' (Hobbes 1972: 183, 385). But natural sociability is nonexistent: natural equality produces social conflict. 'Every man looketh that his companion should value him, at the *same* rate he sets upon *himselfe*,' but the absence of mutual self-recognition produces hostility: 'From this *equality of ability*, ariseth *equality of hope* in attaining our Ends. And therefore if any two men desire the *same thing*, which neverthelesse they cannot both enjoy, they become enemies'. Unless constrained by a 'power able to overawe them all', they live in a condition of war 'of *every man*, against *every man*' (Hobbes 1972: 184–185). Reciprocity attempts to obviate this anarchy, this rivalry of equivalences, by means of identitary self-projection: Men 'conferre all their power and strength upon one Man, or upon an Assembly of men, that may reduce all their Wills, by plurality of voices, unto one Will: which is as much to say, to appoint one man, or Assembly of men, to beare their person'. Thus everyone has an interest in identifying with this structure of government as a means of ensuring their own security. 'More than Consent, or

Concord', this arrangement is tautological: it is 'a reall Unitie of them all, in *one and the same* Person, made by Covenant of *every man* with *every man*'. Making the social, the political and the religious all the same, it ensures the citizen identifies his life with the life of the state: it produces 'that great Leviathan', that '*mortall God*' that in conjunction with the '*immortall God*' ensures peace and security (Hobbes 1972: 227).

In conclusion, the sameness produced by tautological structures is a guarantee of order and rectitude in social, political, or metaphysical terms alike. Its presence in one dimension validates it for the others: as a 'maximally dynamic and constructive copula', Man guarantees their identity. Thus it juxtaposes the ethical-political ideal with ethical-political reality, assimilates human existence to the metaphysical ideal. So the wise man (says Smith) is *like* his Stoical counterpart: he 'endeavours to enter into the views of the great Superintendant of the universe, and to see things in *the same light* in which the divine Being beheld them'. But to him 'all the different events which the course of his providence may bring forth, what to us appear the smallest and the greatest [...], were perfectly *equal*, were *equally* parts of that great chain he had predestined from all eternity, were *equally* the effects of the *same* unerring wisdom, of the *same* universal and boundless benevolence'. Hence, assuming the comprehensive, divine perspective discloses 'to the Stoical wise man, in the *same* manner, [that] all those different events were perfectly *equal'* (Smith 1982: 289–290). Sameness, though vindicating the perfect order of the world in ideal ethical terms, also (duplicitously) permits social affirmation, social homogenisation, according to real social utility.

Sameness and equivalence as ratio

Tautology, an incontrovertible cognitive reference point, is both mutable and rigorous. Sameness, never immediately given or present, is a cognitive preconception. And, as mapping its conceptual field confirms, it can be preconceived in various ways. Its flexibility is its force – especially when produced by rational calculation (cf. the Latin *ratio*; or the English "ratio"). It assesses relative values, proportions, ratios of reciprocity to produce equivalences that transform irreconcilable differences into likenesses.

So for Voltaire in his *Dictionnaire philosophique* (1764 / 1769) equivalence, making repeated differences comparable (identifying religious intolerance as psychopathic behaviour), offers a defining premise: 'fanaticism is to superstition what delirium is to fever, what fury is to anger' (fanaticism ↔ superstition = delirium ↔ fever = fury ↔ anger) (Voltaire 1967: 196). So too a ratio compares and calculates the equivalent values of scientific and ethical knowledge: 'It has taken **centuries** to know part of the laws of **nature**. A **day** suffices for a *philosophe* to know the **duties of man**' (Voltaire 1967: 342); or those of sceptical reason and Christian grace: 'Reason is for the *philosophe* what grace is for the Christian. Grace determines the Christian to act; reason determines the *philosophe*' (reason ↔ *philosophe* = grace ↔ Christian) (Dumarsais 1743/1765). Also, in Rousseau's *Discours sur l'origine et les fondements de l'inégalité parmi les hommes* (1755), it assesses the cognitive value of the extent of human knowledge relative to the knowledge they have of themselves, so 'the *single inscription* on the temple at Delphi [i.e., "to know oneself"] contains a more important and difficult precept than *all the moralists' large tomes* together' (Rousseau 1971: 149).

Similar equivalences (according to Diderot) show that the moralist who focusses on 'singular absurdity' rather than 'rational action' operates just *like* the natural historian: for both the dissection of a single monster, something *unlike* any known other, is 'more useful than studying a hundred specimens all *resembling* each other' [*elle lui sert plus que l'étude de cent individus qui **se ressemblent***] (i.e., moralist = historian of nature; one monster = 100 normal specimens) (Diderot 1994a: 419). And the same calculation informs Pope's observation that, seeing 'A mortal Man unfold all Nature's law', 'Superior beings' 'Admir'd such wisdom in an earthly shape, / And shew'd a NEWTON as we shew an Ape' (Pope 1983: 251). It expresses a ratio (i.e., Superior Beings ↔ Newton = Man ↔ Ape) that aligns Reason with Providence.

For Helvétius in *De l'esprit* (1758), equivalence, treating the ethical and the natural world the same, permits a materialist vindication of the vital rôle of passions in intellectual and social life. 'Passions,' he asserts 'are for morality what in physics is movement: it creates, destroys, conserves, animates everything, and without it everything is dead'. Hence they are the 'productive germ of the mind': 'snatching us away from laziness, they alone endow us with the sustained attention conducive to mental superiority' (passions ↔ morality = movement ↔ physics) (Helvétius 1988: 268, 273, 282; cf. 286). Thus the natural sameness produced by equivalence affirms passion both as an integral part of the natural human condition ordained by God and, therefore, expressing the will animating body and mind. Distinct from occluding social passions such as envy, pride, avariciousness and ambition arising through the development of societies, pleasure and pain persist as physical, materialistic reminders of human necessitousness (Helvétius 1988: 280–290).

Also (in Smith's case) equivalence calibrates the moral aspiration to identify oneself with the 'impartial observer' and the universal moral order: a simple estimated ratio confirms that 'to a real wise man the judicious and well-weighed approbation of a single wise man, gives more heartfelt satisfaction than all the noisy applauses of ten thousand ignorant though enthusiastic admirers' (i.e., 1 wise man = 10,000+ ignorant enthusiasts) (Smith 1982: 253). Thus, as D'Holbach asserted, moral truths can be "arithmetically" demonstrated.

But the flexibility of tautology, its cognitive potential, is illustrated through its capacity to rationalise equivalence between apparently irreconcilable difference: (e.g.) that between *similitude* and genius. For Diderot, *similitude*, the persistence of sameness, threatens the unique transformative legacy of original genius in a given area of knowledge. This legacy declines because genius is vulnerable: unlike other geniuses or prevailing cognitive conventions anyway indifferent to it (Diderot 1994c: 338–339). Conversely, for Helvétius mind is personified by the genius rather than the moralist. Genius deals with more important issues, can coordinate more truths, and so produce more comprehension [*un plus grand ensemble*]. Though not the same as any other human type, the genius still validates sameness. The public enjoys the consequences offered by the vantage point of comprehensive principle. They recognise as a genius someone who provides them with it 'by bringing together an infinity of truths under the *same point of view*' [*en réunissant une infinité de vérités sous le même point de vue*] (Helvétius 1988: 442–443; cf. 108–109). Thus estimated ratios of sameness produced by comprehensive equivalences characterise Enlightenment thinking.

A note on cosmological tautology

The *ratio* of cognitive equivalence – imitating mathematics, geometry and natural science – affirms verifiable inferences established by human reason. These apparently reveal that nature evinces intelligible patterns and laws and (as in Newton's exemplary case) the mind is adequate for comprehending them. But Newton's cosmological system is static, not dynamic. Predicated on the cognitive ideal of complete comprehension [*connaissance maximale, complète*], this paradigm of classical physics 'would reduce becoming to a tautological repetition of the same thing' [*réduirait le devenir à une répétition tautologique du même*] (Prigogine and Stengers 2005: 351). It regards stability as 'the truth of change'; it stresses the 'pre-eminence of permanence' (Prigogine and Stengers 2005: 294, 375). It excludes anything that threatens sameness, anything chaotic, unforeseeable: the irreversibility of time, evolution, chance, thinking, the potentially deviant agency of Mankind itself – anything that might develop de-stabilising, incoherent novelty (what some *philosophes* repudiated as 'Epicureanism'). But since Nature can be viewed only from a standpoint within Nature itself, it is also predicated on an internal contradiction: the intelligible universe it discloses 'renders the fact that we can know and observe it unintelligible' (Prigogine and Stengers 2001: 186). Precisely this comprehensive knowledge that (as D'Alembert intended) 'would disclose the totality of what is real at a glance' [*la totalité du réel serait simultanément visible*], derives from a 'transcendental perspective' [*un point de vue de survol*] that Nature blocks and is, therefore, now (in quantum theory) 'impossible to locate' (Prigogine and Stengers 2005: 313).

Man: A maximally dynamic and constructive copula?

As these textual samples suggest, tautological human self-interest is comprehensive, its conceptual field apparently unlimited. The conceptual schemes of *identity* and *adequacy* assured by the identity principle (A = A) apply universally. Man thus offers a template synchronically and diachronically managing the current state of knowledge, a copula connecting past, present and future generations, a *just medium* in the Great Chain of Being linking the most inferior life-forms with the most superior. In this respect tautology confirms Man as the measure of all things. However, that to prove its *adequacy* the scheme of *identity* must resort to calculating ratios, to estimating various forms of *equivalence, proportion, reciprocity*, and *balance*, apparently affirming its theoretical and practical force, seems rather symptomatic of stress. To put it bluntly, as knowledge develops can "Man" still function as a template or a copula – as the universal measure? Certainly, in metaphysical (theoretical) terms the identity principle assures conceptual coherence in the most antithetical systems, irrespective of the existing world they address. By contrast, in historical (practical) terms it vindicates itself absolutely: ever-changing differences in the existing world reveal the self-same comprehensive coherence.

Mapping the conceptual field (2): Tautology and metaphysics

'All are but parts of one stupendous whole, / Whose body Nature is, and God the soul', asserts Pope: significantly, it is 'chang'd through all, and yet *in all the same*'. To the 'great directing MIND OF ALL' there is 'no high, no low, no great, no small; / He fills, he bounds, connects and *equals all*'. Hence the concluding, immediately self-affirmative reiteration: 'One truth is clear, "Whatever *is, is* RIGHT' (Pope 1983: 249). The main problem for an anthropic metaphysics is its own self-stabilising consistency, an aspiration that is both chimerical, given the labyrinthine heterogeneity of human reality, and indispensable, if human existence is to mean anything. The solution (as Leibniz and Spinoza show) is the recourse to sameness.

Tautology as theodicy

Leibniz's metaphysical world-view foresakes eliding the human and the divine spheres by means of adequacy. Instead, it relates them through other aspects of the same conceptual-semantic field: negotiated equivalences, systems of reciprocity, the self-evidence of proportionate resemblances.

Negotiated equivalences – establishing equitable relationships – underpin theodicy. The omniscience and omnipotence of the creator of the world-machine, of the divine mind that expresses itself artistically in nature, are "saved" by the concept of pre-established harmony. Far from indicating a flaw in the cosmic design, the presence of evil and suffering only accentuates its overall moral and aesthetic perfection (Leibniz 1962a: 114ff; I, §§12–14, 19–26). Hence, confirmed by the evidence of design in nature, by the intricacy of the world-machine, the thought of God's perfection is – in anthropic terms – adequate for appreciating God's transcendental rectitude. Thus, stressed by the repetition of '*propria*' (proper), 'each individual has a share in the perfection of the universe with his or her happiness *proportionate* to [i.e., 'the *equivalent measure* of'] their virtue' [*ut quisque de perfectione universi partem caperet et felicitate propria pro mensura **virtutis propriae**]* (Leibniz 1960/1961a: 307). God, leaving nothing to chance, may 'not be the *same* as us' [***pas semblable*** *à nous*], prone as we are to error (Leibniz 2001c: 230; §XIX). But there are reassuring relationships of *equivalence*: the individual's theological relationship to God is mirrored by the subject's political relationship to his prince (Leibniz 1960/1961a: 307); evinced in whoever acts with perfection, divine providence is the same as [*semblable à*] an excellent geometrician, a good architect, a caring father, a clever mechanic, an erudite author – each type in its own situation performing responsibly to the best of its abilities (Leibniz 2001c: 209–210; §V).

Reciprocity establishes the coherence of Leibniz's world-view. The relationship between oneself (i.e., the soul) and the body projects a transcendent 'dominant unity' that physically and spiritually sustains the world: metaphysics as transcendental self-projection (Leibniz 1960/1961a: 302). Arguing against occasionalism and a crude body-soul dualism, Leibniz stresses their reciprocal relationship: body and abstract thought do act and react on each other (Leibniz 1994a: 151). The soul follows its own, original constitution from the individual standpoint offered by the organised substance (the body) incorporating it. This latter operates reciprocally following the laws of the body-machine according to the soul's intentions. Neither disturbs the other: body and soul operate according to a 'mutual relationship regulated in advance by each substance of the universe' that, enabling them to communicate with each other, establishes their union (Leibniz 1994b: 73–74).

Thus Leibniz's thought expresses itself in models of reciprocity, in an eco-system of already regulated mutual relationships as a means of 'vindicating the ways of God to Man' (Pope 1983: 241). Hence – contrary to Newton's mechanistic view – all matter is inherently dynamic, consisting of a passive force that constitutes its mass and an active force (*entelechy*) that first produces its form. This latter contains a still "live" primitive force, that ensures the *self-same unity* of material forms [*unum per se*], which means there is nothing not sustained by God. Matter contains also a derivative force, a type of impetus through which its form can be altered. This force he has shown '*not* to be conserved the *same* in the *same* body, but, in one way or another being distributed in many, to remain the *same* in all of them' [***non** quidem eandum in eodem corpore conservari, sed tamen, utcunque in pluribus distribuatur,* **eandum in summa manere**] (Leibniz 1960/1961b: 396; cf. Leibniz 1994c: 178). Further, if the soul has the force to act immanently, nothing prevents the *same* force from being inherent in other souls or substances [*nihil prohibet* [...] *naturis substantiarum* **eandem vim** *inesse*]; similarly, with its natural inertia constantly resistant to change, each body evinces a passive force of resistance, 'its mass, everywhere the same in the body in proportion to its size' [*quae in corpore ubique* **eadem magnitudinique** *ejus* **proportionalis** *est*] (Leibniz 1960/1961d: 510). Furthermore, sustained by God as the final cause, these forces operate through the reciprocal relationship of cause and effect, their manifestations testifying to the sufficiency of reason, the principle that nothing happens without a reason *sufficient* (a *proportionate* reason) for it happening (Leibniz 1999b: 1375–1376).

These formations of reciprocity are crystallised metaphorically when the world is conceived as an infinitely complex, intricate machine, a sample of the work of an infinite author (Leibniz 1960/1961b: 396). As in a machine (e.g., clockwork), each component relies on every other for the machine itself to function: that testifies to the wisdom of its creator (Leibniz 1960/1961d: 505). What sustains reciprocity is the accommodation of all created things with each other: even a simple substance has connections that express all others; hence, it itself becomes a 'perpetually living mirror' of the universe' (Leibniz 1962b; 500; §56; cf. Leibniz 2001: 214–215).

The self-evidence of proportionate resemblances generates reciprocity. The cognitive situation already occurs in a world testifying to divine providence, guaranteed by God as its final cause, with everything connected to everything else. Hence, in its own way, from its own perspective, 'the least small body receives some impression of its own of the least change in all the others, however remote and small they may be' (Leibniz 1994d: 195). On the same reciprocal principle, with its multitude of thoughts responsive to everything around it, the soul can be compared with the universe and 'even in some way' with God, 'representing His *infinity finitely*, in its own, imperfect way' [*dont elle représente **finiment l'infinité***] (Leibniz 1994d: 200–201). Hence, too, our knowledge of order, the order 'that we *ourselves* can give to things within our scope in *imitation* of the order God gives to the universe', makes us '*in diminutive resemble* Divinity' [***ressembler en diminutif*** *à la Divinité*] (Leibniz 1994e: 244–245). Establishing proportionate resemblances, these relative equivalences, is self-knowledge, 'this self that thinks, called spirit or soul', that, like the identity-principle formulated by Descartes' *cogito ergo sum*, is far more cognitively self-assured than a reductive empiricism reliant on sense-perception alone (Leibniz 1994e: 239). Knowledge, therefore, always implies self-knowledge: the experience of oneself [*moi*], derived from the body, indicates in the soul an inherent intellectual capacity, an 'indivisible substance' – an already intentional consciousness – that generates these phenomena so that body and soul work in tandem. Self-knowledge, by definition structured for comprehension, models the ontological structure itself: 'substance expresses the universe, minds express God' (Leibniz 1994d: 197–198; Leibniz 2001: 240, 254).

In Leibniz's world-view sameness produces a sublime metaphysical structure that resolves particular difference into overall harmony. In it Mankind plays a crucial role, personifying through the union of body and soul the spiritually dynamic essence of matter itself, replicating in its own comprehensive cognitive situation the transcendental cognitive situation of God, its self-knowledge disclosing to itself its privileged status. At the same time, however, sameness ensures absolutely coercive self-integration. Everything has its pre-ordained place in the perfect meta-structure of the cosmos: anything that demurs – by definition thereby evil or blasphemous – only enhances the perfection it apparently spoils. Offset by the foil of sublimity sameness thus affirms the rectitude of what is – that this is how things are, that this is the way they are.

Tautology and conceptual parsimony

By contrast, in Spinoza tautology ensures conceptual parsimony: the identity principle collapses transcendental differences. This removes the need for ancillary, often figurative constructions of equivalence, reciprocity or resemblance to accommodate them (as in the case of theodicy). This logical strategy surely accounts for his work's continuing resonance. It also both disarms the accusation of atheism and blocks the charge of pantheism. Quite simply: the world can be comprehended in anthropic terms – for this the mind is adequate. This includes God – certainly not as an omniscient and omnipotent author of all things over and above the world, but as the absolute form of already existing substance and essence. Hence, where thinking and being are identical, transcendental difference vanishes, as the following issues – geometrical method, the identity of God and Nature, and their social and political implications – demonstrate.

Geometrical method as a method of understanding nature can also understand human psychology: human psychology is *a priori* an integral part of nature itself. So, for Spinoza, irrational behaviour self-evidently admits rational analysis. Mental and behavioural deviance occurs not through any fault of nature: rather 'Nature is always the *same*, and its virtue and power of acting are everywhere *one and the same*' [*est namque natura* **semper eadem**, *& ubique una,* **eadem**que *ejus virtus, & agendi potentia*]. Consequently 'the laws and rules of Nature, according to which all things happen, and change from one form to another, are *always* and *everywhere* the *same*' [*sunt* **ubique** *et* **semper eadem**]. Hence the inference: 'the way of *understanding* the *nature* of anything, of whatever kind, must also be the *same*, namely through the universal *laws and rules of nature*' [**eadem**que *etiam debet esse ratio* [...] **intelligendi**]. Predicated on the identity principle, this cognitive stance exemplifies the radical, unorthodox character of Spinoza's thinking: he intends to treat 'the nature and powers of the affects, and the power of the mind over them, by the *same* method [**eâdem Methodo**] by which [...] he has treated God and the mind'. Underscored by the repetition of sameness, the geometrical method produces an identitary structure: psychopathology ↔ power of mind = power of mind ↔ God. Thus the comprehensive concept (Nature), like the comprehensive method that works with 'lines, planes and bodies', abolishes transcendental difference (Spinoza 1996: 69; III. Preface; Spinoza 1925a: 138).

In this cognitive stance mind is consistent. The issue is whether or not its capacity for achieving comprehensive certainty and clarity is adequate. Hence the recourse to the geometrical method that guarantees the adequate certainty available to the human mind. Surpassing unreliable opinion and imagination, geometrical reason anticipates the highest form of knowledge, 'intuitive knowledge', which proceeds 'from an *adequate idea* of the formal *essence* of certain attributes of God to the *adequate knowledge* of the formal *essence* of things' [*ab* **adæquatâ ideâ** *essentiæ formalis quorundam* **Dei attributorum** *ad* **adæquatam cognitionem essentiæ rerum**] (Spinoza 1996: 57; III, P40, Schol. 2; Spinoza 1925a: 122).

The identity of God and Nature: Spinoza's conception of thinking and substance underpins the geometrical method, a method that produces mental constructions as the essential structure of things, of extended substances (e.g., the idea of a body and body itself). Hence, his basic premise is tautological: what is *self*-caused [*per causam* **sui**] necessarily exists; substance is conceived of itself [*quod in* **se** *est*]; hence as a substance with infinite attributes, God is an infinite being (Spinoza 1996: 1; Spinoza 1925a: 45). Further, this premise makes otherwise divergent dimensions identical: substance, its attributes, the mutations of finite things, discloses the infinite presence of God; conversely, existing and acting through the 'necessity of his nature', confirmed by the laws of nature (not by miracles) or by the 'same necessities' [*semper* **eâdem** *necessitate sequi*] (such as the always self-same properties of a triangle), God's omnipotence 'has been actual *from eternity* and will remain in the *same* actuality to *eternity'* [*actu* **ab æterno** *fuit, & **in æternum*** *in eâdem actualitate manebit*] (Spinoza 1996: 14; I, P17; Schol. I; Spinoza 1925a: 62). Being what is, God is both substance and thought. That God's intellect is, therefore, not the same as the human, Spinoza takes for granted: as the prior cause of human intellectual and physical existence, God's must be different (Spinoza 1996:15; I, P17, Schol. II; Spinoza 1925a: 62). For his world-view it suffices that 'the essence of man is constituted by certain modifications of God's attributes' (Spinoza 1996: 37; II, P10, Cor.; Spinoza 1925a: 93). Hence, by means of the identity principle and its grammatical structure, the human and the divine converge.

Considering God through his attributes shows that 'the order and connection *of ideas is the same as* the order and connection *of things*' [*Ordo, & connexio* **idearum idem** *est, ac ordo, & connexio* **rerum**], that 'God's power of thinking is *equal* [*æqualis*] to his actual power of action'. But the converse, substance perceived by the infinite intellect, is also true: that 'the *substance thinking* and the *extended substance* are *one and the same* [**una, eademque est substantia**], which is now comprehended under this attribute, now under that'. Hence, whether nature is conceived as the attribute of extension or of thought, it discloses 'one and the *same order*, or one and the *same* connection of *causes,* that is the *same things* follow one another' [*unum,* **eundemque ordinem***, sive unam,* **eandemque causarum** *connexionem, hoc est,* **easdem res** *invicem sequi*] (Spinoza 1996: 35; II, P.7; Spinoza 1925a: 89–90). Thus too, underscored by the syntactical repetition of the same, the transcendental difference that seperates God from His creation vanishes. Conversely, 'by the same reasoning' [***per eandem illam rationem***] but from the human standpoint, Spinoza shows that the 'idea, *or* knowledge of the mind follows in God and is related to God, *in the same way* [**eodem modo**] as the mind is united with the body', itself an attribute of extended substance, and with itself. Since 'thought is an attribute of God', there must then be in God 'an idea both of thought and of all its affections and consequently of the human mind also' (Spinoza 1996: 48; II, P20, 21; Spinoza 1925a: 108–109). The anthropic significance of this deduction is momentous. It ensures that 'our mind, in so far as it perceives things truly, is part of the infinite intellect of God; hence it is as necessary that the *mind's* clear and distinct *ideas are* true as that *God's ideas* are' (Spinoza 1996: 59; II, P43, Schol.; Spinoza 1925a: 125) Thus, with thinking as the *same* essence for God and human beings – with thinking substance and extended substance being identical – transcendental difference is levelled out.

Socio-political implications: According to the identity principle, this radical reconception of human beings in metaphysical thought implies a radical reconception of human existence. The metaphysical abolition of transcendence requires the abolition of the dominant social and political structures it institutionalises for the sake of egalitarianism and democracy. Spinoza is arguing for a society that promotes a mind confidently active rather than resentfully passive, that, rather than foster the domination of 'sad passions' [*tristitia*], recognises that 'the absolute virtue of the mind [...] is understanding', to know God, to strive to 'agree with the whole of nature' (Spinoza 1996: 129; IV, P28; 160; Spinoza 1925a: 228, 276). Here too Spinoza offsets comprehensiveness with conceptual parsimony: the self-same principle, the identity of human and divine reason, produces a political structure that correlates socio-political organisation with the psychopathology of socio-political life and human cognitive potential. In particular this method of gauging the scope for individual self-enlightenment in terms of prevailing social-psychological conditions is persistent (Benasayag and Schmit 2006: 24). Crucially, though, Spinoza's thinking excludes purely nominal types of comprehensive sameness – such as affirming necessarily the contingent variety of human situations, excusing God for the suffering of the world, superimposing on life a uniform, technological armature. Instead, predicated on tautology, it demonstrates that thinking proper to human beings, thinking with intellectual rectitude, must be unorthodox.

Mapping the conceptual field (3): Tautology as history's natural order

'The gen'ral ORDER, since the whole began, / Is kept in Nature, and is kept in Man': hence again the conclusion: 'all our Knowledge is, OURSELVES TO KNOW' (Pope 1983: 246, 279; emphasis in original). Man has for himself a cognitive function: as the universe on a microcosmic scale, he replicates for himself the world he would understand.

If the Natural order really is 'kept in Man', then the order Man creates will replicate the Natural world God created. For 'if there is a God in nature, so there is also in history: for Man too is a part of creation and in its wildest excesses and passions must follow laws that are no less beautiful and excellent than those which move all celestial and terrestrial bodies' (Herder 2013: 468; cf.495, 498; 15; cf. 15.v). The only natural order Man can create is history: '*Man, in a word, has no nature; what he has is … history*. Expressed differently: what nature is to things, history, *res gestae*, is to man' (emphasis in original). Applying to human reality a theological definition formulated by St. Augustine, 'God for whom that is nature which he has done', Ortega y Gasset insists that 'Man, *likewise*, finds that he has no nature other than what he has *himself* done' (Ortega y Gasset 1962: 217).

History, as *ratio*, establishes a measure of equivalence between God and Man. It does so since its sense proves indeterminate, susceptible to conflicting determinations. Whereas a geometrical form (e.g., the properties of a triangle) is always true, historical inferences are revisionistic truths – are themselves historical, determined by history, by historiography. And even if history in the end does make complete, *autochtonous* sense, no-one could verify it: the existence of any human individual is just a minute tile in its comprehensive mosaic. Man, of course, is not. From the Enlightenment perspective Man is *a priori* con-terminous with Western civilisation. That, as its maker, Man Himself provides history with a comprehensive sense-structure, is a natural, tautological inference. Man thus produces in history a knowledge-management technology for himself. This too promotes self-knowledge through self-encounter: Man here too becomes the 'maximally constructive' copula coordinating past, future and present.

The Encyclopédie *as copula between precursors and posterity*

The *Encyclopédie* exemplifies Man's indeterminacy as the precondition of its constructive potential. It defines itself as Modernity, as the inheritor of the intellectual legacy of the Ancients. It also historicizes itself. Having constructed a comprehensive catalogue of human knowledge, the editors obligate themselves to pass it on to posterity for its self-instruction. Their achievement projects itself into the future as progress, as amplified knowledge. Thus history produces – in diachronic order – the human species-solidarity the concept Man proclaims.

Encyclopedic comprehension shows that 'we human beings' need more than just our contemporaries. Motivated by curiosity and pride, and with 'a natural avidity to embrace at once the past, the present, and the future', we desire 'at the *same time* [*en* **même-tems**] to live with those who will follow us, and to have lived with those who have preceded us' (D'Alembert 2011: 92). For the *Encyclopédie* history offers thus a system of classification and order, a component of its knowledge-management technology. History revealing the order in which knowledge developed helps 'us *ourselves* to illuminate [*pour nous éclairer* **nous-mêmes**] the manner by which we must transmit our knowledge to our readers' (D'Alembert 2011: 110) History is a natural and, for this reason, most accessible form of exposition.

The same natural motivation justifies the editors' duty to future humanity. As 'spectators' of the progress of the Sciences and Arts, as their historians, they are concerned 'solely with transmitting them to posterity'. This posterity can then add its discoveries to those already recorded, in order that 'the history of the human mind and its productions goes from age to age until the most distant centuries' [*jusqu'aux siecles les plus reculés*]. Thus historical consciousness equates with a sense of custodianship: earlier centuries had not looked after its accumulated knowledge properly; but at least the editors and contributors now could pass on to their successors knowledge in a far better state than they themselves had received it. Thus they see themselves as agents of Man's cognitive and moral progress. For this reason the *Encyclopédie* could become 'a sanctuary where human knowledge would be sheltered from the times and revolutions' [*un sanctuaire où les connoissances des hommes soient à l'abri des tems & des révolutions*] (D'Alembert 2011: 153). But if the *Encyclopédie* pre-empts its course, history also offers insurance. Aware of the enormity of their task, of its inevitable faults or inadequacies, the editors realise that 'the ultimate perfection of an Encyclopedia is the work of centuries. It required centuries to begin; it will require as many to be complete: but we will be satisfied to have laid the foundation for a useful work' (D'Alembert 2011: 157).

History's order requires progress, its sense the symmetry of past, present and future. With its historicist dynamic the *Encyclopédie* is itself a 'maximally constructive copula'. It enables present humanity to identify with its precursors and its descendents and them to be identified with each other. However much human cognitive concerns progress in history, they remain essentially the same.

Man, the template of historical sense

The conceptual indeterminacy of Man permits the (historical) development of the human species. To orientate itself, it naturally appropriates the ordinary human lifespan for the basis of its comprehensive sense-structure. The meaning of history relies on this sameness – so Pascal (in 1651) asserts 'that the succession of human beings over the course of all the centuries, must be considered as *one and the same* man [*un même homme*] that exists always and learns continuously'. The maturity of this same 'universal man' is to be found, therefore, not with the Ancients, however much their philosophers deserve respect: they in reality represent the childhood of the human species. Since Man (this 'universal man') has over the course of time augmented their knowledge with his scientific experience, he now supersedes the Antiquity otherwise revered in others (Pascal 1963b: 232) – so too for Hume Classical Antiquity disclosed human society 'in its infancy' and history itself 'all the human race, from the beginning of time, [passing], *as it were*, in review before us' (Hume 1971: 560). And so too Herder saw in the Greeks, Romans and 'Hebrews' the 'simple childishness' [*der einfache Kindersinn*] of the human species, so distant now is the stream of history from its source, so much richer now its traditions (Herder 2013: 490; 15.iv).

History thus replicates the natural, biological phases of individual human life in ideal, universal form. This replication also contributes to its knowledge-management technology. As *ratio* this tautological structure *balances out* fundamental faults in Enlightenment thinking, inherent discrepancies between its aspirations and its reality. In so doing it places itself under tremendous stress. The tautological coordination between Man and history can only be figurative. That sustains its conviction: literally it is sheer illusion. That it withstands this stress testifies to its resilience. Sameness provides history with an indispensable purpose: its transcendental design, predicated on Man, offers cognitive compensation for the conflict of differences in the human sphere. More importantly, according to the identity principle (thinking = being), cognitive compensation automatically entails ontological compensation: in this case, the guarantee of a final, ideal order realised historically through Man. Sameness proves indispensable because, suspecting that the Enlightenment would never quite realise itself, its advocates can never relinquish the cognitive and ontological reassurance it apparently dispenses. Historical explanation reveals the persistence of this apprehensive syndrome: the sheer heterogeneity of human behaviour filtered through the self-same preconceived categories (Man, Democracy, Nationalism, etc.) that apparently motivate it or it allegedy exemplifies.

Historical ratio *as cognitive compensation*

With its *balancing out* of cognitive and ontological discrepancies, its calculation [*ratio*] of diachronic *equivalences*, history as compensation takes several forms. For Kant the difference between the ideal and reality of Enlightenment, that he lived in an 'age of Enlightenment' but not in an 'enlightened age', is resolved once the conflicted sociability of the human species equates with a history-making dynamic (Kant 1982b: 59). This equivalence affirms a moral agenda for world history for generations to come, eventually constituting human self-recognition in the form of world-citizenship. Kant bases this historicist scheme on a 'hidden plan of Nature'. The search for *cognitive* compensation (that history must be more than an 'aimless aggregate' [*planloses Aggregat*] of events) necessitates the affirmation of *ontological* reassurance. *Thinking* of history as a system, as the realisation of Providence, might eventually enable the innate potential of the human species to bring a more peaceful, liberated, morally progressive world into *being* (Kant 1982a: 48–49). For Hume (as for Pascal), history uniquely testifies to the advancement of human self-knowledge. After all, 'a man acquainted with history may [...] be said to have lived from the beginning of the world, and to have been making continual additions to his stock of knowledge in every century'. This time, though, history constitutes a *balanced* social knowledge-practice *sui generis*. With the 'man of business' having 'his judgement warped on every occasion by the violence of his passion' and the philosopher with his 'abstract view of the objects' in 'his closets' 'leaving his mind so cold and unmoved', history 'keeps in *a just medium* between these extremes, and places the objects in their *true* point of view' (Hume 1971: 561, 562).

For Lessing history (as *ratio*) reconciles the otherwise irreconcilable: reason and faith. His premiss is that just as education brings out more effectively what Man could have produced by himself for himself, so revelation – through God's intervention in history – brings out more effectively through faith what, expressed as historical endeavour, Man would anyway have discovered for himself through reason (Lessing 1967: 8; §4). For both the human species [*Menschengattung*] and the individual, history consists of three phases of education: the Old Testament as an elementary primer for 'a childish people'; Christ appearing as a more reliable teacher for a more rationally advanced world; and Christianity finally ushering in the age of the 'eternal gospel' of human moral perfection (Lessing 1967: 20, 21, 28; §50, §55 §§85–86). This history relies on a stabilising principle of sameness: the '*same* economy of the *same* God' and always 'the *same* plan for the general education of the human race' [*die **nämliche** Ökonomie des **nämlichen** Gottes. Immer [...] der **nämliche** Plan der allgemeinen Erziehung des Menschengeschlechts*] (Lessing 1967: 29, §88).

History as human self-encounter

For Herder history tautologically affirms the comprehensive assimilation of Man and history: it reinforces the tautology that already made history a technology for Man's self-knowledge. It requires Man not just to *know*, but to *be*, himself. The 'principle law of Nature' imperatively enjoins: 'Man *be* Man!' [*Der Mensch sei Mensch!*] (Herder 2013: 470; 15.i). Already substantiating the concept of Man, the purpose of history is to augment it, to amplify it. Its momentum comes from a discrepancy it exposes between what Man is and what Man could yet become, a discrepancy it can reconcile through human self-realisation, through inspiring Man to cultivate his own essential humanity [*Humanität*]. In this conception, Man does not so much provide a structural template for history (as with Pascal or Hume); rather history evinces a transcendental plan to be realised dynamically only through human self-amplification. God made Man a 'God on Earth', the very 'principle of His effectiveness', set in motion by the necessitousness of the human situation (Herder 2013: 471; 15.i). *Humanität* is, therefore, an identitary construction: what past civilisations have achieved inspires the present to make 'the *same* and better efforts' [*zu ähnlichen und bessern Bestrebungen*]: the 'history of nations thus becomes a competitive guide [*Schule des Wettlaufs*] for achieving the most beautful garland of humanity and human dignity' (Herder 2013: 472; 15.i). This human self-augmentation realises itself through 'proportionate regulation' [*Ebenmaß*] (literally: 'even measure'), a law of Nature that coordinates sameness and difference, simplicity of means and intricacy of effects, economical effort and productive purpose. This 'even measure' is accordingly also an aptitude of Man's soul that through all forms of human existence in all varieties of predicaments governs the current state and future scope of his self-realisation, elusive though the 'fullest enjoyment of existence' it vouchsafes might be. Faced with a disordered, conflicted world, reason in particular offers a principle for producing from it an ordered, '*comprehensive structure* evincing *proportionate regularity* and lasting *beauty*' [*ein* **Ganzes** *mit* **Ebenmaß** *und daurender* **Schönheit**] (Herder 2013: 481, 482–483; 15.iii).

History, therefore, proves tautological in two respects. First, the indispensable premiss is that Man is conterminous and co-existent with the course of history: history is Man's creation. But both Man and history are part of Nature, the expression of a metaphysical order created by God. So, second, recognising the potential of this order both in history and in his reason, Man self-consciously re-invests it in history to realise through his actions the *Humanität* it metaphysically already implies. Hence, Herder's humanist historicism proclaims the very the apotheosis of sameness – since 'wherever in the broad field of history understanding roams, it looks only for *itself* and keeps finding *itself* again' [*suchet er nur* **sich** *und findet* **sich selbst** *wieder*]. Surveying his philosophical heritage, Man, therefore, finds a 'sweet pleasure' in unexpectedly discovering 'traces of a thinking and feeling genius *like himself* [*Spuren eines* **ihm ähnlichen**, *denkenden, empfindenden Genius*]. This productive encounter reveals him as 'my brother, a participant in *the same* world-soul [*Teilnehmer an* **derselben** *Weltseele*], in the *one* human reason, in the *one* human truth' (Herder 2013: 485; 15.iii; emphasis in original). So, whatever the vicissitudes of human life, the essence, purpose, and fate of the human species rest on its understanding and integrity. History thus teaches 'us in our inconsequential form [*in unserer nichtigen Gestalt*] to act according to the eternal natural laws of God'. That ensures that 'everywhere the result of human endeavours is the *same*' [*allenthalben ist das Resultat der Menschenbemühungen* **dasselbe**] (Herder 2013: 500; 15.v).

History: The Enlightenment's self-vindication

Operating with these various types of tautology history is indispensable for Enlightenment thinking. It functions as a knowledge management technology. As *ratio* it reconciles discrepancies between the aspirations of Enlightenment thought and the reality of its circumstances. For purely human affairs and vindicated by Nature's providential reassurance it validates – of necessity – the identity principle, otherwise nothing directly, logically, links human behaviour with the transcendental meaning its disciplinary technology extrapolates from it. Hence, according to the identity principle itself, the tautological forms that support Enlightenment *thinking* need history for the tautological vindication of the Enlightenment's actual *existence*. And so this vindication itself works only if it can guarantee Man's essential, historical sameness. Fortunately, a basic logical premiss does the trick: the identitary proposition, 'a truth beyond all question', formulated by Vico, that 'the world of civil society has certainly been *made by men*, and [...] its principles are therefore to be found within the modifications of *our own human mind*' [*questo mondo civile egli certamente è stato **fatto dagli uomini**, onde se ne possono, perché se ne debbono, ritruovare i principi dentro le modificazioni **della nostra medesima mente umana***] (Vico 1984: 96; §331; 1959: 382; I, iii).[7] Any one human mind can adequately comprehend what other human minds have produced because humanity is essentially the same, certainly nothing 'alien'.

End of tautology

Tautology inevitably fails in practice, whatever its theoretical strength. For thinking the reiteration of the self-same human values might carry conviction: for personal existence it leaves self-reflection both predetermined and overextended. In failing its dynamic changes: personal existence reconfigures self-reflective reason (Rousseau); self-critical reason redefines personal existence (Kant).

Rousseau: The self's broken mould

Autobiography surely exemplifies Mankind as Man's proper study, but Rousseau demonstrates, for example, in his *Confessions* (1782/1789) and *Les rêveries du promeneur solitaire* (1782), that it reconfigures the very concept of tautology. Alluding to Augustine's *Confessions*, Rousseau's autobiography reflects self-re-orientation: its personal candour redefines self-sameness itself. For Rousseau this cannot be recognised by a concept as comprehensive as Man, as the '*homme universel*'. Under the pressure of personal diversity and particularity, the concept itself fragments. In theory comprehensive sameness still frames the personal sense of self; in practice it is experienced negatively as loss, a blend of defiance, alienation and exclusion. Writing his *Confessions*, Rousseau describes as an unprecedented and inimitable undertaking: his intention is 'to show *to those like him* a man in all the veracity of nature' [*montrer **à mes semblables** un homme dans toute la vérité de la nature*], and this (he says) is himself [*cet homme sera **moi***]. But these *semblables*, vindicating ethical propriety and cognitive validity, no longer resemble him: he is made neither like any he has seen nor any that exist. He may not be better than they, but at least he is 'different' [*au moins je suis autre*]. After reading this account of his personal development with its controversies, conflicts, embarrassments, paranoia and persecutions, the reader may judge whether or not nature was justified in breaking the mould that formed him [*si la nature a bien ou mal fait de briser le moule dans lequel elle m'a jeté*] (Rousseau 1968: I, 28).

This sense of exclusion as the negation of sameness is explored further in the *Rêveries*. This starts with the premise that, except for his own self, he lacks all social relationships. Sameness in its negative form henceforth categorises him as a social outcast, as 'a monster, a poisoner, a murderer, the horror of the human race' (Rousseau 1967: 29–30). It enforces renunciation: the conjecture of a providential perspective (generally appreciated by the *philosophes*) signifies real moral destitution: for him as 'a poor unfortunate mortal but impassive as god himself', 'every thing on earth is finished'. Implicitly dismissing Terence's maxim, he asserts that 'everything beyond himself is henceforth for him *foreign*' [*tout ce qui m'est extérieur m'est **étranger** desormais*]. He might as well be on a 'alien planet': 'in this world he has no-one close to him, *no-one like him*, nor any brothers' [*Je n'ai plus en ce monde ni prochain, **ni semblables**, ni frères*] (Rousseau 1967: 34, cf. 36). Abandoning comprehensive knowledge, he studies himself in a state of apprehension and of self-estrangement.[8] In his isolation he interrogates what he himself is [*que suis-je moi-même?*]. Studying oneself no longer motivates the acquisition of universal knowledge from a transcendent, panoramic standpoint, but rather produces an account of oneself to oneself.

Thinking about self-sameness and self-knowledge is thus reconceived: What is the self by itself really worth? Selfhood – a key principle of tautology – proves to be unstable: Rousseau's aim is 'to account for the successive modifications of his soul'. The scientific propriety of this self-study comes not from the constant, abstract certainties of arithmetic or geometry, but from physicists' routine procedures for measuring the atmosphere. Metaphorically, with carefully conducted readings over a long period of time producing results just as reliable as theirs, Rousseau intends 'to apply the barometer to his soul' [*j'appliquerai le baromètre à mon âme*] (Rousseau 1967: 29, 35, 36). The mirror of other minds may be shattered: a machine recording atmospheric pressure offers not a tautological equivalent, but a means of measuring one's fluctuating self-distanciation (Lévi-Strauss 1996: 48–49).

Kant: Tautology or autonomy?

Tautology never dispels misgivings about the adequacy of human comprehension. Evidently it fails to align in practice what it aligns automatically in theory: the universal scope of comprehension and immediately situated cognition. Sameness ensures logical necessity blocks dissenting inferences arising from ordinary experience. Experience feels inferior to the sublime but indifferent logical-metaphysical order that sustains it, particularly since this order derives from a perspective 'impossible to locate'. But what Rousseau experiences as self-estrangement offers Kant the occasion for re-evaluating Enlightenment values. In the world arranged by rational human beings for all their various (social, cultural, political, economic) purposes [*Reich der Zwecke*] every aptitude has its 'market-price', every personality trait an 'affective price', with an *equivalent* exchange-value – everything except for the individual with its 'purpose in his or her own self' [*Zweck an sich*] expressed through moral actions (e.g., keeping a promise) as 'dignity' [*Würde*], an 'inner value' beyond any price, that 'permits no equivalent' [*kein Äquivalent verstattet*], is not *similar* to anything else (Kant 1965: 56–59). However commendable, pity [*Mitleid*], as "suffering with" [*mitleiden*] one's *semblables*, is not by itself effective. As a universal principle of ethical action – i.e., 'as a general disposition towards the well-being of the human species' – it is sublime but, based on a higher standpoint, colder. Trying to reconcile the general principle with relieving the suffering of every single *semblable* one sympathises with would produce emotional fatigue. The kindhearted individual's sense of duty would in truth reduce him or her to a 'sentimental idler' [*ein weichmütiger Müßiggänger*] (Kant 1977b: 835).

The disqualification of moral equivalence and universal identification exposes tautology as inadequate. The proper study of Mankind now means ascertaining the limits of its comprehension. Whatever transcends it – rationalist metaphysics, natural theology, divine providence – must be dismantled; hence, too, the self as constructive copula re-functioned. Metaphysics must, therefore, become a discipline with its own epistemological principles, with its own transcendental logic (Kant 1971: 99; B.80–81). Only then will it become a knowledge-system as valid as mathematics or natural science (Kant 1969: 88ff.; §§40ff.). Though this scientific reduction exposes comprehension's limits, it still affirms Enlightenment intentions: to 'think well' (as Pascal contended), to 'improve understanding' (as Spinoza advocated), to assert cognitive integrity by observing the rules the search for truth requires (cf. Descartes 1996: 2–4, 49–51). Metaphysics thus becomes the transcendental science of the mind itself, elaborating and clarifying its inherent principles (Kant 1971: 54–55; B.24–25).

Dismantling tautology means relinqushing essential selfhood – particularly as the central link in a comprehensive, transcendental scheme. The self is rather 'the most destitute idea' [*die ärmste Vorstellung*] (Kant 1971: B408ff.). Hence, the need to define the mind's limits: its dependence on time and space revealed by an analysis of synthetic *a priori* principles that evaluates the foundations of knowledge (Kant 1971: 56, B.26; 64ff., B.35ff.) – its indecision on crucial problems such as the finite or infinite nature of the world, the constitution of substance, the relationship between causality and freedom, whether or not the world requires a supreme being as the final cause of its existence (the antinomies of pure reason) (Kant 1971: 448ff.); its incapacity for proving the independent existence of God and its reconception of a supreme being as reason's self-generated principle of conceptual coherence (Kant 1971: 557ff., B607ff.). Further, ordinary experience confirms that 'we can think of no object except through categories' (Kant

1971: 186; B.165–166). The world is a synthesis of impressions produced by the imagination from the understanding's in-built cognitive structure supported by analogical synthetic principles: the persistence of substance, causality, and the dynamic, reciprocal co-existence of things perceived (Kant 1971: 115, B102ff.; 164ff., B.150ff.; 183, B.163; 213ff., B.158ff.)

So the world is a phenomenon projected by the natural laws of thought with which the mind operates. Things in themselves [*an sich*] cannot be known. As a comprehensive explanation of consciousness, Kant's transcendental logic precludes a perspective on the world "external" to consciousness. Tautology collapses, the injunction to know oneself invalidated: consciousness of oneself outside one's own self-consciousness is nonexistent. Particularly if (due to the natural 'fallacy of misplaced concreteness') it is seen as something substantive, the self is unknowable (Kant 1971: 275, B.278; cf. Whitehead 1967: 51–55). So, if left to itself, 'correlating with nothing except itself, with the general condition of its consciousness, it can provide nothing other than tautological answers to any questions' [*keine andere als* **tautologische** *Beantwortungen auf alle Fragen geben*]: it would superimpose its own self-conception on the qualities of objects presented to itself, thus presupposing what it intended to discover (Kant 1971: 395, A.366). The self itself does not thus comprehensively identify itself with the multifarious content [*Mannigfaltigkeit*] it experiences (as, e.g., with Vico or D'Alembert). Rather the fundamental identity that constitutes the thinking self derives from its *a priori* synthetic (transcendental) unity. The 'self becomes aware of its identical self' [**Ich** *bin mir also des* **identischen Selbst** *bewußt*] only through the varied content of consciousness that in its inherent unity it recognises as its own (Kant 1971: 144–145; B.134–135). The 'self is only the consciousness of one's thinking' [*das Ich ist nur das Bewußtsein meines Denkens*] (Kant 1971: 394, B.413).

But tautology does survive re-evaluation. 'Knowing oneself' now means not the theoretical sameness of human diversity, but analysing *how* the self knows, *how* it knows anything. 'The *autonomy* of pure reason' is tautological self-sameness refunctioned. Establishing the laws constituting reality for the mental world, it thereby sustains the autonomy of pure practical reason informing the moral law that promotes the highest good in the social world (Kant 1967: 51–52). If 'reason is the permanent condition of free human actions', autonomy invests each self – now that it knows how it knows anything – with the capacity to regulate itself (Kant 1971: 538, B.581). The proper study of Mankind is no longer the self-same *homme universel* but, 'in a pragmatic respect' [*in pragmatischer Hinsicht*], what each self makes of itself, what reality it creates for itself, how it orientates itself in the world it projects (cf. Kant 1980: 511, 673). The purely human sphere of knowledge the critique of pure reason reveals is no longer theoretical, passively surveyed from an (impossible) panoramic vantage-point from without, but demands a social and moral attitude based on reason to sustain it from within. *Autonomy* still retains reason's administrative function, not for aligning knowledge with inscrutable providence, but for one's intellectual and ethical self-consistency, for 'always thinking in unison with oneself' [*Jederzeit* **mit sich selbst einstimmig** *zu denken*] (Kant 1968: 145; 1980: 549).

Deprived by the critique of pure reason of ancillary constructions drawn from rationalist metaphysics, the autonomous self confronts alone its unique cognitive and ethical situation that requires it to assess what it can know, what it should do, and what it may hope for (cf. Kant 1971: 728, B.833). Since self-orientation in the social and political world depends on the rectitude of intellectual self-orientation, *autonomy* works in several ways. It involves having the courage to think for oneself: not automatically to submit to others' socially authoritative regulations; not to bind oneself to doctrinal orthodoxy – not (in other words) to capitulate to the intellectual and social conventions of one's *semblables* just because they are *semblables* (Kant 1982b: 53, 55, 57–58). It means prioritizing the 'needs of reason' [*Bedürfnis der Vernunft*], or resorting to 'rational faith' [*Vernunftglaube*], itself 'a compass to guide the speculative thinker on his wanderings especially in the field of suprasensible [theological] objects' (Kant 1977a: 270–273, 276–277). It requires abandoning the 'impartial observer', and instead developing a sense of duty based on the categorically imperative moral law that is universal not through the comprehensive sameness of a common identity, but through each individual being a representative of the human species committed to its 'species-essential' moral interests (Kant 1967: 94ff.,102). In political terms it involves criticism as both an intellectual and social practice: public reflection by autonomous individuals on the organisation and conduct of social life; the elaboration – demonstrated by aesthetic taste – of consensual forms of judgement (Kant 1971: 677ff. A.738ff.B.766ff.; 1968: 144–147; §40). In the end, autonomy is based on the premise that human existence is not predetermined or pre-empted by metaphysical schemes that transcend it, but is an end in itself [*Zweck an **sich selbst***] (Kant 1967: 102, 151). Rationality as the principle of human though and action, critical questioning as the basic, legitimate form of social behaviour thus foster a culture of autonomy, 'the pre-eminent instrument for establishing order and clarity in unreasoning nature beyond it' (Kant 1968: 300).

Re-functioning tautology also changes the Enlightenment's pragmatic intention. It no longer passes on the naturally ordered, accumulated stock of human erudition to a future humanity already like the past or present. Rather it encourages a form of behaviour, the practice of public criticism, that constantly tests the validity not just of knowledge, but of the social and political behaviour it fosters, thereby in theoretical and practical terms furnishing human self-realisation with its essentially Enlightenment orientation. Far from sameness or equivalence, ensuring that everyone and everything has a pre-ordained place in the perfect meta-structure of the cosmos, *autonomy* establishes human beings as responsible for themselves, in terms not of the history ready-made by them for themselves, but of what they might eventually make of themselves through transgressing prevailing historical limitations (Kant 1980: 625, 634, 635). In this 'age of criticism', nothing is pre-ordained. In a social situation of conflicting self-concerns [*ungesellige Geselligkeit*], self-concern expresses itself in incessant criticism and renegotation (Kant 1971: 7; 688; 1982a: 37). Enlightenment tautology, apparently vindicated, is now redundant.

Various concluding propositions

Tautology: The affirmation of human intelligibility

What a text means derives not just from what it says or implies, but crucially from the conceptual field its thought-style defines – in the diverse samples of Enlightenment thinking explored here, from a grammar of tautology revealed in the consistent repetition of categorical coordinators: e.g., *same* (*like*), *self*; *même, semblable*; *medesimo*; *selber, nämlich, ähnlich, eben, sich*; *idem, ipse*; *autos*. Certainly, that tautology lends itself to diverse, antithetical cognitive standpoints seems unconvincing. But it has to: only by bringing them together through equivalence and reciprocity can it both affirm "Man" as a universal cognitive copula and look unfalsifiable.

But the validity of a conceptual field, here specifically tautology and its cognates, is affirmed less by its (internal) logical rigour than by its three-fold communicative usefulness: the thinking it facilitated for Enlightenment philosophers; the political import of this thinking; the socio-political function of identity and equivalence as basic tropes of cognition, as anthropic characteristics. Crucially, as basic cognitive tropes, identity and equivalence are integral to current thinking (not least while reading Enlightenment texts): they thus abolish the 'historical distance' that apparently separates the world now from the the Enlightenment 'event' (Schmidt 1996: ix). Crucially, too, that identity and equivalence are integral to cognition, does not entail automatic recognition of any particular expression of sameness. Identity may well permit D'Holbach in his *Système social* (1773) to claim that humanity (Man's virtuous conduct) 'is a knot made for binding invisibly the citizen of Paris to that of Pekin' (D'Holbach 2004: 67). The trope currently may well validate his communicative purpose more for its rhetorical effect than its cognitive value. Conversely, identity inhibits a gendered re-functioning of 'Man' and 'Mankind' for communicative purposes, because the underlying conceptual field lacks any sense of current, gendered (or gender-neutral) thought-styles. Those the Enlightenment thought-style marginalized still resorted to its universality – a universality that *a priori* discounted their articularity – to argue for their acceptance. Thus tautology discloses how, superseded by historical developments, the Enlightenment has become historicized, incommensurable in this instance with the identity principle as it currently operates.

The identity principle fails not because it is not falsifiable, but because how logical necessity produces arbitrary heterogeneous arrangements is unclear: 'How is the formal postulate which serves as the *principium sciendi* dependent on, affirmative of the *principium essendi* as it is made manifest in the verb "is"?' (Steiner 1989: 353). For Enlightenment thinkers this dependency is (theoretically) self-evident: with the mind created as part of Nature by Nature, thought and being already harmonise. However, 'the incarnate tautologies between word and object leak' (Steiner 1989: 352). The way things are socially, politically, theologically prove in practice recalcitrant to the way they in theory should be. Perhaps the greatest blow to humanity's self-esteem by its own scientific and philosophical development (and not mentioned by Freud) is the realisation that thinking and being lack any *a priori* interconnection – that 'the world [...] is not complicit in our knowledge,' that 'there is no pre-discursive providence that disposes it in our favour' (Foucault 1971: 55; cf. Freud 1987: 226; §18).

However, to insist on the tautological character of human (self-) knowledge, also proves illusory. If the world does seem complicit in our knowledge, the mind itself ensures it does – in its own, pragmatic self-interest. As James argues, the actual order of the world is its inconceivable 'collateral contemporaneity': 'the world's contents are *given* to each of us in an order so foreign to our subjective interests that we can hardly by an effort of imagination picture to ourselves what it is *like*' (my emphasis). No other option exists but to break this 'real world as it is given objectively' into histories, arts, sciences, since only then do we 'begin to feel at home'. The 'likeness' – the fundamental identity principle, its tautological premise, its comprehensive scope – has first to be constructed: 'We have to break that order altogether – and by picking out from it the items which concern us, and connecting them with others far away, which we say "belong" with them, we are able to make out definite threads of sequence and tendency' (James 1956: 118–119). The Great Chain of Being interconnecting the whole of Nature, yet visible to human beings 'only in some of its continuous sequences', but still ensuring Man's copula function, is one such cognitively pragmatic structure (cf. D'Alembert 2011: 221).

However questionable, however illusory, tautology responds to a deep apprehension of a theoretically anthropocentric world – that 'life can little more supply / Than just to look about us and to die'. 'Expatiating free o'er all this scene of Man', surveying 'A mighty maze! but not without a plan', compensates for existential desolation here barely acknowledged (Pope 1983: 241). As the Enlightenment demonstrates, whatever the communicative ambivalences implicit in the concept 'Man', with its comprehensive cognitive scope and its optimistic outlook, the identity principle alone remains to sustain the paradoxical, otherwise senseless, situation of human existence. Reason enough for the Enlightenment to affirm and re-function what is essential to thought itself: this logically fundamental, existentially indispensable premise of intelligibility.

Identity: History: Enlightenment

That the *Encyclopédie* represents a bequest to posterity for its self-improvement or a 'refuge for human knowledge, securing it against the times and revolutions', affirms historical sameness, presupposes the identity of past, present and future (D'Alembert 2011:153). Guiding intellectual and moral progress, predicated on the template 'Man', this sameness – meant to perpetuate the Enlightenment's comprehensive knowledge – reveals its flawed self-understanding, in two respects: the indeterminacy of the future and the indeterminacy of knowledge.

Citing Diderot, Becker confirms that posterity for the *philosophes equated* with – was the *equivalent* of – Heaven for Christians, 'a promised land, a kind of utopia' (Becker 1960: 119, 122ff.). But projecting sameness as a normative idea into the future is misconceived. As Valéry remarks, no-one can foresee their future state of knowledge: if they could, it would be knowledge known now, not in its future state

(Valéry 1960a: 1068). Moreover, from the perspective of the future, the sameness it requires is now nonexistent: 'that each generation will substantially live amid the conditions governing the lives of its fathers and will transmit those conditions to mould with equal force the lives of its children', is a 'vicious assumption'. The reason is, 'we are living in the first period of human history for which this assumption is false' (Whitehead 1967b: 92–93). Moreover, the Enlightenment's self-projection into the future is self-delusion. Certainly 'the future is there in the present, as a general fact belonging to the nature of things'. However (and unlike the past), 'there are no actual occasions in the future, already constituted', which means 'there are no actual occasions in the future to exercise efficient causation in the present': the future 'has no actuality other than the actuality of present fact' (Whitehead 1967b:194–95). So the comprehensive human self-knowledge the *Encyclopédie* secures against revolutions is not safe from revolutions in knowledge itself. (With its template 'Man' redundant, the *Encyclopédie* becomes a work of academic, antiquarian reference, in its immediate utility long since superseded by the latest version *mathesis universalis*, the Internet search engine.) Its bold intention 'one day to contain all the knowledge of mankind' just concentrates its own self-interest (D'Alembert 2011:145).

Further, the Enlightenment's flawed historical self-understanding has implications for Enlightenment historiography. This substitutes the present (in which the history of the Enlightenment is being written), conceived as the Enlightenment's future, for the pragmatic 'actual occasions' the Enlightenment's future in the eighteenth century lacked. It does so because then the 'actual occasions' that constitute the past can be linked to the present (construed as the Enlightenment's future) by chains of causality reliant on indispensable 'psychic additions' that make this historical identification possible: in this case, 'categorical coordinators', prerequisite for any historical reconstruction to make sense, for producing intelligible causality (Whitehead 1967b: 195; Whitehead 1920: 29–30).[9] Hence, irrespective of whether the historian advocates or rejects its values, the Enlightenment is construed in relation to the present as a "legacy", "bequest", "forerunner" or (most frequently) "process" or "project", the present seeing itself as its "heir".

History compensated the Enlightenment for the discrepancy between the rational order of the world in theory (i.e., in thought) and its conflicted structure in practice (i.e., as it exists). It demonstrated change and conflict (in practice) as ultimately vindicating the Enlightenment's agenda (in theory). But history itself is a tautological structure that above all knows itself. It too is predicated on sameness: whatever happens, it is all the same, all history.[10] It accounts for things being the way they were so that they are now how they have got to be. It elicits meaning from its heterogeneous materials by means of categorical coordinators it *a priori* invests in it. The Enlightenment is a (historical) process only because the connection between past and present is to start with styled as "process". The Enlightenment is hardly "historically distant" if history still operates with its thought-style within the same conceptual field – if it relies on the same tautological premise and the same identitary logic 'to get more of a grip on what the ideas of the Enlightenment *actually were*' so striving for 'a genuine *balance*' between 'ideas [i.e., *thought*] and their socio-political context [i.e., *existence / practice*]', to 'understand just what it was' (Israel 2006: v; Pagden 2013: xiv). Hence, while claiming (in theory) to promote on the basis of Enlightenment values the cultural amelioration of the human species, Enlightenment historiography – never moving from where it starts – produces (in practice) its own tautological redundancy. The Enlightenment (Pagden concludes) may well have been 'about creating a field of values, political, social, and moral, based upon a detached and scrupulous understanding – as far as the mind is capable – of *what it means to be human*', but historical comprehension still leaves no-one any clearer about what 'being human' means. Hence, the disciplinary correction and academic admonition: '*we* are *all, inescapably*, the heirs [cf. "legacy"] of the architects of the Enlightenment "science of man"' (Pagden 2013: 343, 351). But precisely this constricting intention of one age with its doctrinal conventions – including now the incommensurable thought-conventions of the eighteenth-century Enlightenment – to prevent subsequent ages from broadening their knowledge and so becoming more enlightened, Kant had already described as 'a crime against human nature' (Kant 1982b: 57–58). Pre-emptively occluding the horizon of consciousness, historical precedent subverts the indispensable indeterminacy of the future, the precondition for hope, the hope for something different.

'Man' the measure?

With its tautological premise the identity principle (A = A) invites mathematical conceptualisations: equivalences, ratios, proportions. It requires also a measure, a common scale of measurement, to assess their relative values. For this purpose God or a Supreme Being is useless: infinity and eternity defy measure: 'he fills, he bounds, connects and *equals all*' (Pope 1983: 249). So necessarily the calculation of equivalences, ratios, proportions falls to Man (hence the recourse to geometrical methods): 'the gen'ral ORDER [...] is kept in Nature and is kept in Man' (Pope 1983: 246). Hence the conviction supporting Mankind's 'proper study' – already attributed to Protagoras in Plato's *Theaetetus* – that 'Man is the measure of all things' (Plato 2002: 41; 152A).

Measuring seems to be an anthropic trait: essential for a sense of time and space – vindicating Man as a template that orders knowledge, placing it and dating it; but also endemic in socio-economic intercourse, in its 'unsocial sociability', where individuals measure themselves against each other (cf. Nietzsche 1988b: 306; II, §8). Hence, for Nietzsche, working out measures and equivalences, their exchange and underlying reciprocal values, was the basic preoccupation of thought, 'to a certain extent the very meaning of thinking'. Suggesting that '*Mensch*' derives from 'measure', he defines the human being as 'essentially an animal that estimates' [*das abschätzende Tier an sich*] (Nietzsche 1988b: 306; II, §8). For Hegel, to achieve certain knowledge, consciousness has to produce from within itself a scale of measurement [*Maßstab*] that in its experience aligns concepts and their corresponding objects (Hegel 1979: 75ff.).

Yet doubt remains: Does the human sphere where nothing is alien permit anything to be measured? 'Is there any measure on Earth? [*Gibt es auf Erden ein Maß*]' asked the mentally ill Hölderlin in the draft of a poem in 1823, already recognising there was none (Hölderlin 2014: 674).[11] And Kant deplored the lack of progress towards metaphysics becoming a science, attracting those unable to distinguish themselves in other disciplines because it lacked any 'sure measure and weight to tell the difference between thoroughness and superficial chatter' [*kein sicheres Maß und Gewicht vorhanden* [...], *um Gründlichkeit von seichtem Geschwätze zu unterscheiden*] (Kant 1969: 3).

If the world lacks a comprehensive measure, human beings must produce a world their own scale measures. The universe could be seen as an artefact of God, as a sublime 'natural machine' [*machina naturalis*] or 'world-machine' [*machina rerum*] (Leibniz 1960/1961d: 504-5). The human equivalent would be a complex structure – a 'mega-machine' [*ein großer **Automat***] driven by its self-generating dynamic; an 'apparatus' [*Ge-stell*] discovering and organising resources for human existence (Marx 2005: 401ff.; Heidegger 1967a: 22–23). The product of the human mind, this human world would be automatically comprehensible, automatically manageable, as Vico's *New Science* claims. That would make technology the new science: the *New Science* confirms history as a comprehensive way of managing the world, as a form of technology, a technology of technologies.[12]

Here Man truly comes to know Himself: his technological world is self-made. The creation of a self-regulating, global biosphere proves integral to the Enlightenment's tautological thought-style. Here reason is already assimilated to how things 'are as we find them' – *das Vorfindliche* (to use Horkheimer's and Adorno's term); this assimilation confirms the world as its own measure, knowledge as constant reiteration and thinking as tautology (Horkheimer and Adorno 2003a: 49). Reason, driving the technology of bureaucratic administration, validates itself in its self-sameness in the methodologies, analyses, regulations, protocols, procedures, reports and histories it generates.

Thus the Enlightenment thought-style permits the tautological relationship between thinking and being to turn positivistic. As Husserl remarks: 'sciences based merely on fact' [*bloße Tatsachenwissenschaften*] produce 'people concerned merely with facts' [*bloße Tatsachenmenschen*] (Husserl 2012: 5–6). The *philosophe* diversifies into specific social types, with specific social-cognitive, administrative functions: the intellectually honest, self-accountable academic; the expert, 'methodically gifted technician'; the 'objective person' not motivated by autonomy but content to mirror whatever they encounter; the 'resources manager' – occupations all instrumentalizing reason as a 'type of office-machine dispensing analytical inferences' [*eine Art Büromaschine, die analytische Urteile zurichtet*] (cf. Weber 1988: 608, 613; Husserl 2012: 61; Nietzsche 1988a: 135 §207; Heidegger 1967a: 26; Horkheimer 2003c: 327).

The *Encyclopédie* intended to produce all kinds of new advantages in society such as increasing the number of scientists and artists in the population (D'Alembert 2011: 158). And the Enlightenment has increased the population of administrators, managers, experts, and technocrats. Once a strategy of provocation, this intention now serves an affirmative knowledge-management technology. Reason drives expert thinking in conformity with existing managerial-supervisory behaviour in national and global political and economic institutions which naturally sustains the world as it is, as it has got to be. The Enlightenment does make up the fabric of contemporary life. With its tautological thought-style it becomes ever more comprehensive, ever more like itself, ever more affirmative.

Identity and comprehensive order

'Bourgeois thinking is dominated by the idea of the equivalent' – precisely what enables incommensurable values to be considered *alike* (Horkheimer and Adorno 2003a: 30). Thus identity – the self-equivalent – numbs the apprehension that no absolute human measure exists. Human comprehension is the cognitive practice that affirms its incessant identity construction: 'to comprehend would be to assimilate – in the literal sense of the verb: to make similar to itself [*rendre semblable à soi*] – what at first presents itself as different, to transform difference into identity'. From the humanist perspective, therefore, 'similitude is essential [...] confirmed by comprehension itself conceived as a process of identification' (Pouillon: 90–91).

The tautological dynamic of reason thus generates sameness: it enforces 'the law of what is always the same' [*Gesetz der Immergleichheit*] (Adorno 1982: 51). But this proposition also works in reverse. Suppose sameness was the political, ethical, cognitive intention because it alone vindicated human existence without recourse to supportive ancillary constructions, whether from a metaphysical or a theological world-design. The authority of reason would, therefore, affirm the power, authority and momentum a state, an institution, a society, an agent gives to itself: its autonomy, its auto-finality, its self-affirmation (cf. Derrida 2003: 30–31). In political terms it would project structures of integration: 'the values of selfhood and togetherness, resemblance, simultaneity, congregation, also simulacrum, simulation and assimilation' (cf. Derrida 2003: 32). 'The idea of force (*kratos*), power, and control' would basically constitute the 'concept of self- hood' [*le concept d'ipséité*] (Derrida 2003: 38).

In both cases, sameness characterises whatever human beings undertake, since, as Aristotle explains, 'all artifical things are generated either from something which bears the same name [...] or from a part of themselves which bears the same name as themselves' (Aristotle 1996: 350–351; 1034 a 20). And this principle, as 'comprehensive identitary logic' [*logique ensembliste identitaire*] structures human society and, therefore, human behaviour, just as the 'self-sameness of its object' [*Selbigkeit ihres Gegenstandes*] structures the foundation of disciplinary (calculable) knowledge and, therefore, human cognition (Castoriadis 1975: 303ff., 311–313; Heidegger 2002: 13).[13]

Identity, as the relationship between oneself and oneself, may well affirm personal autonomy – a crucial Enlightenment value. It is, though, offset by the fundamental immobility, the repressive non-differentiation it also guarantees: 'What is merely identical with itself, is unhappy' [*Was bloß identisch ist mit sich, ist ohne Glück*] (Adorno 1977: 538).

Self-encounter, common humanity, or ...

The Enlightenment apparently culminates in a cognitive situation with no exit. As Condillac remarked: 'we can never can get outside of ourselves; and it is only ever our thinking we perceive' [*Nous ne sortons point de nous mêmes; et ce n'est jamais que notre propre pensée que nous apercevons*] (Condillac 2014: 69). But this – and nothing else – is the foundation of its affirmative value asserted still (e.g., by an eminent historian) as 'the common humanity that has *always bound* us together, that *still binds* us together today, and that *will continue to bind* us together in the future' (Cannadine 2013: 264). But here too – with its authoritarian tone of academic admonition – the thought betrays itself: its moral idealism subverted by the metaphor of coercion ('*bind*'), its undemonstrable historicism pre-empting the future.

In fact, self-encounter and a common, human identity are fraught with risk. The world created by the mind, operating on technological rationality, has a treacherous appearance [*einen trügerischen Schein*]. It is as though, as 'lords of the Earth', human beings can 'only ever encounter themselves' [*als begegne der Mensch überall nur noch sich selbst*]. But (Heidegger continues) human beings are so implicated in the technological apparatus indispensable to their existence that they are self-alienated: they cannot even encounter only themselves any longer [*darum niemals nur sich selbst begegnen kann*] (Heidegger 1967a: 26–27). As Valéry observes, the world created by human rationality is hazardous not just because no-one can know their future state of knowledge, but also because impelled by the speed of thought, hence constantly eluding comprehension, it produces a 'crisis of the unforeseen' (Valéry 1960a: 1065). Thus 'the specialized nature of modern expertise contributes directly to the erratic, runaway character of modernity' (Giddens 1991: 30).

Conversely, the self-encounter produced by 'Man', 'the proper study of Mankind', suggests also something banal: the inability to cope with the ever accumulating burden of self-knowledge, the same old thing. The euphoria of Enlightened self-discovery soon fades: 'Relieved of its material ties, humanity for the first time confronts itself, with nothing else to do [*sans rien d'autre à faire*] but to think of itself [*songer à soi*]: and it realizes it is *bored*' (Halévy 1997: ix, 52–53 (emphasis in original)). This boredom also produces self-estrangement.

Self-encounter through common humanity is affirmed because there is nothing else: there is either humanity – or else nothing. The 'nothing else' is here decisive: the individual reduced to 'merely an observation post in strange territory' [*Un homme n'est qu'une poste d'observation perdu dans l'étrangeté*], hence to a 'pointless passion' [*l'homme est une passion inutile*] with "humanity" the beguiling façade of this desolation (Valéry 1960b: 721; Sartre 2010: 662). However, dialectically acknowledged by Terence ('nothing alien' [*nihil alienum*]), the estrangement that is nothing, that implies nothing else, discovered by Rousseau in the unsparing candour of autobiographical self-assessment, and vindicated (e.g.) by Valéry and Sartre, always shadowed the moral idealism of a self-identical humanity, predicated as this is on tautological redundancy.

Revolutions in knowledge produce reconceptions of human nature. Transformations in the environment due to humanity's own potential produce physiological and psychological mutations: that human nature is 'always the same' is no longer credible (Valéry 1960a: 1061). Still, this intimation of the frailty of human existence in a unique biosphere in a sublimely indifferent cosmos re-orientates thinking. The lack of complicity of the world in human knowledge, the assertion of non-identity, offers hope. Ultimately, particularly in desolate circumstances (as Rousseau discovered), being conscious means existing at a distance from oneself (not identifying with oneself) It means finding oneself different to oneself [*je suis autre*], wondering what this other self-hood means for oneself [*que suis-je moi-même?*]. This distance is ensured by nothingness: nothing prevents self-realisation (Sartre 2010: 114). So existing for oneself means not coinciding with oneself: self-knowledge can arise, therefore, only from 'finding oneself as unknown, as divided from oneself' (Valéry 1960b: 733).

Sustained by the apprehension induced by the frailty of the human sphere, thinking enlightens when it thus dispels the illusion of comprehensive identity projected by the conceit that Man himself is a 'maximally dynamic and constructive copula', when it discloses that its humanistic ethic, in failing to realise itself, cancels its Cartesian premise (*je pense donc je suis*) (Lévi-Strauss 1996: 48, 50, 53). Precisely this resistance to sameness, this self-distanciation, resulting from Rousseau's 'arrogant thinking and a solitary, aggrieved existence', exerts a 'subversive force', its potential hitherto unprecedented. This would produce a credible "science of man", an anthropology – formulated as a fluid chiasmus not as a repetitive, tautological assertion – that would 'explore the society of nature in order from there to reflect on the nature of society' [*rechercher la société de la nature pour y méditer sur la nature de la société*] ((Lévi-Strauss 1996: 52).

The Enlightenment always meant something useful, something pragmatic, not purely theoretical. 'Thinking for oneself' – as advocated by Kant – intended human beings to use knowledge to create for themselves what they want to be, to produce their own nature, not to receive it conceptually pre-packaged in historical shrink-wrapping. New forms of behaviour, new cognitive practices produce new realities (though were it possible to define them now, they would not be new). Still, better for enlightening practices to confront an indeterminate future than for the Enlightenment to signify a project meaningful only in its always postponed fulfilment. Better to see it intimated now pragmatically in the perpetration of small but significant 'acts of deviance' [*kleine abweichende Handlungen*]; but also cognitively in developing mental 'resistance' to the way things are, in 'the effort no longer to let oneself be deceived' (Nietzsche 1988c: 141–142; III, §149; Horkheimer 2003b: 318).

Better still: to see it in a practice for anyone *at any time*: not just to 'think for oneself', but – in apprehensive circumstances the ultimate self-challenge – to 'work at thinking better'.

Notes

1 On 'thought style' and 'thought collective' as concepts, see Benda 1948 and Fleck 1980.
2 Translations are my own unless otherwise indicated.
3 My emphasis (*italics*) in quotations unless indication to the contrary.

4 'Man' and 'Mankind' in this essay reflect the rules of Enlightenment discourse: as central terms in that discourse they produce tautology as a conceptual field. They, therefore, cannot be reformulated in current gender-neutral language to adapt them to current thinking. That demonstrates that they are not automatically commensurable with current thinking. In any case, the recourse to identitary structures in current thinking (even if formulated in gender-neutral language) makes it incommensurable with current realities (cf. Tautology: the affirmation of human intelligibility; and Identity: history: Enlightenment, above).

5 The rather non-literal (and for the dramatic genre more feasible) translation in the Loeb edition (loc. cit.) inverts the sentiment expressed: 'I'm human, and I regard no human business as other people's'.

6 *Semblable* normally translates as 'fellow-creature', but this lacks the sense of similarity the French word connotes.

7 In Italian the adjective *medesimo, -a* means 'same'. The Englsh translation '*own* human mind' fails to register the sense of sameness in the original.

8 On the distinction between comprehension and apprehension as modes of knowledge, see Davies 2006: 65ff., 254.

9 On categorical coordinators invested by the mind into historical material to produce in it patterns of causal relationships and identities, see Davies 2010: 167, 186; 2016: 90ff.

10 For examples of the equivalences and ratios history constructs, see Davies 2006: 81ff., 88–89, 152ff.; 2010: 65ff., 188.

11 In a commentary on Hölderlin's poetic draft, Heidegger explores the significance of measure for human existence (cf. Heidegger 1967b; cf. Marx 1986).

12 For a background to this argument, see Davies 2006: 126ff.

13 '*Logique ensembliste identitaire*' is – with its thematical derivation – more precisely translated as 'set-theoretical identity logic'. But Castoriadis employs it for showing society organised in total by groups the members of which are identified and constituted by their common features (cf. Davies 2006: 81–84).

References

Adorno, T. W. 1977. 'Sexualtabus und Recht heute' [1963], in *Kulturkritk und Gesellschaft II*, edited by R. Tiedemann et al. Frankfurt am Main: suhrkamp taschenbuch wissenschaft, pp. 533–554.

—. 1979. 'Kultur und Verwaltung' [1960], in *Soziologische Schriften I*, edited by R. Tiedemann et al. Frankfurt am Main: suhrkamp taschenbuch wissenschaft, pp.122–146.

—. 1982. *Negative Dialektik* [1966], 3rd edn. Frankfurt am Main: suhrkamp taschenbuch wissenschaft.

Aquinas, T. 1998. *Selected Writings*, edited and translated by R. McInerny. London: Penguin Classics.

Aristotle. 1996. *Metaphysics. Books I–IX*, translated by H. Tredennick. Loeb Classical Library. Cambridge, MA and London, England: Harvard University Press.

Becker, C. L. 1960. *The Heavenly City of the Eighteenth-Century Philosophers* [1932]. New Haven and London: Yale University Press.

Benasayag, M. and Schmit, G. 2006. *Les passions tristes. Souffrance psychique et crise sociale*. Paris: Les Éditions La Découverte.

Benda, J. 1948. *Du style d'idées. Réflexions sur la pensée*. Paris: NRF / Gallimard.

Bergson, H. 1982. *Essais sur les données immédiates de la conscience*. Paris: Quadriges / Presses Universitaires de France.

Cannadine, D. 2013. *The Undivided Past: History Beyond Our Differences*. London: Allen Lane.

Cassirer, E. 1963. *Rousseau, Kant, Goethe* [1945], translated by J. Gutmann et al., introduction by P. Gay. Harper Torchbooks. New York: Harper & Row.

Castoriadis, C. 1975. *L'Institution imaginaire de la société*, 5th edn. Paris: Éditions du Seuil.

Condillac, E. B. 2014. *Essai sur l'origine des connaissances humaines* [1746], edited by J. C. Pariente and M. Pécharman. Paris: J.Vrin.

D'Alembert, J. 2011. *Discours préliminaire de l'Encyclopédie et articles de l'Encyclopédie*, edited by M. Groult. Champion Classiques. Paris: Honoré Champion.

Davies, M. L. 2006. *Historics: What History Dominates Contemporary Society*. Abingdon: Routledge.

—. 2010. *Imprisoned by History: Aspects of Historicized Life*. New York: Routledge.

—. 2016. *How History Works: The Reconstitution of a Human Science*. Abingdon: Routledge.

Derrida, J. 2003. *Voyous: Deux essais sur la raison*. Paris: Éditions Galilée.

Descartes, R. 1966. *Discours de la méthode* [1637], edited by G. Rodis-Lewis. Paris: Garnier Flammarion.

—. 1996. *Règles pour la direction de l'esprit* [1627–1628], edited by J. Sirven. Paris: Vrin.

—. 1627–1628. *Regulae ad directionem ingenii* at http://www2.ac-toulouse.fr/philosophie/textesdephilosophes.htm (accessed 26 May 2015).

D'Holbach, P.-H. T. 2004. *Système social ou Principes naturels de la Morale & de la Politique avec un Examen de l'Influence du Gouvernement sur les Mœurs* [1773], in *Œuvres philosophiques 1773–1790*, edited by J.-P. Jackson. Paris: Coda, pp. 5–314.

Diderot, D. (1994a). 'Encyclopédie' [1755], in *Œuvres. Tome I Philosophie*, edited by L. Versini. Paris: Éditions Robert Laffont, pp. 363–436.

—. (1994b). 'Système des connaissances humaines' [1750], in *Œuvres. Tome I Philosophie*, pp. 225–237.

—. (1994c). 'Éclectisme' [1755], in *Œuvres. Tome I Philosophie*, pp. 300–362.

—. (1994d). 'Pensées sur l'interprétation de la nature' [1753], in *Œuvres. Tome I Philosophie*, pp. 553–600.

Dumarsais, C. C. 1743/1765. L'article 'Philosophe' de l' *Encyclopédie* at http://www.lettres.ac-versailles.fr/spip.php?article382 (accessed 9 June 2015).

—. 1988. *Des Tropes ou des différents sens, Figure et vingt autres articles de l'Encyclopédie, suivi de l'Abrégé des Tropes de l'abbé Ducros*, edited by F. Douay-Soublin. Paris: Critiques Flammarion.

Fleck, L. 1980. *Entstehung und Entwicklung einer wissenschaftlichen Tatsache: Einführung in die Lehre vom Denkstil und Denkkollektiv*, edited by L. Schäfer and T. Schelle. Frankfurt am Main: suhrkamp taschenbuch wissenschaft.

Foucault, M. 1971. *L'ordre du discours*. Paris: Gallimard.

Freud, S. 1987. *Vorlesungen zur Einführung in die Psychoanalyse* [1917]. Frankfurt am Main: Fischer Taschenbuch Verlag.

Gay, P. 1971. *The Party of Humanity: Essays in the French Enlightenment*. New York: W. W. Norton & Company.

Giddens, A. 1991. *Modernity and Self-Identity: Self and Society in the Late Modern Age*. Cambridge: Polity Press.

Gray, J. 1997. *Enlightenment's Wake: Politics and Culture at the Close of the Modern Age*. London: Routledge.

Halévy, D. 1997. *Histoire de quatre ans 1997–2001* [1903], preface by F. Rouvillois. Paris: Éditions Kimé.

Hegel, G. W. F. 1979. *Phänomenologie des Geistes* [1807], in *Theorie Werkausgabe* III. Frankfurt am Main: Suhrkamp Verlag.

Heidegger, M. 1967a. 'Die Frage nach der Technik' [1954], in *Vorträge und Aufsätze. Teil I*. Pfullingen: Neske, pp. 5–36.

—. 1967b. '… dichterisch wohnet der Mensch…' [1951], in *Vorträge und Ausätze. Teil II*. Pfullingen: Neske, pp. 61–78.
—. 2002. *Identität und Differenz*. 12th edn. Stuttgart: Klett-Cotta.
Helvétius, C.-A. 1988. *De l'esprit* [1758]. Corpus des Œuvres de Philosophie en Langue Française. Paris: Fayard.
Herder, J. G. 2013. *Ideen zur Philosophie der Geschichte der Menschheit* [1784–1791], edited by M. Holzinger. Berlin: Holzinger.
Hobbes, T. 1972. *Leviathan* [1651], edited by C. B. Macpherson. Harmondsworth: Pelican Classics.
Hölderlin, F. 2014. 'In lieblicher Bläue…' [1823], in *Gesammelte Werke*, edited by H. J. Balmes, 2nd edn. Frankfurt am Main: Fischer Taschenbuch Verlag, pp. 673–675.
Horkheimer, M. 2003a. *Dialektik der Aufklärung* [1944/1947], in *Gesammelte Schriften*, edited by A. Schmidt and G. Schmid Noerr. Frankfurt am Main: Fischer Taschenbuch Verlag, V, pp. 11–290.
—. 2003b. 'Autoritärer Staat' [1940/1942], in ed. cit., V, pp. 293–319.
—. 2003c. 'Vernunft und Selbsterhaltung' [1942], in ed. cit., V, pp. 320–350.
Hume, D. 1971. 'Of the Study of History', in *Essays Moral, Political, and Literary* [1741/1742]. The World's Classics. Oxford: Oxford University Press, pp. 558–562.
Husserl, E. 2009. *Logische Untersuchungen* [1900–1901/1913], edited by E. Ströker. Philosopische Bibliothek. Hamburg: Meiner.
—. 2012. *Die Krisis der europäischen Wissenschaften und die transzendentale Phänomenologie* [1936], edited by E. Ströker. Philosopische Bibliothek. Hamburg: Meiner.
Israel, J. I. 2006. *Enlightenment Conteste:. Philosophy, Modernity, and the Emancipation of Man 1670–1752*. Oxford: Oxford University Press.
James, W. 1956. *The Will to Believe and Other Essays in Popular Philosophy: Human Immortality: Two Supposed Objections to the Doctrine* [1897/1898]. New York: Dover Publications.
Kant, I. 1965. *Grundlegung zur Metaphysik der Sitten* [1785], edited by K. Vorländer. Philosopische Bibliothek. Hamburg: Meiner.
—. 1967. *Kritik der praktischen Vernunft* [1797], edited by K. Vorländer. Philosopische Bibliothek. Hamburg: Meiner.
—. 1968. *Kritik der Urteilskraft* [1799], edited by K. Vorländer. Philosopische Bibliothek. Hamburg: Meiner.
—. 1969. *Prolegomena zu einer jeden künftigen Metaphysik, die als Wissenschaft wird auftreten können* [1783], edited by K. Vorländer. Philosopische Bibliothek. Hamburg: Meiner.
—. 1971. *Kritik der reinen Vernunft* [1781/1787], edited by R. Schmidt. Philosopische Bibliothek. Hamburg: Meiner.
—. 1977a. 'Was heißt: sich im Denken orientieren?' [1786], in *Werkausgabe*, edited by W. Weischedel. Frankfurt am Main: suhrkamp taschenbuch wissenschaft, V, pp. 265–283.
—. 1977b. *Beobachtungen über das Gefühl des Schönen und Erhabenen* [1764], in *Werkausgabe*, II, pp. 823–884.
—. 1980. *Anthropologie in pragmatischer Hinsicht* [1798/1800], in *Werkausgabe*, XII, pp. 395–690.
—. 1982a. 'Idee zu einer allgemeinen Geschichte in weltbürgerlicher Absicht' [1784], in *Werkausgabe*, XI, pp. 31–50.
—. 1982b. 'Beantwortung der Frage: Was ist Aufklärung?' [1784], in *Werkausgabe*, XI, pp. 51–61.
Kirk, G. S. and Raven, J. E. 1969. *The Presocratic Philosophers: A Critical History with a Selection of Texts*. Cambridge: Cambridge University Press.
Leibniz, G. W. 1960/1961a. 'De rerum originatione radicali' [1697], in *Die philosophischen Schriften von Gottfried Wilhelm Leibniz*, edited by C. J. Gerhardt. 7 vols. Hildesheim: Georg Olms Verlagsbuchhandlung, VII, pp. 302–308.

—. 1960/1961b. 'Ohne Überschrift, enthaltend den Anfang einer Abhandlung Leibnizens in Betreff der Philosophie des Descartes, datirt Maji 1702', in *Die philosophischen Schriften von Gottfried Wilhelm Leibniz*, ed. cit., IV, pp. 393–400.

—. 1960/1961c. 'Briefwechsel zwischen Leibniz und Conring' [1670–1678] in *Die philosophischen Schriften von Gottfried Wilhelm Leibniz*, ed. cit., I, pp. 153–206.

—. 1960/1961d: 'De ipsa natura sive de vi insita actionibusque Creaturum, pro Dynamicis suis confirmandis illustrandisque' [1698], in *Die philosophischen Schriften von Gottfried Wilhelm Leibniz*, ed. cit., IV, pp. 504–517.

—. 1962a. *Essais de Théodicée sur la bonté de dieu, la liberté de l'homme et l'origine du mal* [1710], in *Essais de Théodicée. Suivi de Monadologie*, edited by J. Jalabert. Paris: Aubier Éditions Montaigne, pp.7–472.

—. 1962b. 'La Monadologie,' [1714] in *Essais de Théodicée: Suivi de Monadologie*, edited by J. Jalabert, Paris: Aubier Éditions Montaigne, pp. 473–506.

—. 1994a. 'Addition à l'explication du système nouveau touchant l'union de l'âme et du corps envoyée à Paris à l'occasion d'un livre intitulé connaissance de soi-même' [1698/1700], in *Système nouveau de la nature et de la communication des substances et autres textes 1690–1703*, edited by C. Frémont. Paris: GF-Flammarion, pp. 145–155.

—. 1994b. 'Système nouveau de la nature et de la communication des substances aussi bien que de l'union qu'il y a entre l'âme et le corps' [1695–1696], in *Système nouveau de la nature et de la communication des substances et autres textes 1690–1703*, edited by C. Frémont. Paris: GF-Flammarion, pp. 61–90.

—. 1994c. '[De la nature du corps et de la force motrice]' [1702], in *Système nouveau de la nature et de la communication des substances et autres textes 1690–1703*, ed. cit., pp. 171–187.

—. 1994d. 'Réponse aux Réflexions contenues dans la seconde édition du Dictionnaire critique de M. Bayle, article Rotarius, sur le système de l'harmonie préétablie' [1702/1703] in *Système nouveau de la nature et de la communication des substances et autres textes 1690–1703*, ed, cit., pp. 189–215.

—. 1994e. 'Lettre touchant ce qui est indépendant des sens et de la matière 1702,' in *Système nouveau de la nature et de la communication des substances et autres textes 1690-1703*, ed. cit., pp. 233–247.

—. 1999a. 'De libertate, contingentia et serie causarum, providentia' [1689], in *Akademie Ausgabe*, edited by Akademie der Wissenschaften zu Göttingen, vol. VI, 4B, pp. 1653–9, http://www.uni-muenster.de/Leibniz/DatenVI4/VI4b3.pdf (accessed 19 June 2015).

—. 1999b. 'Conversatio cum domino episcopo stenonio de libertate 27. November (7. Dezember) 1677' in *Akademie Ausgabe*, vol. VI, 4B, pp. 1375–1383, http://www.uni-muenster.de/Leibniz/DatenVI4/VI4b1.pdf (accessed 19 June 2015).

—. 2001. *Discours de métaphysique* [1686], in *Discours de métaphysique et autres textes*, edited by C. Frémont. Paris: Flammarion, pp. 201–272.

Levi-Strauss, C. 1996. 'Jean-Jacques Rousseau, fondateur des sciences de l'homme' [1962], in *Anthropologie structurale deux*. Paris: Plon, pp. 45–56.

Lessing, G.E. 1967. 'Die Erziehung des Menschengeschlechts' [1777], in *Die Erziehung des Menschengeschlechts und andere Schriften*, afterword by H. Thielicke. Stuttgart: Philip Reclam, Jun., pp. 7–31.

Lovejoy, A.O. 1965. *The Great Chain of Being: A Study in the History of an Idea*. Harper Torchbooks. New York: Harper & Row.

Marx, K. 2005. *Das Kapital. Kritik der politischen Ökonomie. Erster Band* [1867], edited Rosa Luxemburg Stiftung. Berlin: Karl Dietz Verlag.

Marx, W. 1986. *Gibt es auf Erden ein Maß?* Frankfurt am Main: Fischer Taschenbuch Verlag.

Nietzsche, F. (1988a) *Jenseits von Gut und Böse. Vorspiel einer Philosophie der Zukunft* [1886], in *Kritische Studienausgabe*, V, edited by G. Colli and M. Montinari, 2nd revised edn. Berlin and New York: Walter de Gruyter, Munich: DTV, pp. 9–243.

—. (1988b) *Zur Genealogie der Moral. Eine Streitschrift* [1887], in ed. cit., V, 245–412.

—. 1988c. *Morgenröte* [1881 /1887], in ed. cit., III, pp. 9–331.

Ortega y Gasset, J. 1962. 'History as a System,' in *History as a System and Other Essays Toward a Philosophy of History*, afterword by J. W. Miller. The Nortion Library. New York and London: W.W. Norton & Company, pp. 165–233.

Pagden, A. 2013. *The Enlightenment and Why It Still Matters*. Oxford: Oxford University Press.

Pascal, B. 1963a. *Pensées* [1670], in *Œuvres complètes*, preface by H. Gouhier, edited by L. Lafuma. Paris: Éditions du Seuil, pp. 493–649.

—. 1963b. 'Préface, Sur le Traité du vide' [1651], in *Œuvres complètes*, ed. cit., pp. 230–232.

Plato. 2002. *Theaetetus*, in *Theaetetus. Sophist*, translated by H. N. Fowler. Loeb Classical Library, Cambridge, MA and London: Harvard University Press, pp. 1–257.

Pope, A. 1983. *An Essay on Man* [1733/1734], in *Poetical Works*, edited by H. Davis, introduction by P. Rogers. Oxford and New York: Oxford University Press, pp. 239–279.

Pouillon, J. 1987. 'L' Œuvre de Claude Lévi-Strauss,' in Lévi-Strauss, C., *Race et histoire*. Folio essais. Paris: Denoël, pp. 87–127.

Prigogine, I. and Stengers, I. 2001. *Entre le temps et l'éternité*. Paris: Champs / Flammarion.

—. 2005. *La nouvelle alliance: Métamorphose de la science*. Folio essais. Paris: Gallimard.

Pufendorf, S. 1991. *On the Duty of Man and Citizen According to Natural Law* [1673], edited by J. Tully, translated by M. Silverstone. Cambridge: Cambridge University Press.

Quintilian. 2001. *The Orator's Education*, edited and translated by D. A. Russell. Loeb Classical Library, 5. vols. Cambridge, MA and London: Harvard University Press.

Reed, T.J. 2015. *Light in Germany: Scenes from an Unknown Enlightenment*. Chicago and London: Chicago University Press.

Rousseau, J.-J. 1967. *Les rêveries du promeneur solitaire* [1782], edited by J. Grenier. Livre de Poche. Paris: Éditions Gallimard.

—. 1968. *Confessions* [1782/1789], edited by J. Guéhenno. 2 vols. Livre de Poche: Paris Éditions Gallimard.

—. 1971. *Discourse sur l'origine et les fondements de l'inégalité parmi les hommes* [1755], in *Discours sur les sciences et les arts: Discourse sur l'origine et les fondements de l'inégalité parmi les hommes*, edited by J. Roger. Paris: Garnier-Flammarion.

Sartre, J.-P. 2010. *L'Être et le néant: Essai d'ontologie phénoménologique* [1943], edited by E. Elkaïm-Sartre. Coll. Tel. Paris: Gallimard.

Schmidt, J. (ed.). 1996. *What Is Enlightenment? Eighteenth-Century Answers and Twentieth-Century Questions*. Berkeley and Los Angeles. California University Press.

Smith, A. 1982. *The Theory of Moral Sentiments* [1759], edited by D. D. Raphael and A. L. Macfie. Indianapolis: Liberty Classics.

Spinoza, B. 1925a. *Ethica* [1677], in *Opera*, edited by C. Gebhardt. 4 vols. Heidelberg: Carl Winters Universitätsbuchhandlung, II, pp. 41–308.

—. 1925b. *Epistolae*, in *Opera*, ed. cit., IV, pp.1–342.

—. 1996. *Ethics*, edited and translated by E. Curley, introduction by S. Hampshire. London: Penguin Classics.

Spitzer, L. 1963. *Classical and Christian Ideas of World Harmony*, edited by A. G. Hatcher, foreword by R. Wellek. Baltimore: Johns Hopkins Press.

Steiner, G. 1997. 'The Great Tautology' [1992], in *No Passion Spent: Essays 1978–1996*. London and Boston: Faber & Faber, pp. 348–360.

Terence. 2001. 'The Self-Tormentor', in *The Woman of Andros, the Self Tormentor, the Eunuch*, translated and edited by J. Barsby. Loeb Classical Library. Cambridge, MA and London: Harvard University Press, pp. 171–303.

Valéry, P. 1960a. 'Notre Destin et les Lettres' [1937], in *Œuvres II*, edited by J. Hytier. Bibliothèque de ls Pléiade. Paris: Éditions Gallimard, pp. 1059–1076.

—. 1960b. *Analecta* [1926], in *Œuvres II*, pp. 700–749.
Vico, G. 1984. *The New Science of Giambattista Vico: Unabridged Translation of the Third Edition (1744) with the addition of the 'Practic of the New Science'*, translated by T. G. Bergin and M. H. Fisch. Ithaca and London: Cornell University Press.
—. 1959. *La Scienza Nuova Secondo l'Edizione del MDCCXLIV*, in *Opere*, edited by P. Rossi. Milan; Rizzole Editore, pp. 237–860.
—. 1993. *On Humanistic Education (Six Inaugural Orations, 1699–1707) from the Definitive Latin Text, Introduction, and Notes by G. G. Visconti*, translated by G. A. Pinton and A. W. Shippee, introduction by D. P. Verene. Ithaca and London: Cornell University Press.
Voltaire. 1967. *Dictionnaire philosophique* [1764 /1769], preface Étiemble, edited by R. Naves and J. Benda. Paris: Éditions Garnier.
Wahl, J. 2004. *Vers le concret. Études d'histoire de la philosophie contemporaine. William James, Whitehead, Gabriel Marcel* [1932]. Paris: Librairie Philosophique J. Vrin.
Weber, M. 1988. 'Wissenschaft als Beruf' [1919], in *Gesammelte Aufsätze zur Wissenschaftslehre*, edited by J. Winckelmann, Uni-Taschenbücher. Tübingen: J.C.B. Mohr (Paul Siebeck), pp. 582–613.
Whitehead, A. N. 1920. *The Concept of Nature*. Cambridge: Cambridge University Press.
—. 1967a. *Science and the Modern World* [1925]. New York: The Free Press.
—. 1967b. *Adventures of Ideas* 1933]. New York: The Free Press.

INDEX

abortion 123
academic self-interest 2, 13
academic work 1–2
adoption 173–186
Adorno, T. W. 115, 117, 118, 203, 261
Africans 157
alienation 203
Allott, P. 17–19
American Revolution 32, 70, 79, 82
analytical philosophy 32
anamnestic reason 114–118
'An Answer to the Question: What Is Enlightenment?' (Kant) 32–35, 46, 48
Anderson, B. 132
Anderson, E. 96
anomic suicide 195
anomie 196
antagonism 194, 196, 198
antagonistic relations 189
anthropocentrism 16, 40, 114
anthropology 153, 189, 198–203
anti-encyclopedism 213–219
anti-philosophes 209, 212, 213–219
anti-Semitism 156
apperception 36
a priori 36, 40, 41
Aquinas, T. 190, 230
Arendt, H. 23, 53, 54, 60–63; on following conscience 50–53, 61–63; post-totalitarian reflection of 49–50
Aristotle 5, 190, 230, 261
Artemjeva, O. 59–60
atomisation 194, 196, 197, 198, 199

Auschwitz 117
autonomy 23, 252–255

barbarians 154–155
Barbeyrac, J. 70
Bauman, Z. 122
Beauvoir, S. de 164
Beck, U. 123
Becker, G. S. 200
Benedict XVI 105–106, 113–114, 119; *see also* Ratzinger, J.
Benjamin, W. 115, 117
Berlin, I. 130–133, 210–211, 221, 222
Bernier, F. 158–159
Bernstein, R. J. 54, 55–56
Bertrand, E. 73, 77
biological origin 174
Bloch, E. 10, 115
Blum, L. 64n10
Blumenbach, J. F. 159, 160
Böckenförde, E.-W. 110
Bologna School 107
Book of Job 117
Boudon, R. 201–202
Bourdieu, P. 123, 201, 202
Buffon, Comte de 160–161
Burlamaqui, J.-J. 70
Butler, J. 158

Calvinism 77
capitalism 17, 118, 123, 124
Cartesian method 78–79
cartoon controversy 123, 124–130, 134

caste system 156
categorical imperative 23, 35, 38, 40–43, 45, 46, 53–56, 58, 60, 255
Catholic Church 105–119, 141–142, 146, 156
Catholicism 24, 78, 105–119
causality 253, 254
Choderlos de Laclos 143
Christianity 73, 76–78, 105–119, 133, 141–142, 249
civil disobedience 23, 51, 61–63
civilised intercourse 191–192
civil liberty 33–34
civil society 80–81, 99, 191, 193
clericalism 78
Code of Humanity 69–84
codification 79
cognition 256, 261
Cohen, H. 156
collective action 201
colliding values 130–131, 132
colonialism 157
Columbus, C. 156
commodity thinking 10
common good 89
common humanity 262–263
common sense 77
concepts 5
conceptual parsimony 243–246
Condorcet, M. de 11, 12, 14, 88, 149
conscience 50–53, 61, 64n14, 77
consciousness 18–19, 36, 254
Constant, B. 57
convents 142, 146
Copernican revolution 36
cosmological tautology 240
cosmopolitanism 40, 44, 45, 47, 122
Counter-Enlightenment 2, 24–25, 209–223; concepts of 211–213; in eighteenth century 213–220
courtier 191–192
Crenshaw, K. 153
criminal law 79, 80
critical thinking 88
criticism of criticisms 87–88
cultural capital 202
cultural progress 123

Daughter from Danang 173–174
death penalty 80
Debray, R. 122–123
Declaration of Independence 70, 82
Declaration of the Rights of Man 79, 82
De Felice, F.-B. 69–84

de Gouges, O. 162
de Jaucourt, L. 73, 77, 81
Deleuze, G. 5, 6, 14
deliberative democracy 24, 86–100; background on 90–92; Dewey and 87, 89–90, 92, 94–98; Enlightenment thought and 86–100; Habermas and 87, 90, 92–94, 98–100; legitimacy and 91; practicality and feasibility of 98–99
deliberative polling 99
Delon, M. 219
democracy 49, 82, 128–129, 133; deliberative 86–100; discourse theory of 87, 92–94; legitimacy and 91; participatory 89; radical 92, 100; as social enquiry 95, 96
democratic theory 87, 90–92, 96, 98
d'Epinay, L. 144–145
Der Findling (Kleist) 174–175, 181–186
Derrida, J. 261
Descartes, R. 230, 243
Dewey, J. 87, 89–90, 92, 94–98, 189
Dialectics of Enlightenment 116–117, 118
Diderot, D. 7, 10, 19, 22, 32, 143–144, 146–147, 227, 239
dignity 35, 40, 43, 45, 48
discourse theory 87, 92–94
diversity 94, 254
divine laws 77
Divine Revelation 88
documentary values 6–10, 19–21
dogmatism 50
Dryden, J. 155
Durkheim, E. 195–196
duty 51, 53–63

ecclesiology 113
eclecticism 22–23
economic science 199–201, 202
education, women's 139–149
egoistic suicide 195
Eichmann, trial of 53–56, 58, 64n8
emancipatory reason 116
Empiricists 95
Encyclopédie 209, 213–215, 234, 247, 257–258, 260–261
encyclopedism 69–84, 213–219, 227
Enlightenment: academic evaluation of 13–14; adoption and 173–186; Christianity and 105–119; definition of 4–5, 32–35; deliberative democrats as heirs to 86–100; as discourse 126–129;

documentary value of 6–10; European identity and 131–134; finality 7, 11–16; future of 258; historical self-projection of 11–15; historiography 7–11, 13–14, 18, 257–259; as incomplete 15–16; at individual level 31, 35–39; interest in 1–2; Kant and 31–64, 235, 248–249, 252–255; legacy of 11–12, 122–124, 130–131, 174; meaning of 1–4; phases of 87–90; principles of 33; racism and 153–154; science and 32, 88; sexism and 153–154; spirit of 1–2; tautology and 227–263; at universal level 31, 39–42; unsocial sociability and 188–203; women's education during 139–149
Enlightenment values 1, 2, 4
environmental categorical imperative 43
environmental problems 43
epistemological level 36
equality 237
equivalence 238–241, 246, 248–249, 253, 256–258
ethical level 36–37
ethical values 8–10, 12
Eurocentrism 155, 160–161
European identity 122, 131–134, 155
evil 37
experimentation 5–6
Eze, E. C. 154, 157, 158, 160

faith 109
familial kinships 181
fanaticism 213, 217, 238
femininity 161–162
Fénelon, F. 140, 144
Ferrone, V. 4, 23
figures of speech 229–230
Fishkin, J. 99
Fleury, C. 144
Formey, J.-H.-S. 73
Forster, G. 159, 160
Fortuyn, P. 123
Foucault, M. 7, 176–177, 222–223
Frankfurt School 116
freedom 33–34, 46, 110, 253
freedom of expression 123–129, 131, 134
freedom of thought 32–33, 48–50, 77
free will 37, 38–39, 40, 46
Frege, G. 32
French Revolution 32, 70, 79, 82, 149, 162, 212
Freron, E. C. 214
future, indeterminancy of the 257–258

Gaudium et spes 107
Gay, P. 217
gender: differences 163–164; Enlightenment thought and 153–154, 157–158, 161–165; history of 161–164; identity 162; inequality 24, 139–149; roles 162–165; sexism and 156; women's education 139–149
General Will 89
genius 143, 145, 239–240
genocide 60–63
geometrical method 244
ghost detainees 123
Gilbert, N.-J.-L. 214, 215
globalisation 122
God 73, 77, 80, 82, 95, 108, 111–112, 117, 156, 243–246, 249, 250, 259
Goldthorpe, J. 202
good 37
governesses 146
government, legitimacy 89, 90, 91, 97, 98
Great Community 97
Great Society 97
Grotius, 78
group distinctions 192–194
Guattari, F. 5, 6, 14
Gustave III 72–73

Habermas, J. 87, 90, 92–94, 98–100, 110–112, 118
habitus 201, 202
Hacking, I. 199
Hamites 157
Hegelian-Marxist tradition 112
Helvétius 235, 236, 239–240
Herder, J. G. 248, 249, 250
historical development 42
historical-dialectical materialism 116
historical knowledge 4, 5
historical process 12–13, 33, 258
historicism 5–7, 12, 14–17, 249
historicist determinism 17
historiography 13–14, 18, 257–259
history 5–7, 251, 257–259; as human self-encounter 249–250; Kant's philosophy of 40–42, 45–47; tautology and 246–251
history of ideas 154, 158–164
Hobbes, T. 81, 191, 193, 233, 235, 237
Horkheimer, M. 260, 261
human action 34, 37
human capital 200, 202
human dignity 35, 40, 43, 45, 48
humanism 1, 2, 3, 14, 77
humanity 250

human nature 18, 31, 35–40, 42, 46, 158, 164, 188–189, 262–263
human relationships 5
human self-equivalence 235–238
human society 80–81
Hume, D. 2, 31, 249
Husserl, E. 260

idealism 19, 32
ideal speech situation 87, 93
ideas, history of 154
identity 24, 240–241, 256–259, 261–263
identity principle 10, 232–235, 240–241, 245–246, 256–257, 259
immaturity 38, 48–50
imperialism 155, 157
independent thinking 32–33, 48–50, 51
individual level, Enlightenment at 31, 35–39
individual rights 79–80
institutional corruption 24
international cooperation 31, 39, 42–47
inter-religious dialogue 119
intersectionality 153–158, 165
irrationalism 122, 222
Islamic scarf controversy 123
Israel, J. I. 4, 5, 13, 14

Jefferson, T. 82, 83–84
John Paul II 119
Judaic tradition 117
jusnaturalism 78–82
justice 88

Kant, I. 3, 7, 11, 17, 31–64, 235, 248–249, 263; 'An Answer to the Question: What Is Enlightenment?' 32–35, 46, 48; compared with Arendt 49–53; doctrine of international cooperation and 44–46; on gender 163–165; on human nature 35–37, 38–39; on immaturity 48–50; individual level of Enlightenment and 35–39; influence of 32; introduction to 31–32; Nazism and 53–56; on obedience to law 50–63; philosophical teachings of 32–35; philosophy of history of 40–42, 45, 46–47; on race 159, 160; Ratzinger and 109; on reason 86, 90; system of universal values 42–44, 45; tautology and 252–255; universal level of Enlightenment and 39–42; on unsocial sociability 189–194
Kittler, F. 177
Kleist, H. von 174–175, 181–186

knowledge 16–17, 36, 90, 232–234; instrumental theory of 95–96; metaphysical 109–110; self-knowledge 232–234, 243, 249, 252, 257; spectator theory of 95; useful 227–229

Lafont, C. 91, 94
La Harpe, J.-F. 214
Lamennais, 195
La Tour-Landry, G. de 141
Lausten, C. B. 54–55
law(s) 24, 34; civil disobedience and 23, 51, 61–63; criminal 79, 80; discourse theory of 87; divine 77; legitimacy of 91, 92–94; moral 56–63, 71, 77; natural 69–84, 236–237, 254; of nature 37; obedience to 49, 50–53, 54–63
legitimacy 87, 89–94, 97, 98
Leibniz, G. W. 230, 241–242, 243
Le Masson de Granges, D. 218
Le Rond d'Alembert, J. 16, 146
Lessing, G. E. 174–181, 185, 186, 249
Lettres persanes (Montesquieu) 21
liberalism 198
liberation theology 112–113
liberty *see* freedom
liberty of speech *see* freedom of expression
Linnaeus, C. 159, 160
Lippmann, W. 96
Locke, J. 81, 88–89
Lohenstein, D. C. von 155
Louden, 9
lumières 213–219
Luther, M. 163
lying 57–60

Maillane, D. de 74
Maistre, J. de 194
Mandeville, B. 192–193
Manin, B. 91
Man/Mankind 234–235, 240–241, 246, 248–250, 254, 256, 259–261, 262
Mannheim, K. 6
market socialisation 192
Marx, K. 196–198
Marxism 112–116, 194
masculinity 161–162
Masseau, D. 212
maturity 48–50, 60
McMahon, D. 212
memory 117–118
metaphysics 32, 90, 109–110, 117, 241–246, 253

Metz, J. B. 105, 106, 112–119
Middle Ages 156
Mill, J. S. 199–200
Mingard, G. 74, 77, 80, 82
minipublics 98–99
modernity 5, 7–13, 18, 19, 90, 100, 105, 106, 123, 262; Christianity and 105–119; Counter-Enlightenment and 210–211, 221; definition of 108
monarchy 82
Montaigne, M. de 155, 191
Montesquieu 21, 143
moral behaviour 38, 40
moral dilemmas 59
moral idealism 8
moral identity 42
moralism 191–192
morality 24, 40, 42–43, 54–55, 71–72, 77, 88, 110
moral law 56–63, 71, 77
moral philosophy 76–77
Morin, E. 132–133
multiculturalism 127
mutual self-recognition 236–238

narrative 4–5
Nathan der Weise (Lessing) 174–181, 186
natural history 159
naturalistic fallacies 24, 153, 154, 156–158, 162, 164
natural laws 37, 236–237, 254
natural rights 69–84, 88
Nature/nature 35, 157, 240, 244–245, 246, 249, 250, 259; state of 80–81, 89
Nazism 49, 51–56, 58, 60–61, 64n8, 64n11, 156
negative liberty 110, 113
negotiated equivalences 241
neo-capitalism 123, 124
New Political Theology 112–119
New World 156
Nicole, P. 192
Nietzsche, F. 259
nihilism 3
Nisbet, R. 194
noble savage 155
nominalism 109, 117
Norton, R. E. 222
Nussbaum, M. C. 2

obedience 33–34, 39, 46, 49, 50–63
Olson, M. 201
Operation Babylift 173–174
oppression 81–82

original sin 157
Other/Otherness 108–109, 154–158

Pagden, A. 1, 2, 4, 8, 11–15, 123, 132, 259
Panckoucke, C.-J. 82–83
parsimony, conceptual 243–246
participatory democracy 89
party 217–218
passivity 52–53
Péguy, C. 20–21
perpetual peace 31, 40, 44, 45, 47
personal freedom 23
philosophes 24–25, 209, 212, 213–219, 257–258
philosophy 2, 5, 6, 11, 18–19; analytical 32; history of 154; jusnaturalism 76–77; moral 76–77; political 41, 118; theology and 106
Plato 88, 141
pluralism 94, 117, 118, 119, 131
Plutarch 147
political economy 199
political philosophy 41, 118
political power 88–89, 90, 97, 190
Pope, A. 155, 229–230, 239, 241, 246, 257, 259
Popper, K. R. 14, 16–17
posterity 247
Postman, N. 123
postmodernism 108, 122, 123–124, 222
practical reason 55
pragmatism 87, 89–90, 95–98
praxis 108, 109, 113, 117, 119
precursors 247
private reason 50
progress 10, 139, 247
property rights 80
proportionate resemblances 242–243
Protestantism 73–74, 76–78, 133, 142
public deliberation 90, 96, 98–99
public opinion 93
public reason 48, 50, 51, 52
pure grammar 229
pure reason 33–36, 38–39, 254
Putnam, H. 87–90, 97

Querelle des femmes 139–149

race/racism 153–154, 156–161
radical democracy 92, 100
ratio 238–240, 246, 248–249
rationalism 78–79
Rationalists 95

rationality 3, 23, 41, 87–90, 109–110, 115, 118
rational judgement 33–34, 46
Ratzinger, J. 105–114, 119
Rawls, J. 110, 111, 118, 119
reading, act of 20–22
reason 24, 33–41, 48, 51–55, 86; anamnestic 114–118; Dewey on 90, 92; emancipatory 116; faith and 249; Habermas on 92, 94; Kant on 90, 254; Metz on 117–118; Ratzinger on 108–112; truth and 106–107
reciprocity 236–237, 242–243
reflective transcendence 87–88
religion 24, 77–78, 105–119; *see also* Christianity
religious conflict 24
religious tolerance 124, 127, 129
Renaissance 32, 155
republican revolutions 32
resemblances 242–243
Riballier 148
Rochefoucauld, F. de La. 191–192
Romanticism 88
Rorty, R. 123
Rose, F. 124–125
Rousseau, J.-J. 86, 89, 143, 145, 146, 147, 148, 155, 185, 193, 238–239, 251–252

sameness 230–233, 235–240, 243, 245–246, 248–249, 252, 257–258, 261
savages 154–155
Schmidt, J. 211
Schmitt, C. 60, 64n11, 116
Schnadelbach, H. 220
Schneider, H. 179
scholasticism 88
Schopenhauer, A. 188
Schumpeter, J. 90
science 20, 32, 88, 157, 260
scientific method 88, 90
scientific progress 115
scientific racism 156, 157, 159–160
scientific revolution 157
Second Vatican Council 105–108, 115
secularisation 112, 114, 115, 158
self-consciousness 36
self-encounter 262–263
selfhood 253
self-interest 2, 133, 134, 191, 192, 199–201, 229–230, 240–241
self-knowledge 232–234, 243, 249, 252, 257
self-same principle 245–246
semblables 232–234, 252, 253, 255

sex/gender 153–154, 156–158, 161–165
sexism 154, 156
Silber, J. 55–56
similitude 239–240
sin 24
Sisyphus 15–16
slavery 80, 160
Smith, A. 193, 233, 237
sociability 24, 188–203
social capital 202
social contract 88, 90, 192, 193
Social Darwinism 156
social enquiry 95, 96
social identity 42
social science 198–203
social theory 201–202
sociology 194–195
Socrates 88
Soemmerring, S. T. 160, 161
Spinoza, B. 243–246
spiritual freedom 33–34
state: of nature 80–81, 89; political origin of 80
Sternhell, Z. 222
strong public 93
studiousness 2
Sturm und Drang 221
subjective unity of consciousness 36
suffering, memory of 117–118
suicide 195

tautology 227–263; conceptual parsimony and 243–246; cosmological 240; end of 251–255; as history's natural order 246–251; human intelligibility and 256–257; metaphysics and 241–246; as theodicy 241–243
technology 260
terrorism 123
theodicy 241–243
theology 106–119
thinking, act of 3, 5
Thoreau, H. 51
Tibi, B. 123
Todorov, T. 1, 122
tolerance 124, 127, 129, 131, 134
totalitarianism 17, 19, 23, 49, 51–52, 63, 109
tradition 118
transcendence, reflective 87–88
transcendental subject 37
transcendental unity of self-consciousness 36
transnational adoption 173–174
Tridentine reform 141–142

trust proxies 99
truth 57–60, 94, 106–109, 113, 119, 230
tutelage 33, 34, 38, 49

Ugilt, R. 54–55
universalism 118, 122
universality 235–236
universal level, Enlightenment at 31, 39–42
universal values 42–44, 45
unsocial sociability 24, 188–203
useful knowledge 227–229

Valéry, P. 21, 262, 263
values: colliding 130–131, 132; universal 42–44, 45
van Gogh, T. 123
Vattel, E. de 70
Vico, G. 234
Vietnam War 173–174

virtue 3
Voltaire 31, 143–146, 214, 218, 238
von Mohl, R. 198

weak public 93
Weber, M. 8–9
Whitehead, A. N. 7, 23, 258
Williams, B. 154
Wolff, C. 70
women, role of, in society 140
women's education 139–149
women's rights 123
world-citizenship 17, 33, 35, 40, 43–44, 45, 47, 249
world-civil society 31, 40, 43–44, 45, 47

xenophobia 155

Žižek, S. 59